이름	
수험번호	

실전 모의고사 ▸ 1

TOEIC®

JN413164

Test of English for International Communication

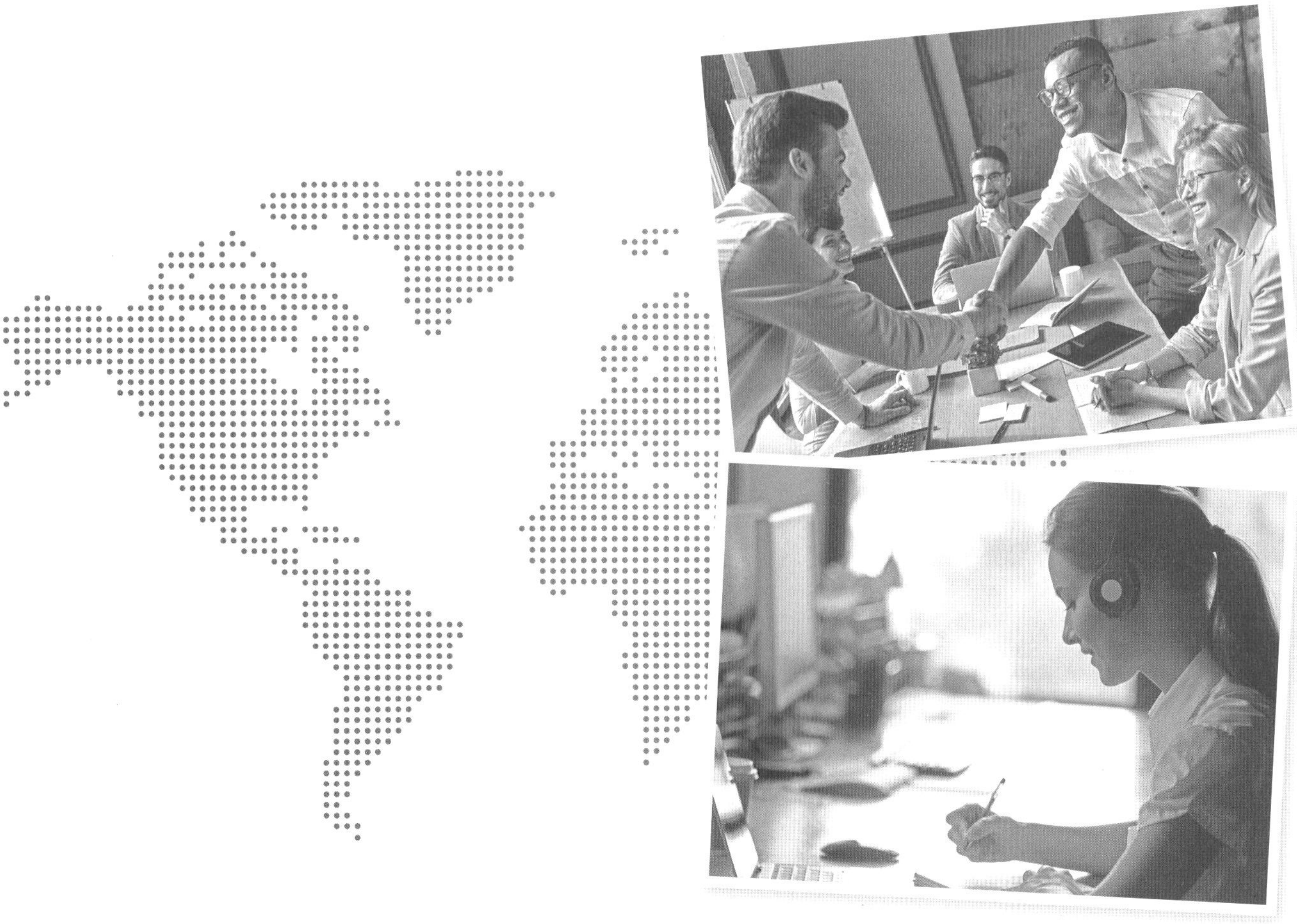

LISTENING TEST

In the Listening test, you will be asked to demonstrate how well you understand spoken English. The entire Listening test will last approximately 45 minutes. There are four parts, and directions are given for each part. You must mark your answers on the separate answer sheet. Do not write your answers in the test book.

PART 1

Directions: For each question in this part, you will hear four statements about a picture in your test book. When you hear the statements, you must select the one statement that best describes what you see in the picture. Then find the number of the question on your answer sheet and mark your answer. The statements will not be printed in your test book and will be spoken only one time.

Statement (B), "The man is working at a desk," is the best description of the picture, so you should select answer (B) and mark it on your answer sheet.

MP3 듣기 

1.

2.

GO ON TO THE NEXT PAGE

3.

SUMMER TIME
APRICOT ALE
FARMER JON'S
OATMEAL STOUT

4.

TOASTIES
JACKET POTATOES
Cheese
Beans
Coleslaw
Tuna mayo
2.95 - 1 filling
extra fillings
50p each
PANINI'S 3.95 each

5.

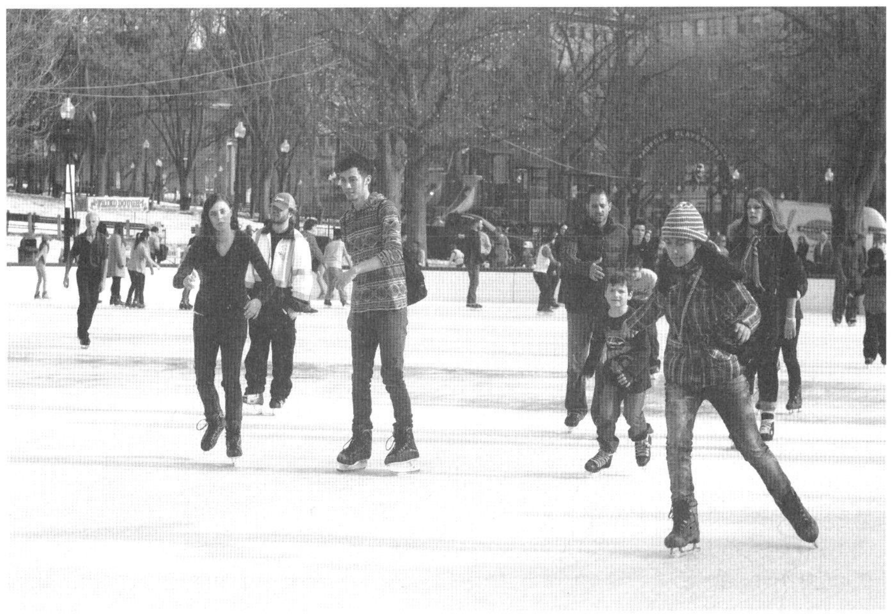

6.

GO ON TO THE NEXT PAGE

PART 2

Directions: You will hear a question or statement and three responses spoken in English. They will not be printed in your test book and will be spoken only one time. Select the best response to the question or statement and mark the letter (A), (B), or (C) on your answer sheet.

7. Mark your answer on your answer sheet.

8. Mark your answer on your answer sheet.

9. Mark your answer on your answer sheet.

10. Mark your answer on your answer sheet.

11. Mark your answer on your answer sheet.

12. Mark your answer on your answer sheet.

13. Mark your answer on your answer sheet.

14. Mark your answer on your answer sheet.

15. Mark your answer on your answer sheet.

16. Mark your answer on your answer sheet.

17. Mark your answer on your answer sheet.

18. Mark your answer on your answer sheet.

19. Mark your answer on your answer sheet.

20. Mark your answer on your answer sheet.

21. Mark your answer on your answer sheet.

22. Mark your answer on your answer sheet.

23. Mark your answer on your answer sheet.

24. Mark your answer on your answer sheet.

25. Mark your answer on your answer sheet.

26. Mark your answer on your answer sheet.

27. Mark your answer on your answer sheet.

28. Mark your answer on your answer sheet.

29. Mark your answer on your answer sheet.

30. Mark your answer on your answer sheet.

31. Mark your answer on your answer sheet.

PART 3

Directions: You will hear some conversations between two or more people. You will be asked to answer three questions about what the speakers say in each conversation. Select the best response to each question and mark the letter (A), (B), (C), or (D) on your answer sheet. The conversations will not be printed in your test book and will be spoken only one time.

32. What is mentioned about the new restaurant?

(A) It has a luxurious interior.
(B) It is within walking distance.
(C) It opened yesterday.
(D) It serves Italian food.

33. What will take place tomorrow?

(A) An opening ceremony
(B) A farewell banquet
(C) An interview for a position
(D) A company picnic

34. What time does the man suggest for the party?

(A) At 4:00 P.M.
(B) At 5:00 P.M.
(C) At 6:00 P.M.
(D) At 7:00 P.M.

---

35. Who is the man?

(A) A reporter
(B) A clothing designer
(C) A researcher
(D) A store owner

36. What is NOT a characteristic of the fabric being mentioned?

(A) It is light.
(B) It is waterproof.
(C) It is thin.
(D) It is warm.

37. When does the man say will the fabric be ready for sale?

(A) In a month
(B) In one year
(C) In two years
(D) In three years

38. What are the speakers discussing?

(A) Changing the type of service
(B) Registering a secret code number
(C) Cancelling cable services
(D) Unblocking channels

39. What was the woman's problem?

(A) She forgot her secret code number.
(B) She found too many violent channels.
(C) The repairman didn't come on time.
(D) She couldn't see some of the channels.

40. According to the man, what was the reason for the woman's problem?

(A) The cable was inserted incorrectly.
(B) Some channels require a secret code number.
(C) Her child spilled juice on the cable box.
(D) The instruction book had several pages missing.

---

41. What are the speakers mainly discussing?

(A) An employee evaluation
(B) A foreign country
(C) A sales strategy
(D) A job opportunity

42. Who most likely is the woman?

(A) A business owner
(B) A potential employee
(C) A language instructor
(D) A travel agent

43. What does the woman imply when she says, "Not at all"?

(A) She wants to work abroad.
(B) She has not signed the contract.
(C) She does not speak a foreign language.
(D) She wants to attend a sales meeting.

GO ON TO THE NEXT PAGE

44. What does the man say about Shawn Gomez?

(A) He has lived in a foreign country.
(B) He has more experience than required.
(C) He does not want to travel often.
(D) He applied for several positions.

45. What does Selena suggest doing?

(A) Building a new shopping center overseas
(B) Relocating the company's headquarters
(C) Recommending a candidate for another position
(D) Advertising job openings in a newspaper

46. What will happen in Tokyo in a week?

(A) A computer system will be upgraded.
(B) A phone interview will be conducted.
(C) A construction project will begin.
(D) An annual event will be held.

---

47. Who most likely are the speakers?

(A) Building inspectors
(B) Home builders
(C) Personnel employees
(D) Professional gardeners

48. What does the man mean when he says, "That's not good"?

(A) A budget might not be approved.
(B) Some materials are out of stock.
(C) Heavy rains are forecast.
(D) A project might not be finished on time.

49. What do the speakers decide to do?

(A) Cancel an order
(B) Purchase from another supplier
(C) Hire more workers
(D) Contact a client

50. What kind of business do the speakers work for?

(A) A butcher's
(B) A farm
(C) A laboratory
(D) A restaurant

51. What are customers concerned about?

(A) The pricing of some dishes
(B) The ingredients in the food
(C) The cleanliness of the restaurant
(D) The hours of opening

52. What does the woman ask the man to do?

(A) Search for a new supplier
(B) Open a new branch
(C) Design a new menu
(D) Distribute a survey

---

53. Where most likely does the man work?

(A) At an energy station
(B) At a training company
(C) At an advertising firm
(D) At a manufacturing plant

54. Why does the man say he requested a consultation?

(A) Some members of staff need retraining.
(B) An expense has become too costly.
(C) A building needs to be demolished.
(D) Some equipment needs to be replaced.

55. What does the woman suggest doing first?

(A) Analyzing a process
(B) Relocating to a different plant
(C) Moving some manufacturing equipment
(D) Creating a budget

56. What is the man asked to do?

(A) Provide a new password
(B) Assist with getting online
(C) Help writing an e-mail
(D) Analyze some data

57. What was the problem?

(A) The computer was broken.
(B) The e-mail address was wrong.
(C) The password had been changed.
(D) The connection was wrong.

58. Why does the woman say, "Is that all"?

(A) She found an e-mail address.
(B) She understood the problem.
(C) She fixed the laptop.
(D) She had to restart the computer.

---

59. Why is the man calling?

(A) He thinks an excess charge is wrong.
(B) He did not receive an invoice.
(C) Some drill parts are missing.
(D) He wants a newer component.

60. What does the woman say is missing?

(A) Some tool components
(B) A credit card authorization
(C) Correct contact details
(D) The original packaging

61. What does the woman say her supervisor can do?

(A) Waive a fee
(B) Locate a replacement
(C) Change a booking
(D) Review a product

62. According to the woman, what has Jenx Chemicals requested?

(A) A reduced price
(B) An extended deadline
(C) An emergency meeting
(D) A revised product

63. What problem does the man mention?

(A) His team is not available.
(B) He does not have the required skills.
(C) He has prior commitments.
(D) The factory is closed.

64. What does the woman say she will arrange?

(A) New equipment for workers
(B) Free transport for employees
(C) Access to work areas
(D) Training for temporary workers

GO ON TO THE NEXT PAGE

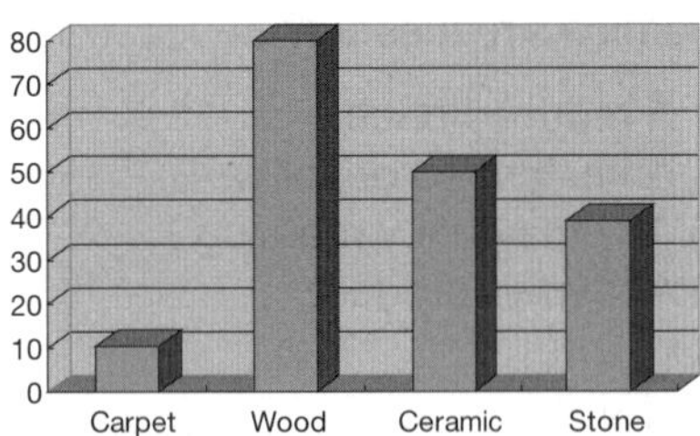

MENU		
Item	Tray for 20	Each Additional Tray
Greek Salad	$100	$50
BBQ Tacos	$200	$150

65. Which material is the best seller in the store?

(A) Carpet
(B) Bamboo
(C) Hardwood
(D) Ceramic

66. Look at the graphic. Which material will the man investigate?

(A) Carpet
(B) Wood
(C) Ceramic
(D) Stone

67. What does the man mention about bamboo flooring?

(A) It is easy to clean.
(B) It is environmentally friendly.
(C) It is affordable.
(D) It is durable.

68. What problem does the woman mention?

(A) A rain shower is forecast.
(B) Not many people have replied.
(C) A supplier has raised its prices.
(D) A restaurant does not accept reservations.

69. What will the woman probably do next?

(A) Contact a catering company
(B) Pay a bill
(C) Call a party planner
(D) Cancel an event

70. Look at the graphic. How much is it for the entire catering order?

(A) $100
(B) $200
(C) $300
(D) $450

PART 4

Directions: You will hear some talks given by a single speaker. You will be asked to answer three questions about what the speaker says in each talk. Select the best response to each question and mark the letter (A), (B), (C), or (D) on your answer sheet. The talks will not be printed in your test book and will be spoken only one time.

71. What are listeners encouraged to do?

(A) Conserve energy
(B) Work in daylight
(C) Share office space
(D) Reduce the cost of living

72. Who is Peter Bow?

(A) A lighting expert
(B) An accountant
(C) An office administrator
(D) A maintenance manager

73. According to the speaker, why is the change being made?

(A) To reduce energy expenditure
(B) To promote recycling practices
(C) To help employees
(D) To recruit staff

---

74. What is the topic of the study?

(A) How to beat insomnia
(B) The health effects of sleep patterns
(C) Better ways to exercise
(D) Sleeping in a strange environment

75. How long will the study last?

(A) For 2 months
(B) For 3 months
(C) For 6 months
(D) For a year

76. What will volunteers be required to do according to the passage?

(A) Take a suitability test at the university
(B) Reside much of their time at the center
(C) Submit an application form in person
(D) Monitor their own progress through surveys

77. What is the purpose of the message?

(A) To allay a customer's worries
(B) To confirm a shipment address
(C) To advertise a fleet of cars
(D) To announce a company change

78. What kind of company is Preston?

(A) A construction firm
(B) An Internet provider
(C) A pharmaceutical company
(D) A car rental service

79. According to the speaker, what will Preston do this week?

(A) Merge with a competitor
(B) Open a new branch
(C) Send a letter to customers
(D) Answer questions on a Web site

---

80. What change has the company recently made?

(A) It has adopted a strict recycling policy.
(B) It has moved to a more spacious office.
(C) It has replaced a service provider.
(D) It has hired additional employees.

81. What does the speaker mean when he says, "But it's going to be different with the new company"?

(A) Uncomfortable furniture will be replaced.
(B) Problems regarding insufficient office space will be resolved.
(C) The company will purchase new office equipment.
(D) Employees will not need to do paperwork.

82. What are listeners encouraged to do?

(A) Read a list
(B) E-mail a supplier
(C) Conserve paper
(D) Work overtime

GO ON TO THE NEXT PAGE

83. What is the purpose of the talk?

(A) To clarify weekly sales achievements
(B) To explain a company policy
(C) To revise budget plans
(D) To describe the recruitment process

84. What are employees reminded to do in advance?

(A) Prepare necessary paperwork
(B) Request customer approval
(C) Pay for items up front
(D) Check the cost of items

85. What are employees asked to provide?

(A) Expense application forms
(B) Contact information
(C) Copies of receipts
(D) Proof of returned items

---

86. What is the theme of the exhibition?

(A) Modern architectural technology
(B) Use of traditional materials
(C) Plastic manufacturing in Switzerland
(D) Gardens of the future

87. Who is Jean Paul Glisson?

(A) An outdoor enthusiast
(B) An architect
(C) An exhibition official
(D) A landscape architect

88. What are visitors invited to do?

(A) Indicate a preference
(B) Take a brochure
(C) Ask for an estimate
(D) Take photographs

89. What is the topic of the training session?

(A) Online references
(B) Web design
(C) Computer software
(D) Home building

90. What does the speaker mean when he says, "So I'd really like you to take her place"?

(A) There was a computer malfunction.
(B) Some equipment needs to be installed.
(C) He wants the listener to lead a workshop.
(D) The listener needs to meet a deadline.

91. What will the caller probably do next?

(A) Send an agenda
(B) Visit a hospital
(C) Plan an event
(D) Call tech support

Meeting Schedule	
Kali Hawk	10:00 A.M.
Hank Harris	11:00 A.M.
Alexandra Park	1:00 P.M.
Shawn Smith	2:00 P.M.

92. Why is the speaker congratulating Shawn?

(A) He has won an award.
(B) He has met a deadline.
(C) He has developed a new product.
(D) He has been promoted at work.

93. Look at the graphic. According to the revised schedule, who will give a presentation at 2 P.M. on Monday?

(A) Kali Hawk
(B) Hank Harris
(C) Alexandra Park
(D) Shawn Smith

94. What is the topic of Kali's presentation?

(A) A marketing strategy
(B) A product launch
(C) A new advertisement
(D) A product budget

Employee Directory	
Name	Extension
Winona Brown	09
Kathryn Newton	19
Annette Heaton	21
Mckenna Grace	45

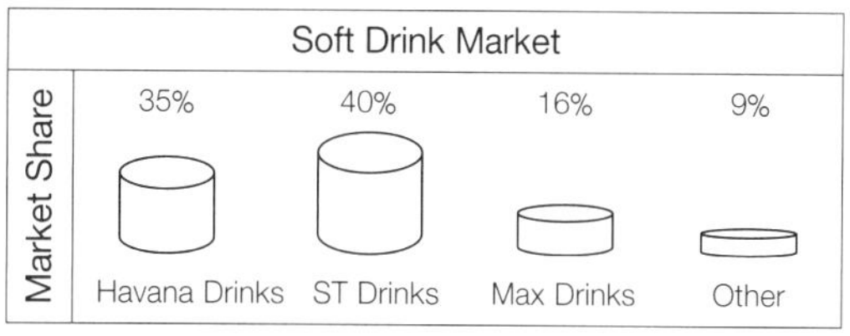

95. What is the main purpose of the message?

(A) To respond to an inquiry
(B) To request a document
(C) To explain a new policy
(D) To provide contact information

96. What is mentioned about Annette Heaton?

(A) She is on a business trip.
(B) She runs her own business.
(C) She reviews expense reports.
(D) She works in the payroll department.

97. Look at the graphic. Which extension will the listener probably dial?

(A) 09
(B) 19
(C) 21
(D) 45

Soft Drink Market

Market Share	Havana Drinks	ST Drinks	Max Drinks	Other
	35%	40%	16%	9%

98. Which department does the speaker work in?

(A) Sales
(B) Personnel
(C) Advertising
(D) Product development

99. Look at the graphic. How much market share did the man's company have last quarter?

(A) 9%
(B) 16%
(C) 35%
(D) 40%

100. According to the speaker, what will happen on May 20th?

(A) A merger will take place.
(B) The division head will get a promotion.
(C) A new product will be introduced.
(D) Employees will submit proposals.

This is the end of the Listening test. Turn to Part 5 in your test book.

GO ON TO THE NEXT PAGE

READING TEST

In the Reading test, you will read a variety of texts and answer several different types of reading comprehension questions. The entire Reading test will last 75 minutes. There are three parts, and directions are given for each part. You are encouraged to answer as many questions as possible within the time allowed.

You must mark your answers on the separate answer sheet. Do not write your answers in your test book.

PART 5

Directions: A word or phrase is missing in each of the sentences below. Four answer choices are given below each sentence. Select the best answer to complete the sentence. Then mark the letter (A), (B), (C), or (D) on your answer sheet.

101. Patients whose operations are delayed for more ------- three months may be entitled to compensation.

(A) of
(B) from
(C) as
(D) than

102. Upon ------- of this email, please let me know if you are available to attend.

(A) receipt
(B) request
(C) entry
(D) appear

103. Please return all keys to the reception before ------- the hotel.

(A) leaves
(B) leaving
(C) left
(D) leave

104. Thanks to meticulous work by Luiz Damez, the project was finished ------- without delay and within budget.

(A) successfully
(B) successful
(C) succeeded
(D) success

105. The Campion List of Hotel Retreats should be a welcome ------- to any establishment.

(A) output
(B) addition
(C) response
(D) treatment

106. Please give ------- a list of the new roster for next week.

(A) everyone
(B) anyone
(C) themselves
(D) which

107. Following a minor fault, the new air conditioning for the main office was ------- commissioned and installed.

(A) finally
(B) rarely
(C) exactly
(D) immensely

108. His good ------- to detail allowed him to notice the small, yet potentially dangerous error in the product's design.

(A) attention
(B) attendant
(C) attended
(D) attends

109. Cutbacks were announced last month but will not come into effect ------- April 2.

(A) behind
(B) until
(C) against
(D) during

110. To comply with catering legislation, food must be kept in ------- airtight and clean containers.

(A) honorable
(B) positive
(C) approved
(D) increased

111. Eyewitnesses were urged to say ------- they saw, regardless of how trivial the information may appear to them.

(A) anywhere
(B) whatever
(C) whenever
(D) nothing

112. Selena Ahmed's rise to marketing manager was ------- her determination to make the Conservative Party succeed.

(A) due to
(B) so that
(C) whereas
(D) because

113. Loueen Morrison's artistic style is ------- by her extensive use of simple colors.

(A) recognizing
(B) recognize
(C) recognizable
(D) recognizably

114. The company merger will ------- affect business and offer new inroads into the South American market.

(A) favoring
(B) favored
(C) favorable
(D) favorably

115. The simplest way to enhance the ------- of your old automobile is to clean it regularly and use wax polish on the paintwork.

(A) appearance
(B) control
(C) improvement
(D) instruction

116. Worksly Appliances is proud to launch the Twospin, the washing machine with the best energy efficiency rating of ------- washing machine to date.

(A) each
(B) some
(C) any
(D) few

117. In the last year, the Winter Gardens Creative Committee has been introducing ------- that are compatible with other organizations in the region.

(A) to measure
(B) measure
(C) measuring
(D) measures

118. Ansar Community Center will donate the money raised from its annual charity sale ------- the erection of a new statue.

(A) about
(B) within
(C) towards
(D) except

119. While New Street Bridge will be closed for ------- renovations, commuters in Cheltenham will be redirected through Queen Street.

(A) structuralize
(B) structural
(C) structurally
(D) structure

120. Visiting several cities every year, the Touring Actors Roadshows ------- thousands of people.

(A) remain
(B) explore
(C) attract
(D) attend

GO ON TO THE NEXT PAGE

121. The underground car park will be ------- unavailable to residents as the concrete floor surface is being cleaned.

(A) temporarily
(B) previously
(C) constructively
(D) stylishly

122. MJ Consulting offers ------- solutions to combating security threats on laptop computers.

(A) innovates
(B) innovative
(C) innovate
(D) innovatively

123. Fire fighters must be accompanied by two ------- when entering a potentially dangerous building.

(A) precaution
(B) emergency
(C) colleagues
(D) personnel

124. As the job requires presenting complex figures at meetings, ------- candidates with extensive power-point experience will be considered.

(A) only
(B) moreover
(C) but
(D) unless

125. In her latest broadcast, award-winning presenter Grace Anjam follows the daily life of a ------- in Tehran.

(A) correspondence
(B) corresponding
(C) correspondent
(D) correspond

126. Due mainly to its ------- high position in the league tables, Shackley United has been promoted to the next division in the South West League.

(A) reluctantly
(B) potentially
(C) evenly
(D) consistently

127. To cement relationships with the newly-acquired company, Smithson Inc, management is offering ------- training programs.

(A) cooperated
(B) cooperative
(C) cooperate
(D) cooperatively

128. Reusable packaging is becoming a normal sight in restaurants as recent surveys show that recycling ------- are important to diners.

(A) compositions
(B) effects
(C) creations
(D) practices

129. ------- exceeded the company's expectations in terms of turnover and profitability, all employees in Rosside Corporation's financial department were awarded an extra day's holiday.

(A) Having
(B) To have
(C) Being
(D) To be

130. Special needs children at the Hamton Hospital are entitled to free ------- to local theater.

(A) admission
(B) movement
(C) connection
(D) exchange

PART 6

Directions: Read the texts that follow. A word, phrase, or sentence is missing in parts of each text. Four answer choices for each question are given below the text. Select the best answer to complete the text. Then mark the letter (A), (B), (C), or (D) on your answer sheet.

Questions 131-134 refer to the following memo.

To: All staff members
From: Luke Perry
Date: May 21

As the holiday season is coming, we hope to take this chance to remind all of you of the company's policy regarding gifts which appear on page 5 of your employee handbook. So as to promote professional -------, all staff members are prohibited from accepting gifts. **131.**

------- this policy, a "gift" is defined as any item given from other retailers, clients, prospective employees, or others with a professional relationship with Konove Products. **132.**

-------. Other benefits, such as gift certificates or free samples, are also defined as gifts. **133.** Employees are held ------- for making retailers and other clients aware of this policy. **134.**

Thank you,

Luke Perry
Public Affairs Director, SH Products

131. (A) integrity
(B) intuition
(C) enactment
(D) sensitivity

132. (A) Regardless of
(B) Under
(C) Beyond
(D) With

133. (A) The gift items range from small promotional items to show tickets and luxury items.
(B) In that case, all employees are asked to report what they've received to their supervisors.
(C) But it is often very hard to recognize who the recipient is.
(D) Alternatively, you get to write an appreciation letter to them.

134. (A) accounting
(B) accounts
(C) accountably
(D) accountable

GO ON TO THE NEXT PAGE

Questions 135–138 refer to the following announcement.

New Vacation Policy

At several recent board meetings, the need to change our ------- (135.) vacation policy has been continually addressed. At present, only employees who have been working both part time and full time for more than 12 months are eligible to ------- (136.) vacation requests. The company, ------- (137.), will now accept vacation requests if an employee has been working for at least 3 months. This updated policy will take effect on August 1. Moreover, an additional two days of paid leave can be used each year for personal business. ------- (138.).

135. (A) existing
(B) exists
(C) existed
(D) existence

136. (A) confirm
(B) fulfill
(C) ensure
(D) submit

137. (A) however
(B) besides
(C) otherwise
(D) namely

138. (A) We hope that you will keep doing business with us.
(B) This month's board meeting will begin at 11 A.M.
(C) Full-time employees are eligible to apply for internal promotion.
(D) This will be allowed only upon approval by your team manager.

Questions 139-142 refer to the following memo.

To: All Harper International Employees
From: Noah Harpster, Administration Manager

A protest against the government's decision to construct an apartment complex near Coronado Bridge is scheduled to take place on Adam Avenue at 6:00 P.M. today.

There will be more than 3,000 people protesting on Adam Avenue which is across from Harper International Inc. As a ------- (**139.**) measure, senior management has decided to let employees depart work by 5:30 P.M. today. -------- (**140.**). Please make sure -------- (**141.**) your immediate supervisor before leaving, via telephone or e-mail.

Employees who get hourly rates are required to clock out as usual at departure.

All department heads should make proper adjustments to review and ------- (**142.**) timekeeping approval to guarantee hourly employees receive pay without any problems.

Noah Harpster

139. (A) careful
(B) precautionary
(C) replaceable
(D) immovable

140. (A) We think an early departure will help our employees avoid the congestion.
(B) The apartment complex needs to be renovated for safety reasons.
(C) Management will review each application before the second interview.
(D) During rush hour, you can park your vehicle on the street near the building.

141. (A) that contact
(B) contacting
(C) to contact
(D) will contact

142. (A) completing
(B) completed
(C) complete
(D) completion

GO ON TO THE NEXT PAGE

Questions 143-146 refer to the following e-mail.

To: Ryan Yerdon
From: Customer Service Center
Date: June 4
Subject: Your order

Thank you for your purchase of a table from our online store. Since you purchased the item during the sale, it cannot be refunded or exchanged unless it is damaged in -------.
143.

Our delivery truck service prides itself on ------- that customers receive their orders undamaged.
144.

------- If the item doesn't meet your expectations after using it, please let us know what is the matter
145.
so that we can address it. Your ------- is always greatly appreciated.
146.

Thank you for doing business with us again.

Sincerely,

Juno Temple, Customer Service Representative

143. (A) usage
(B) display
(C) payment
(D) transit

144. (A) ensuring
(B) ensured
(C) ensures
(D) ensure

145. (A) Unfortunately, problems sometimes arise.
(B) You should select your preferred delivery option.
(C) The assembly manual included is very confusing.
(D) Our customer service center is open 24 hours a day.

146. (A) donation
(B) feedback
(C) invitation
(D) transaction

PART 7

Directions: In this part you will read a selection of texts, such as magazine and newspaper articles, e-mails, and instant messages. Each text or set of texts is followed by several questions. Select the best answer for each question and mark the letter (A), (B), (C), or (D) on your answer sheet.

Questions 147-148 refer to the following letter.

Genghis

9 Piazza Place•Amerte Bay•New Zealand

January 3

Ms. Jillian Naymar
Flecken Drive, 112 Minster Road
Wellington, New Zealand

Dear Ms. Naymar,

Allow me to congratulate you on becoming an elite member of the Genghis Clothing Store Club. This new card grants you 20% off of all goods purchased either in store or from our Web site. This includes all women's clothing, menswear and children's items. We will also send you details about exclusive deals. Members of the Genghis Club also get exclusive first viewing of our new collections which are introduced at the beginning of every season. You can get amazing discounts of up to 30% on certain items.

As a club member, you may also take advantage of our automatic billing service, which allows you to pay your amount due each month directly from your bank account. Of course, members may still pay by check through the mail or by credit card. Go to www.genghis.com.nz/activate or call 555-0154 to activate your membership and start saving today!

Sincerely,

Jorge Hernandez
Jorge Hernandez
Customer Service Department

147. For whom is the letter intended?

(A) A fitness club member
(B) A clothing store customer
(C) A customer service representative
(D) A credit card company clerk

148. What is a benefit the club members receive?

(A) They can have their Genghis bills paid automatically.
(B) They receive a cash bonus after 20 purchases.
(C) They receive a new card every month.
(D) They can access a members-only area on the Web site.

GO ON TO THE NEXT PAGE

Questions 149-150 refer to the following text message chain.

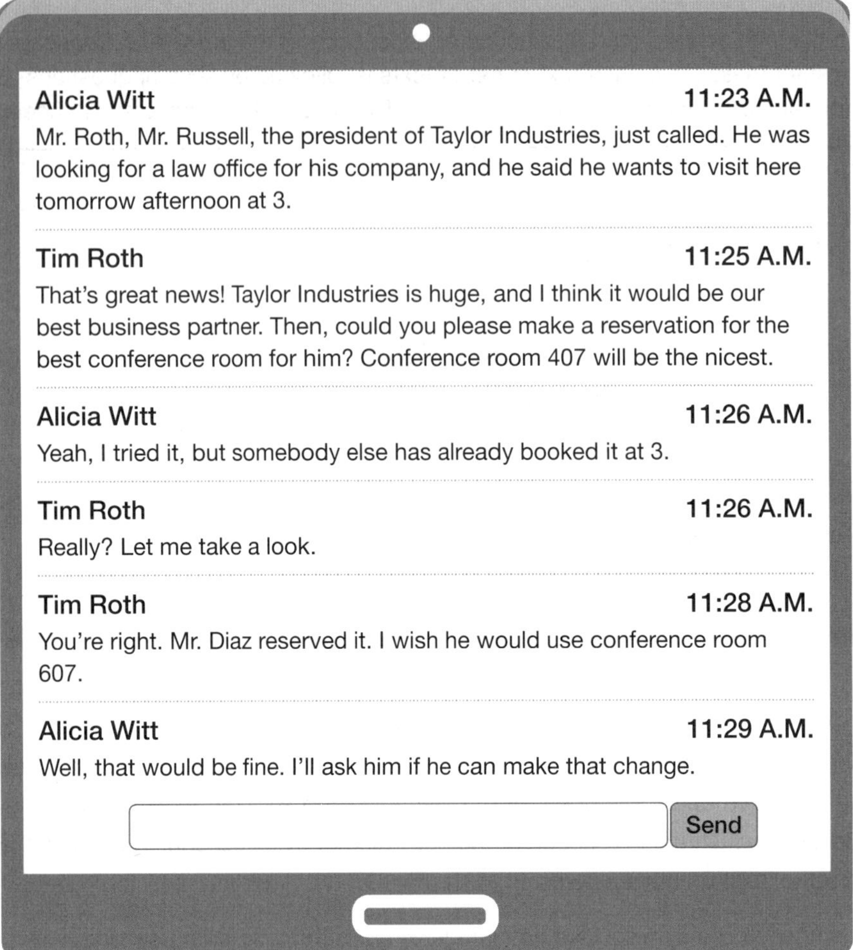

Alicia Witt **11:23 A.M.**
Mr. Roth, Mr. Russell, the president of Taylor Industries, just called. He was looking for a law office for his company, and he said he wants to visit here tomorrow afternoon at 3.

Tim Roth **11:25 A.M.**
That's great news! Taylor Industries is huge, and I think it would be our best business partner. Then, could you please make a reservation for the best conference room for him? Conference room 407 will be the nicest.

Alicia Witt **11:26 A.M.**
Yeah, I tried it, but somebody else has already booked it at 3.

Tim Roth **11:26 A.M.**
Really? Let me take a look.

Tim Roth **11:28 A.M.**
You're right. Mr. Diaz reserved it. I wish he would use conference room 607.

Alicia Witt **11:29 A.M.**
Well, that would be fine. I'll ask him if he can make that change.

149. Where do Mr. Roth and Ms. Witt most likely work?

(A) At a law firm
(B) At a publishing house
(C) At an entertainment company
(D) At an advertising company

150. At 11:29 A.M., what does Ms. Witt most likely mean when she writes, "Well, that would be fine"?

(A) She needs to call her coworker.
(B) She wants Mr. Roth to reserve the location.
(C) She wants Mr. Diaz to accept the change.
(D) She needs to change a schedule for a meeting.

Questions 151-153 refer to the following notice.

Notice for Helsinki Public Train Passengers

Because of surface restructuring and track repairs to part of the Oslo Railroad, a number of public train services will be severely disrupted in the week beginning 3 July and continuing through 17 July. Travelers are urged to make alternative travel arrangements during this period. Normal train services are expected to resume after 17 July.

	Route	Departure	Dates
34	Itäväylä to Viipuri	Every hour	Running as scheduled
36	Länsiväylä to Main Struss	Every hour	Not in Service: 6 July – 9 July
37	Espoo to Vantaa,	Every hour	Not in Service: 3 July – 8 July
45	Kauniainen to Turku	Every half hour	Running as scheduled
51	Tallinn to Sappo	Every hour	Not in Service: 11 July – 15 July
58	Helsinki to Oslo	Every hour	Not in Service: 13 July – 17 July

Refer to the regular schedule for departure and route information.

For more information, visit our Web site at www.helsinkitrains.org or email to info@helsinkitrains.org.

151. What is the notice about?

(A) A temporary change in train service
(B) The addition of new travel routes
(C) The renovation of some old trains
(D) A price increase in train travel

152. According to the notice, what track is undergoing maintenance?

(A) Oslo Railroad
(B) Sappo Railroad
(C) Tallinn Railroad
(D) Turku Railroad

153. Which train is scheduled to run most frequently?

(A) Train 34
(B) Train 36
(C) Train 45
(D) Train 58

Questions 154-155 refer to the following information.

Relocation and Care

When potted shrubs and plants are moved to new locations, special care is vital to ensure that they arrive without injury and flourish in their new habitat. Carry all plants by their pots, as picking them up by their tops or trunks may injure the roots. Follow the watering instructions in the directions-for-care leaflet for the exact type of plant you have bought. These leaflets are complimentary and can be found near the checkout registers.

154. For whom is the information primarily intended?

(A) People selling containers
(B) People purchasing plants
(C) Safety consultants
(D) Store managers

155. What is available at no cost?

(A) Delivery
(B) Boxes
(C) Written instructions
(D) Seed packets

Questions 156-157 refer to the following advertisement.

Jade's Jewelry Company

22 Thesman Street
Holland

Jade's Jewelry Company is holding a relocation sale.

Holland's most exclusive jewelry store is relocating to larger premises (361 Rue Francais). To mark the occasion, we're offering massive reductions on all stock throughout the store.

All jewelry will be discounted by 50 percent or more.

Bring this advertisement with you and get a further 10 percent discount on sale prices.

Hurry in! Sale ends on March 12.

- Current location: 22 Thesman Street
- New location: 361 Rue Francais, opens on April 22

For directions to our current and new location,
visit us online or call us at (+44) 555-2281.

156. What is mentioned about Jade's Jewelry Company?

(A) It is moving premises.
(B) It holds monthly sales.
(C) It is going out of business.
(D) It specializes in men's accessories.

157. What is indicated in the advertisement?

(A) The sale will end before the opening of the new store.
(B) Jade's Jewelry Company will expand overseas next year.
(C) The 10 percent discount will be available only to items that are not on sale.
(D) More shoppers will buy online from Jade's Jewelry Company.

Questions 158-159 refer to the following letter.

Keffen Pharmaceuticals

January 28

Dear Mr. Obangeh,

We received your letter dated January 21 regarding the position of research assistant at Keffen Pharmaceuticals. As mentioned in the job advertisement, we were only accepting completed applications until January 14. The standard of qualified applicants was extremely high and we have offered the position another candidate. However, I would like you to be aware that I found your résumé very impressive and I have kept it on file. I am especially fascinated by your current position as an intern at Milo Labs, as this is where I began my career.

Thank you again for your interest in Keffen Pharmaceuticals. I will contact you if we have any other openings for research assistants here at Keffen Pharmaceuticals in the near future.

Regards,
Addison Morris
Addison Morris
Senior Researcher

158. Why was the letter written?

(A) To explain that a vacant position has been filled
(B) To confirm the details of an interview
(C) To describe the responsibilities of an intern
(D) To request an updated résumé

159. What is mentioned about Mr. Obangeh?

(A) He currently has a job.
(B) His application was declined for lack of experience.
(C) He is applying for a position as chief researcher.
(D) His work experience is not relevant.

Questions 160-162 refer to the following advertisement.

The Forest Glade Gallery

On Sunday, May 18, join us for our annual organic food and plant sale. We have floral collections donated by local garden centers. All profits go to support the gallery lecture series and exhibits. Admission to the gallery is free of charge during the sale.

The Forest Glade Gallery was established twenty-five years ago by the family of the late artist and ceramicist Ernst Steinberg. The gallery houses an outstanding collection of artifacts and pottery collected over the course of the artist's travels, as well as various paintings by other renowned artists. Its beautifully landscaped gardens include a water fountain and picturesque sculptures, set out along the various walking paths.

The gallery gift shop will offer a 15 percent discount on items purchased during the plant sale. Gallery hours are from 10 AM to 5:30 PM, Monday to Friday. Weekend hours are 11 AM to 4 PM. (Current exhibitions include *The Landscapes* of Alicia Merton and are open to the public during regular gallery hours through the month of May.) For more information, visit www.forestgladegallery.org.

160. What is being advertised?

(A) A lecture by Ernst Steinberg
(B) A sale of ceramics
(C) A fundraising sale
(D) A grand opening

161. What can be indicated about the Forest Glade Gallery?

(A) It is re-arranging its exhibits.
(B) It was established by an artist's family.
(C) It offers classes in ceramics.
(D) It was recently landscaped.

162. What is NOT scheduled to happen at the Forest Glade Gallery on May 18?

(A) The gallery will remain open until 9:00 P.M.
(B) Ceramic objects will be on display.
(C) There will be a discount on prices in the gallery gift shop.
(D) Admission to the gallery will be free of charge.

GO ON TO THE NEXT PAGE

Questions 163-166 refer to the following online chat discussion.

Jason Lee [4:31 P.M.]	Good afternoon. I want everyone to talk about the opinions of staff members at your branch after the announcement of the restructuring.
Brie James [4:33 P.M.]	Right after the initial announcement, they felt uncomfortable, but seemed to gradually calm down. They are keeping a close eye on future changes.
Mary Goggin [4:34 P.M.]	Staff members here expect that the restructuring will involve some staff arrangements and massive layoffs. Due to the severe economic recession, employees are worried about any changes that might happen.
Chris Messina [4:35 P.M.]	I'm careful to say something about this issue to my employees. I have nothing to say to them without further information.
Jason Lee [4:36 P.M.]	We're working on it. After the decisions are made roughly in May through a meeting of department heads, I'll consult in more detail with you.
Mary Goggin [4:37 P.M.]	In June, some of our offices might be filled with moving boxes. I have mixed feelings.
Jason Lee [4:38 P.M.]	Until the restructuring is complete, your cooperation is greatly needed. If you have any other questions, please feel free to contact me.

Send

163. Why did Mr. Lee send the message?

(A) To schedule a meeting
(B) To announce possible plans
(C) To find out employees' opinions
(D) To confirm schedules for office relocation

164. At 4:36 P.M., what does Mr. Lee most likely mean when he writes, "We're working on it"?

(A) The work hours has been extended significantly.
(B) Several offices will be closed soon.
(C) He meets regularly with CEOs.
(D) The managers are gathering more detailed information.

165. When will the branches receive an update?

(A) In May
(B) In June
(C) In July
(D) In August

166. What are the branch managers expected to do?

(A) Hire new employees
(B) Ask questions at any time
(C) Provide new identification cards
(D) Order office equipment

Questions 167-170 refer to the following letter.

Jim Thomas
980 Alm Street
Denver, CO 80247

Dear Mr. Thomas:

I have booked the date for my arrival at the Colorado Nova Factory. – [1] –. I will be arriving at Denver International Airport on Monday, October 24 at 4:00 P.M. You do not need to worry about a place for me to stay. I have booked a room at the local Holiday Motel.

I am looking forward to walking the floor of the factory. Also, I am interested in viewing the health records and the safety records of the employees. – [2] –. We will be instigating a new safety program in the workplace at the beginning of next year. I am also excited about seeing the factory's new fluorescent lights product line. – [3] –. I believe that this is a great product for the new market that will be opening overseas in the coming years as countries develop.

As always, I am looking forward to seeing you again. I will see you on the 24th. – [4] –.

Sincerely,
Arthur Clark

167. What is the letter about?

(A) Mr. Clark's visit to the Colorado Nova Factory
(B) Mr. Clark's visit to corporate headquarters
(C) The new production of fluorescent lights
(D) The new market opening overseas

168. What will the company do early next year?

(A) Check health records
(B) Start a safety program in the workplace
(C) Produce fluorescent lights
(D) Fire some employees

169. In which of the positions marked [1], [2], [3], and [4] does the following sentence best belong?

"There has been concern at corporate headquarters that safety in the workplace is in need of improvement."

(A) [1]
(B) [2]
(C) [3]
(D) [4]

170. What is NOT mentioned in the letter?

(A) How long Mr. Clark is staying
(B) When Mr. Clark is arriving
(C) New markets opening overseas
(D) Where Mr. Clark is staying

Questions 171-175 refer to the following letter.

May 14

Lui Chin
Tien Corporation
1005 Szechuan Province
China 00354

Dear Mr. Chin,

Thank you for subscribing to Suitan Service for broadband and telephone services for your office. We have arranged for an engineer to connect the service at 9 A.M. on May 17. We hope this is convenient for you. – [1] –.

The terms of the contract state that we will provide you with broadband and telephone services for a period of 24 months; installation is $30 and the fixed rate contract for the services is $25 per month. The installation fee will be billed separately. – [2] –. After two years, you will be charged at a rate of $40 per month. If you cancel before the end of the contract period, this will be considered a breach of contract, which incurs a penalty of $75. A copy of the contract is enclosed. – [3] –.

You will receive a bill at the end of each month, and payment must be received within fourteen days via bank transfer, direct debit or in person. Your nearest Suitan Service office is located at 992 Canton Street in the High Street opposite the Shanghai Bank. – [4] –. Thank you for your business.

Sincerely,
Lassi Virente
Lassi Virente
Suitan Account Manager

171. Where is Mr. Chin having an Internet connection installed?

(A) At his store
(B) At his office
(C) At his house
(D) At his café

172. In which of the positions marked [1], [2], [3], and [4] does the following sentence best belong?

"As our engineer has many installations that day, please contact us the day before to confirm the schedule."

(A) [1]
(B) [2]
(C) [3]
(D) [4]

173. After two years of service, how much will Mr. Chin be expected to pay each month?

(A) $30
(B) $40
(C) $75
(D) $100

174. According to the letter, why might Mr. Chin receive an additional charge?

(A) For losing his account password
(B) For submitting the incorrect payment details
(C) For canceling a direct debit
(D) For breaking his service agreement

175. When will Mr. Chin's first Suitan Service payment be due?

(A) May 10
(B) May 14
(C) June 14
(D) June 31

GO ON TO THE NEXT PAGE

Questions 176-180 refer to the following letter and e-mail.

October 2

Anwar Singh
Denham Corporation
41 Mumbai Street
Peshwar Province
Delhi, India

Dear Mr. Singh,

At Abbeycom, we are committed to responsibly recycling all your packaging, industrial waste, and other disposables. We have an extensive collection network and efficient technologies that keep our costs low and our services competitive. With depots in three countries, we have the means to process material on a large and continuous scale.

As the account manager responsible for one of the biggest recycling companies in India, we are concerned about where and what you may recycle. Please take a look at the enclosed brochure about Abbeycom as a guide to disposing your recyclable waste. For further information about the quality of our business, I advise you to check the testimonials from a number of satisfied companies within the brochure. If you wish to discuss your company's specific requirements, please contact me. Or if you prefer, speak with Harri Chai in our Delhi office.

Sincerely,
Kumar Barhi
Kumar Barhi
Senior Account Manager
Enclosed

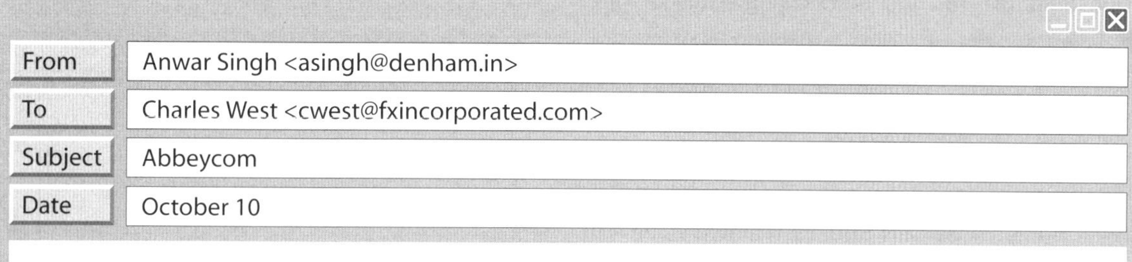

From: Anwar Singh <asingh@denham.in>
To: Charles West <cwest@fxincorporated.com>
Subject: Abbeycom
Date: October 10

I am the facilities manager for the Denham Corporation in Delhi. We are looking to partner with Abbeycom to recycle our industrial waste and packaging. Before I decide to speak to Abbeycom, I would be interested in your opinion.

I understand that your organization uses Abbeycom to collect manufacturing waste from your various international factories. I am especially concerned with your operations in Massaua. Abbeycom transports from that city to its processing plant in Lajan, where our collected waste would also be sent. I would be interested to find out whether they collect materials on time and are reliable with their collections. I welcome any additional information you provide.

Sincerely,

Anwar Singh
Facilities manager, Delhi office

176. What is the purpose of the letter?

(A) To offer a discount to a loyal client
(B) To describe new environmental regulations
(C) To promote a recycling service
(D) To recommend a brand of industrial equipment

177. According to the letter, how does Abbeycom stay competitive?

(A) It operates state-of-the-art facilities.
(B) It uses cheap shipment methods.
(C) It transports products overnight.
(D) It recycles garbage into new products.

178. Who most likely is the regional representative for Abbeycom?

(A) Anwar Singh
(B) Kumar Barhi
(C) Charles West
(D) Harri Chai

179. Where did Mr. Singh most likely get Mr. West's contact information?

(A) From an Indian business network
(B) From a colleague of Mr. Chai
(C) From Abbeycom's Web site
(D) From Abbeycom's list of testimonials

180. What concerns Mr. Singh about Abbeycom?

(A) The reliability of its services
(B) The extra fees that may be added
(C) The shipment operation overseas
(D) The length of time it has been in business

GO ON TO THE NEXT PAGE

Questions 181-185 refer to following e-mails.

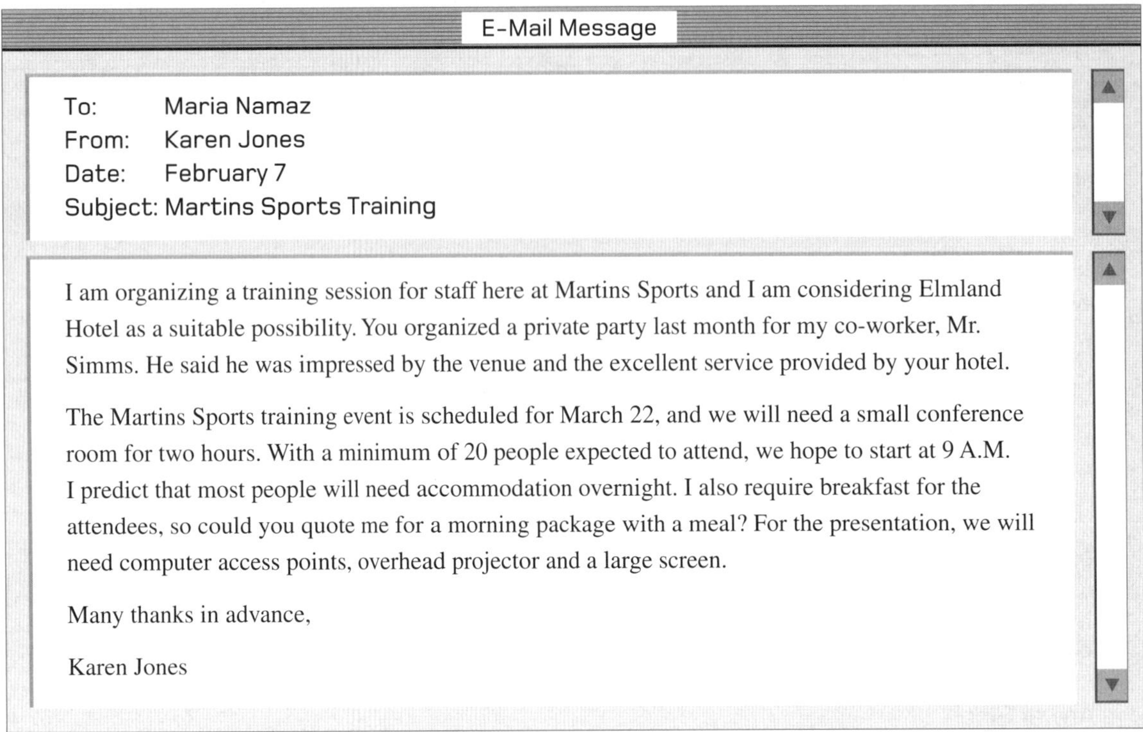

E-Mail Message

To: Maria Namaz
From: Karen Jones
Date: February 7
Subject: Martins Sports Training

I am organizing a training session for staff here at Martins Sports and I am considering Elmland Hotel as a suitable possibility. You organized a private party last month for my co-worker, Mr. Simms. He said he was impressed by the venue and the excellent service provided by your hotel.

The Martins Sports training event is scheduled for March 22, and we will need a small conference room for two hours. With a minimum of 20 people expected to attend, we hope to start at 9 A.M. I predict that most people will need accommodation overnight. I also require breakfast for the attendees, so could you quote me for a morning package with a meal? For the presentation, we will need computer access points, overhead projector and a large screen.

Many thanks in advance,

Karen Jones

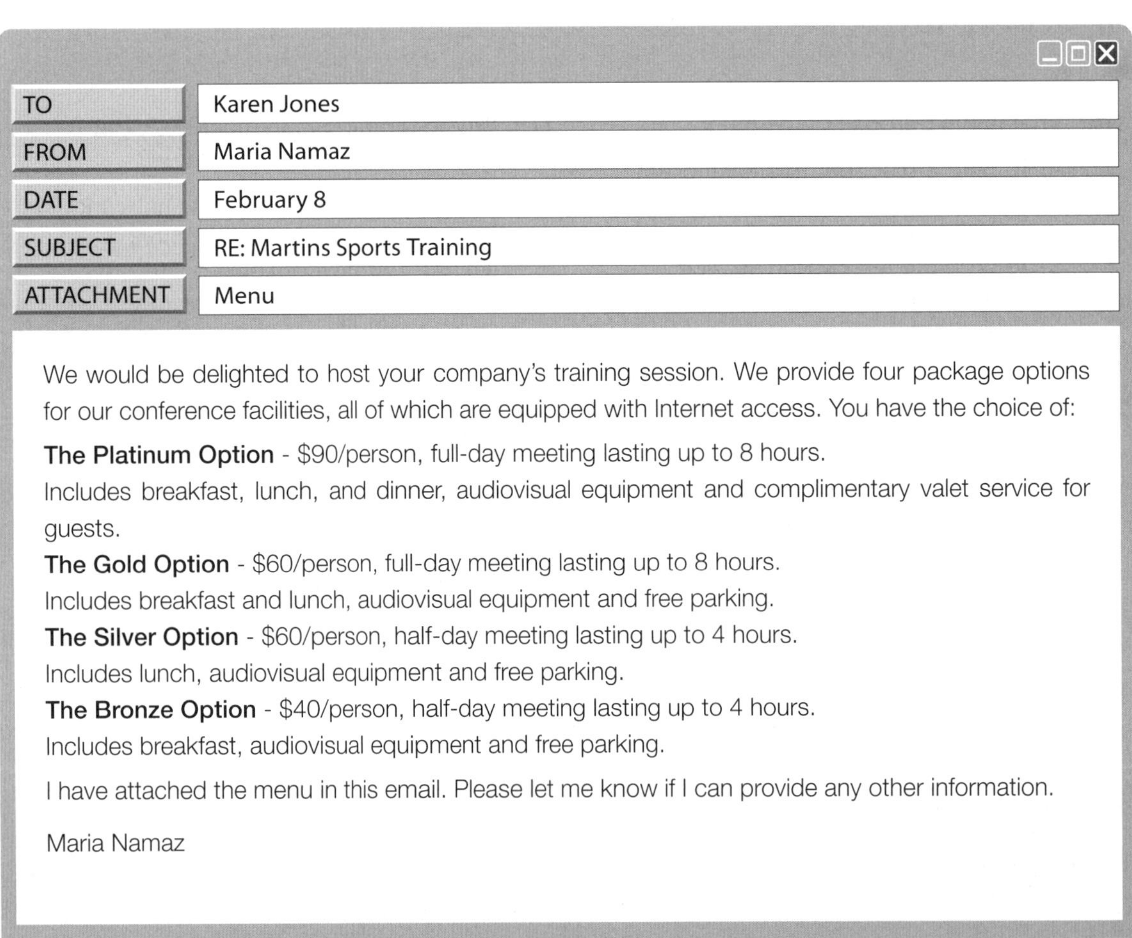

TO	Karen Jones
FROM	Maria Namaz
DATE	February 8
SUBJECT	RE: Martins Sports Training
ATTACHMENT	Menu

We would be delighted to host your company's training session. We provide four package options for our conference facilities, all of which are equipped with Internet access. You have the choice of:

The Platinum Option - $90/person, full-day meeting lasting up to 8 hours.
Includes breakfast, lunch, and dinner, audiovisual equipment and complimentary valet service for guests.

The Gold Option - $60/person, full-day meeting lasting up to 8 hours.
Includes breakfast and lunch, audiovisual equipment and free parking.

The Silver Option - $60/person, half-day meeting lasting up to 4 hours.
Includes lunch, audiovisual equipment and free parking.

The Bronze Option - $40/person, half-day meeting lasting up to 4 hours.
Includes breakfast, audiovisual equipment and free parking.

I have attached the menu in this email. Please let me know if I can provide any other information.

Maria Namaz

181. What is the purpose of the first e-mail?

(A) To send out party invitations
(B) To correct a mistake on the registration form
(C) To confirm a reservation date
(D) To inquire about options for a meeting

182. What is suggested about the seminar?

(A) A film will be shown in the morning.
(B) Participants are employed in a variety of industries.
(C) It was originally scheduled for another venue.
(D) It will feature a presentation.

183. What is indicated about Ms. Namaz?

(A) She was recommended by a coworker of Ms. Jones.
(B) She recently began working at the Elmland Hotel.
(C) She previously worked for Martins Sports.
(D) She designed the Elmland Hotel's catering menu.

184. What is NOT mentioned as a feature of the meeting packages?

(A) Free parking for hotel guests
(B) Internet access in the conference room
(C) Price discounts on rooms for participants
(D) Audiovisual equipment for the meeting room

185. What package best meets the needs of Martins Sports?

(A) The Gold Option
(B) The Bronze Option
(C) The Silver Option
(D) The Platinum Option

GO ON TO THE NEXT PAGE

Questions 186-190 refer to the following memo, document, and report.

To: All branch managers
From: GLN Bank, Headquarters
Date: March 3
Subject: Preparation for the Launching of Green Card

The Green Card is one of our bank's latest credit card services. It will go on the market on the 16th of this month.

For that matter, all bank personnel should be familiar with the terms and conditions related to the Green Card. Although these specifics are not prepared yet, you can check the final version of all the relevant information by tomorrow morning.

Furthermore, all branch managers are obligated to submit an evaluation report on the Green Card products after a month of its launching.

Green Card

Terms and Conditions

* All bank staff members must be fully aware of the terms and conditions of the Green Card products.
  1) Clients must have an initial deposit of $100.
  2) Clients should fill out the application form.
  3) Product beneficiaries must also have an income at least $5,000 a month.
  4) Card recipients must present identification such as below:
     — Company identification card, driver's license, passport
* Clients interested in joining the service must be properly informed of the rules stated above.

To: All employees
From: GLN Bank, Seattle branch
Date: April 20
Subject: Green Card Update

Attention: Please secure a copy of this message for your reference. After the launching of the Green Card, we have experienced a couple of problems, such as:

1. Customers complaining of inoperative cards or the cards not being registered on the main system.
2. Minors requesting cards with driver's license. (Note: A driver's license can be obtained at the age of 16. However, credit cards are not available to clients until they are the age of 20.)

We have learned valuable lessons from the past month and this will help us improve our plans for the future. We have to be more thorough and not make the same mistakes again. So we are planning to have a seminar on the Green Card products. We hope that this seminar can be the foundation for our need to provide high-quality service to our clients.

Jeffrey Donovan
Seattle branch

186. What is the purpose of the memo?

(A) To tell employees to sell the new card product
(B) To request opinions about the Green Card
(C) To inquire about consumers' response to the new product
(D) To inform all branch managers of the near future plan

187. What is requested of the branch managers?

(A) Sell the new product on site to customers
(B) Submit the assessment of the new product
(C) Brainstorm a card design by the end of this month
(D) Attract more of the affiliating companies

188. What is NOT requested of a customer who wants Green Card products?

(A) Presentation of ID card
(B) An initial deposit
(C) Regular income
(D) Property asset

189. Which of the following is NOT identified about product launching?

(A) Some of the cards were not operating.
(B) The product was launched in early April.
(C) A workshop is scheduled after the launch of the product.
(D) Minors were requesting to be entitled to a card.

190. What is being suggested by Mr. Donovan?

(A) That the employees attend a training session
(B) That the number of sales representatives be increased
(C) That the bank's closing time be adjusted
(D) That employees have as much experience as possible

GO ON TO THE NEXT PAGE

Questions 191-195 refer to the following flyer, coupon, and fax.

Blue Table Catering Services

For your next event, put your worries aside and call Blue Table Catering Services to prepare gourmet food with a delicate presentation.

We offer you

- Full service catering, from set-up to clean-up
- Various menu options
- Trained and courteous servers
- A variety of tableware
- Decorating specialists

If you plan to host a huge event, you can use the enclosed special coupons. Please enjoy the incredible benefits within a limited period.

For further questions, please make a phone call at 555-6524, or send a fax to 555-6527 or visit our Web site at www.bluetable.com.

Blue Table Catering Services

Special Discount Coupon

We are offering the best and perfect service to you!

Please cut out the coupon below and feel free to use it for your own needs.

20% discount on rates for events serving more than **200 people** **July 1 ~ August 31**	30% discount on rates for events serving more than **300 people** **July 1 ~ August 31**

To: Blue Table Catering Services
From: Eva Tennant
Date: June 20
Subject: Catering Estimates

I would like to host a 4th of July outing for my employees and their families. I have 100 employees, and if they bring all their family members, it will be around 220 to 250 people. A simple and classic type of 4th of July menu with BBQ, small sandwiches and finger foods would be nice.

Before I make a formal request, I would like to know about the approximate price and menu choices for the event I am planning. Also, is it possible to get a 25% discount if my guests go over the number of 250?

Please call me on my mobile phone at 014-555-0987 and let me know.

Thank you very much.

Eva Tennant

191. What is NOT being offered by Blue Table Catering Services?

(A) Experts on decorations
(B) A wide choice of dishware
(C) Etiquette learning service
(D) Abundant menu choices

192. In the flyer, the word "delicate" in paragraph 1, line 2, is closest in meaning to

(A) bright
(B) graceful
(C) expensive
(D) weak

193. For whom is Ms. Tennant planning an event?

(A) Her friends
(B) Her clients
(C) Her grandparents
(D) Her colleagues and their families

194. How much discount can Ms. Tennant get for the event?

(A) 10%
(B) 20%
(C) 25%
(D) 30%

195. How does Ms. Tennant want to be contacted by Blue Table Catering Services?

(A) By fax
(B) By phone
(C) By a visit to her office
(D) By e-mail

GO ON TO THE NEXT PAGE

Questions 196-200 refer to the following e-mail, letter, and schedule.

To: Paul Dooley <dooley@alpine.net>
From: Martin Donovan <donovan@chc.com>
Date: December 20
Subject: Proposed Schedule

Hello, Paul.

It looks like we've run into a bit of a snag. We received your proposed construction schedule for the McKee development, and management is not satisfied with it. Either my manager, Sean Grady, or one of our project coordinators will be formally contacting your boss in a day or so, but I just wanted to give you a heads-up about the specific problems.

The first is the long delay between the scheduled delivery of the plumbing and wiring components and the beginning of the installation process. They want to know what kind of storage will be in place to prevent potential weather damage during the ten days between delivery and installation. The second is the weeklong break in the middle of the project, which was neither previously mentioned nor approved. And finally, the opening ceremony is meant to occur on the first of June, but your final day of construction is scheduled later than that. I hope your company is flexible with the schedule so that we can find some middle ground.

Martin

December 26, 2019

Jennifer Wiener
Seattle Housing Corporation
61 White Creek Lane

Dear Ms. Wiener:

In response to your letter dated December 21 regarding the McKee housing development, I can offer the following solutions. First of all, accommodating your plans to hold the opening ceremony on June 1 is not a problem. We can simply condense our final inspection process from six to three days. As for the plumbing and wiring components, there are no on-site storage facilities—materials waiting to be used are simply covered by waterproof tarps. While we are unable to alter the scheduled installation starting date of May 1 for the components in question, we can, with your approval, change their delivery date. Finally, the mid-project break is non-negotiable. It is union mandated and set to coincide with the time required for the concrete foundations to dry and set.

Sincerely,

Jeremy Piven
Premium Construction

McKee Housing Development – Final Construction Schedule

Date	Task	Date	Task
1/18 to 2/10	Leveling and preparation of the site	4/28	Delivery of plumbing and wiring components
2/10 to 2/20	Application of concrete for foundations	5/1 to 5/15	Installation of plumbing and wiring components
2/21 to 2/28	Break period	5/16 to 5/28	Interior and exterior finishing touches
3/1 to 4/30	General construction of building frames	5/29 to 5/31	Final inspection

196. What is the purpose of the e-mail?

(A) To apologize for a delay in a schedule
(B) To notify someone of an upcoming ceremony
(C) To complain about faulty construction
(D) To warn someone about a potential problem

197. Who most likely is Jennifer Wiener?

(A) Martin Donovan's manager
(B) Sean Grady's boss
(C) A building inspector
(D) A project coordinator

198. What was the delivery date for plumbing and wiring components in the original schedule?

(A) April 1
(B) April 20
(C) May 1
(D) May 15

199. What does Mr. Piven say about the weeklong break?

(A) It will be shortened.
(B) It will be pushed back.
(C) It cannot be changed.
(D) It does not apply to this project.

200. What was the final date of construction in the original schedule?

(A) May 28
(B) May 29
(C) June 1
(D) June 3

Stop! This is the end of the test. If you finish before time is called, you may go back to Parts 5, 6, and 7 and check your work.

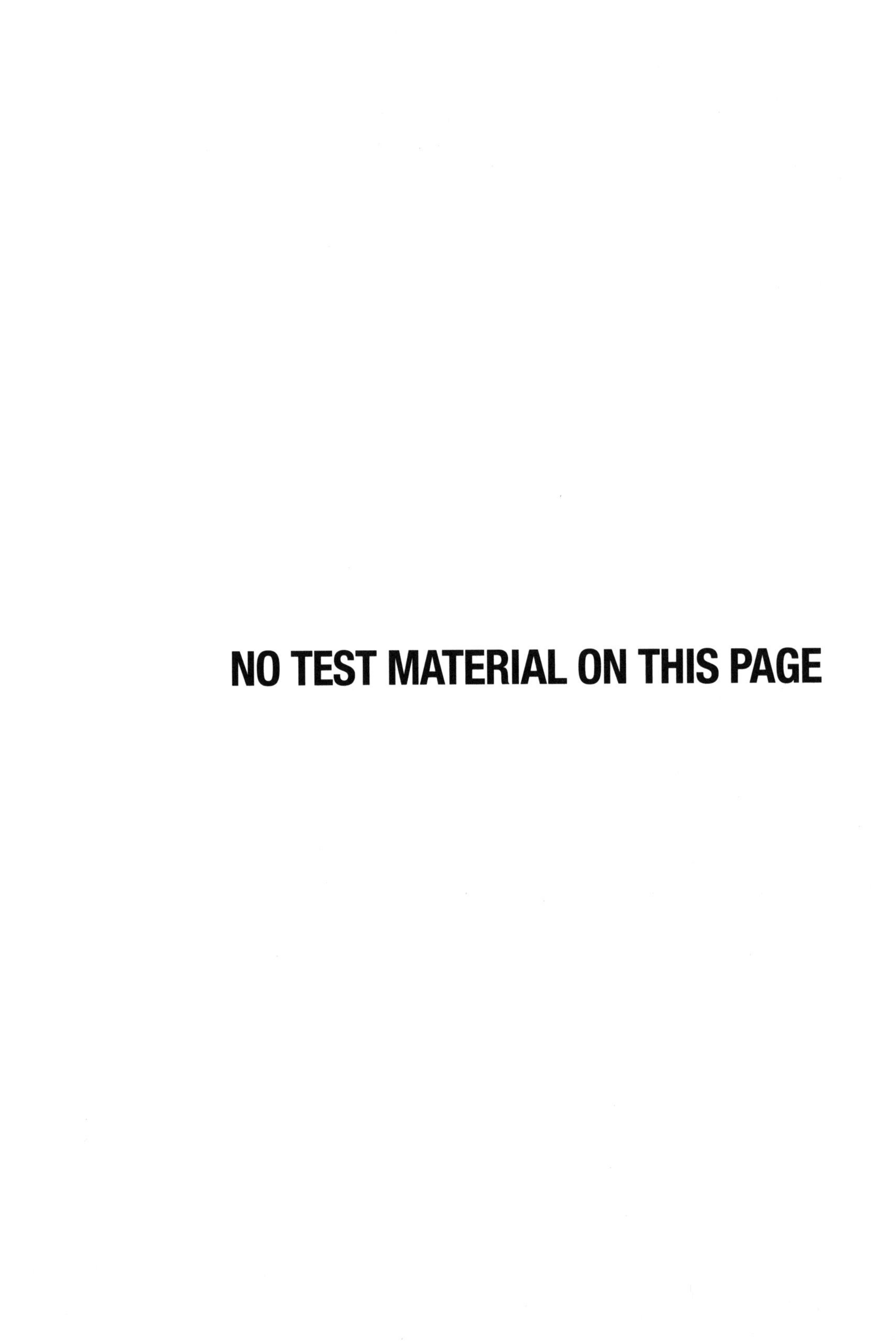

NO TEST MATERIAL ON THIS PAGE

ANSWER SHEET

수험번호						

Actual **Test 1**

성명	한글	
	한자	
	영자	

좌석번호
Ⓐ Ⓑ Ⓒ Ⓓ Ⓔ
① ② ③ ④ ⑤ ⑥ ⑦

응시일자 : 년 월 일

LISTENING (Part I~IV)

NO.	ANSWER				NO.	ANSWER				NO.	ANSWER				NO.	ANSWER				NO.	ANSWER			
	A	B	C	D		A	B	C	D		A	B	C	D		A	B	C	D		A	B	C	D
1	Ⓐ	Ⓑ	Ⓒ	Ⓓ	21	Ⓐ	Ⓑ	Ⓒ		41	Ⓐ	Ⓑ	Ⓒ	Ⓓ	61	Ⓐ	Ⓑ	Ⓒ	Ⓓ	81	Ⓐ	Ⓑ	Ⓒ	Ⓓ
2	Ⓐ	Ⓑ	Ⓒ	Ⓓ	22	Ⓐ	Ⓑ	Ⓒ		42	Ⓐ	Ⓑ	Ⓒ	Ⓓ	62	Ⓐ	Ⓑ	Ⓒ	Ⓓ	82	Ⓐ	Ⓑ	Ⓒ	Ⓓ
3	Ⓐ	Ⓑ	Ⓒ	Ⓓ	23	Ⓐ	Ⓑ	Ⓒ		43	Ⓐ	Ⓑ	Ⓒ	Ⓓ	63	Ⓐ	Ⓑ	Ⓒ	Ⓓ	83	Ⓐ	Ⓑ	Ⓒ	Ⓓ
4	Ⓐ	Ⓑ	Ⓒ	Ⓓ	24	Ⓐ	Ⓑ	Ⓒ		44	Ⓐ	Ⓑ	Ⓒ	Ⓓ	64	Ⓐ	Ⓑ	Ⓒ	Ⓓ	84	Ⓐ	Ⓑ	Ⓒ	Ⓓ
5	Ⓐ	Ⓑ	Ⓒ	Ⓓ	25	Ⓐ	Ⓑ	Ⓒ		45	Ⓐ	Ⓑ	Ⓒ	Ⓓ	65	Ⓐ	Ⓑ	Ⓒ	Ⓓ	85	Ⓐ	Ⓑ	Ⓒ	Ⓓ
6	Ⓐ	Ⓑ	Ⓒ	Ⓓ	26	Ⓐ	Ⓑ	Ⓒ		46	Ⓐ	Ⓑ	Ⓒ	Ⓓ	66	Ⓐ	Ⓑ	Ⓒ	Ⓓ	86	Ⓐ	Ⓑ	Ⓒ	Ⓓ
7	Ⓐ	Ⓑ	Ⓒ		27	Ⓐ	Ⓑ	Ⓒ		47	Ⓐ	Ⓑ	Ⓒ	Ⓓ	67	Ⓐ	Ⓑ	Ⓒ	Ⓓ	87	Ⓐ	Ⓑ	Ⓒ	Ⓓ
8	Ⓐ	Ⓑ	Ⓒ		28	Ⓐ	Ⓑ	Ⓒ		48	Ⓐ	Ⓑ	Ⓒ	Ⓓ	68	Ⓐ	Ⓑ	Ⓒ	Ⓓ	88	Ⓐ	Ⓑ	Ⓒ	Ⓓ
9	Ⓐ	Ⓑ	Ⓒ		29	Ⓐ	Ⓑ	Ⓒ		49	Ⓐ	Ⓑ	Ⓒ	Ⓓ	69	Ⓐ	Ⓑ	Ⓒ	Ⓓ	89	Ⓐ	Ⓑ	Ⓒ	Ⓓ
10	Ⓐ	Ⓑ	Ⓒ		30	Ⓐ	Ⓑ	Ⓒ		50	Ⓐ	Ⓑ	Ⓒ	Ⓓ	70	Ⓐ	Ⓑ	Ⓒ	Ⓓ	90	Ⓐ	Ⓑ	Ⓒ	Ⓓ
11	Ⓐ	Ⓑ	Ⓒ		31	Ⓐ	Ⓑ	Ⓒ		51	Ⓐ	Ⓑ	Ⓒ	Ⓓ	71	Ⓐ	Ⓑ	Ⓒ	Ⓓ	91	Ⓐ	Ⓑ	Ⓒ	Ⓓ
12	Ⓐ	Ⓑ	Ⓒ		32	Ⓐ	Ⓑ	Ⓒ	Ⓓ	52	Ⓐ	Ⓑ	Ⓒ	Ⓓ	72	Ⓐ	Ⓑ	Ⓒ	Ⓓ	92	Ⓐ	Ⓑ	Ⓒ	Ⓓ
13	Ⓐ	Ⓑ	Ⓒ		33	Ⓐ	Ⓑ	Ⓒ	Ⓓ	53	Ⓐ	Ⓑ	Ⓒ	Ⓓ	73	Ⓐ	Ⓑ	Ⓒ	Ⓓ	93	Ⓐ	Ⓑ	Ⓒ	Ⓓ
14	Ⓐ	Ⓑ	Ⓒ		34	Ⓐ	Ⓑ	Ⓒ	Ⓓ	54	Ⓐ	Ⓑ	Ⓒ	Ⓓ	74	Ⓐ	Ⓑ	Ⓒ	Ⓓ	94	Ⓐ	Ⓑ	Ⓒ	Ⓓ
15	Ⓐ	Ⓑ	Ⓒ		35	Ⓐ	Ⓑ	Ⓒ	Ⓓ	55	Ⓐ	Ⓑ	Ⓒ	Ⓓ	75	Ⓐ	Ⓑ	Ⓒ	Ⓓ	95	Ⓐ	Ⓑ	Ⓒ	Ⓓ
16	Ⓐ	Ⓑ	Ⓒ		36	Ⓐ	Ⓑ	Ⓒ	Ⓓ	56	Ⓐ	Ⓑ	Ⓒ	Ⓓ	76	Ⓐ	Ⓑ	Ⓒ	Ⓓ	96	Ⓐ	Ⓑ	Ⓒ	Ⓓ
17	Ⓐ	Ⓑ	Ⓒ		37	Ⓐ	Ⓑ	Ⓒ	Ⓓ	57	Ⓐ	Ⓑ	Ⓒ	Ⓓ	77	Ⓐ	Ⓑ	Ⓒ	Ⓓ	97	Ⓐ	Ⓑ	Ⓒ	Ⓓ
18	Ⓐ	Ⓑ	Ⓒ		38	Ⓐ	Ⓑ	Ⓒ	Ⓓ	58	Ⓐ	Ⓑ	Ⓒ	Ⓓ	78	Ⓐ	Ⓑ	Ⓒ	Ⓓ	98	Ⓐ	Ⓑ	Ⓒ	Ⓓ
19	Ⓐ	Ⓑ	Ⓒ		39	Ⓐ	Ⓑ	Ⓒ	Ⓓ	59	Ⓐ	Ⓑ	Ⓒ	Ⓓ	79	Ⓐ	Ⓑ	Ⓒ	Ⓓ	99	Ⓐ	Ⓑ	Ⓒ	Ⓓ
20	Ⓐ	Ⓑ	Ⓒ		40	Ⓐ	Ⓑ	Ⓒ	Ⓓ	60	Ⓐ	Ⓑ	Ⓒ	Ⓓ	80	Ⓐ	Ⓑ	Ⓒ	Ⓓ	100	Ⓐ	Ⓑ	Ⓒ	Ⓓ

READING (Part V~VII)

NO.	ANSWER				NO.	ANSWER				NO.	ANSWER				NO.	ANSWER				NO.	ANSWER			
	A	B	C	D		A	B	C	D		A	B	C	D		A	B	C	D		A	B	C	D
101	Ⓐ	Ⓑ	Ⓒ	Ⓓ	121	Ⓐ	Ⓑ	Ⓒ	Ⓓ	141	Ⓐ	Ⓑ	Ⓒ	Ⓓ	161	Ⓐ	Ⓑ	Ⓒ	Ⓓ	181	Ⓐ	Ⓑ	Ⓒ	Ⓓ
102	Ⓐ	Ⓑ	Ⓒ	Ⓓ	122	Ⓐ	Ⓑ	Ⓒ	Ⓓ	142	Ⓐ	Ⓑ	Ⓒ	Ⓓ	162	Ⓐ	Ⓑ	Ⓒ	Ⓓ	182	Ⓐ	Ⓑ	Ⓒ	Ⓓ
103	Ⓐ	Ⓑ	Ⓒ	Ⓓ	123	Ⓐ	Ⓑ	Ⓒ	Ⓓ	143	Ⓐ	Ⓑ	Ⓒ	Ⓓ	163	Ⓐ	Ⓑ	Ⓒ	Ⓓ	183	Ⓐ	Ⓑ	Ⓒ	Ⓓ
104	Ⓐ	Ⓑ	Ⓒ	Ⓓ	124	Ⓐ	Ⓑ	Ⓒ	Ⓓ	144	Ⓐ	Ⓑ	Ⓒ	Ⓓ	164	Ⓐ	Ⓑ	Ⓒ	Ⓓ	184	Ⓐ	Ⓑ	Ⓒ	Ⓓ
105	Ⓐ	Ⓑ	Ⓒ	Ⓓ	125	Ⓐ	Ⓑ	Ⓒ	Ⓓ	145	Ⓐ	Ⓑ	Ⓒ	Ⓓ	165	Ⓐ	Ⓑ	Ⓒ	Ⓓ	185	Ⓐ	Ⓑ	Ⓒ	Ⓓ
106	Ⓐ	Ⓑ	Ⓒ	Ⓓ	126	Ⓐ	Ⓑ	Ⓒ	Ⓓ	146	Ⓐ	Ⓑ	Ⓒ	Ⓓ	166	Ⓐ	Ⓑ	Ⓒ	Ⓓ	186	Ⓐ	Ⓑ	Ⓒ	Ⓓ
107	Ⓐ	Ⓑ	Ⓒ	Ⓓ	127	Ⓐ	Ⓑ	Ⓒ	Ⓓ	147	Ⓐ	Ⓑ	Ⓒ	Ⓓ	167	Ⓐ	Ⓑ	Ⓒ	Ⓓ	187	Ⓐ	Ⓑ	Ⓒ	Ⓓ
108	Ⓐ	Ⓑ	Ⓒ	Ⓓ	128	Ⓐ	Ⓑ	Ⓒ	Ⓓ	148	Ⓐ	Ⓑ	Ⓒ	Ⓓ	168	Ⓐ	Ⓑ	Ⓒ	Ⓓ	188	Ⓐ	Ⓑ	Ⓒ	Ⓓ
109	Ⓐ	Ⓑ	Ⓒ	Ⓓ	129	Ⓐ	Ⓑ	Ⓒ	Ⓓ	149	Ⓐ	Ⓑ	Ⓒ	Ⓓ	169	Ⓐ	Ⓑ	Ⓒ	Ⓓ	189	Ⓐ	Ⓑ	Ⓒ	Ⓓ
110	Ⓐ	Ⓑ	Ⓒ	Ⓓ	130	Ⓐ	Ⓑ	Ⓒ	Ⓓ	150	Ⓐ	Ⓑ	Ⓒ	Ⓓ	170	Ⓐ	Ⓑ	Ⓒ	Ⓓ	190	Ⓐ	Ⓑ	Ⓒ	Ⓓ
111	Ⓐ	Ⓑ	Ⓒ	Ⓓ	131	Ⓐ	Ⓑ	Ⓒ	Ⓓ	151	Ⓐ	Ⓑ	Ⓒ	Ⓓ	171	Ⓐ	Ⓑ	Ⓒ	Ⓓ	191	Ⓐ	Ⓑ	Ⓒ	Ⓓ
112	Ⓐ	Ⓑ	Ⓒ	Ⓓ	132	Ⓐ	Ⓑ	Ⓒ	Ⓓ	152	Ⓐ	Ⓑ	Ⓒ	Ⓓ	172	Ⓐ	Ⓑ	Ⓒ	Ⓓ	192	Ⓐ	Ⓑ	Ⓒ	Ⓓ
113	Ⓐ	Ⓑ	Ⓒ	Ⓓ	133	Ⓐ	Ⓑ	Ⓒ	Ⓓ	153	Ⓐ	Ⓑ	Ⓒ	Ⓓ	173	Ⓐ	Ⓑ	Ⓒ	Ⓓ	193	Ⓐ	Ⓑ	Ⓒ	Ⓓ
114	Ⓐ	Ⓑ	Ⓒ	Ⓓ	134	Ⓐ	Ⓑ	Ⓒ	Ⓓ	154	Ⓐ	Ⓑ	Ⓒ	Ⓓ	174	Ⓐ	Ⓑ	Ⓒ	Ⓓ	194	Ⓐ	Ⓑ	Ⓒ	Ⓓ
115	Ⓐ	Ⓑ	Ⓒ	Ⓓ	135	Ⓐ	Ⓑ	Ⓒ	Ⓓ	155	Ⓐ	Ⓑ	Ⓒ	Ⓓ	175	Ⓐ	Ⓑ	Ⓒ	Ⓓ	195	Ⓐ	Ⓑ	Ⓒ	Ⓓ
116	Ⓐ	Ⓑ	Ⓒ	Ⓓ	136	Ⓐ	Ⓑ	Ⓒ	Ⓓ	156	Ⓐ	Ⓑ	Ⓒ	Ⓓ	176	Ⓐ	Ⓑ	Ⓒ	Ⓓ	196	Ⓐ	Ⓑ	Ⓒ	Ⓓ
117	Ⓐ	Ⓑ	Ⓒ	Ⓓ	137	Ⓐ	Ⓑ	Ⓒ	Ⓓ	157	Ⓐ	Ⓑ	Ⓒ	Ⓓ	177	Ⓐ	Ⓑ	Ⓒ	Ⓓ	197	Ⓐ	Ⓑ	Ⓒ	Ⓓ
118	Ⓐ	Ⓑ	Ⓒ	Ⓓ	138	Ⓐ	Ⓑ	Ⓒ	Ⓓ	158	Ⓐ	Ⓑ	Ⓒ	Ⓓ	178	Ⓐ	Ⓑ	Ⓒ	Ⓓ	198	Ⓐ	Ⓑ	Ⓒ	Ⓓ
119	Ⓐ	Ⓑ	Ⓒ	Ⓓ	139	Ⓐ	Ⓑ	Ⓒ	Ⓓ	159	Ⓐ	Ⓑ	Ⓒ	Ⓓ	179	Ⓐ	Ⓑ	Ⓒ	Ⓓ	199	Ⓐ	Ⓑ	Ⓒ	Ⓓ
120	Ⓐ	Ⓑ	Ⓒ	Ⓓ	140	Ⓐ	Ⓑ	Ⓒ	Ⓓ	160	Ⓐ	Ⓑ	Ⓒ	Ⓓ	180	Ⓐ	Ⓑ	Ⓒ	Ⓓ	200	Ⓐ	Ⓑ	Ⓒ	Ⓓ

1. 사용 필기구 : 컴퓨터용 연필(연필을 제외한 사인펜, 볼펜 등은 사용 절대 불가)
2. 잘못된 필기구 사용과 〈보기〉의 올바른 표기 이외의 잘못된 표기로 한 경우에는 당 위원회의 OMR기기가 판독한 결과에 따르며 그 결과는 본인 책임입니다. 1개의 정답만 골라 아래의 올바른 표기대로 정확히 표기하여야 합니다.
   〈보기〉 올바른 표기 : ● 잘못된 표기 : ✔ ✖ ◍
3. 답안지는 컴퓨터로 처리되므로 훼손하시면 안 되며, 상단의 타이밍마크(▮▮▮▮)부분을 찢거나, 낙서 등을 하면 본인에게 불이익이 발생할 수 있습니다.
4. 감독관의 확인이 없거나 시험 종료 후에 답안 작성을 계속할 경우 시험 무효 처리됩니다.

*서약 내용을 읽으시고 확인란에 반드시 서명하십시오.

서 약	확 인
본인은 TOEIC 시험 문제의 일부 또는 전부를 유출하거나 어떠한 형태로든 타인에게 누설 공개하지 않을 것이며 인터넷 또는 인쇄물 등을 이용해 유포하거나 참고 자료로 활용하지 않을 것입니다. 또한 TOEIC 시험 부정 행위 처리 규정을 준수할 것을 서약합니다.	

ANSWER SHEET

수험번호						

Actual **Test 2**

성명	한글	
	한자	
	영자	

좌석번호
Ⓐ Ⓑ Ⓒ Ⓓ Ⓔ
① ② ③ ④ ⑤ ⑥ ⑦

응시일자 : 년 월 일

LISTENING (Part I~IV)

NO.	ANSWER				NO.	ANSWER				NO.	ANSWER				NO.	ANSWER				NO.	ANSWER			
	A	B	C	D		A	B	C	D		A	B	C	D		A	B	C	D		A	B	C	D
1	Ⓐ	Ⓑ	Ⓒ	Ⓓ	21	Ⓐ	Ⓑ	Ⓒ		41	Ⓐ	Ⓑ	Ⓒ	Ⓓ	61	Ⓐ	Ⓑ	Ⓒ	Ⓓ	81	Ⓐ	Ⓑ	Ⓒ	Ⓓ
2	Ⓐ	Ⓑ	Ⓒ	Ⓓ	22	Ⓐ	Ⓑ	Ⓒ		42	Ⓐ	Ⓑ	Ⓒ	Ⓓ	62	Ⓐ	Ⓑ	Ⓒ	Ⓓ	82	Ⓐ	Ⓑ	Ⓒ	Ⓓ
3	Ⓐ	Ⓑ	Ⓒ	Ⓓ	23	Ⓐ	Ⓑ	Ⓒ		43	Ⓐ	Ⓑ	Ⓒ	Ⓓ	63	Ⓐ	Ⓑ	Ⓒ	Ⓓ	83	Ⓐ	Ⓑ	Ⓒ	Ⓓ
4	Ⓐ	Ⓑ	Ⓒ	Ⓓ	24	Ⓐ	Ⓑ	Ⓒ		44	Ⓐ	Ⓑ	Ⓒ	Ⓓ	64	Ⓐ	Ⓑ	Ⓒ	Ⓓ	84	Ⓐ	Ⓑ	Ⓒ	Ⓓ
5	Ⓐ	Ⓑ	Ⓒ	Ⓓ	25	Ⓐ	Ⓑ	Ⓒ		45	Ⓐ	Ⓑ	Ⓒ	Ⓓ	65	Ⓐ	Ⓑ	Ⓒ	Ⓓ	85	Ⓐ	Ⓑ	Ⓒ	Ⓓ
6	Ⓐ	Ⓑ	Ⓒ	Ⓓ	26	Ⓐ	Ⓑ	Ⓒ		46	Ⓐ	Ⓑ	Ⓒ	Ⓓ	66	Ⓐ	Ⓑ	Ⓒ	Ⓓ	86	Ⓐ	Ⓑ	Ⓒ	Ⓓ
7	Ⓐ	Ⓑ	Ⓒ		27	Ⓐ	Ⓑ	Ⓒ		47	Ⓐ	Ⓑ	Ⓒ	Ⓓ	67	Ⓐ	Ⓑ	Ⓒ	Ⓓ	87	Ⓐ	Ⓑ	Ⓒ	Ⓓ
8	Ⓐ	Ⓑ	Ⓒ		28	Ⓐ	Ⓑ	Ⓒ		48	Ⓐ	Ⓑ	Ⓒ	Ⓓ	68	Ⓐ	Ⓑ	Ⓒ	Ⓓ	88	Ⓐ	Ⓑ	Ⓒ	Ⓓ
9	Ⓐ	Ⓑ	Ⓒ		29	Ⓐ	Ⓑ	Ⓒ		49	Ⓐ	Ⓑ	Ⓒ	Ⓓ	69	Ⓐ	Ⓑ	Ⓒ	Ⓓ	89	Ⓐ	Ⓑ	Ⓒ	Ⓓ
10	Ⓐ	Ⓑ	Ⓒ		30	Ⓐ	Ⓑ	Ⓒ		50	Ⓐ	Ⓑ	Ⓒ	Ⓓ	70	Ⓐ	Ⓑ	Ⓒ	Ⓓ	90	Ⓐ	Ⓑ	Ⓒ	Ⓓ
11	Ⓐ	Ⓑ	Ⓒ		31	Ⓐ	Ⓑ	Ⓒ		51	Ⓐ	Ⓑ	Ⓒ	Ⓓ	71	Ⓐ	Ⓑ	Ⓒ	Ⓓ	91	Ⓐ	Ⓑ	Ⓒ	Ⓓ
12	Ⓐ	Ⓑ	Ⓒ		32	Ⓐ	Ⓑ	Ⓒ	Ⓓ	52	Ⓐ	Ⓑ	Ⓒ	Ⓓ	72	Ⓐ	Ⓑ	Ⓒ	Ⓓ	92	Ⓐ	Ⓑ	Ⓒ	Ⓓ
13	Ⓐ	Ⓑ	Ⓒ		33	Ⓐ	Ⓑ	Ⓒ	Ⓓ	53	Ⓐ	Ⓑ	Ⓒ	Ⓓ	73	Ⓐ	Ⓑ	Ⓒ	Ⓓ	93	Ⓐ	Ⓑ	Ⓒ	Ⓓ
14	Ⓐ	Ⓑ	Ⓒ		34	Ⓐ	Ⓑ	Ⓒ	Ⓓ	54	Ⓐ	Ⓑ	Ⓒ	Ⓓ	74	Ⓐ	Ⓑ	Ⓒ	Ⓓ	94	Ⓐ	Ⓑ	Ⓒ	Ⓓ
15	Ⓐ	Ⓑ	Ⓒ		35	Ⓐ	Ⓑ	Ⓒ	Ⓓ	55	Ⓐ	Ⓑ	Ⓒ	Ⓓ	75	Ⓐ	Ⓑ	Ⓒ	Ⓓ	95	Ⓐ	Ⓑ	Ⓒ	Ⓓ
16	Ⓐ	Ⓑ	Ⓒ		36	Ⓐ	Ⓑ	Ⓒ	Ⓓ	56	Ⓐ	Ⓑ	Ⓒ	Ⓓ	76	Ⓐ	Ⓑ	Ⓒ	Ⓓ	96	Ⓐ	Ⓑ	Ⓒ	Ⓓ
17	Ⓐ	Ⓑ	Ⓒ		37	Ⓐ	Ⓑ	Ⓒ	Ⓓ	57	Ⓐ	Ⓑ	Ⓒ	Ⓓ	77	Ⓐ	Ⓑ	Ⓒ	Ⓓ	97	Ⓐ	Ⓑ	Ⓒ	Ⓓ
18	Ⓐ	Ⓑ	Ⓒ		38	Ⓐ	Ⓑ	Ⓒ	Ⓓ	58	Ⓐ	Ⓑ	Ⓒ	Ⓓ	78	Ⓐ	Ⓑ	Ⓒ	Ⓓ	98	Ⓐ	Ⓑ	Ⓒ	Ⓓ
19	Ⓐ	Ⓑ	Ⓒ		39	Ⓐ	Ⓑ	Ⓒ	Ⓓ	59	Ⓐ	Ⓑ	Ⓒ	Ⓓ	79	Ⓐ	Ⓑ	Ⓒ	Ⓓ	99	Ⓐ	Ⓑ	Ⓒ	Ⓓ
20	Ⓐ	Ⓑ	Ⓒ		40	Ⓐ	Ⓑ	Ⓒ	Ⓓ	60	Ⓐ	Ⓑ	Ⓒ	Ⓓ	80	Ⓐ	Ⓑ	Ⓒ	Ⓓ	100	Ⓐ	Ⓑ	Ⓒ	Ⓓ

READING (Part V~VII)

NO.	ANSWER				NO.	ANSWER				NO.	ANSWER				NO.	ANSWER				NO.	ANSWER			
	A	B	C	D		A	B	C	D		A	B	C	D		A	B	C	D		A	B	C	D
101	Ⓐ	Ⓑ	Ⓒ	Ⓓ	121	Ⓐ	Ⓑ	Ⓒ	Ⓓ	141	Ⓐ	Ⓑ	Ⓒ	Ⓓ	161	Ⓐ	Ⓑ	Ⓒ	Ⓓ	181	Ⓐ	Ⓑ	Ⓒ	Ⓓ
102	Ⓐ	Ⓑ	Ⓒ	Ⓓ	122	Ⓐ	Ⓑ	Ⓒ	Ⓓ	142	Ⓐ	Ⓑ	Ⓒ	Ⓓ	162	Ⓐ	Ⓑ	Ⓒ	Ⓓ	182	Ⓐ	Ⓑ	Ⓒ	Ⓓ
103	Ⓐ	Ⓑ	Ⓒ	Ⓓ	123	Ⓐ	Ⓑ	Ⓒ	Ⓓ	143	Ⓐ	Ⓑ	Ⓒ	Ⓓ	163	Ⓐ	Ⓑ	Ⓒ	Ⓓ	183	Ⓐ	Ⓑ	Ⓒ	Ⓓ
104	Ⓐ	Ⓑ	Ⓒ	Ⓓ	124	Ⓐ	Ⓑ	Ⓒ	Ⓓ	144	Ⓐ	Ⓑ	Ⓒ	Ⓓ	164	Ⓐ	Ⓑ	Ⓒ	Ⓓ	184	Ⓐ	Ⓑ	Ⓒ	Ⓓ
105	Ⓐ	Ⓑ	Ⓒ	Ⓓ	125	Ⓐ	Ⓑ	Ⓒ	Ⓓ	145	Ⓐ	Ⓑ	Ⓒ	Ⓓ	165	Ⓐ	Ⓑ	Ⓒ	Ⓓ	185	Ⓐ	Ⓑ	Ⓒ	Ⓓ
106	Ⓐ	Ⓑ	Ⓒ	Ⓓ	126	Ⓐ	Ⓑ	Ⓒ	Ⓓ	146	Ⓐ	Ⓑ	Ⓒ	Ⓓ	166	Ⓐ	Ⓑ	Ⓒ	Ⓓ	186	Ⓐ	Ⓑ	Ⓒ	Ⓓ
107	Ⓐ	Ⓑ	Ⓒ	Ⓓ	127	Ⓐ	Ⓑ	Ⓒ	Ⓓ	147	Ⓐ	Ⓑ	Ⓒ	Ⓓ	167	Ⓐ	Ⓑ	Ⓒ	Ⓓ	187	Ⓐ	Ⓑ	Ⓒ	Ⓓ
108	Ⓐ	Ⓑ	Ⓒ	Ⓓ	128	Ⓐ	Ⓑ	Ⓒ	Ⓓ	148	Ⓐ	Ⓑ	Ⓒ	Ⓓ	168	Ⓐ	Ⓑ	Ⓒ	Ⓓ	188	Ⓐ	Ⓑ	Ⓒ	Ⓓ
109	Ⓐ	Ⓑ	Ⓒ	Ⓓ	129	Ⓐ	Ⓑ	Ⓒ	Ⓓ	149	Ⓐ	Ⓑ	Ⓒ	Ⓓ	169	Ⓐ	Ⓑ	Ⓒ	Ⓓ	189	Ⓐ	Ⓑ	Ⓒ	Ⓓ
110	Ⓐ	Ⓑ	Ⓒ	Ⓓ	130	Ⓐ	Ⓑ	Ⓒ	Ⓓ	150	Ⓐ	Ⓑ	Ⓒ	Ⓓ	170	Ⓐ	Ⓑ	Ⓒ	Ⓓ	190	Ⓐ	Ⓑ	Ⓒ	Ⓓ
111	Ⓐ	Ⓑ	Ⓒ	Ⓓ	131	Ⓐ	Ⓑ	Ⓒ	Ⓓ	151	Ⓐ	Ⓑ	Ⓒ	Ⓓ	171	Ⓐ	Ⓑ	Ⓒ	Ⓓ	191	Ⓐ	Ⓑ	Ⓒ	Ⓓ
112	Ⓐ	Ⓑ	Ⓒ	Ⓓ	132	Ⓐ	Ⓑ	Ⓒ	Ⓓ	152	Ⓐ	Ⓑ	Ⓒ	Ⓓ	172	Ⓐ	Ⓑ	Ⓒ	Ⓓ	192	Ⓐ	Ⓑ	Ⓒ	Ⓓ
113	Ⓐ	Ⓑ	Ⓒ	Ⓓ	133	Ⓐ	Ⓑ	Ⓒ	Ⓓ	153	Ⓐ	Ⓑ	Ⓒ	Ⓓ	173	Ⓐ	Ⓑ	Ⓒ	Ⓓ	193	Ⓐ	Ⓑ	Ⓒ	Ⓓ
114	Ⓐ	Ⓑ	Ⓒ	Ⓓ	134	Ⓐ	Ⓑ	Ⓒ	Ⓓ	154	Ⓐ	Ⓑ	Ⓒ	Ⓓ	174	Ⓐ	Ⓑ	Ⓒ	Ⓓ	194	Ⓐ	Ⓑ	Ⓒ	Ⓓ
115	Ⓐ	Ⓑ	Ⓒ	Ⓓ	135	Ⓐ	Ⓑ	Ⓒ	Ⓓ	155	Ⓐ	Ⓑ	Ⓒ	Ⓓ	175	Ⓐ	Ⓑ	Ⓒ	Ⓓ	195	Ⓐ	Ⓑ	Ⓒ	Ⓓ
116	Ⓐ	Ⓑ	Ⓒ	Ⓓ	136	Ⓐ	Ⓑ	Ⓒ	Ⓓ	156	Ⓐ	Ⓑ	Ⓒ	Ⓓ	176	Ⓐ	Ⓑ	Ⓒ	Ⓓ	196	Ⓐ	Ⓑ	Ⓒ	Ⓓ
117	Ⓐ	Ⓑ	Ⓒ	Ⓓ	137	Ⓐ	Ⓑ	Ⓒ	Ⓓ	157	Ⓐ	Ⓑ	Ⓒ	Ⓓ	177	Ⓐ	Ⓑ	Ⓒ	Ⓓ	197	Ⓐ	Ⓑ	Ⓒ	Ⓓ
118	Ⓐ	Ⓑ	Ⓒ	Ⓓ	138	Ⓐ	Ⓑ	Ⓒ	Ⓓ	158	Ⓐ	Ⓑ	Ⓒ	Ⓓ	178	Ⓐ	Ⓑ	Ⓒ	Ⓓ	198	Ⓐ	Ⓑ	Ⓒ	Ⓓ
119	Ⓐ	Ⓑ	Ⓒ	Ⓓ	139	Ⓐ	Ⓑ	Ⓒ	Ⓓ	159	Ⓐ	Ⓑ	Ⓒ	Ⓓ	179	Ⓐ	Ⓑ	Ⓒ	Ⓓ	199	Ⓐ	Ⓑ	Ⓒ	Ⓓ
120	Ⓐ	Ⓑ	Ⓒ	Ⓓ	140	Ⓐ	Ⓑ	Ⓒ	Ⓓ	160	Ⓐ	Ⓑ	Ⓒ	Ⓓ	180	Ⓐ	Ⓑ	Ⓒ	Ⓓ	200	Ⓐ	Ⓑ	Ⓒ	Ⓓ

1. 사용 필기구 : 컴퓨터용 연필(연필을 제외한 사인펜, 볼펜 등은 사용 절대 불가)
2. 잘못된 필기구 사용과 〈보기〉의 올바른 표기 이외의 잘못된 표기로 한 경우에는 당 위원회의 OMR기기가 판독한 결과에 따르며 그 결과는 본인 책임입니다. 1개의 정답만 골라 아래의 올바른 표기대로 정확히 표기하여야 합니다.
   〈보기〉 올바른 표기 : ● 잘못된 표기 : ✓ ⊗ ◍
3. 답안지는 컴퓨터로 처리되므로 훼손하시면 안 되며, 상단의 타이밍마크(▌▌▌▌)부분을 찢거나, 낙서 등을 하면 본인에게 불이익이 발생할 수 있습니다.
4. 감독관의 확인이 없거나 시험 종료 후에 답안 작성을 계속할 경우 시험 무효 처리됩니다.

*서약 내용을 읽으시고 확인란에 반드시 서명하십시오.

서 약	확 인
본인은 TOEIC 시험 문제의 일부 또는 전부를 유출하거나 어떠한 형태로든 타인에게 누설 공개하지 않을 것이며 인터넷 또는 인쇄물 등을 이용해 유포하거나 참고 자료로 활용하지 않을 것입니다. 또한 TOEIC 시험 부정 행위 처리 규정을 준수할 것을 서약합니다.	

ANSWER SHEET

수험번호						

응시일자 : 년 월 일

Actual **Test 3**

성명	한글	
	한자	
	영자	

좌석번호
Ⓐ Ⓑ Ⓒ Ⓓ Ⓔ ① ② ③ ④ ⑤ ⑥ ⑦

LISTENING (Part I~IV)

NO.	ANSWER				NO.	ANSWER				NO.	ANSWER				NO.	ANSWER				NO.	ANSWER			
	A	B	C	D		A	B	C	D		A	B	C	D		A	B	C	D		A	B	C	D
1	Ⓐ	Ⓑ	Ⓒ	Ⓓ	21	Ⓐ	Ⓑ	Ⓒ		41	Ⓐ	Ⓑ	Ⓒ	Ⓓ	61	Ⓐ	Ⓑ	Ⓒ	Ⓓ	81	Ⓐ	Ⓑ	Ⓒ	Ⓓ
2	Ⓐ	Ⓑ	Ⓒ	Ⓓ	22	Ⓐ	Ⓑ	Ⓒ		42	Ⓐ	Ⓑ	Ⓒ	Ⓓ	62	Ⓐ	Ⓑ	Ⓒ	Ⓓ	82	Ⓐ	Ⓑ	Ⓒ	Ⓓ
3	Ⓐ	Ⓑ	Ⓒ	Ⓓ	23	Ⓐ	Ⓑ	Ⓒ		43	Ⓐ	Ⓑ	Ⓒ	Ⓓ	63	Ⓐ	Ⓑ	Ⓒ	Ⓓ	83	Ⓐ	Ⓑ	Ⓒ	Ⓓ
4	Ⓐ	Ⓑ	Ⓒ	Ⓓ	24	Ⓐ	Ⓑ	Ⓒ		44	Ⓐ	Ⓑ	Ⓒ	Ⓓ	64	Ⓐ	Ⓑ	Ⓒ	Ⓓ	84	Ⓐ	Ⓑ	Ⓒ	Ⓓ
5	Ⓐ	Ⓑ	Ⓒ	Ⓓ	25	Ⓐ	Ⓑ	Ⓒ		45	Ⓐ	Ⓑ	Ⓒ	Ⓓ	65	Ⓐ	Ⓑ	Ⓒ	Ⓓ	85	Ⓐ	Ⓑ	Ⓒ	Ⓓ
6	Ⓐ	Ⓑ	Ⓒ	Ⓓ	26	Ⓐ	Ⓑ	Ⓒ		46	Ⓐ	Ⓑ	Ⓒ	Ⓓ	66	Ⓐ	Ⓑ	Ⓒ	Ⓓ	86	Ⓐ	Ⓑ	Ⓒ	Ⓓ
7	Ⓐ	Ⓑ	Ⓒ		27	Ⓐ	Ⓑ	Ⓒ		47	Ⓐ	Ⓑ	Ⓒ	Ⓓ	67	Ⓐ	Ⓑ	Ⓒ	Ⓓ	87	Ⓐ	Ⓑ	Ⓒ	Ⓓ
8	Ⓐ	Ⓑ	Ⓒ		28	Ⓐ	Ⓑ	Ⓒ		48	Ⓐ	Ⓑ	Ⓒ	Ⓓ	68	Ⓐ	Ⓑ	Ⓒ	Ⓓ	88	Ⓐ	Ⓑ	Ⓒ	Ⓓ
9	Ⓐ	Ⓑ	Ⓒ		29	Ⓐ	Ⓑ	Ⓒ		49	Ⓐ	Ⓑ	Ⓒ	Ⓓ	69	Ⓐ	Ⓑ	Ⓒ	Ⓓ	89	Ⓐ	Ⓑ	Ⓒ	Ⓓ
10	Ⓐ	Ⓑ	Ⓒ		30	Ⓐ	Ⓑ	Ⓒ		50	Ⓐ	Ⓑ	Ⓒ	Ⓓ	70	Ⓐ	Ⓑ	Ⓒ	Ⓓ	90	Ⓐ	Ⓑ	Ⓒ	Ⓓ
11	Ⓐ	Ⓑ	Ⓒ		31	Ⓐ	Ⓑ	Ⓒ		51	Ⓐ	Ⓑ	Ⓒ	Ⓓ	71	Ⓐ	Ⓑ	Ⓒ	Ⓓ	91	Ⓐ	Ⓑ	Ⓒ	Ⓓ
12	Ⓐ	Ⓑ	Ⓒ		32	Ⓐ	Ⓑ	Ⓒ	Ⓓ	52	Ⓐ	Ⓑ	Ⓒ	Ⓓ	72	Ⓐ	Ⓑ	Ⓒ	Ⓓ	92	Ⓐ	Ⓑ	Ⓒ	Ⓓ
13	Ⓐ	Ⓑ	Ⓒ		33	Ⓐ	Ⓑ	Ⓒ	Ⓓ	53	Ⓐ	Ⓑ	Ⓒ	Ⓓ	73	Ⓐ	Ⓑ	Ⓒ	Ⓓ	93	Ⓐ	Ⓑ	Ⓒ	Ⓓ
14	Ⓐ	Ⓑ	Ⓒ		34	Ⓐ	Ⓑ	Ⓒ	Ⓓ	54	Ⓐ	Ⓑ	Ⓒ	Ⓓ	74	Ⓐ	Ⓑ	Ⓒ	Ⓓ	94	Ⓐ	Ⓑ	Ⓒ	Ⓓ
15	Ⓐ	Ⓑ	Ⓒ		35	Ⓐ	Ⓑ	Ⓒ	Ⓓ	55	Ⓐ	Ⓑ	Ⓒ	Ⓓ	75	Ⓐ	Ⓑ	Ⓒ	Ⓓ	95	Ⓐ	Ⓑ	Ⓒ	Ⓓ
16	Ⓐ	Ⓑ	Ⓒ		36	Ⓐ	Ⓑ	Ⓒ	Ⓓ	56	Ⓐ	Ⓑ	Ⓒ	Ⓓ	76	Ⓐ	Ⓑ	Ⓒ	Ⓓ	96	Ⓐ	Ⓑ	Ⓒ	Ⓓ
17	Ⓐ	Ⓑ	Ⓒ		37	Ⓐ	Ⓑ	Ⓒ	Ⓓ	57	Ⓐ	Ⓑ	Ⓒ	Ⓓ	77	Ⓐ	Ⓑ	Ⓒ	Ⓓ	97	Ⓐ	Ⓑ	Ⓒ	Ⓓ
18	Ⓐ	Ⓑ	Ⓒ		38	Ⓐ	Ⓑ	Ⓒ	Ⓓ	58	Ⓐ	Ⓑ	Ⓒ	Ⓓ	78	Ⓐ	Ⓑ	Ⓒ	Ⓓ	98	Ⓐ	Ⓑ	Ⓒ	Ⓓ
19	Ⓐ	Ⓑ	Ⓒ		39	Ⓐ	Ⓑ	Ⓒ	Ⓓ	59	Ⓐ	Ⓑ	Ⓒ	Ⓓ	79	Ⓐ	Ⓑ	Ⓒ	Ⓓ	99	Ⓐ	Ⓑ	Ⓒ	Ⓓ
20	Ⓐ	Ⓑ	Ⓒ		40	Ⓐ	Ⓑ	Ⓒ	Ⓓ	60	Ⓐ	Ⓑ	Ⓒ	Ⓓ	80	Ⓐ	Ⓑ	Ⓒ	Ⓓ	100	Ⓐ	Ⓑ	Ⓒ	Ⓓ

READING (Part V~VII)

NO.	ANSWER				NO.	ANSWER				NO.	ANSWER				NO.	ANSWER				NO.	ANSWER			
	A	B	C	D		A	B	C	D		A	B	C	D		A	B	C	D		A	B	C	D
101	Ⓐ	Ⓑ	Ⓒ	Ⓓ	121	Ⓐ	Ⓑ	Ⓒ	Ⓓ	141	Ⓐ	Ⓑ	Ⓒ	Ⓓ	161	Ⓐ	Ⓑ	Ⓒ	Ⓓ	181	Ⓐ	Ⓑ	Ⓒ	Ⓓ
102	Ⓐ	Ⓑ	Ⓒ	Ⓓ	122	Ⓐ	Ⓑ	Ⓒ	Ⓓ	142	Ⓐ	Ⓑ	Ⓒ	Ⓓ	162	Ⓐ	Ⓑ	Ⓒ	Ⓓ	182	Ⓐ	Ⓑ	Ⓒ	Ⓓ
103	Ⓐ	Ⓑ	Ⓒ	Ⓓ	123	Ⓐ	Ⓑ	Ⓒ	Ⓓ	143	Ⓐ	Ⓑ	Ⓒ	Ⓓ	163	Ⓐ	Ⓑ	Ⓒ	Ⓓ	183	Ⓐ	Ⓑ	Ⓒ	Ⓓ
104	Ⓐ	Ⓑ	Ⓒ	Ⓓ	124	Ⓐ	Ⓑ	Ⓒ	Ⓓ	144	Ⓐ	Ⓑ	Ⓒ	Ⓓ	164	Ⓐ	Ⓑ	Ⓒ	Ⓓ	184	Ⓐ	Ⓑ	Ⓒ	Ⓓ
105	Ⓐ	Ⓑ	Ⓒ	Ⓓ	125	Ⓐ	Ⓑ	Ⓒ	Ⓓ	145	Ⓐ	Ⓑ	Ⓒ	Ⓓ	165	Ⓐ	Ⓑ	Ⓒ	Ⓓ	185	Ⓐ	Ⓑ	Ⓒ	Ⓓ
106	Ⓐ	Ⓑ	Ⓒ	Ⓓ	126	Ⓐ	Ⓑ	Ⓒ	Ⓓ	146	Ⓐ	Ⓑ	Ⓒ	Ⓓ	166	Ⓐ	Ⓑ	Ⓒ	Ⓓ	186	Ⓐ	Ⓑ	Ⓒ	Ⓓ
107	Ⓐ	Ⓑ	Ⓒ	Ⓓ	127	Ⓐ	Ⓑ	Ⓒ	Ⓓ	147	Ⓐ	Ⓑ	Ⓒ	Ⓓ	167	Ⓐ	Ⓑ	Ⓒ	Ⓓ	187	Ⓐ	Ⓑ	Ⓒ	Ⓓ
108	Ⓐ	Ⓑ	Ⓒ	Ⓓ	128	Ⓐ	Ⓑ	Ⓒ	Ⓓ	148	Ⓐ	Ⓑ	Ⓒ	Ⓓ	168	Ⓐ	Ⓑ	Ⓒ	Ⓓ	188	Ⓐ	Ⓑ	Ⓒ	Ⓓ
109	Ⓐ	Ⓑ	Ⓒ	Ⓓ	129	Ⓐ	Ⓑ	Ⓒ	Ⓓ	149	Ⓐ	Ⓑ	Ⓒ	Ⓓ	169	Ⓐ	Ⓑ	Ⓒ	Ⓓ	189	Ⓐ	Ⓑ	Ⓒ	Ⓓ
110	Ⓐ	Ⓑ	Ⓒ	Ⓓ	130	Ⓐ	Ⓑ	Ⓒ	Ⓓ	150	Ⓐ	Ⓑ	Ⓒ	Ⓓ	170	Ⓐ	Ⓑ	Ⓒ	Ⓓ	190	Ⓐ	Ⓑ	Ⓒ	Ⓓ
111	Ⓐ	Ⓑ	Ⓒ	Ⓓ	131	Ⓐ	Ⓑ	Ⓒ	Ⓓ	151	Ⓐ	Ⓑ	Ⓒ	Ⓓ	171	Ⓐ	Ⓑ	Ⓒ	Ⓓ	191	Ⓐ	Ⓑ	Ⓒ	Ⓓ
112	Ⓐ	Ⓑ	Ⓒ	Ⓓ	132	Ⓐ	Ⓑ	Ⓒ	Ⓓ	152	Ⓐ	Ⓑ	Ⓒ	Ⓓ	172	Ⓐ	Ⓑ	Ⓒ	Ⓓ	192	Ⓐ	Ⓑ	Ⓒ	Ⓓ
113	Ⓐ	Ⓑ	Ⓒ	Ⓓ	133	Ⓐ	Ⓑ	Ⓒ	Ⓓ	153	Ⓐ	Ⓑ	Ⓒ	Ⓓ	173	Ⓐ	Ⓑ	Ⓒ	Ⓓ	193	Ⓐ	Ⓑ	Ⓒ	Ⓓ
114	Ⓐ	Ⓑ	Ⓒ	Ⓓ	134	Ⓐ	Ⓑ	Ⓒ	Ⓓ	154	Ⓐ	Ⓑ	Ⓒ	Ⓓ	174	Ⓐ	Ⓑ	Ⓒ	Ⓓ	194	Ⓐ	Ⓑ	Ⓒ	Ⓓ
115	Ⓐ	Ⓑ	Ⓒ	Ⓓ	135	Ⓐ	Ⓑ	Ⓒ	Ⓓ	155	Ⓐ	Ⓑ	Ⓒ	Ⓓ	175	Ⓐ	Ⓑ	Ⓒ	Ⓓ	195	Ⓐ	Ⓑ	Ⓒ	Ⓓ
116	Ⓐ	Ⓑ	Ⓒ	Ⓓ	136	Ⓐ	Ⓑ	Ⓒ	Ⓓ	156	Ⓐ	Ⓑ	Ⓒ	Ⓓ	176	Ⓐ	Ⓑ	Ⓒ	Ⓓ	196	Ⓐ	Ⓑ	Ⓒ	Ⓓ
117	Ⓐ	Ⓑ	Ⓒ	Ⓓ	137	Ⓐ	Ⓑ	Ⓒ	Ⓓ	157	Ⓐ	Ⓑ	Ⓒ	Ⓓ	177	Ⓐ	Ⓑ	Ⓒ	Ⓓ	197	Ⓐ	Ⓑ	Ⓒ	Ⓓ
118	Ⓐ	Ⓑ	Ⓒ	Ⓓ	138	Ⓐ	Ⓑ	Ⓒ	Ⓓ	158	Ⓐ	Ⓑ	Ⓒ	Ⓓ	178	Ⓐ	Ⓑ	Ⓒ	Ⓓ	198	Ⓐ	Ⓑ	Ⓒ	Ⓓ
119	Ⓐ	Ⓑ	Ⓒ	Ⓓ	139	Ⓐ	Ⓑ	Ⓒ	Ⓓ	159	Ⓐ	Ⓑ	Ⓒ	Ⓓ	179	Ⓐ	Ⓑ	Ⓒ	Ⓓ	199	Ⓐ	Ⓑ	Ⓒ	Ⓓ
120	Ⓐ	Ⓑ	Ⓒ	Ⓓ	140	Ⓐ	Ⓑ	Ⓒ	Ⓓ	160	Ⓐ	Ⓑ	Ⓒ	Ⓓ	180	Ⓐ	Ⓑ	Ⓒ	Ⓓ	200	Ⓐ	Ⓑ	Ⓒ	Ⓓ

1. 사용 필기구 : 컴퓨터용 연필(연필을 제외한 사인펜, 볼펜 등은 사용 절대 불가)
2. 잘못된 필기구 사용과 〈보기〉의 올바른 표기 이외의 잘못된 표기로 한 경우에는 당 위원회의 OMR기기가 판독한 결과에 따르며 그 결과는 본인 책임입니다. 1개의 정답만 골라 아래의 올바른 표기대로 정확히 표기하여야 합니다.
   〈보기〉 올바른 표기 : ● 잘못된 표기 : ✓ ✗ ◍
3. 답안지는 컴퓨터로 처리되므로 훼손하시면 안 되며, 상단의 타이밍마크(❙❙❙❙)부분을 찢거나, 낙서 등을 하면 본인에게 불이익이 발생할 수 있습니다.
4. 감독관의 확인이 없거나 시험 종료 후에 답안 작성을 계속할 경우 시험 무효 처리됩니다.

*서약 내용을 읽으시고 확인란에 반드시 서명하십시오.

서 약	확 인
본인은 TOEIC 시험 문제의 일부 또는 전부를 유출하거나 어떠한 형태로든 타인에게 누설 공개하지 않을 것이며 인터넷 또는 인쇄물 등을 이용해 유포하거나 참고 자료로 활용하지 않을 것입니다. 또한 TOEIC 시험 부정 행위 처리 규정을 준수할 것을 서약합니다.	

TOEIC® 점수 환산표

정답수	Listening Comprehension	정답수	Reading Comprehension
96-100	480-495	96-100	460-495
91-95	435-490	91-95	410-475
86-90	395-450	86-90	380-430
81-85	355-415	81-85	355-400
76-80	325-375	76-80	325-375
71-75	295-340	71-75	295-345
66-70	265-315	66-70	265-315
61-65	240-285	61-65	235-285
56-60	215-260	56-60	205-255
51-55	190-235	51-55	175-225
46-50	160-210	46-50	150-195
41-45	135-180	41-45	120-170
36-40	110-155	36-40	100-140
31-35	85-130	31-35	75-120
26-30	70-105	26-30	55-100
21-25	50-90	21-25	40-80
16-20	35-75	16-20	30-65
11-15	20-55	11-15	20-50
6-10	15-40	6-10	15-35
1-5	5-20	1-5	5-20
0	5	0	5

나혼자 끝내는 新토익 FINAL 실전 모의고사 3회분

지은이 넥서스토익연구소
펴낸이 임상진
펴낸곳 (주)넥서스

초판 1쇄 발행 2019년 6월 24일
초판 10쇄 발행 2024년 4월 1일

출판신고 1992년 4월 3일 제311-2002-2호
10880 경기도 파주시 지목로 5
Tel (02)330-5500 Fax (02)330-5555

ISBN 979-11-6165-640-3 13740

나혼자 끝내는 新 토익

FINAL 실전 3회분 모의고사

新토익 실전 모의고사 3회분 + 정답/스크립트 해석/해설 제공 + 실전용·복습용 2종 MP3

MP3 듣기
정답 자동 채점

★ 실제 시험지 형태 그대로, 신토익 실전 모의고사 3회분 수록

★ 문제의 키워드를 단숨에 파악하는 알짜 해석·해설

★ 실전용 · 복습용 버전의 2종 MP3 무료 다운로드 >> QR코드 & 홈페이지 다운로드

★ 문제풀이 후 바로 채점할 수 있는 자동 채점 방식 제공 >> QR코드

★ 신토익 빈출 어휘 리스트제공 >> www.nexusbook.com

이름	
수험번호	

실전 모의고사 ▸▸ 2

TOEIC®

Test of English for International Communication

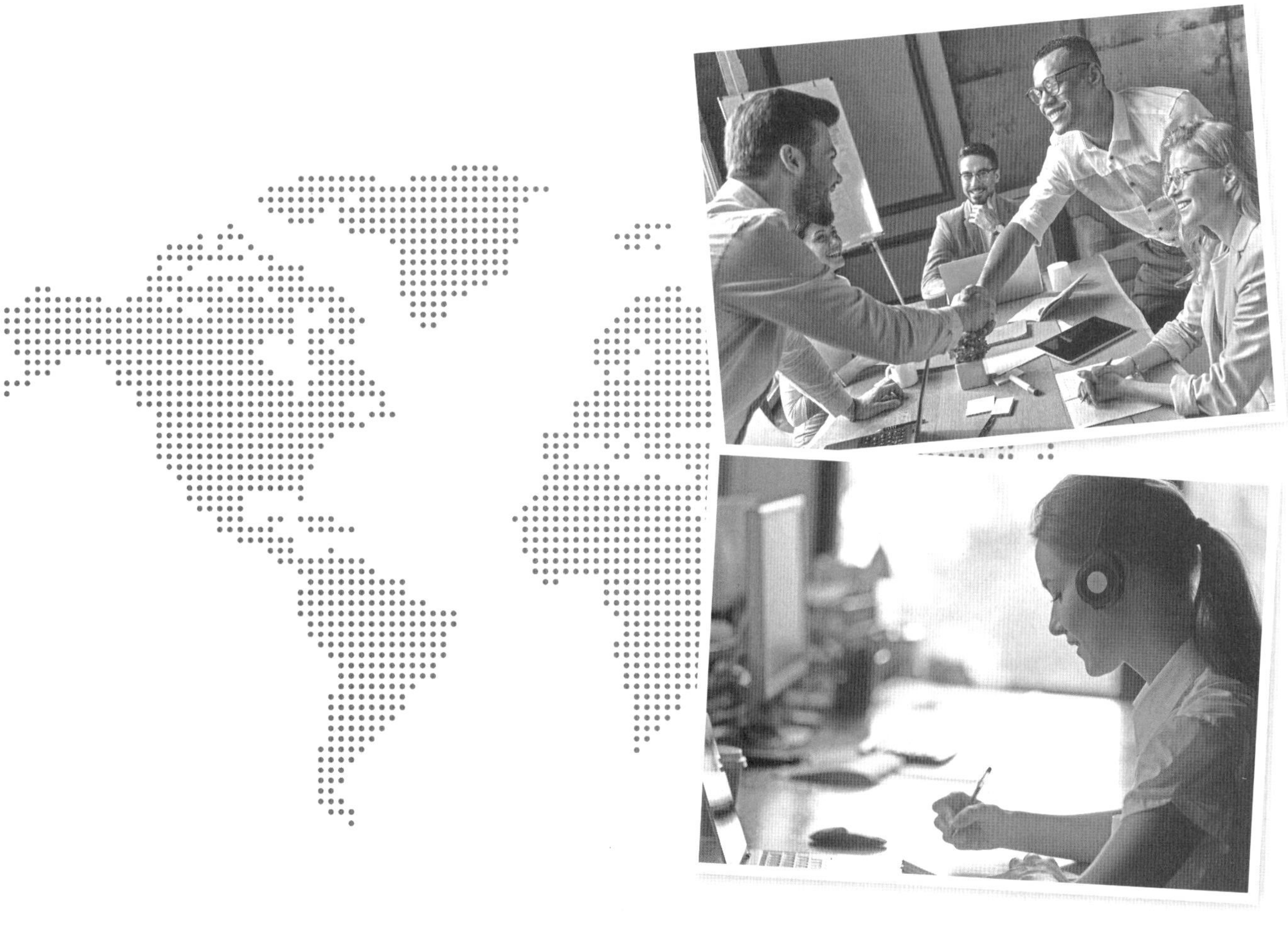

LISTENING TEST

In the Listening test, you will be asked to demonstrate how well you understand spoken English. The entire Listening test will last approximately 45 minutes. There are four parts, and directions are given for each part. You must mark your answers on the separate answer sheet. Do not write your answers in the test book.

PART 1

Directions: For each question in this part, you will hear four statements about a picture in your test book. When you hear the statements, you must select the one statement that best describes what you see in the picture. Then find the number of the question on your answer sheet and mark your answer. The statements will not be printed in your test book and will be spoken only one time.

Statement (B), "The man is working at a desk," is the best description of the picture, so you should select answer (B) and mark it on your answer sheet.

MP3 듣기 

1.

2.

GO ON TO THE NEXT PAGE

3.

4.

5.

6.

GO ON TO THE NEXT PAGE

PART 2

Directions: You will hear a question or statement and three responses spoken in English. They will not be printed in your test book and will be spoken only one time. Select the best response to the question or statement and mark the letter (A), (B), or (C) on your answer sheet.

7. Mark your answer on your answer sheet.

8. Mark your answer on your answer sheet.

9. Mark your answer on your answer sheet.

10. Mark your answer on your answer sheet.

11. Mark your answer on your answer sheet.

12. Mark your answer on your answer sheet.

13. Mark your answer on your answer sheet.

14. Mark your answer on your answer sheet.

15. Mark your answer on your answer sheet.

16. Mark your answer on your answer sheet.

17. Mark your answer on your answer sheet.

18. Mark your answer on your answer sheet.

19. Mark your answer on your answer sheet.

20. Mark your answer on your answer sheet.

21. Mark your answer on your answer sheet.

22. Mark your answer on your answer sheet.

23. Mark your answer on your answer sheet.

24. Mark your answer on your answer sheet.

25. Mark your answer on your answer sheet.

26. Mark your answer on your answer sheet.

27. Mark your answer on your answer sheet.

28. Mark your answer on your answer sheet.

29. Mark your answer on your answer sheet.

30. Mark your answer on your answer sheet.

31. Mark your answer on your answer sheet.

PART 3

Directions: You will hear some conversations between two or more people. You will be asked to answer three questions about what the speakers say in each conversation. Select the best response to each question and mark the letter (A), (B), (C), or (D) on your answer sheet. The conversations will not be printed in your test book and will be spoken only one time.

32. What time does the event start?

(A) At noon
(B) At 1 o'clock
(C) At 2 o'clock
(D) At 3 o'clock

33. What does the woman tell the man to do?

(A) Wait while the room is being prepared
(B) Buy some juice for the attendees
(C) Come back tomorrow
(D) Remember the correct time

34. What will the man do next?

(A) Find a café
(B) Give a lecture
(C) Clean the room
(D) Go to the lounge

---

35. Where are the speakers now?

(A) At a natural forest
(B) At an art museum
(C) At an educational institution
(D) At a gift shop

36. What does the woman ask about?

(A) Business hours
(B) Group rates
(C) Discounts for students
(D) Prices of souvenirs

37. What does the man suggest?

(A) Buying an annual ticket
(B) Visiting the special exhibit
(C) Shopping for souvenirs
(D) Coming early for admission

38. Why did Mr. Wilder call?

(A) To change the deadline date
(B) To invite the woman to the store
(C) To express his concern about the construction
(D) To inquire about the materials

39. What does the man tell the woman?

(A) They can meet the due date.
(B) They need a larger space.
(C) They are over budget.
(D) They need an extra month.

40. What will the man do next?

(A) Stop building the foundation
(B) Repaint the department store
(C) Check the schedule
(D) Contact Mr. Wilder

---

41. What are the speakers mainly discussing?

(A) The location of a promotional event
(B) The opening of a new factory
(C) The shipment of some goods
(D) The cause of a power failure

42. What does the woman imply when she says, "I'm relieved to hear that"?

(A) She is happy that a delivery will arrive on time.
(B) She is satisfied with the quality of some products.
(C) She feels better after receiving treatment.
(D) She likes to hear other people's opinions.

43. According to the woman, what will happen next week?

(A) A factory tour
(B) A trade show
(C) A demonstration
(D) A promotional event

GO ON TO THE NEXT PAGE

44. Where does the woman most likely work?

(A) At a moving company
(B) At a financial firm
(C) At an office supply store
(D) At a property development company

45. What does the man imply when he says, "Thanks for all your hard work, Ms. Pearce"?

(A) He has received a discount.
(B) He is satisfied with his office relocation.
(C) He wants the woman to try harder.
(D) A renovation project is ahead of schedule.

46. What does the woman ask the man about?

(A) How to get to a meeting room
(B) The cost of a special service
(C) Where to place a container
(D) The name of a company

---

47. What is scheduled to begin today?

(A) Some repair work
(B) A sporting event
(C) Building renovations
(D) A new theater production

48. According to Paul, what might delay the scheduled repairs?

(A) Labor costs
(B) Special events
(C) Changes in the weather
(D) Complaints from local residents

49. Why is traffic congestion expected at night?

(A) Some road crews are off sick.
(B) A bridge is not fully open to traffic.
(C) Many people are attending an event.
(D) Several cars are involved in an accident.

50. Where do the speakers work?

(A) At a library
(B) At a university
(C) At a software lab
(D) At a computer store

51. What does the new software do?

(A) It translates written text to spoken words.
(B) It assesses student fitness.
(C) It helps provide better feedback.
(D) It analyzes people's speech.

52. What does the man ask the woman to do?

(A) Write a summary
(B) Upgrade a computer
(C) Register for a workshop
(D) Bring back some information

---

53. Where do the speakers most likely work?

(A) At a relocation company
(B) At a clothing store
(C) At an international law firm
(D) At a design company

54. What does the woman recommend doing?

(A) Recruiting an overseas agent
(B) Promoting designs online
(C) Publishing a brochure
(D) Hiring a domestic sales team

55. What has the man done?

(A) Joined the board of trustees
(B) Arranged an appointment
(C) Prepared a portfolio
(D) Booked a flight

56. What did the man ask the woman to do in his e-mail?

(A) Contact the board of directors
(B) Provide some feedback on his work
(C) Offer some presentation materials
(D) Confirm the length of a presentation

57. What does the woman mean when she says, "I'll leave that to you"?

(A) She plans to give an item to the man.
(B) She does not intend to stay for much longer.
(C) She will not accompany the man.
(D) She will allow the man to make a decision.

58. What does the woman suggest?

(A) Contacting a coworker
(B) Increasing a budget
(C) Adding a visual aid
(D) Shortening a document

---

59. What industry do the speakers work in?

(A) Graphic design
(B) Television programming
(C) Global media
(D) Online advertising

60. How did the man find out about the job?

(A) From a recruitment agency
(B) From a corporate Web site
(C) From a newspaper advertisement
(D) From a colleague

61. What will the woman discuss next?

(A) Pension benefits
(B) Working hours
(C) Employment rights
(D) Relocation expenses

62. What are the speakers mainly discussing?

(A) A city funding project
(B) An educational program
(C) A must-have wooden toy
(D) A best-selling electronic game

63. What gave the woman the idea for her product?

(A) Watching her nephew
(B) Talking with colleagues
(C) Reading a magazine feature
(D) Visiting a games fair

64. How was the woman able to launch her business?

(A) By requesting foreign distributors
(B) By using another company's funding
(C) By advertising at game conventions
(D) By hiring inexpensive labor

GO ON TO THE NEXT PAGE

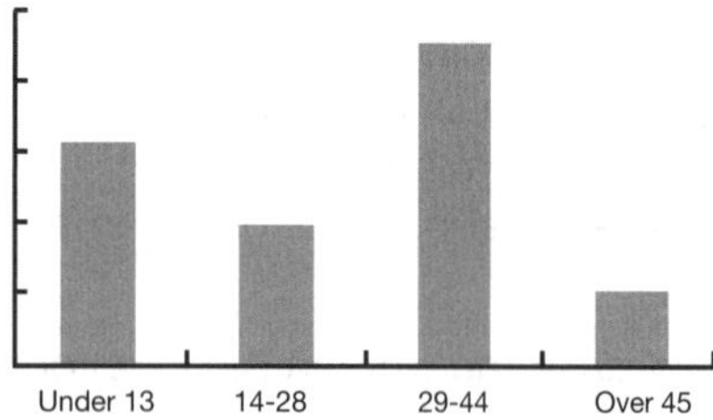

65. Where do the speakers most likely work?
(A) At a fitness club
(B) At an art gallery
(C) At a graphic design firm
(D) At a community center

66. What are the speakers mainly discussing?
(A) A family membership
(B) Promoting a new program
(C) A schedule change
(D) The results of a recent survey

67. Look at the graphic. Which age group wants the center to offer more classes?
(A) Under 13
(B) 14-28
(C) 29-44
(D) Over 45

City Sights of LA		
	Adult	Senior/Student
Half Day City Tour	$50	$25
Full Day City Tour	$120	$84

68. What is the man asking about?
(A) A sightseeing tour
(B) A concert schedule
(C) A famous artist
(D) Directions to an attraction

69. According to the woman, what is included in the full-day city tour?
(A) A museum tour
(B) A seafood lunch
(C) A ferry ride
(D) A Broadway show

70. Look at the graphic. How much will the man pay for a tour?
(A) $25
(B) $50
(C) $84
(D) $120

PART 4

Directions: You will hear some talks given by a single speaker. You will be asked to answer three questions about what the speaker says in each talk. Select the best response to each question and mark the letter (A), (B), (C), or (D) on your answer sheet. The talks will not be printed in your test book and will be spoken only one time.

71. Why is the speaker calling?

(A) To cancel a meeting
(B) To ask for a quote
(C) To query a design
(D) To criticize a co-worker

72. What did the speaker initially want to remodel?

(A) The garden
(B) The kitchen
(C) The foundations
(D) The bedroom

73. Who did the speaker give Ms. Reinhard's phone number to?

(A) His colleague
(B) His partner
(C) A gardener
(D) A designer

---

74. What will happen in Henman Falls this summer?

(A) Community meetings will be held.
(B) The economy will be analyzed.
(C) A range of clothing will be introduced.
(D) A new factory will be opened.

75. Who is Jin Sun?

(A) A business owner
(B) A factory worker
(C) A business expert
(D) The president of a company

76. What will Jin Sun discuss?

(A) Local job opportunities
(B) Increasing taxes
(C) Traffic delays
(D) Education costs

77. Who most likely is the speaker?

(A) A student
(B) A car park attendant
(C) A real estate agent
(D) A lawyer

78. What is the purpose of the call?

(A) To query a transaction
(B) To undertake research
(C) To confirm an appointment
(D) To rent a vehicle

79. Where will the speaker be waiting?

(A) At the main entrance
(B) At the rear entrance
(C) At the gymnasium
(D) At the house

---

80. What kind of event is taking place?

(A) An opening ceremony
(B) An annual conference
(C) A company outing
(D) An awards dinner

81. What is Dr. Adams famous for?

(A) Receiving a prestigious award
(B) Having written a series of books
(C) Developing a successful marketing strategy
(D) Expanding her own business overseas

82. What does the speaker mean when he says, "So please hold your questions until the end"?

(A) The audience should not interrupt the speaker.
(B) The audience should not leave their seats.
(C) The audience should applaud the speaker.
(D) The audience should answer some questions.

GO ON TO THE NEXT PAGE

83. What are the listeners attending?

(A) A cooking class
(B) A research group
(C) A marketing session
(D) A job interview

84. What does the speaker ask the listeners to do?

(A) Ask questions
(B) Turn off appliances
(C) Clean up the area
(D) Fill in a form

85. Why are listeners directed to the common room?

(A) To taste some food
(B) To take refreshments
(C) To talk with the tutor
(D) To exchange contact info

---

86. What is the company trying to do?

(A) Offload some timber
(B) Hire more employees
(C) Find new partners
(D) Improve customer service

87. What are listeners asked to do?

(A) Make referrals
(B) Work extra shifts
(C) Recruit family members
(D) Fill in a survey

88. What incentive is mentioned?

(A) A financial bonus
(B) Extra vacation days
(C) Promotion at work
(D) Recognition on the company Web site

89. Where did the speaker meet Jake Johnson?

(A) At a trade fair
(B) At a business meeting
(C) At a seminar
(D) At a press conference

90. What is the purpose of the message?

(A) To exchange some devices
(B) To arrange for an event
(C) To make a complaint
(D) To apologize for being late

91. What does the speaker mean when she says, "So I really hope it is in your possession"?

(A) She would like to buy a new computer.
(B) She does not want to pay an extra fee.
(C) She hopes her computer hasn't gone missing.
(D) She wants to arrive at work on time.

---

92. What type of business is the speaker calling?

(A) A gardening company
(B) A roofing company
(C) An auto repair shop
(D) A home-improvement store

93. What does the speaker mean when he says, "And even more rain is forecast for the weekend"?

(A) A repair person will be late.
(B) He cannot keep windows open.
(C) A problem will get worse.
(D) He will have to change his schedule.

94. What does the speaker ask the listener to do?

(A) Visit his office
(B) Deliver some items to his home
(C) Call him back
(D) Give him a discount

List of Catering Companies	
Company	Price Quote
1. Jude Catering	$2,500
2. O'Hara Catering	$5,000
3. Art of Catering	$6,000
4. Shawn Catering	$3,000

95. What event will the company hold?

(A) A retirement party
(B) An awards banquet
(C) A press conference
(D) An annual convention

96. What does the speaker mention about Jude Catering?

(A) The food was not good.
(B) The service was excellent.
(C) The price was expensive.
(D) The employees are well trained.

97. Look at the graphic. Which company does the speaker want to hire?

(A) Jude Catering
(B) O'Hara Catering
(C) Art of Catering
(D) Shawn Catering

Best Sellers in science-fiction novel (April)
1. *Broken Stars* by Arron Shiver
2. *Life* by Sam Neill
3. *Unknown* by Ray Stevenson
4. *Orbit 2020* by Paul Schneider

98. Where most likely does the speaker work?

(A) At a television station
(B) At a bookstore
(C) At a publishing firm
(D) At an advertising agency

99. What are listeners asked to do?

(A) Help with some preparations
(B) Make travel arrangements
(C) Meet a project deadline
(D) Donate money to a charity

100. Look at the graphic. According to the speaker, which book will become the best seller in May?

(A) *Broken Stars*
(B) *Life*
(C) *Unknown*
(D) *Orbit 2020*

This is the end of the Listening test. Turn to Part 5 in your test book.

GO ON TO THE NEXT PAGE

READING TEST

In the Reading test, you will read a variety of texts and answer several different types of reading comprehension questions. The entire Reading test will last 75 minutes. There are three parts, and directions are given for each part. You are encouraged to answer as many questions as possible within the time allowed.

You must mark your answers on the separate answer sheet. Do not write your answers in your test book.

PART 5

Directions: A word or phrase is missing in each of the sentences below. Four answer choices are given below each sentence. Select the best answer to complete the sentence. Then mark the letter (A), (B), (C), or (D) on your answer sheet.

101. The ------- cost approximation for the plan to widen Pretoria Road had to be extended by 15 percent.

(A) originally
(B) origin
(C) origins
(D) original

102. Passengers are expected to ------- a ticket and an authentic form of identification to the airport reception.

(A) presents
(B) presenting
(C) presented
(D) present

103. Because the demand for raw materials has risen -------, Tzi Rai Coatings raised the recommended retail cost of its paints.

(A) sharpen
(B) sharpness
(C) sharply
(D) sharp

104. Check the proposed ------- arrangement and let me know what alterations you think should be made.

(A) seated
(B) seating
(C) seats
(D) seat

105. The plays of seven ------- playwrights will be performed at Hainan Province's annual arts competition.

(A) differences
(B) different
(C) differently
(D) difference

106. Mr. Akkinuoye's ------- book, *Sleeping Through Tomorrow*, will be published in paperback starting on December 30.

(A) more recently
(B) most recently
(C) more recent
(D) most recent

107. Since choosing organic farming options last year, Parson and Boatman's Orchard has ------- trebled its profit margin.

(A) almost
(B) while
(C) until
(D) after

108. Given the increasing number of ------- applications for the position, Barkhad Industries will interview only the most exceptional candidates.

(A) qualifies
(B) qualifications
(C) qualify
(D) qualified

109. Odin Hermod Inc.'s recruiting manager normally negotiates ------- with prospective employees when delivering job offers.

(A) discounts
(B) salaries
(C) returns
(D) revenues

110. Please remove all delicate items ------- as the package may have moved during transit.

(A) slightly
(B) relatively
(C) carefully
(D) powerlessly

111. Barcelona Broadcast Television has ------- expanded its operating area, which now reaches all of Sant Andreu and Les Corts.

(A) substantially
(B) substantiated
(C) substance
(D) substantial

112. Rodriguez Rail passengers may ------- food and beverages from the refreshment carriage situated to the rear of each train.

(A) invest
(B) spend
(C) shop
(D) purchase

113. Because of higher-than-predicted profits in the last nine months, Giampanidou Designs is understandably ------- about its expansion.

(A) devoted
(B) optimistic
(C) impressive
(D) ample

114. To certify if Ms. Kurilenko is ready for promotion to factory manager, her boss has been ------- monitoring her output.

(A) routinely
(B) correctively
(C) availably
(D) approximately

115. A penalty is ------- for products returned after the date printed on the rental contract.

(A) obliged
(B) summoned
(C) imposed
(D) dispensed

116. Ms. Belham has decided against flying business class, although the company will provide ------- with the ticket.

(A) she
(B) her
(C) hers
(D) herself

117. The Bringham Group intends to help its customers make ------- that will provide a secure future.

(A) investments
(B) invests
(C) invested
(D) investing

118. Our trained consultants can ------- you with speaking in public.

(A) assist
(B) lend
(C) tell
(D) explain

119. In a newspaper article, award winning playwright Bert Tong said that he changed the ending of the plot in his first play several times ------- submitting the finished script to the actors.

(A) regarding
(B) except for
(C) just as
(D) before

120. Ms. Gonzalez, ------- made the food for the retirement party, will email her invoice tomorrow.

(A) who
(B) that
(C) whose
(D) which

GO ON TO THE NEXT PAGE

121. Financial analysts have been disappointed by how ------- Klein Fashion has lost customers.

(A) tightly
(B) quickly
(C) strongly
(D) usually

122. In April, Grensworth Farm sold more ------- twice as much produce as they had sold in March.

(A) so
(B) as
(C) over
(D) than

123. Princeton's Glass Container provides better technology and lasts longer than other ------- brands.

(A) had led
(B) leading
(C) to lead
(D) leads

124. When the bottles behind the bar are ------- gone, the bar staff should order more.

(A) nearly
(B) nearest
(C) neared
(D) nears

125. Tickets ------- through Amdram's website are liable to a $2.50 surcharge.

(A) acquired
(B) valued
(C) fined
(D) signed

126. Please tell Mr. Brown that he has ------- the end of the day to submit his February expense report.

(A) as
(B) along
(C) until
(D) so

127. Anderson Wholesale is the only ------- of premium home appliances for the Greendale community.

(A) distributor
(B) distributed
(C) distribution
(D) distributing

128. Le Chang Cafe serves excellent fish dishes caught ------- in the local river.

(A) exclusively
(B) fluently
(C) heavily
(D) slightly

129. Fire alarms will be tested between 7 AM and 6 PM next Monday ------- routine maintenance.

(A) as for
(B) since
(C) for
(D) among

130. Asmar International College's annual budget includes a ------- increase in spending for the sports and leisure departments.

(A) sharpen
(B) sharply
(C) sharp
(D) sharpness

PART 6

Directions: Read the texts that follow. A word, phrase, or sentence is missing in parts of each text. Four answer choices for each question are given below the text. Select the best answer to complete the text. Then mark the letter (A), (B), (C), or (D) on your answer sheet.

Questions 131-134 refer to the following memo.

From: John Magaro
To: All employees
Date: October 20
Subject: Server maintenance

This memo is to notify all employees of a temporary ------- (**131.**) of e-mail service beginning tomorrow due to server maintenance. The maintenance work is expected to last until October 30. Because you cannot have access to your company's e-mail account during the work, ------- (**132.**) contact with clients and colleagues should be made through a different e-mail account. ------- (**133.**). Previous works included installing security doors to all offices and surveillance cameras in the main lobby. The e-mail service will be back to ------- (**134.**) as of November 1.

Thank you for your cooperation.

John Magaro, Manager of Technical Support Department

131. (A) transition
(B) absence
(C) interruption
(D) decline

132. (A) every
(B) this
(C) others
(D) some

133. (A) You need to show your identification badge to security personnel.
(B) Our company has recently upgraded its order filling process.
(C) The demand for highly trained maintenance staff has been increasing.
(D) This is the last in the series of extensive maintenance works.

134. (A) normal
(B) plan
(C) direction
(D) original

GO ON TO THE NEXT PAGE

Questions 135–138 refer to the following e-mail.

From: Kate Burton <burton@harper.com>
To: All employees
Subject: Lecture series
Date: January 8

Hi, everyone,

As you already were notified at the staff meeting, the -------(135.) speaker for the March lecture series is Jessica Sparks. Ms. Sparks is president of KS Inc. and one of the most popular SF authors. I had the chance to hear her at the technology conference three months ago, and I -------(136.) her presentation very enlightening and insightful. She willingly accepted our offer to deliver a presentation about her newly released book *A message from the future* at the Tokyo Future Fair. -------(137.). I would, therefore, recommend reserving seats at least 3 weeks prior to the event. I'm -------(138.) this event will be more successful than ever! I hope you won't miss out on this great opportunity.

Sincerely,

Kate Burton

135. (A) feature
(B) featuring
(C) features
(D) featured

136. (A) will found
(B) could have found
(C) found
(D) am finding

137. (A) I expect higher turnout than usual from overseas branches this time.
(B) Each presentation should not exceed 30 minutes in length.
(C) A list of participating authors can be found at the company's Web site.
(D) It was a great honor to host such a successful event.

138. (A) possible
(B) qualified
(C) confirmed
(D) confident

Questions 139-142 refer to the following notice.

Attention Tenants!

-------. (139.) While under the lease terms and conditions, each party has 15 days to give the other notice of intent whether or not to renew the lease, we are extending you the courtesy of early notice of an increase in rent as follows:

I would like each of you to continue as my tenants, but an increase of $150 will be applied to the new lease term. The rent is currently $1,500 and under the terms of the new lease agreement, will need to increase ------- (140.) $1,650. Renewal of the lease will be ------- (141.) on your 15 days' written notice that you intend to renew.

During this period, we will perform an inspection of the home no later than April 10 for purposes of ------- (142.) the statement of condition. And the relevant party will address any items needing maintenance or repair. We hope that you have settled into the home and the neighborhood.

139. (A) As discussed, you will now be able to sell your home.
(B) We are pleased to send you the revised contract.
(C) As you know, your lease of our property expires on April 1.
(D) Effective immediately, all tenants should report any problems.

140. (A) to
(B) by
(C) upon
(D) toward

141. (A) responsive
(B) eligible
(C) contingent
(D) insolvent

142. (A) updating
(B) updates
(C) updated
(D) update

GO ON TO THE NEXT PAGE

Questions 143–146 refer to the following e-mail.

To: Cameron Seely <cameronseely@efron.com>
From: Sam Humphrey <shumphrey@efron.com>
Date: August 15
Subject: Your Move

Dear Cameron,

-------. I'm sure you will be a valuable addition to our department. On your very first day
143.
here, we are holding a weekly staff meeting, where you will have the opportunity to meet your colleagues as well as company executives. Shortly after the meeting, you will be given your identification badge which you should present to security personnel every time -------- company facilities.
144.

Do you have -------- questions or requests before you arrive here? -------, please call one of our representatives at 031-555-7890 or email me at shumphrey@efron.com.
145. 146.

Jay Holden

143. (A) To commemorate your 10 years of service, we will be holding a party.
(B) I was very excited to hear that you'll be joining us here in the European branch.
(C) Our company will be expanding the facilities to include a couple of meeting rooms.
(D) Several promising candidates are being considered for the final-round interview.

144. (A) you access
(B) to access
(C) access
(D) accessible

145. (A) main
(B) any
(C) this
(D) so

146. (A) In addition
(B) For instance
(C) In the end
(D) If so

PART 7

Directions: In this part you will read a selection of texts, such as magazine and newspaper articles, e-mails, and instant messages. Each text or set of texts is followed by several questions. Select the best answer for each question and mark the letter (A), (B), (C), or (D) on your answer sheet.

Questions 147-148 refer to the following information.

Victory Athletic, Inc.

Here is a summary of your recent order.
You can also view your updated order details at www.vathletic.com.
Thank you for trading with us.

Order Details

Customer Name : The Glen Hill Golf & Country Club
Customer Number : LJ2378CM

Order Number : 105-3675384-3692230
Date Placed : Dec. 12
Date Filled : Dec. 17

Item : Customized caps with the company logo
Color : Black and white
Size : Adjustable
Quantity : 300

147. What kind of company is Victory Athletic, Inc.?

(A) A news reporting agency
(B) A tracking courier service
(C) A sports apparel manufacturer
(D) A business document outsourcing company

148. When is the order date?

(A) December 12
(B) December 13
(C) December 17
(D) December 30

GO ON TO THE NEXT PAGE

Questions 149-150 refer to the following notice.

Town Agenda

"Town Agenda" is published in the weekend edition of the *Art & Life* magazine in order to promote various local events and activities in Cleveland. If you would like to submit a story idea or event notification, please direct your e-mail to Jim Campbell at jimc@anl.com or by fax at 440-555-9123. Postal mail is also available at the address listed below. To guarantee the publication of your submissions, please send them by Wednesday morning of each week. However, we have no specific deadline. We expect that "Town Agenda" contains up-to-date information about upcoming cultural events and exciting activities in the city.

Art & Life
12200 Fairhill Road
Cleveland, OH 44120-1058

149. What is the purpose of the notice?

(A) To send a story idea to a journalist
(B) To promote community events and activities
(C) To request submissions to a magazine
(D) To increase the circulation of *Art & Life* magazine

150. What is indicated about Town Agenda?

(A) It promotes professional opportunities in all areas of the arts.
(B) It delivers local news about events and activities every day.
(C) It does not have any submission deadline.
(D) It guarantees a response from local residents.

Questions 151-153 refer to the following letter.

Wildlife Rehabilitation Organization (WRO)

PO Box 1004, Grantham, Lincolnshire MG11 0AG

December 5

Alexis Ramsdell
President
Watson Nature Foundation
Michelin House, 81 Fulham Road, London, SW3 6RD, United Kingdom

Dear Mr. Ramsdell,

I am writing to express my sincere appreciation for your sponsorship of the 17th Annual Wildlife Festival on behalf of Wildlife Rehabilitation Organization.
The number of participants at the Annual Wildlife Festival has greatly increased in the past few years, so we had to search for an ideal place to accommodate more participants and volunteers this year. The Grand Valley Hotel was much more spacious and pleasant than the WRO main conference room where we held last year's conference. Thanks to your generous donations, this year's event was a huge success. We would not have been able to hold such a successful event without your help.

Thank you again for your contribution and support.

Sincerely,
Rob Hulls
President and CEO

151. Why did Mr. Hulls write to Mr. Ramsdell?

(A) To promote a wildlife conservation group
(B) To reserve a meeting space for the annual event
(C) To demonstrate gratitude for the generous donation
(D) To improve infrastructure for a sponsorship opportunity

152. What can be inferred about Mr. Ramsdell?

(A) He organizes the Wildlife Festival every year.
(B) He is committed to Wildlife Rehabilitation.
(C) He is a frequent supporter of various charities.
(D) He founded the Wildlife Rehabilitation Organization.

153. What is NOT mentioned about the annual Wildlife Festival?

(A) It is to benefit the Wildlife Rehabilitation Organization.
(B) It is getting more attention from a lot of people.
(C) It is sponsored by Watson Nature Foundation.
(D) It is held at the same location every year.

Questions 154-155 refer to the following text message chain.

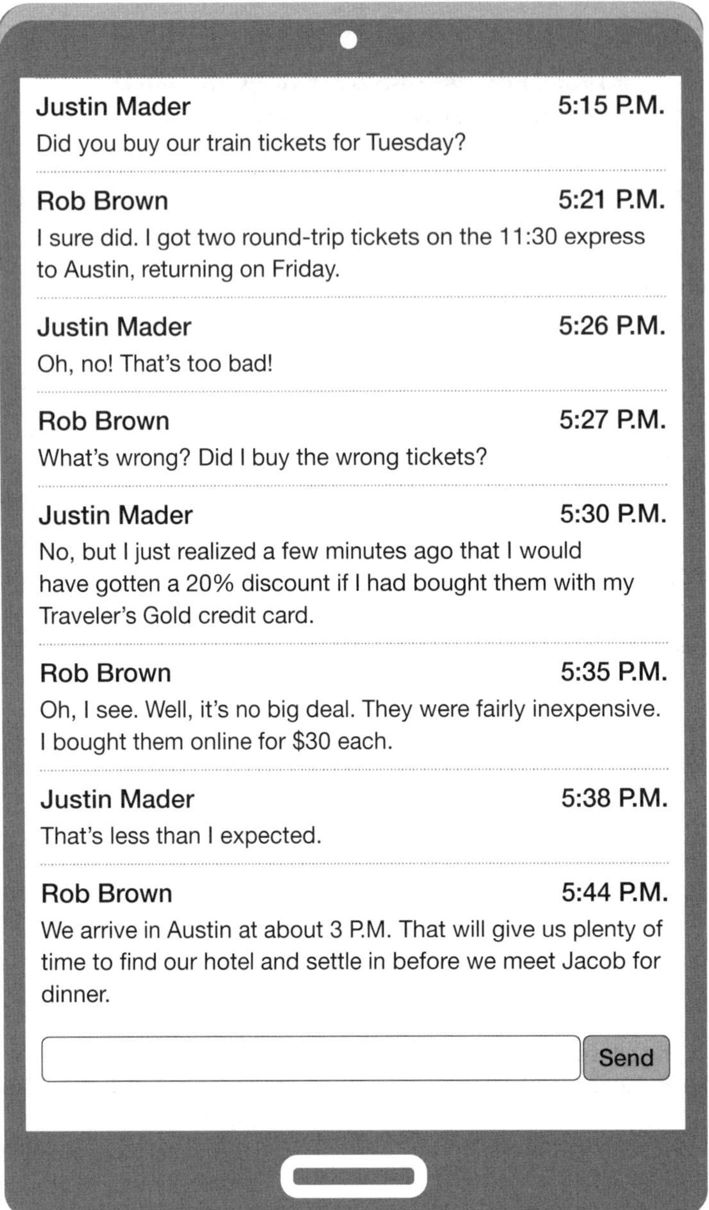
Justin Mader 5:15 P.M.
Did you buy our train tickets for Tuesday?

Rob Brown 5:21 P.M.
I sure did. I got two round-trip tickets on the 11:30 express to Austin, returning on Friday.

Justin Mader 5:26 P.M.
Oh, no! That's too bad!

Rob Brown 5:27 P.M.
What's wrong? Did I buy the wrong tickets?

Justin Mader 5:30 P.M.
No, but I just realized a few minutes ago that I would have gotten a 20% discount if I had bought them with my Traveler's Gold credit card.

Rob Brown 5:35 P.M.
Oh, I see. Well, it's no big deal. They were fairly inexpensive. I bought them online for $30 each.

Justin Mader 5:38 P.M.
That's less than I expected.

Rob Brown 5:44 P.M.
We arrive in Austin at about 3 P.M. That will give us plenty of time to find our hotel and settle in before we meet Jacob for dinner.

154. What is NOT suggested about Mr. Mader and Mr. Brown?

(A) Their train tickets cost a total of $60.
(B) Their destination is Austin.
(C) They will arrive in the afternoon.
(D) They will stay for one week.

155. At 5:35 P.M., what does Mr. Brown mean when he writes, "It's no big deal"?

(A) The ticket price seems too high.
(B) The problem is not significant.
(C) The credit card was not accepted.
(D) The trip is not important.

Questions 156-158 refer to the following advertisement.

**If you have a career interest in writing,
we have the appropriate tools to successfully guide you.**

Writersclinic.com has Internet-based courses that will help you advance your writing skills and find your creativity talents. Your goal may be to perfect writing poetry, short stories, novels, or even scripts. All of these can be done at the comfort of your home.

We offer three-month courses led by top authors. They will modify the instructions and materials to tailor your needs. You will get personal feedback and comments on strategies to perfect your writing. All participants will be able to have a discussion with each other to compare ideas and writing opinions.

Wanting to have strong writing skills? Do not wait any longer! Visit us at our Web site and register by December 31 to receive a 20% discount on all classes that begin in January.

For more information, visit us right now at writersclinic.com, or give us a call at 555-1352.

www.writersclinic.com

156. For whom is this advertisement intended?

(A) People looking for travel guides
(B) People working in teaching clinic
(C) People interested in career writing
(D) People running a successful business

157. Which is NOT an advantage of these classes?

(A) Personalized attention
(B) Free online registration
(C) Sharing ideas with participants
(D) Lectures by professional writers

158. What is given to the people who register by the end of the year?

(A) Discounts on all courses
(B) Free materials for classes
(C) Free counseling with instructors
(D) Detailed information about classes

GO ON TO THE NEXT PAGE

Questions 159-161 refer to the following notice.

Lockers & Laundry Service

If you lose your locker key, you will be responsible for the $10 key replacement fee. A $25 lock replacement fee will be charged if the lock needs to be changed. A lost or misplaced laundry bag will be exchanged at a fee of $15. Please notify our front desk staff on duty as soon as possible and then complete a missing key form if you lose your locker key.

Workout clothes need to be placed in your laundry bag and closed tightly. It will reduce a chance of yours getting lost. There is a laundry basket at the entrance to the laundry room for men and at the entrance to the shower room for women. Your clean laundry will be returned to your locker within 24 hours.

NOTE: Leaving your expensive clothes or shoes in a laundry bag is not recommended. Secure all your personal belongings in your locker when you leave the fitness center.

JAY'S FITNESS CENTER DOES NOT ASSUME ANY LIABILITIES OR RESPONSIBILITIES FOR LOST OR STOLEN ITEMS.

JAY'S FITNESS

159. Where is the notice most likely to be found?

(A) At a clothing store
(B) At a hotel
(C) At a laundry
(D) At a gym

160. What should people do first if they lose or misplace their locker key?

(A) Fill out a missing form
(B) Request a locker change
(C) Report it to an employee
(D) Pay $10 for replacement

161. Where will the clean workout clothes be returned to?

(A) The locker
(B) The front desk
(C) The laundry bag
(D) The laundry basket

Questions 162-164 refer to the following letter.

Best Offer Factory

Mose Denmon
3828 Reeves Street
Appleton, WI 54913

Dear Mr. Denmon,

We sincerely apologize for the mistake with your order. We have heard that the electric shaver was damaged when you received it. Our company has a strong reputation for unparalleled customer service and we are happy to replace it with a new one, the same item as you ordered.

We have already sent a replacement along with a pre-paid return label for your convenience. You will receive it within 3-5 business days. When you receive the new electric shaver, please make sure that the item is in good condition before signing to accept the delivery. If you send the damaged electric shaver to us, we will make a claim with the courier company.

I am extremely sorry for the inconvenience once again. You are always our valuable customer. Thank you very much for your business.

Sincerely yours,

Mellisa Paulding
Customer Service Representative
Best Offer Factory

162. What problem happened to Mr. Denmon?

(A) An order was not processed.
(B) A broken item was delivered.
(C) A replacement was not provided.
(D) An ordered item was out of stock.

163. What was sent with a new electric shaver?

(A) A return code
(B) A new claim form
(C) A descriptive label
(D) A pre-paid return kit

164. What will Mr. Denmon probably do?

(A) File a complaint
(B) Place a new order
(C) Call Ms. Paulding again
(D) Return the damaged item

GO ON TO THE NEXT PAGE

Questions 165-166 refer to the following online chat discussion.

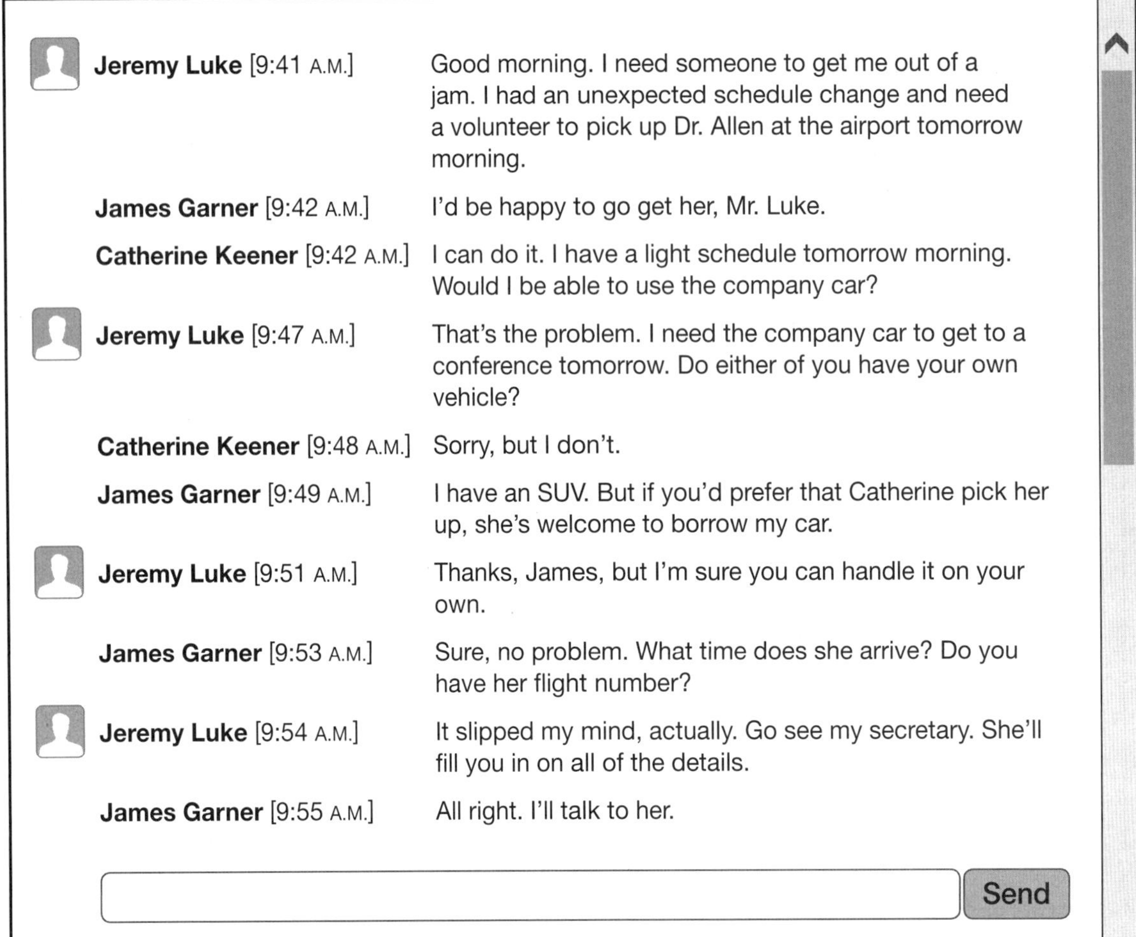

Jeremy Luke [9:41 A.M.]	Good morning. I need someone to get me out of a jam. I had an unexpected schedule change and need a volunteer to pick up Dr. Allen at the airport tomorrow morning.
James Garner [9:42 A.M.]	I'd be happy to go get her, Mr. Luke.
Catherine Keener [9:42 A.M.]	I can do it. I have a light schedule tomorrow morning. Would I be able to use the company car?
Jeremy Luke [9:47 A.M.]	That's the problem. I need the company car to get to a conference tomorrow. Do either of you have your own vehicle?
Catherine Keener [9:48 A.M.]	Sorry, but I don't.
James Garner [9:49 A.M.]	I have an SUV. But if you'd prefer that Catherine pick her up, she's welcome to borrow my car.
Jeremy Luke [9:51 A.M.]	Thanks, James, but I'm sure you can handle it on your own.
James Garner [9:53 A.M.]	Sure, no problem. What time does she arrive? Do you have her flight number?
Jeremy Luke [9:54 A.M.]	It slipped my mind, actually. Go see my secretary. She'll fill you in on all of the details.
James Garner [9:55 A.M.]	All right. I'll talk to her.

Send

165. What will Mr. Garner most likely do next?

(A) Obtain the flight information
(B) Drive his SUV to the airport
(C) Contact Dr. Allen
(D) Return to his home

166. At 9:41 A.M., what does Mr. Luke mean when he writes, "I need someone to get me out of a jam"?

(A) He is stuck in traffic.
(B) He wants some data.
(C) He requires assistance.
(D) He is worried about a project.

Questions 167-170 refer to the following letter.

Joseph Kidman
Acquisitions Department
Reingold Accounting
19188 6th Avenue
Detroit, MI 48207

Dear Mr. Kidman:

It was a pleasure to meet with you and your staff at your Detroit office last Friday. As per our discussion about providing security equipment and monitoring services to your company, I'm sending you a formal price estimate that has been approved by our CEO. – [1] –. Although the scale of the services we would be providing to your company fail to meet the threshold for this discount, our CEO has agreed to extend it in anticipation of your company's forecasted growth. – [2] –. If you agree to these terms, the discount will be in place for one year from the signing of the contract. – [3] –. After this period has expired, we will only continue to offer the bulk discount if your company's required services have met or surpassed our standard minimum. – [4] –. Please review the attached estimate and get back to me at your earliest convenience.

Sincerely,

Patrick Jensen
Houseman Security Services

167. What is the purpose of this letter?

(A) To follow up on a meeting
(B) To introduce a new service
(C) To reject a proposal
(D) To request a confirmation

168. What is suggested as being included with this letter?

(A) A letter of introduction
(B) A cost approximation
(C) A revised contract
(D) A product list

169. In which of the positions marked [1], [2], [3], and [4] does the following sentence best fit?

"These prices reflect the 15% bulk discount we offer to our larger customers."

(A) [1]
(B) [2]
(C) [3]
(D) [4]

170. What will happen after one year if an agreement is reached?

(A) The bulk discount will be increased.
(B) The contract will be automatically renewed.
(C) The CEO will request another meeting.
(D) The contract's terms will be reassessed.

GO ON TO THE NEXT PAGE

Questions 171-175 refer to the following letter.

Carlson Business Travel
23 Ivan Street
Lexington, MA 02420-1437

September 10

Darrell Crompton
4534 Romano St.
Cambridge, MA 02141

Dear Mr. Crompton,

This letter is in response to your recent request for a change to your itinerary as we discussed it on the phone. Your flight to Portland from Boston on October 2 has been cancelled and a flight on Tuesday, October 12 at 10:20 AM has been booked for you. – [1] –. You will arrive at 6:40 PM as planned in Portland, Oregon. This is a transfer flight that stops in Houston, TX for an hour before taking off to Portland. This reservation will be cancelled if you don't confirm this flight within seven days of this notice. – [2] –.

I have booked a room at Great Western Hotel in the downtown area, which serves breakfast. October 15 on Friday is the check-out date. You can use any equipment such as a fax machine, a copier, a printer and a laptop computer in the hotel business center. – [3] –. I have also reserved a meeting room available on October 13, the date you requested. However, there will be a scheduled maintenance on the cable network from October 13 to October 14 according to the hotel management. All guests will be unable to access the Internet from anywhere in the hotel: guest rooms, hotel lobby, meeting spaces, even the business center for 24 hours. If this is a serious problem for you, please let me know immediately. – [4] –.

Please call me back at your earliest convenience if you want to confirm the flight and the hotel reservation provided. Thank you for your understanding and my sincerest apologies for any troubles this may have caused you in the schedule.

Sincerely,
Sandra Stafford
Customer Support Manager

171. What did Mr. Crompton probably ask Ms. Stafford to do on the phone?

(A) Recommend a new resort
(B) Report on itinerary changes
(C) Inquire about hotel accessibility
(D) Reschedule a flight

172. When does the flight to Portland leave?

(A) October 2
(B) October 12
(C) October 13
(D) October 14

173. In which of the positions marked [1], [2], [3], and [4] does the following sentence best fit?

"I will search for another hotel so as not to disturb your business."

(A) [1]
(B) [2]
(C) [3]
(D) [4]

174. Why should Mr. Crompton contact Ms. Stafford as soon as possible?

(A) To apply for using the hotel's office equipment
(B) To perform a scheduled maintenance
(C) To provide accommodations options
(D) To confirm the travel itinerary

175. What concern is being addressed by this letter?

(A) A temporary Internet disruption
(B) A reservation of the meeting room
(C) A closure of the hotel business center
(D) A problem with access to the meeting room

Questions 176-180 refer to the following report and e-mail.

Temp Agency

3rd floor, 35 Ashdown Road, Caterham
Phone: 414-555-4465
Fax: 414-555-6693

Name: Austin Smith
Beginning Date: Feb 8

Temp Agency Representative: Inge Bleckman
Assignment: Carlton Banking Group

Day	Date	Start	Finish	Hr/ Min
Mon	Feb 8	7:00 A.M.	4:30 P.M.	8/30
Tue	Feb 9	7:00 A.M.	7:30 P.M.	11/30
Wed	Feb 10	8:30 A.M.	5:30 P.M.	8/00
Thur	Feb 11	7:00 A.M.	4:00 P.M.	8/00
Fri	Feb 12	7:30 A.M.	5:00 P.M.	8/30
			Total	44/30

Signature: *Austin Smith*   Date: Feb 15

* Employees must take two half-hour breaks each day, which are unpaid.

* Employees must obtain written approval from their appointed line managers if they work over time (more than 45 hours per week); managers are to e-mail Temp Agency's representative.

To: Austin Smith
From: Inge Bleckman
C.C: Cleo Ratton
Subject: Weekly Work Report
Date: February 16

I'm writing about the weekly work report you submitted for the temporary placement you had last week at Carlton Banking Group. You appear to have forgotten to notify us of the additional hours you worked. Cleo Ratton contacted us to ask for our permission to allow you to help out after work at a company function in the evening of Feb 9. However, these three extra hours have not been recorded on your work log. If you amend your work report to reflect three overtime hours, I would be happy to approve it for you. We would like to ensure that you are properly paid.

176. What does the information in the work record suggest about Mr. Smith?

(A) He finished work every evening at 5 P.M.
(B) He submitted his work record every day.
(C) His work schedule was the same every day.
(D) He has two half hour breaks every day.

177. According to the email, for what day did Mr. Smith incorrectly record his work hours?

(A) Monday
(B) Tuesday
(C) Wednesday
(D) Friday

178. Who most likely is Ms. Ratton?

(A) A permanent employee
(B) A manager at Carlton Banking Group
(C) A recruitment manager
(D) A temp agency representative

179. In the e-mail, the word "reflect" in paragraph 1, line 6 is closest in meaning to

(A) indicate
(B) return
(C) copy
(D) allow

180. What does Ms. Bleckman ask Mr. Smith to do?

(A) Accept a different work placement
(B) Renew his contract with Temp Agency
(C) Assist with a company celebration
(D) Make changes to his work record

GO ON TO THE NEXT PAGE

Questions 181-185 refer to the following Web site and e-mail.

WWW.HAMIDZAFREEN.UK

About the Concert | About the Performer | **Events and Appearances** | Praise for Hamid's Work

UK Dates

- **May 21-22: Sigmund Center, Edinburgh**
  Concert starts every evening at 7:00 P.M. For more information or to purchase tickets, visit www.edevents/concert.
- **May 24: Carlson University, Clearwater**
  Events begin at 5:00 P.M. Autograph session follows at 7:30 P.M.
- **May 26: Carron Theater, Liverpool**
  Call ticket office at (0161) 555-5734 for details.
- **May 28: Halton Conference Center, Manchester**
  Those who book tickets for Mr. Zafreen's event will be eligible for a 15 percent discount on their accommodations at HCC if they book by April 17. Contact Maria Callan at (0181) 555-3567.

Tickets for all of these concerts must be booked directly via the individual venues and not through this Web site. All events include a concert and a question-and-answer session. Check each event description for details. To invite Mr. Zafreen to perform in your area, contact Mark Wall at mwall@hamidzafreen.uk.

Last updated on May 13.

From: srider@cccharity.com
To: mwall@hamidzafreen.uk
Date: June 3
Subject: Upcoming concert

Dear Mr. Wall,

I met Mr. Zafreen last month at his engagement at the Halton Conference Center. During our meeting, we talked about the possibility of him performing at a charity function for which I am the committee chair. He seemed agreeable to the idea but suggested I speak to you regarding his availability.

The annual Flyford Charity Function is sponsored by the Animal Protection League. It will take place September 15-18 at the National Indoor Arena in Birmingham. I would like to know if Mr. Zafreen would be able to perform on the evening of September 16 as part of our international line-up of performing artists.

Travel and one night hotel accommodation would be covered by our sponsors. We cannot provide any additional payment for participating, unfortunately. However, Mr. Zafreen would have a one-day unlimited use of the National Indoor Arena's facilities on the day he is scheduled to perform. If he wishes to stay for the rest of the event, we can arrange a discounted rate at the hotel.

Please confirm Mr. Zafreen's availability no later than July 21. In the meantime, please let me know if you have any questions.

Regards,
Steve Rider

181. Who most likely is Mr. Zafreen?

(A) A writer
(B) A performer
(C) A charity worker
(D) A convention organizer

182. What is indicated on the Web site about the May events?

(A) Autograph signings will take place after every event.
(B) Tickets cannot be purchased through Mr. Zafreen's Web site.
(C) They all take place in Liverpool.
(D) There are plenty of tickets available.

183. Where did Mr. Rider meet Mr. Zafreen?

(A) In Liverpool
(B) In Edinburgh
(C) In Manchester
(D) In Clearwater

184. What is the purpose of Mr. Rider's email?

(A) To arrange payment for members of a musical group
(B) To invite an artist to give a performance
(C) To update to hotel accommodation
(D) To order tickets for a concert performance

185. When would Mr. Zafreen be able to use the National Indoor Arena's facilities for free?

(A) On September 18
(B) On September 17
(C) On September 16
(D) On September 15

GO ON TO THE NEXT PAGE

Questions 186-190 refer to the following announcement, e-mail, and form.

Attention! Library Staff Members!

The 5th annual International Library Association Conference has been scheduled for August 7 in Melbourne, Australia. We are looking for four volunteers to represent our institution at this event. You will be required to spend three days in Australia, with two additional travel days, and, upon returning, you will be expected to make a variety of presentations related to the information you obtain at the conference. Round-trip air fare and a private room at the Meriton Hotel for two nights will be provided by the university. However, attendees must pay for their own food, and they will not be compensated for any additional expenses incurred. If you are interested in taking part or would like more information, please contact Kevin James at kjames@uta.edu by this Friday.

To : Kevin James <kjames@uta.edu>
From: Mel Brooks <mbrooks@uta.edu>
Date: June 10
Subject: ILA Conference

Hello, Mr. James.

I'm writing to express my interest in attending this year's ILA conference on behalf of the university library. As you may remember, we attended the third ILA conference in London together, although I missed last year's Denver conference due to a schedule conflict. This year's event caught my eye, as I have family in Melbourne. However, I do have a few special requests. First, I'd prefer to leave from Miami rather than Richmond. I don't believe this would affect the ticket price. Also, would it be possible to stay at the Space Hotel rather than the Meriton Hotel? The reason is that the Meriton is quite far from my parents' home, which I would like to visit. Finally, I would like to add two vacation days to the end of the trip, so I can spend more time with my family. I promise I would be prepared to make a presentation about the conference the following Monday. Thanks for considering my requests!

Mel Brooks

Australia Arrival Card

Name:	Mel Brooks
Citizenship:	American
Number of accompanying members:	0
Passport Number:	00237181
Length of stay:	six days
Main purpose of visit:	attending a conference
Address in Australia:	Meriton Hotel, Melbourne
Port of Embarkation:	Miami, America
Aircraft or vessel number:	Air Australia Flight 13

186. In the announcement, the word "compensated" in paragraph 1, line 7, is closest in meaning to

(A) paid back
(B) included in
(C) consulted on
(D) questioned about

187. What is indicated as a requirement of conference attendees?

(A) They must use their vacation time.
(B) They must share a hotel room.
(C) They must share what they learn.
(D) They must speak at the conference.

188. What is indicated about Mr. Brooks?

(A) He attends the ILA conference every year.
(B) He no longer works at the university library.
(C) He has previously met Mr. James.
(D) He is a citizen of Australia.

189. Where was the fourth annual ILA conference held?

(A) Melbourne
(B) London
(C) Denver
(D) Miami

190. Which of Mr. Brooks' requests did Mr. James deny?

(A) Attending the conference
(B) Switching to another hotel
(C) Taking additional days off
(D) Leaving from a different airport

GO ON TO THE NEXT PAGE

Questions 191-195 refer to the following information, review, and e-mail.

Important Update for Capital Bank Customers

Our downtown branch located on Sixth Avenue will be closed for renovations from April 16th to May 12th. The two ATMs located in the lobby will still be accessible, but customers wishing to speak to a bank representative will have to visit our other downtown branch, which can be found on the corner of Second Avenue and Virginia Street. We regret the inconvenience but are pleased to announce that the Sixth Avenue branch will be updated into a state-of-the-art, customer-friendly facility, with sofas, conference tables and touch-screen information modules. This will result in a banking experience that is faster, more comfortable, and more enjoyable for all of our customers. At the same time, the branch will retain the classic traditional features of the century-old building in which it is located. You can find more details about our renovation plans on the Capital Bank Web site.

Instant Customer Reviews – Washington – Banking and Finance

In case you haven't heard, the Capital Bank on Sixth Avenue has finally reopened, and I can tell you that it has undergone a complete transformation. It looks more like a breakroom at a tech start-up than a traditional bank. Although the new layout was off-putting at first, I quickly learned to love it. The old number-ticket dispensers have been replaced with touch screens, and the clerks are no longer hidden behind a big counter—they come right out and deal with you face to face. While the lobby ATMs are the same old models, there are three brand new ones inside the branch itself. There are even pastries and free coffee to indulge in while you wait. I was pretty frustrated when their renovations ran several weeks longer than they had announced, but it was worth the wait!

William Mercado – Capital Bank customer since 2016

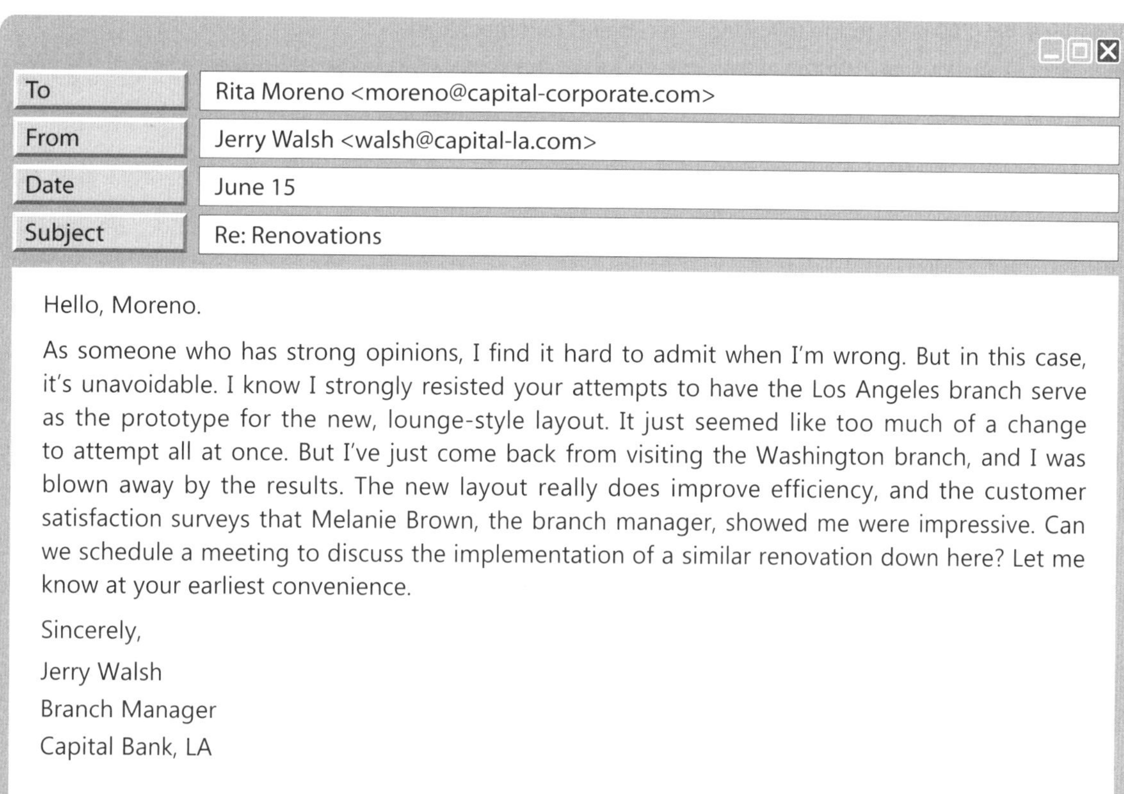

To: Rita Moreno <moreno@capital-corporate.com>
From: Jerry Walsh <walsh@capital-la.com>
Date: June 15
Subject: Re: Renovations

Hello, Moreno.

As someone who has strong opinions, I find it hard to admit when I'm wrong. But in this case, it's unavoidable. I know I strongly resisted your attempts to have the Los Angeles branch serve as the prototype for the new, lounge-style layout. It just seemed like too much of a change to attempt all at once. But I've just come back from visiting the Washington branch, and I was blown away by the results. The new layout really does improve efficiency, and the customer satisfaction surveys that Melanie Brown, the branch manager, showed me were impressive. Can we schedule a meeting to discuss the implementation of a similar renovation down here? Let me know at your earliest convenience.

Sincerely,

Jerry Walsh
Branch Manager
Capital Bank, LA

191. What is NOT indicated about the Capital Bank on Sixth Avenue?

(A) It was scheduled to reopen in May.
(B) It has a pair of ATMs in its lobby.
(C) It is moving to Second Avenue.
(D) It is located in an older building.

192. What does Mr. Mercado indicate as the cause of his annoyance?

(A) An unexpectedly lengthy closure
(B) A surprisingly rude bank staff
(C) A lack of new technology
(D) An inconvenient location

193. How many ATMs does the Sixth Avenue Apex Bank have after its renovation?

(A) None
(B) 2
(C) 3
(D) 5

194. What was Mr. Walsh's original opinion of the change to a new bank style?

(A) He was excited about it.
(B) He felt it was too extreme.
(C) He thought it cost too much.
(D) He was concerned about safety.

195. What does Mr. Walsh want Ms. Moreno to do?

(A) Apologize for her rude behavior
(B) Take a tour of the Washington branch
(C) Conduct a customer satisfaction survey
(D) Talk with him about renovating his branch

GO ON TO THE NEXT PAGE

Questions 196-200 refer to the following e-mails and text message.

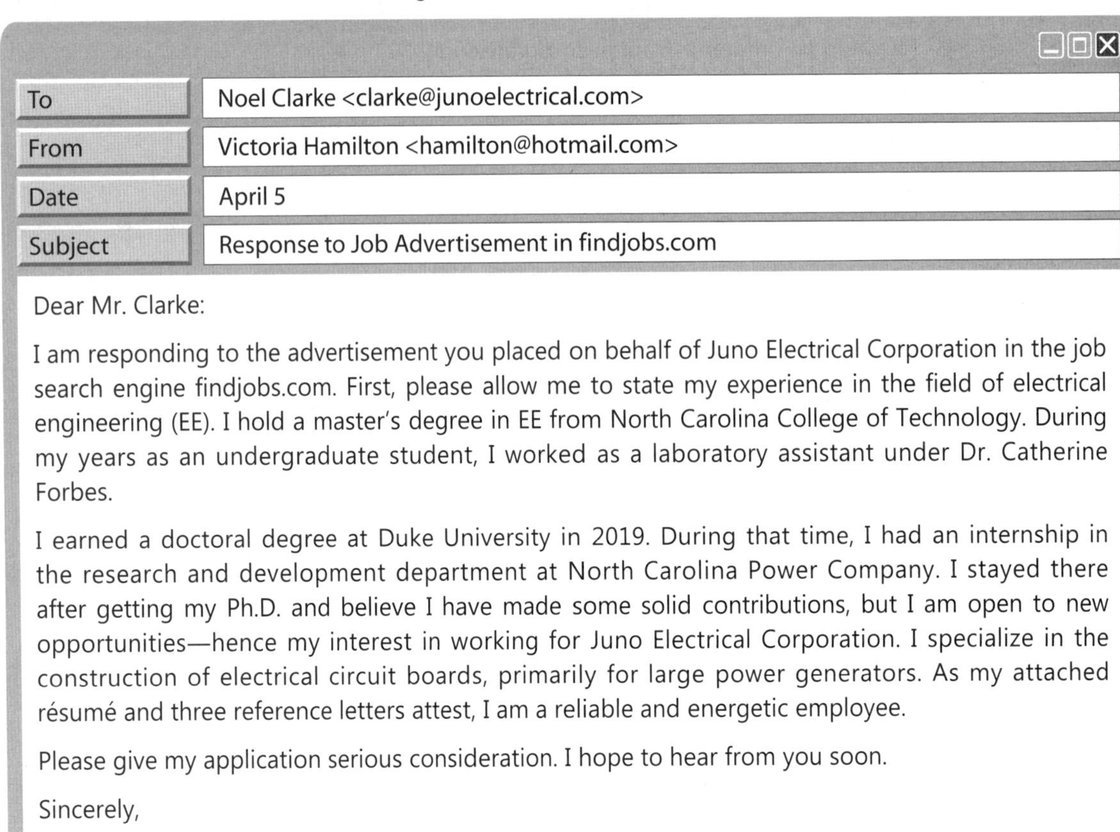

To: Noel Clarke <clarke@junoelectrical.com>
From: Victoria Hamilton <hamilton@hotmail.com>
Date: April 5
Subject: Response to Job Advertisement in findjobs.com

Dear Mr. Clarke:

I am responding to the advertisement you placed on behalf of Juno Electrical Corporation in the job search engine findjobs.com. First, please allow me to state my experience in the field of electrical engineering (EE). I hold a master's degree in EE from North Carolina College of Technology. During my years as an undergraduate student, I worked as a laboratory assistant under Dr. Catherine Forbes.

I earned a doctoral degree at Duke University in 2019. During that time, I had an internship in the research and development department at North Carolina Power Company. I stayed there after getting my Ph.D. and believe I have made some solid contributions, but I am open to new opportunities—hence my interest in working for Juno Electrical Corporation. I specialize in the construction of electrical circuit boards, primarily for large power generators. As my attached résumé and three reference letters attest, I am a reliable and energetic employee.

Please give my application serious consideration. I hope to hear from you soon.

Sincerely,
Victoria Hamilton

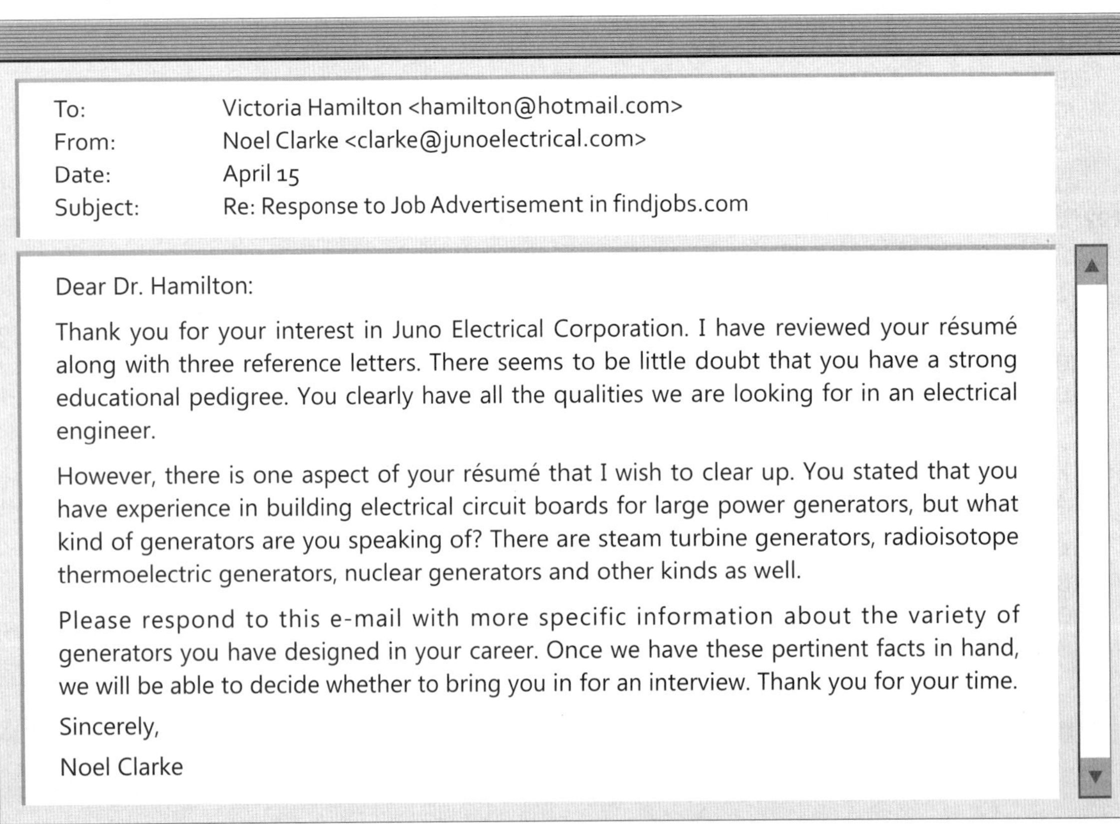

To: Victoria Hamilton <hamilton@hotmail.com>
From: Noel Clarke <clarke@junoelectrical.com>
Date: April 15
Subject: Re: Response to Job Advertisement in findjobs.com

Dear Dr. Hamilton:

Thank you for your interest in Juno Electrical Corporation. I have reviewed your résumé along with three reference letters. There seems to be little doubt that you have a strong educational pedigree. You clearly have all the qualities we are looking for in an electrical engineer.

However, there is one aspect of your résumé that I wish to clear up. You stated that you have experience in building electrical circuit boards for large power generators, but what kind of generators are you speaking of? There are steam turbine generators, radioisotope thermoelectric generators, nuclear generators and other kinds as well.

Please respond to this e-mail with more specific information about the variety of generators you have designed in your career. Once we have these pertinent facts in hand, we will be able to decide whether to bring you in for an interview. Thank you for your time.

Sincerely,
Noel Clarke

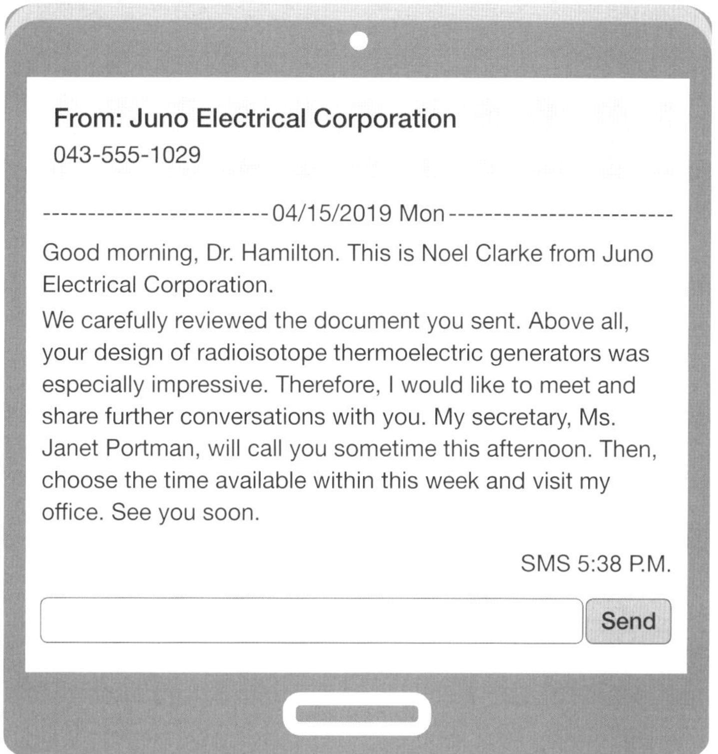
From: Juno Electrical Corporation
043-555-1029

------------------------- 04/15/2019 Mon -------------------------

Good morning, Dr. Hamilton. This is Noel Clarke from Juno Electrical Corporation.

We carefully reviewed the document you sent. Above all, your design of radioisotope thermoelectric generators was especially impressive. Therefore, I would like to meet and share further conversations with you. My secretary, Ms. Janet Portman, will call you sometime this afternoon. Then, choose the time available within this week and visit my office. See you soon.

SMS 5:38 P.M.

196. Who is Noel Clarke?

(A) A student at North Carolina College of Technology
(B) A worker at North Carolina Power Company
(C) An agent at findjobs.com
(D) An employee at Juno Electrical Corporation

197. What does Dr. Hamilton specialize in?

(A) Public relations
(B) Assisting Dr. Forbes
(C) Teaching graduate students
(D) Designing electrical circuit boards

198. What specific information does Mr. Clarke ask for?

(A) When Dr. Hamilton may come in for an interview
(B) The topic of Dr. Hamilton's Ph.D. dissertation
(C) Dr. Hamilton's educational background
(D) Information about electrical generators

199. What is suggested by the text message?

(A) Mr. Clarke has worked with Dr. Hamilton many times.
(B) Juno Electrical Corporation will launch a new product in April.
(C) Dr. Hamilton sent an e-mail to Mr. Clarke on April 15.
(D) Mr. Clarke has recently been hired as a manager.

200. What can be inferred about Dr. Hamilton?

(A) She works at North Carolina Power Company permanently.
(B) She submitted a résumé and application form to findjobs.com.
(C) She received a great deal of help from the classified ads.
(D) She will talk with Ms. Portman on the phone.

Stop! This is the end of the test. If you finish before time is called, you may go back to Parts 5, 6, and 7 and check your work.

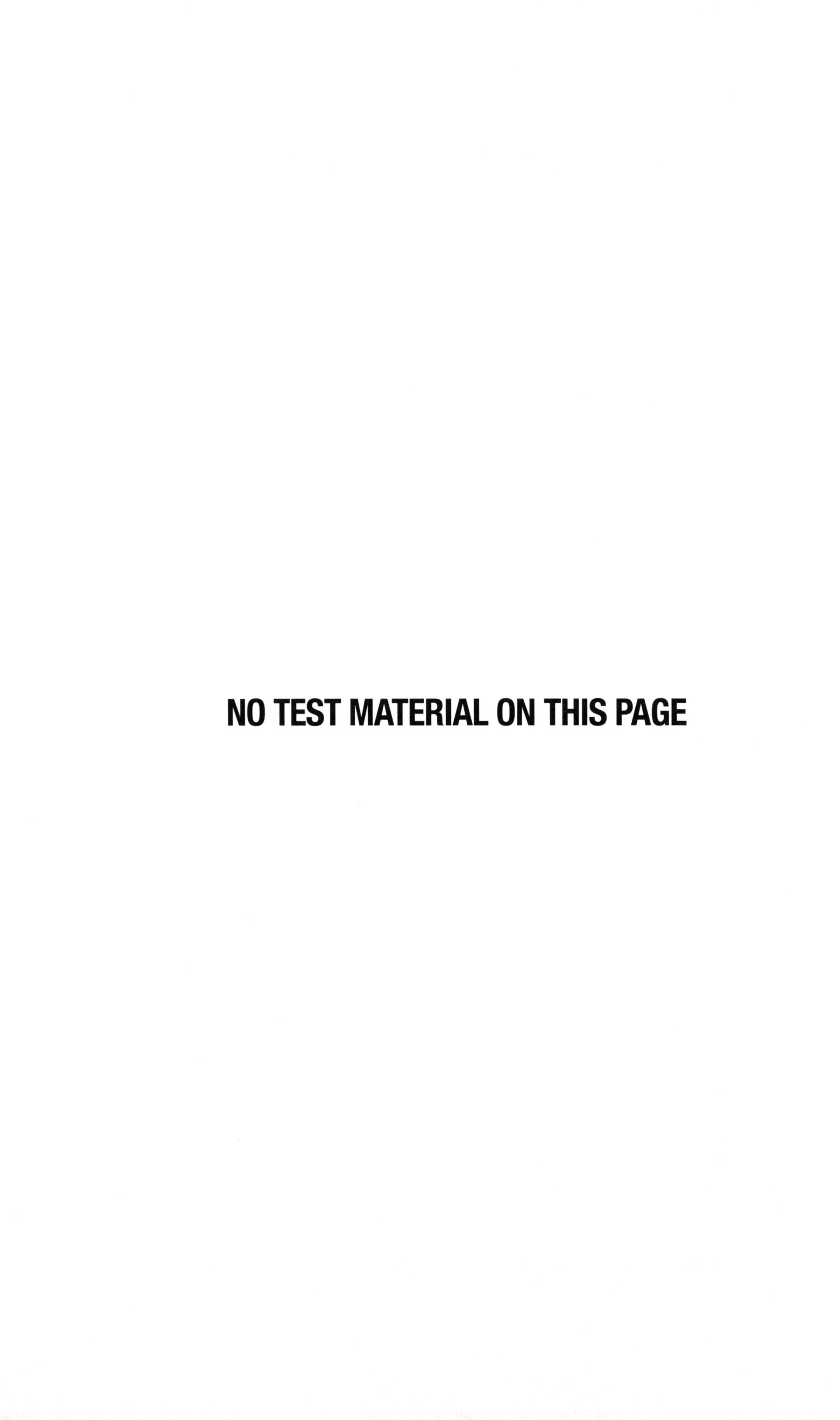
NO TEST MATERIAL ON THIS PAGE

ANSWER SHEET

Actual **Test 1**

수험번호						

응시일자 : 년 월 일

성명	한글	
	한자	
	영자	

좌석번호
Ⓐ Ⓑ Ⓒ Ⓓ Ⓔ ① ② ③ ④ ⑤ ⑥ ⑦

LISTENING (Part I~IV)

NO.	ANSWER				NO.	ANSWER				NO.	ANSWER				NO.	ANSWER				NO.	ANSWER			
	A	B	C	D		A	B	C	D		A	B	C	D		A	B	C	D		A	B	C	D
1	Ⓐ	Ⓑ	Ⓒ	Ⓓ	21	Ⓐ	Ⓑ	Ⓒ		41	Ⓐ	Ⓑ	Ⓒ	Ⓓ	61	Ⓐ	Ⓑ	Ⓒ	Ⓓ	81	Ⓐ	Ⓑ	Ⓒ	Ⓓ
2	Ⓐ	Ⓑ	Ⓒ	Ⓓ	22	Ⓐ	Ⓑ	Ⓒ		42	Ⓐ	Ⓑ	Ⓒ	Ⓓ	62	Ⓐ	Ⓑ	Ⓒ	Ⓓ	82	Ⓐ	Ⓑ	Ⓒ	Ⓓ
3	Ⓐ	Ⓑ	Ⓒ	Ⓓ	23	Ⓐ	Ⓑ	Ⓒ		43	Ⓐ	Ⓑ	Ⓒ	Ⓓ	63	Ⓐ	Ⓑ	Ⓒ	Ⓓ	83	Ⓐ	Ⓑ	Ⓒ	Ⓓ
4	Ⓐ	Ⓑ	Ⓒ	Ⓓ	24	Ⓐ	Ⓑ	Ⓒ		44	Ⓐ	Ⓑ	Ⓒ	Ⓓ	64	Ⓐ	Ⓑ	Ⓒ	Ⓓ	84	Ⓐ	Ⓑ	Ⓒ	Ⓓ
5	Ⓐ	Ⓑ	Ⓒ	Ⓓ	25	Ⓐ	Ⓑ	Ⓒ		45	Ⓐ	Ⓑ	Ⓒ	Ⓓ	65	Ⓐ	Ⓑ	Ⓒ	Ⓓ	85	Ⓐ	Ⓑ	Ⓒ	Ⓓ
6	Ⓐ	Ⓑ	Ⓒ	Ⓓ	26	Ⓐ	Ⓑ	Ⓒ		46	Ⓐ	Ⓑ	Ⓒ	Ⓓ	66	Ⓐ	Ⓑ	Ⓒ	Ⓓ	86	Ⓐ	Ⓑ	Ⓒ	Ⓓ
7	Ⓐ	Ⓑ	Ⓒ		27	Ⓐ	Ⓑ	Ⓒ		47	Ⓐ	Ⓑ	Ⓒ	Ⓓ	67	Ⓐ	Ⓑ	Ⓒ	Ⓓ	87	Ⓐ	Ⓑ	Ⓒ	Ⓓ
8	Ⓐ	Ⓑ	Ⓒ		28	Ⓐ	Ⓑ	Ⓒ		48	Ⓐ	Ⓑ	Ⓒ	Ⓓ	68	Ⓐ	Ⓑ	Ⓒ	Ⓓ	88	Ⓐ	Ⓑ	Ⓒ	Ⓓ
9	Ⓐ	Ⓑ	Ⓒ		29	Ⓐ	Ⓑ	Ⓒ		49	Ⓐ	Ⓑ	Ⓒ	Ⓓ	69	Ⓐ	Ⓑ	Ⓒ	Ⓓ	89	Ⓐ	Ⓑ	Ⓒ	Ⓓ
10	Ⓐ	Ⓑ	Ⓒ		30	Ⓐ	Ⓑ	Ⓒ		50	Ⓐ	Ⓑ	Ⓒ	Ⓓ	70	Ⓐ	Ⓑ	Ⓒ	Ⓓ	90	Ⓐ	Ⓑ	Ⓒ	Ⓓ
11	Ⓐ	Ⓑ	Ⓒ		31	Ⓐ	Ⓑ	Ⓒ		51	Ⓐ	Ⓑ	Ⓒ	Ⓓ	71	Ⓐ	Ⓑ	Ⓒ	Ⓓ	91	Ⓐ	Ⓑ	Ⓒ	Ⓓ
12	Ⓐ	Ⓑ	Ⓒ		32	Ⓐ	Ⓑ	Ⓒ	Ⓓ	52	Ⓐ	Ⓑ	Ⓒ	Ⓓ	72	Ⓐ	Ⓑ	Ⓒ	Ⓓ	92	Ⓐ	Ⓑ	Ⓒ	Ⓓ
13	Ⓐ	Ⓑ	Ⓒ		33	Ⓐ	Ⓑ	Ⓒ	Ⓓ	53	Ⓐ	Ⓑ	Ⓒ	Ⓓ	73	Ⓐ	Ⓑ	Ⓒ	Ⓓ	93	Ⓐ	Ⓑ	Ⓒ	Ⓓ
14	Ⓐ	Ⓑ	Ⓒ		34	Ⓐ	Ⓑ	Ⓒ	Ⓓ	54	Ⓐ	Ⓑ	Ⓒ	Ⓓ	74	Ⓐ	Ⓑ	Ⓒ	Ⓓ	94	Ⓐ	Ⓑ	Ⓒ	Ⓓ
15	Ⓐ	Ⓑ	Ⓒ		35	Ⓐ	Ⓑ	Ⓒ	Ⓓ	55	Ⓐ	Ⓑ	Ⓒ	Ⓓ	75	Ⓐ	Ⓑ	Ⓒ	Ⓓ	95	Ⓐ	Ⓑ	Ⓒ	Ⓓ
16	Ⓐ	Ⓑ	Ⓒ		36	Ⓐ	Ⓑ	Ⓒ	Ⓓ	56	Ⓐ	Ⓑ	Ⓒ	Ⓓ	76	Ⓐ	Ⓑ	Ⓒ	Ⓓ	96	Ⓐ	Ⓑ	Ⓒ	Ⓓ
17	Ⓐ	Ⓑ	Ⓒ		37	Ⓐ	Ⓑ	Ⓒ	Ⓓ	57	Ⓐ	Ⓑ	Ⓒ	Ⓓ	77	Ⓐ	Ⓑ	Ⓒ	Ⓓ	97	Ⓐ	Ⓑ	Ⓒ	Ⓓ
18	Ⓐ	Ⓑ	Ⓒ		38	Ⓐ	Ⓑ	Ⓒ	Ⓓ	58	Ⓐ	Ⓑ	Ⓒ	Ⓓ	78	Ⓐ	Ⓑ	Ⓒ	Ⓓ	98	Ⓐ	Ⓑ	Ⓒ	Ⓓ
19	Ⓐ	Ⓑ	Ⓒ		39	Ⓐ	Ⓑ	Ⓒ	Ⓓ	59	Ⓐ	Ⓑ	Ⓒ	Ⓓ	79	Ⓐ	Ⓑ	Ⓒ	Ⓓ	99	Ⓐ	Ⓑ	Ⓒ	Ⓓ
20	Ⓐ	Ⓑ	Ⓒ		40	Ⓐ	Ⓑ	Ⓒ	Ⓓ	60	Ⓐ	Ⓑ	Ⓒ	Ⓓ	80	Ⓐ	Ⓑ	Ⓒ	Ⓓ	100	Ⓐ	Ⓑ	Ⓒ	Ⓓ

READING (Part V~VII)

NO.	ANSWER				NO.	ANSWER				NO.	ANSWER				NO.	ANSWER				NO.	ANSWER			
	A	B	C	D		A	B	C	D		A	B	C	D		A	B	C	D		A	B	C	D
101	Ⓐ	Ⓑ	Ⓒ	Ⓓ	121	Ⓐ	Ⓑ	Ⓒ	Ⓓ	141	Ⓐ	Ⓑ	Ⓒ	Ⓓ	161	Ⓐ	Ⓑ	Ⓒ	Ⓓ	181	Ⓐ	Ⓑ	Ⓒ	Ⓓ
102	Ⓐ	Ⓑ	Ⓒ	Ⓓ	122	Ⓐ	Ⓑ	Ⓒ	Ⓓ	142	Ⓐ	Ⓑ	Ⓒ	Ⓓ	162	Ⓐ	Ⓑ	Ⓒ	Ⓓ	182	Ⓐ	Ⓑ	Ⓒ	Ⓓ
103	Ⓐ	Ⓑ	Ⓒ	Ⓓ	123	Ⓐ	Ⓑ	Ⓒ	Ⓓ	143	Ⓐ	Ⓑ	Ⓒ	Ⓓ	163	Ⓐ	Ⓑ	Ⓒ	Ⓓ	183	Ⓐ	Ⓑ	Ⓒ	Ⓓ
104	Ⓐ	Ⓑ	Ⓒ	Ⓓ	124	Ⓐ	Ⓑ	Ⓒ	Ⓓ	144	Ⓐ	Ⓑ	Ⓒ	Ⓓ	164	Ⓐ	Ⓑ	Ⓒ	Ⓓ	184	Ⓐ	Ⓑ	Ⓒ	Ⓓ
105	Ⓐ	Ⓑ	Ⓒ	Ⓓ	125	Ⓐ	Ⓑ	Ⓒ	Ⓓ	145	Ⓐ	Ⓑ	Ⓒ	Ⓓ	165	Ⓐ	Ⓑ	Ⓒ	Ⓓ	185	Ⓐ	Ⓑ	Ⓒ	Ⓓ
106	Ⓐ	Ⓑ	Ⓒ	Ⓓ	126	Ⓐ	Ⓑ	Ⓒ	Ⓓ	146	Ⓐ	Ⓑ	Ⓒ	Ⓓ	166	Ⓐ	Ⓑ	Ⓒ	Ⓓ	186	Ⓐ	Ⓑ	Ⓒ	Ⓓ
107	Ⓐ	Ⓑ	Ⓒ	Ⓓ	127	Ⓐ	Ⓑ	Ⓒ	Ⓓ	147	Ⓐ	Ⓑ	Ⓒ	Ⓓ	167	Ⓐ	Ⓑ	Ⓒ	Ⓓ	187	Ⓐ	Ⓑ	Ⓒ	Ⓓ
108	Ⓐ	Ⓑ	Ⓒ	Ⓓ	128	Ⓐ	Ⓑ	Ⓒ	Ⓓ	148	Ⓐ	Ⓑ	Ⓒ	Ⓓ	168	Ⓐ	Ⓑ	Ⓒ	Ⓓ	188	Ⓐ	Ⓑ	Ⓒ	Ⓓ
109	Ⓐ	Ⓑ	Ⓒ	Ⓓ	129	Ⓐ	Ⓑ	Ⓒ	Ⓓ	149	Ⓐ	Ⓑ	Ⓒ	Ⓓ	169	Ⓐ	Ⓑ	Ⓒ	Ⓓ	189	Ⓐ	Ⓑ	Ⓒ	Ⓓ
110	Ⓐ	Ⓑ	Ⓒ	Ⓓ	130	Ⓐ	Ⓑ	Ⓒ	Ⓓ	150	Ⓐ	Ⓑ	Ⓒ	Ⓓ	170	Ⓐ	Ⓑ	Ⓒ	Ⓓ	190	Ⓐ	Ⓑ	Ⓒ	Ⓓ
111	Ⓐ	Ⓑ	Ⓒ	Ⓓ	131	Ⓐ	Ⓑ	Ⓒ	Ⓓ	151	Ⓐ	Ⓑ	Ⓒ	Ⓓ	171	Ⓐ	Ⓑ	Ⓒ	Ⓓ	191	Ⓐ	Ⓑ	Ⓒ	Ⓓ
112	Ⓐ	Ⓑ	Ⓒ	Ⓓ	132	Ⓐ	Ⓑ	Ⓒ	Ⓓ	152	Ⓐ	Ⓑ	Ⓒ	Ⓓ	172	Ⓐ	Ⓑ	Ⓒ	Ⓓ	192	Ⓐ	Ⓑ	Ⓒ	Ⓓ
113	Ⓐ	Ⓑ	Ⓒ	Ⓓ	133	Ⓐ	Ⓑ	Ⓒ	Ⓓ	153	Ⓐ	Ⓑ	Ⓒ	Ⓓ	173	Ⓐ	Ⓑ	Ⓒ	Ⓓ	193	Ⓐ	Ⓑ	Ⓒ	Ⓓ
114	Ⓐ	Ⓑ	Ⓒ	Ⓓ	134	Ⓐ	Ⓑ	Ⓒ	Ⓓ	154	Ⓐ	Ⓑ	Ⓒ	Ⓓ	174	Ⓐ	Ⓑ	Ⓒ	Ⓓ	194	Ⓐ	Ⓑ	Ⓒ	Ⓓ
115	Ⓐ	Ⓑ	Ⓒ	Ⓓ	135	Ⓐ	Ⓑ	Ⓒ	Ⓓ	155	Ⓐ	Ⓑ	Ⓒ	Ⓓ	175	Ⓐ	Ⓑ	Ⓒ	Ⓓ	195	Ⓐ	Ⓑ	Ⓒ	Ⓓ
116	Ⓐ	Ⓑ	Ⓒ	Ⓓ	136	Ⓐ	Ⓑ	Ⓒ	Ⓓ	156	Ⓐ	Ⓑ	Ⓒ	Ⓓ	176	Ⓐ	Ⓑ	Ⓒ	Ⓓ	196	Ⓐ	Ⓑ	Ⓒ	Ⓓ
117	Ⓐ	Ⓑ	Ⓒ	Ⓓ	137	Ⓐ	Ⓑ	Ⓒ	Ⓓ	157	Ⓐ	Ⓑ	Ⓒ	Ⓓ	177	Ⓐ	Ⓑ	Ⓒ	Ⓓ	197	Ⓐ	Ⓑ	Ⓒ	Ⓓ
118	Ⓐ	Ⓑ	Ⓒ	Ⓓ	138	Ⓐ	Ⓑ	Ⓒ	Ⓓ	158	Ⓐ	Ⓑ	Ⓒ	Ⓓ	178	Ⓐ	Ⓑ	Ⓒ	Ⓓ	198	Ⓐ	Ⓑ	Ⓒ	Ⓓ
119	Ⓐ	Ⓑ	Ⓒ	Ⓓ	139	Ⓐ	Ⓑ	Ⓒ	Ⓓ	159	Ⓐ	Ⓑ	Ⓒ	Ⓓ	179	Ⓐ	Ⓑ	Ⓒ	Ⓓ	199	Ⓐ	Ⓑ	Ⓒ	Ⓓ
120	Ⓐ	Ⓑ	Ⓒ	Ⓓ	140	Ⓐ	Ⓑ	Ⓒ	Ⓓ	160	Ⓐ	Ⓑ	Ⓒ	Ⓓ	180	Ⓐ	Ⓑ	Ⓒ	Ⓓ	200	Ⓐ	Ⓑ	Ⓒ	Ⓓ

1. 사용 필기구 : 컴퓨터용 연필(연필을 제외한 사인펜, 볼펜 등은 사용 절대 불가)
2. 잘못된 필기구 사용과 〈보기〉의 올바른 표기 이외의 잘못된 표기로 한 경우에는 당 위원회의 OMR기기가 판독한 결과에 따르며 그 결과는 본인 책임입니다. 1개의 정답만 골라 아래의 올바른 표기대로 정확히 표기하여야 합니다.
   〈보기〉 올바른 표기 : ● 잘못된 표기 : ✔ ✖ ▨
3. 답안지는 컴퓨터로 처리되므로 훼손하시면 안 되며, 상단의 타이밍마크(▌▌▌▌)부분을 찢거나, 낙서 등을 하면 본인에게 불이익이 발생할 수 있습니다.
4. 감독관의 확인이 없거나 시험 종료 후에 답안 작성을 계속할 경우 시험 무효 처리됩니다.

*서약 내용을 읽으시고 확인란에 반드시 서명하십시오.

서 약	확 인
본인은 TOEIC 시험 문제의 일부 또는 전부를 유출하거나 어떠한 형태로든 타인에게 누설 공개하지 않을 것이며 인터넷 또는 인쇄물 등을 이용해 유포하거나 참고 자료로 활용하지 않을 것입니다. 또한 TOEIC 시험 부정 행위 처리 규정을 준수할 것을 서약합니다.	

ANSWER SHEET

수험번호						

Actual **Test 2**

성명	한글	
	한자	
	영자	

좌석번호
Ⓐ Ⓑ Ⓒ Ⓓ Ⓔ ① ② ③ ④ ⑤ ⑥ ⑦

응시일자 : 년 월 일

LISTENING (Part I~IV)

NO.	ANSWER				NO.	ANSWER				NO.	ANSWER				NO.	ANSWER				NO.	ANSWER			
	A	B	C	D		A	B	C	D		A	B	C	D		A	B	C	D		A	B	C	D
1	Ⓐ	Ⓑ	Ⓒ	Ⓓ	21	Ⓐ	Ⓑ	Ⓒ		41	Ⓐ	Ⓑ	Ⓒ	Ⓓ	61	Ⓐ	Ⓑ	Ⓒ	Ⓓ	81	Ⓐ	Ⓑ	Ⓒ	Ⓓ
2	Ⓐ	Ⓑ	Ⓒ	Ⓓ	22	Ⓐ	Ⓑ	Ⓒ		42	Ⓐ	Ⓑ	Ⓒ	Ⓓ	62	Ⓐ	Ⓑ	Ⓒ	Ⓓ	82	Ⓐ	Ⓑ	Ⓒ	Ⓓ
3	Ⓐ	Ⓑ	Ⓒ	Ⓓ	23	Ⓐ	Ⓑ	Ⓒ		43	Ⓐ	Ⓑ	Ⓒ	Ⓓ	63	Ⓐ	Ⓑ	Ⓒ	Ⓓ	83	Ⓐ	Ⓑ	Ⓒ	Ⓓ
4	Ⓐ	Ⓑ	Ⓒ	Ⓓ	24	Ⓐ	Ⓑ	Ⓒ		44	Ⓐ	Ⓑ	Ⓒ	Ⓓ	64	Ⓐ	Ⓑ	Ⓒ	Ⓓ	84	Ⓐ	Ⓑ	Ⓒ	Ⓓ
5	Ⓐ	Ⓑ	Ⓒ	Ⓓ	25	Ⓐ	Ⓑ	Ⓒ		45	Ⓐ	Ⓑ	Ⓒ	Ⓓ	65	Ⓐ	Ⓑ	Ⓒ	Ⓓ	85	Ⓐ	Ⓑ	Ⓒ	Ⓓ
6	Ⓐ	Ⓑ	Ⓒ	Ⓓ	26	Ⓐ	Ⓑ	Ⓒ		46	Ⓐ	Ⓑ	Ⓒ	Ⓓ	66	Ⓐ	Ⓑ	Ⓒ	Ⓓ	86	Ⓐ	Ⓑ	Ⓒ	Ⓓ
7	Ⓐ	Ⓑ	Ⓒ		27	Ⓐ	Ⓑ	Ⓒ		47	Ⓐ	Ⓑ	Ⓒ	Ⓓ	67	Ⓐ	Ⓑ	Ⓒ	Ⓓ	87	Ⓐ	Ⓑ	Ⓒ	Ⓓ
8	Ⓐ	Ⓑ	Ⓒ		28	Ⓐ	Ⓑ	Ⓒ		48	Ⓐ	Ⓑ	Ⓒ	Ⓓ	68	Ⓐ	Ⓑ	Ⓒ	Ⓓ	88	Ⓐ	Ⓑ	Ⓒ	Ⓓ
9	Ⓐ	Ⓑ	Ⓒ		29	Ⓐ	Ⓑ	Ⓒ		49	Ⓐ	Ⓑ	Ⓒ	Ⓓ	69	Ⓐ	Ⓑ	Ⓒ	Ⓓ	89	Ⓐ	Ⓑ	Ⓒ	Ⓓ
10	Ⓐ	Ⓑ	Ⓒ		30	Ⓐ	Ⓑ	Ⓒ		50	Ⓐ	Ⓑ	Ⓒ	Ⓓ	70	Ⓐ	Ⓑ	Ⓒ	Ⓓ	90	Ⓐ	Ⓑ	Ⓒ	Ⓓ
11	Ⓐ	Ⓑ	Ⓒ		31	Ⓐ	Ⓑ	Ⓒ		51	Ⓐ	Ⓑ	Ⓒ	Ⓓ	71	Ⓐ	Ⓑ	Ⓒ	Ⓓ	91	Ⓐ	Ⓑ	Ⓒ	Ⓓ
12	Ⓐ	Ⓑ	Ⓒ		32	Ⓐ	Ⓑ	Ⓒ	Ⓓ	52	Ⓐ	Ⓑ	Ⓒ	Ⓓ	72	Ⓐ	Ⓑ	Ⓒ	Ⓓ	92	Ⓐ	Ⓑ	Ⓒ	Ⓓ
13	Ⓐ	Ⓑ	Ⓒ		33	Ⓐ	Ⓑ	Ⓒ	Ⓓ	53	Ⓐ	Ⓑ	Ⓒ	Ⓓ	73	Ⓐ	Ⓑ	Ⓒ	Ⓓ	93	Ⓐ	Ⓑ	Ⓒ	Ⓓ
14	Ⓐ	Ⓑ	Ⓒ		34	Ⓐ	Ⓑ	Ⓒ	Ⓓ	54	Ⓐ	Ⓑ	Ⓒ	Ⓓ	74	Ⓐ	Ⓑ	Ⓒ	Ⓓ	94	Ⓐ	Ⓑ	Ⓒ	Ⓓ
15	Ⓐ	Ⓑ	Ⓒ		35	Ⓐ	Ⓑ	Ⓒ	Ⓓ	55	Ⓐ	Ⓑ	Ⓒ	Ⓓ	75	Ⓐ	Ⓑ	Ⓒ	Ⓓ	95	Ⓐ	Ⓑ	Ⓒ	Ⓓ
16	Ⓐ	Ⓑ	Ⓒ		36	Ⓐ	Ⓑ	Ⓒ	Ⓓ	56	Ⓐ	Ⓑ	Ⓒ	Ⓓ	76	Ⓐ	Ⓑ	Ⓒ	Ⓓ	96	Ⓐ	Ⓑ	Ⓒ	Ⓓ
17	Ⓐ	Ⓑ	Ⓒ		37	Ⓐ	Ⓑ	Ⓒ	Ⓓ	57	Ⓐ	Ⓑ	Ⓒ	Ⓓ	77	Ⓐ	Ⓑ	Ⓒ	Ⓓ	97	Ⓐ	Ⓑ	Ⓒ	Ⓓ
18	Ⓐ	Ⓑ	Ⓒ		38	Ⓐ	Ⓑ	Ⓒ	Ⓓ	58	Ⓐ	Ⓑ	Ⓒ	Ⓓ	78	Ⓐ	Ⓑ	Ⓒ	Ⓓ	98	Ⓐ	Ⓑ	Ⓒ	Ⓓ
19	Ⓐ	Ⓑ	Ⓒ		39	Ⓐ	Ⓑ	Ⓒ	Ⓓ	59	Ⓐ	Ⓑ	Ⓒ	Ⓓ	79	Ⓐ	Ⓑ	Ⓒ	Ⓓ	99	Ⓐ	Ⓑ	Ⓒ	Ⓓ
20	Ⓐ	Ⓑ	Ⓒ		40	Ⓐ	Ⓑ	Ⓒ	Ⓓ	60	Ⓐ	Ⓑ	Ⓒ	Ⓓ	80	Ⓐ	Ⓑ	Ⓒ	Ⓓ	100	Ⓐ	Ⓑ	Ⓒ	Ⓓ

READING (Part V~VII)

NO.	ANSWER				NO.	ANSWER				NO.	ANSWER				NO.	ANSWER				NO.	ANSWER			
	A	B	C	D		A	B	C	D		A	B	C	D		A	B	C	D		A	B	C	D
101	Ⓐ	Ⓑ	Ⓒ	Ⓓ	121	Ⓐ	Ⓑ	Ⓒ	Ⓓ	141	Ⓐ	Ⓑ	Ⓒ	Ⓓ	161	Ⓐ	Ⓑ	Ⓒ	Ⓓ	181	Ⓐ	Ⓑ	Ⓒ	Ⓓ
102	Ⓐ	Ⓑ	Ⓒ	Ⓓ	122	Ⓐ	Ⓑ	Ⓒ	Ⓓ	142	Ⓐ	Ⓑ	Ⓒ	Ⓓ	162	Ⓐ	Ⓑ	Ⓒ	Ⓓ	182	Ⓐ	Ⓑ	Ⓒ	Ⓓ
103	Ⓐ	Ⓑ	Ⓒ	Ⓓ	123	Ⓐ	Ⓑ	Ⓒ	Ⓓ	143	Ⓐ	Ⓑ	Ⓒ	Ⓓ	163	Ⓐ	Ⓑ	Ⓒ	Ⓓ	183	Ⓐ	Ⓑ	Ⓒ	Ⓓ
104	Ⓐ	Ⓑ	Ⓒ	Ⓓ	124	Ⓐ	Ⓑ	Ⓒ	Ⓓ	144	Ⓐ	Ⓑ	Ⓒ	Ⓓ	164	Ⓐ	Ⓑ	Ⓒ	Ⓓ	184	Ⓐ	Ⓑ	Ⓒ	Ⓓ
105	Ⓐ	Ⓑ	Ⓒ	Ⓓ	125	Ⓐ	Ⓑ	Ⓒ	Ⓓ	145	Ⓐ	Ⓑ	Ⓒ	Ⓓ	165	Ⓐ	Ⓑ	Ⓒ	Ⓓ	185	Ⓐ	Ⓑ	Ⓒ	Ⓓ
106	Ⓐ	Ⓑ	Ⓒ	Ⓓ	126	Ⓐ	Ⓑ	Ⓒ	Ⓓ	146	Ⓐ	Ⓑ	Ⓒ	Ⓓ	166	Ⓐ	Ⓑ	Ⓒ	Ⓓ	186	Ⓐ	Ⓑ	Ⓒ	Ⓓ
107	Ⓐ	Ⓑ	Ⓒ	Ⓓ	127	Ⓐ	Ⓑ	Ⓒ	Ⓓ	147	Ⓐ	Ⓑ	Ⓒ	Ⓓ	167	Ⓐ	Ⓑ	Ⓒ	Ⓓ	187	Ⓐ	Ⓑ	Ⓒ	Ⓓ
108	Ⓐ	Ⓑ	Ⓒ	Ⓓ	128	Ⓐ	Ⓑ	Ⓒ	Ⓓ	148	Ⓐ	Ⓑ	Ⓒ	Ⓓ	168	Ⓐ	Ⓑ	Ⓒ	Ⓓ	188	Ⓐ	Ⓑ	Ⓒ	Ⓓ
109	Ⓐ	Ⓑ	Ⓒ	Ⓓ	129	Ⓐ	Ⓑ	Ⓒ	Ⓓ	149	Ⓐ	Ⓑ	Ⓒ	Ⓓ	169	Ⓐ	Ⓑ	Ⓒ	Ⓓ	189	Ⓐ	Ⓑ	Ⓒ	Ⓓ
110	Ⓐ	Ⓑ	Ⓒ	Ⓓ	130	Ⓐ	Ⓑ	Ⓒ	Ⓓ	150	Ⓐ	Ⓑ	Ⓒ	Ⓓ	170	Ⓐ	Ⓑ	Ⓒ	Ⓓ	190	Ⓐ	Ⓑ	Ⓒ	Ⓓ
111	Ⓐ	Ⓑ	Ⓒ	Ⓓ	131	Ⓐ	Ⓑ	Ⓒ	Ⓓ	151	Ⓐ	Ⓑ	Ⓒ	Ⓓ	171	Ⓐ	Ⓑ	Ⓒ	Ⓓ	191	Ⓐ	Ⓑ	Ⓒ	Ⓓ
112	Ⓐ	Ⓑ	Ⓒ	Ⓓ	132	Ⓐ	Ⓑ	Ⓒ	Ⓓ	152	Ⓐ	Ⓑ	Ⓒ	Ⓓ	172	Ⓐ	Ⓑ	Ⓒ	Ⓓ	192	Ⓐ	Ⓑ	Ⓒ	Ⓓ
113	Ⓐ	Ⓑ	Ⓒ	Ⓓ	133	Ⓐ	Ⓑ	Ⓒ	Ⓓ	153	Ⓐ	Ⓑ	Ⓒ	Ⓓ	173	Ⓐ	Ⓑ	Ⓒ	Ⓓ	193	Ⓐ	Ⓑ	Ⓒ	Ⓓ
114	Ⓐ	Ⓑ	Ⓒ	Ⓓ	134	Ⓐ	Ⓑ	Ⓒ	Ⓓ	154	Ⓐ	Ⓑ	Ⓒ	Ⓓ	174	Ⓐ	Ⓑ	Ⓒ	Ⓓ	194	Ⓐ	Ⓑ	Ⓒ	Ⓓ
115	Ⓐ	Ⓑ	Ⓒ	Ⓓ	135	Ⓐ	Ⓑ	Ⓒ	Ⓓ	155	Ⓐ	Ⓑ	Ⓒ	Ⓓ	175	Ⓐ	Ⓑ	Ⓒ	Ⓓ	195	Ⓐ	Ⓑ	Ⓒ	Ⓓ
116	Ⓐ	Ⓑ	Ⓒ	Ⓓ	136	Ⓐ	Ⓑ	Ⓒ	Ⓓ	156	Ⓐ	Ⓑ	Ⓒ	Ⓓ	176	Ⓐ	Ⓑ	Ⓒ	Ⓓ	196	Ⓐ	Ⓑ	Ⓒ	Ⓓ
117	Ⓐ	Ⓑ	Ⓒ	Ⓓ	137	Ⓐ	Ⓑ	Ⓒ	Ⓓ	157	Ⓐ	Ⓑ	Ⓒ	Ⓓ	177	Ⓐ	Ⓑ	Ⓒ	Ⓓ	197	Ⓐ	Ⓑ	Ⓒ	Ⓓ
118	Ⓐ	Ⓑ	Ⓒ	Ⓓ	138	Ⓐ	Ⓑ	Ⓒ	Ⓓ	158	Ⓐ	Ⓑ	Ⓒ	Ⓓ	178	Ⓐ	Ⓑ	Ⓒ	Ⓓ	198	Ⓐ	Ⓑ	Ⓒ	Ⓓ
119	Ⓐ	Ⓑ	Ⓒ	Ⓓ	139	Ⓐ	Ⓑ	Ⓒ	Ⓓ	159	Ⓐ	Ⓑ	Ⓒ	Ⓓ	179	Ⓐ	Ⓑ	Ⓒ	Ⓓ	199	Ⓐ	Ⓑ	Ⓒ	Ⓓ
120	Ⓐ	Ⓑ	Ⓒ	Ⓓ	140	Ⓐ	Ⓑ	Ⓒ	Ⓓ	160	Ⓐ	Ⓑ	Ⓒ	Ⓓ	180	Ⓐ	Ⓑ	Ⓒ	Ⓓ	200	Ⓐ	Ⓑ	Ⓒ	Ⓓ

1. 사용 필기구 : 컴퓨터용 연필(연필을 제외한 사인펜, 볼펜 등은 사용 절대 불가)
2. 잘못된 필기구 사용과 〈보기〉의 올바른 표기 이외의 잘못된 표기로 한 경우에는 당 위원회의 OMR기기가 판독한 결과에 따르며 그 결과는 본인 책임입니다. 1개의 정답만 골라 아래의 올바른 표기대로 정확히 표기하여야 합니다.
〈보기〉 올바른 표기 : ● 잘못된 표기 : ✅ ✖ ◍
3. 답안지는 컴퓨터로 처리되므로 훼손하시면 안 되며, 상단의 타이밍마크(▮▮▮▮)부분을 찢거나, 낙서 등을 하면 본인에게 불이익이 발생할 수 있습니다.
4. 감독관의 확인이 없거나 시험 종료 후에 답안 작성을 계속할 경우 시험 무효 처리됩니다.

*서약 내용을 읽으시고 확인란에 반드시 서명하십시오.

서 약	확 인
본인은 TOEIC 시험 문제의 일부 또는 전부를 유출하거나 어떠한 형태로든 타인에게 누설 공개하지 않을 것이며 인터넷 또는 인쇄물 등을 이용해 유포하거나 참고 자료로 활용하지 않을 것입니다. 또한 TOEIC 시험 부정 행위 처리 규정을 준수할 것을 서약합니다.	

ANSWER SHEET

수험번호

응시일자 :　　　년　　　월　　　일

Actual **Test 3**

성명	
한글	
한자	
영자	

좌석번호
Ⓐ Ⓑ Ⓒ Ⓓ Ⓔ
① ② ③ ④ ⑤ ⑥ ⑦

LISTENING (Part I~IV)

NO.	ANSWER				NO.	ANSWER				NO.	ANSWER				NO.	ANSWER				NO.	ANSWER			
	A	B	C	D		A	B	C	D		A	B	C	D		A	B	C	D		A	B	C	D
1	Ⓐ	Ⓑ	Ⓒ	Ⓓ	21	Ⓐ	Ⓑ	Ⓒ		41	Ⓐ	Ⓑ	Ⓒ	Ⓓ	61	Ⓐ	Ⓑ	Ⓒ	Ⓓ	81	Ⓐ	Ⓑ	Ⓒ	Ⓓ
2	Ⓐ	Ⓑ	Ⓒ	Ⓓ	22	Ⓐ	Ⓑ	Ⓒ		42	Ⓐ	Ⓑ	Ⓒ	Ⓓ	62	Ⓐ	Ⓑ	Ⓒ	Ⓓ	82	Ⓐ	Ⓑ	Ⓒ	Ⓓ
3	Ⓐ	Ⓑ	Ⓒ	Ⓓ	23	Ⓐ	Ⓑ	Ⓒ		43	Ⓐ	Ⓑ	Ⓒ	Ⓓ	63	Ⓐ	Ⓑ	Ⓒ	Ⓓ	83	Ⓐ	Ⓑ	Ⓒ	Ⓓ
4	Ⓐ	Ⓑ	Ⓒ	Ⓓ	24	Ⓐ	Ⓑ	Ⓒ		44	Ⓐ	Ⓑ	Ⓒ	Ⓓ	64	Ⓐ	Ⓑ	Ⓒ	Ⓓ	84	Ⓐ	Ⓑ	Ⓒ	Ⓓ
5	Ⓐ	Ⓑ	Ⓒ	Ⓓ	25	Ⓐ	Ⓑ	Ⓒ		45	Ⓐ	Ⓑ	Ⓒ	Ⓓ	65	Ⓐ	Ⓑ	Ⓒ	Ⓓ	85	Ⓐ	Ⓑ	Ⓒ	Ⓓ
6	Ⓐ	Ⓑ	Ⓒ	Ⓓ	26	Ⓐ	Ⓑ	Ⓒ		46	Ⓐ	Ⓑ	Ⓒ	Ⓓ	66	Ⓐ	Ⓑ	Ⓒ	Ⓓ	86	Ⓐ	Ⓑ	Ⓒ	Ⓓ
7	Ⓐ	Ⓑ	Ⓒ		27	Ⓐ	Ⓑ	Ⓒ		47	Ⓐ	Ⓑ	Ⓒ	Ⓓ	67	Ⓐ	Ⓑ	Ⓒ	Ⓓ	87	Ⓐ	Ⓑ	Ⓒ	Ⓓ
8	Ⓐ	Ⓑ	Ⓒ		28	Ⓐ	Ⓑ	Ⓒ		48	Ⓐ	Ⓑ	Ⓒ	Ⓓ	68	Ⓐ	Ⓑ	Ⓒ	Ⓓ	88	Ⓐ	Ⓑ	Ⓒ	Ⓓ
9	Ⓐ	Ⓑ	Ⓒ		29	Ⓐ	Ⓑ	Ⓒ		49	Ⓐ	Ⓑ	Ⓒ	Ⓓ	69	Ⓐ	Ⓑ	Ⓒ	Ⓓ	89	Ⓐ	Ⓑ	Ⓒ	Ⓓ
10	Ⓐ	Ⓑ	Ⓒ		30	Ⓐ	Ⓑ	Ⓒ		50	Ⓐ	Ⓑ	Ⓒ	Ⓓ	70	Ⓐ	Ⓑ	Ⓒ	Ⓓ	90	Ⓐ	Ⓑ	Ⓒ	Ⓓ
11	Ⓐ	Ⓑ	Ⓒ		31	Ⓐ	Ⓑ	Ⓒ		51	Ⓐ	Ⓑ	Ⓒ	Ⓓ	71	Ⓐ	Ⓑ	Ⓒ	Ⓓ	91	Ⓐ	Ⓑ	Ⓒ	Ⓓ
12	Ⓐ	Ⓑ	Ⓒ		32	Ⓐ	Ⓑ	Ⓒ	Ⓓ	52	Ⓐ	Ⓑ	Ⓒ	Ⓓ	72	Ⓐ	Ⓑ	Ⓒ	Ⓓ	92	Ⓐ	Ⓑ	Ⓒ	Ⓓ
13	Ⓐ	Ⓑ	Ⓒ		33	Ⓐ	Ⓑ	Ⓒ	Ⓓ	53	Ⓐ	Ⓑ	Ⓒ	Ⓓ	73	Ⓐ	Ⓑ	Ⓒ	Ⓓ	93	Ⓐ	Ⓑ	Ⓒ	Ⓓ
14	Ⓐ	Ⓑ	Ⓒ		34	Ⓐ	Ⓑ	Ⓒ	Ⓓ	54	Ⓐ	Ⓑ	Ⓒ	Ⓓ	74	Ⓐ	Ⓑ	Ⓒ	Ⓓ	94	Ⓐ	Ⓑ	Ⓒ	Ⓓ
15	Ⓐ	Ⓑ	Ⓒ		35	Ⓐ	Ⓑ	Ⓒ	Ⓓ	55	Ⓐ	Ⓑ	Ⓒ	Ⓓ	75	Ⓐ	Ⓑ	Ⓒ	Ⓓ	95	Ⓐ	Ⓑ	Ⓒ	Ⓓ
16	Ⓐ	Ⓑ	Ⓒ		36	Ⓐ	Ⓑ	Ⓒ	Ⓓ	56	Ⓐ	Ⓑ	Ⓒ	Ⓓ	76	Ⓐ	Ⓑ	Ⓒ	Ⓓ	96	Ⓐ	Ⓑ	Ⓒ	Ⓓ
17	Ⓐ	Ⓑ	Ⓒ		37	Ⓐ	Ⓑ	Ⓒ	Ⓓ	57	Ⓐ	Ⓑ	Ⓒ	Ⓓ	77	Ⓐ	Ⓑ	Ⓒ	Ⓓ	97	Ⓐ	Ⓑ	Ⓒ	Ⓓ
18	Ⓐ	Ⓑ	Ⓒ		38	Ⓐ	Ⓑ	Ⓒ	Ⓓ	58	Ⓐ	Ⓑ	Ⓒ	Ⓓ	78	Ⓐ	Ⓑ	Ⓒ	Ⓓ	98	Ⓐ	Ⓑ	Ⓒ	Ⓓ
19	Ⓐ	Ⓑ	Ⓒ		39	Ⓐ	Ⓑ	Ⓒ	Ⓓ	59	Ⓐ	Ⓑ	Ⓒ	Ⓓ	79	Ⓐ	Ⓑ	Ⓒ	Ⓓ	99	Ⓐ	Ⓑ	Ⓒ	Ⓓ
20	Ⓐ	Ⓑ	Ⓒ		40	Ⓐ	Ⓑ	Ⓒ	Ⓓ	60	Ⓐ	Ⓑ	Ⓒ	Ⓓ	80	Ⓐ	Ⓑ	Ⓒ	Ⓓ	100	Ⓐ	Ⓑ	Ⓒ	Ⓓ

READING (Part V~VII)

NO.	ANSWER				NO.	ANSWER				NO.	ANSWER				NO.	ANSWER				NO.	ANSWER			
	A	B	C	D		A	B	C	D		A	B	C	D		A	B	C	D		A	B	C	D
101	Ⓐ	Ⓑ	Ⓒ	Ⓓ	121	Ⓐ	Ⓑ	Ⓒ	Ⓓ	141	Ⓐ	Ⓑ	Ⓒ	Ⓓ	161	Ⓐ	Ⓑ	Ⓒ	Ⓓ	181	Ⓐ	Ⓑ	Ⓒ	Ⓓ
102	Ⓐ	Ⓑ	Ⓒ	Ⓓ	122	Ⓐ	Ⓑ	Ⓒ	Ⓓ	142	Ⓐ	Ⓑ	Ⓒ	Ⓓ	162	Ⓐ	Ⓑ	Ⓒ	Ⓓ	182	Ⓐ	Ⓑ	Ⓒ	Ⓓ
103	Ⓐ	Ⓑ	Ⓒ	Ⓓ	123	Ⓐ	Ⓑ	Ⓒ	Ⓓ	143	Ⓐ	Ⓑ	Ⓒ	Ⓓ	163	Ⓐ	Ⓑ	Ⓒ	Ⓓ	183	Ⓐ	Ⓑ	Ⓒ	Ⓓ
104	Ⓐ	Ⓑ	Ⓒ	Ⓓ	124	Ⓐ	Ⓑ	Ⓒ	Ⓓ	144	Ⓐ	Ⓑ	Ⓒ	Ⓓ	164	Ⓐ	Ⓑ	Ⓒ	Ⓓ	184	Ⓐ	Ⓑ	Ⓒ	Ⓓ
105	Ⓐ	Ⓑ	Ⓒ	Ⓓ	125	Ⓐ	Ⓑ	Ⓒ	Ⓓ	145	Ⓐ	Ⓑ	Ⓒ	Ⓓ	165	Ⓐ	Ⓑ	Ⓒ	Ⓓ	185	Ⓐ	Ⓑ	Ⓒ	Ⓓ
106	Ⓐ	Ⓑ	Ⓒ	Ⓓ	126	Ⓐ	Ⓑ	Ⓒ	Ⓓ	146	Ⓐ	Ⓑ	Ⓒ	Ⓓ	166	Ⓐ	Ⓑ	Ⓒ	Ⓓ	186	Ⓐ	Ⓑ	Ⓒ	Ⓓ
107	Ⓐ	Ⓑ	Ⓒ	Ⓓ	127	Ⓐ	Ⓑ	Ⓒ	Ⓓ	147	Ⓐ	Ⓑ	Ⓒ	Ⓓ	167	Ⓐ	Ⓑ	Ⓒ	Ⓓ	187	Ⓐ	Ⓑ	Ⓒ	Ⓓ
108	Ⓐ	Ⓑ	Ⓒ	Ⓓ	128	Ⓐ	Ⓑ	Ⓒ	Ⓓ	148	Ⓐ	Ⓑ	Ⓒ	Ⓓ	168	Ⓐ	Ⓑ	Ⓒ	Ⓓ	188	Ⓐ	Ⓑ	Ⓒ	Ⓓ
109	Ⓐ	Ⓑ	Ⓒ	Ⓓ	129	Ⓐ	Ⓑ	Ⓒ	Ⓓ	149	Ⓐ	Ⓑ	Ⓒ	Ⓓ	169	Ⓐ	Ⓑ	Ⓒ	Ⓓ	189	Ⓐ	Ⓑ	Ⓒ	Ⓓ
110	Ⓐ	Ⓑ	Ⓒ	Ⓓ	130	Ⓐ	Ⓑ	Ⓒ	Ⓓ	150	Ⓐ	Ⓑ	Ⓒ	Ⓓ	170	Ⓐ	Ⓑ	Ⓒ	Ⓓ	190	Ⓐ	Ⓑ	Ⓒ	Ⓓ
111	Ⓐ	Ⓑ	Ⓒ	Ⓓ	131	Ⓐ	Ⓑ	Ⓒ	Ⓓ	151	Ⓐ	Ⓑ	Ⓒ	Ⓓ	171	Ⓐ	Ⓑ	Ⓒ	Ⓓ	191	Ⓐ	Ⓑ	Ⓒ	Ⓓ
112	Ⓐ	Ⓑ	Ⓒ	Ⓓ	132	Ⓐ	Ⓑ	Ⓒ	Ⓓ	152	Ⓐ	Ⓑ	Ⓒ	Ⓓ	172	Ⓐ	Ⓑ	Ⓒ	Ⓓ	192	Ⓐ	Ⓑ	Ⓒ	Ⓓ
113	Ⓐ	Ⓑ	Ⓒ	Ⓓ	133	Ⓐ	Ⓑ	Ⓒ	Ⓓ	153	Ⓐ	Ⓑ	Ⓒ	Ⓓ	173	Ⓐ	Ⓑ	Ⓒ	Ⓓ	193	Ⓐ	Ⓑ	Ⓒ	Ⓓ
114	Ⓐ	Ⓑ	Ⓒ	Ⓓ	134	Ⓐ	Ⓑ	Ⓒ	Ⓓ	154	Ⓐ	Ⓑ	Ⓒ	Ⓓ	174	Ⓐ	Ⓑ	Ⓒ	Ⓓ	194	Ⓐ	Ⓑ	Ⓒ	Ⓓ
115	Ⓐ	Ⓑ	Ⓒ	Ⓓ	135	Ⓐ	Ⓑ	Ⓒ	Ⓓ	155	Ⓐ	Ⓑ	Ⓒ	Ⓓ	175	Ⓐ	Ⓑ	Ⓒ	Ⓓ	195	Ⓐ	Ⓑ	Ⓒ	Ⓓ
116	Ⓐ	Ⓑ	Ⓒ	Ⓓ	136	Ⓐ	Ⓑ	Ⓒ	Ⓓ	156	Ⓐ	Ⓑ	Ⓒ	Ⓓ	176	Ⓐ	Ⓑ	Ⓒ	Ⓓ	196	Ⓐ	Ⓑ	Ⓒ	Ⓓ
117	Ⓐ	Ⓑ	Ⓒ	Ⓓ	137	Ⓐ	Ⓑ	Ⓒ	Ⓓ	157	Ⓐ	Ⓑ	Ⓒ	Ⓓ	177	Ⓐ	Ⓑ	Ⓒ	Ⓓ	197	Ⓐ	Ⓑ	Ⓒ	Ⓓ
118	Ⓐ	Ⓑ	Ⓒ	Ⓓ	138	Ⓐ	Ⓑ	Ⓒ	Ⓓ	158	Ⓐ	Ⓑ	Ⓒ	Ⓓ	178	Ⓐ	Ⓑ	Ⓒ	Ⓓ	198	Ⓐ	Ⓑ	Ⓒ	Ⓓ
119	Ⓐ	Ⓑ	Ⓒ	Ⓓ	139	Ⓐ	Ⓑ	Ⓒ	Ⓓ	159	Ⓐ	Ⓑ	Ⓒ	Ⓓ	179	Ⓐ	Ⓑ	Ⓒ	Ⓓ	199	Ⓐ	Ⓑ	Ⓒ	Ⓓ
120	Ⓐ	Ⓑ	Ⓒ	Ⓓ	140	Ⓐ	Ⓑ	Ⓒ	Ⓓ	160	Ⓐ	Ⓑ	Ⓒ	Ⓓ	180	Ⓐ	Ⓑ	Ⓒ	Ⓓ	200	Ⓐ	Ⓑ	Ⓒ	Ⓓ

1. 사용 필기구 : 컴퓨터용 연필(연필을 제외한 사인펜, 볼펜 등은 사용 절대 불가)
2. 잘못된 필기구 사용과 〈보기〉의 올바른 표기 이외의 잘못된 표기로 한 경우에는 당 위원회의 OMR기기가 판독한 결과에 따르며 그 결과는 본인 책임입니다. 1개의 정답만 골라 아래의 올바른 표기대로 정확히 표기하여야 합니다.
   〈보기〉 올바른 표기 : ●　　잘못된 표기 : ✓ ✗ ◍
3. 답안지는 컴퓨터로 처리되므로 훼손하시면 안 되며, 상단의 타이밍마크(▮▮▮▮)부분을 찢거나, 낙서 등을 하면 본인에게 불이익이 발생할 수 있습니다.
4. 감독관의 확인이 없거나 시험 종료 후에 답안 작성을 계속할 경우 시험 무효 처리됩니다.

*서약 내용을 읽으시고 확인란에 반드시 서명하십시오.

서　약	확 인
본인은 TOEIC 시험 문제의 일부 또는 전부를 유출하거나 어떠한 형태로든 타인에게 누설 공개하지 않을 것이며 인터넷 또는 인쇄물 등을 이용해 유포하거나 참고 자료로 활용하지 않을 것입니다. 또한 TOEIC 시험 부정 행위 처리 규정을 준수할 것을 서약합니다.	

TOEIC® 점수 환산표

정답수	Listening Comprehension	정답수	Reading Comprehension
96-100	480-495	96-100	460-495
91-95	435-490	91-95	410-475
86-90	395-450	86-90	380-430
81-85	355-415	81-85	355-400
76-80	325-375	76-80	325-375
71-75	295-340	71-75	295-345
66-70	265-315	66-70	265-315
61-65	240-285	61-65	235-285
56-60	215-260	56-60	205-255
51-55	190-235	51-55	175-225
46-50	160-210	46-50	150-195
41-45	135-180	41-45	120-170
36-40	110-155	36-40	100-140
31-35	85-130	31-35	75-120
26-30	70-105	26-30	55-100
21-25	50-90	21-25	40-80
16-20	35-75	16-20	30-65
11-15	20-55	11-15	20-50
6-10	15-40	6-10	15-35
1-5	5-20	1-5	5-20
0	5	0	5

나혼자 끝내는 新토익 FINAL 실전 모의고사 3회분

지은이 넥서스토익연구소
펴낸이 임상진
펴낸곳 (주)넥서스

출판신고 1992년 4월 3일 제311-2002-2호
10880 경기도 파주시 지목로 5
Tel (02)330-5500 Fax (02)330-5555

ISBN 979-11-6165-640-3 13740

가격은 뒤표지에 있습니다.
잘못 만들어진 책은 구입처에서 바꾸어 드립니다.

이 도서의 국립중앙도서관 출판예정도서목록(CIP)은
서지정보유통지원시스템 홈페이지(http://seoji.nl.go.kr)와
국가자료공동목록시스템(http://www.nl.go.kr/kolisnet)에서 이용하실 수
있습니다.
(CIP제어번호 : CIP2019022664)

www.nexusbook.com

나혼자 끝내는 新 토익

FINAL 실전 모의고사

3회분

新토익 실전 모의고사 3회분 + 정답/스크립트 해석/해설 제공 + 실전용·복습용 2종 MP3

MP3 듣기
정답 자동 채점

★ 실제 시험지 형태 그대로, 신토익 실전 모의고사 3회분 수록

★ 문제의 키워드를 단숨에 파악하는 알짜 해석·해설

★ 실전용 · 복습용 버전의 2종 MP3 무료 다운로드 >> QR코드 & 홈페이지 다운로드

★ 문제풀이 후 바로 채점할 수 있는 자동 채점 방식 제공 >> QR코드

★ 신토익 빈출 어휘 리스트 제공 >> www.nexusbook.com

이름	
수험번호	

실전 모의고사 ▸▸ 3

TOEIC®

Test of English for International Communication

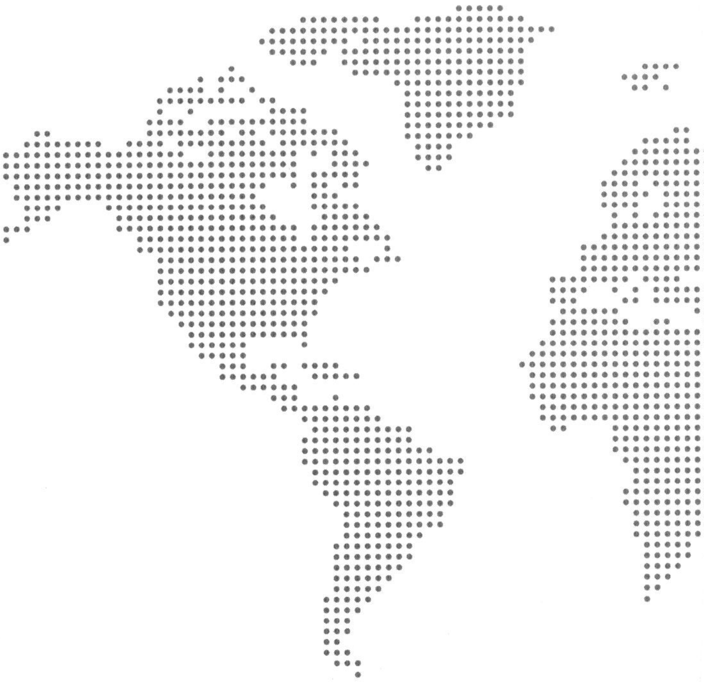

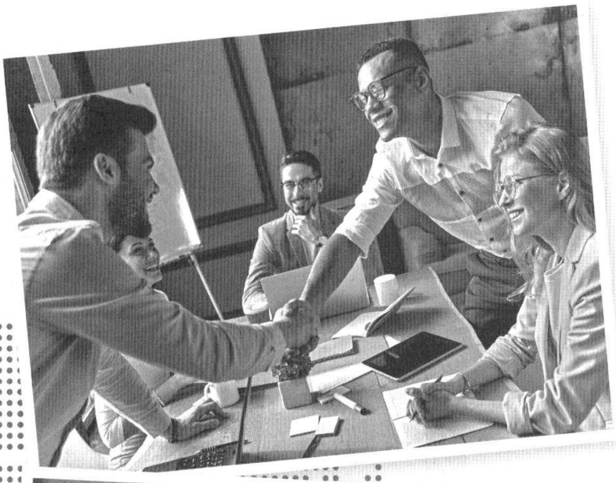

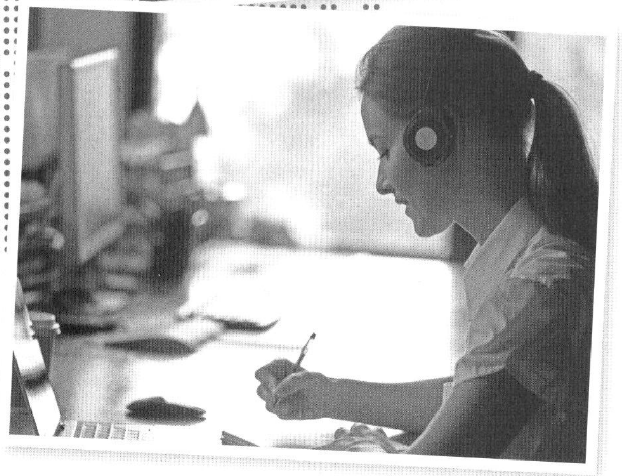

LISTENING TEST

In the Listening test, you will be asked to demonstrate how well you understand spoken English. The entire Listening test will last approximately 45 minutes. There are four parts, and directions are given for each part. You must mark your answers on the separate answer sheet. Do not write your answers in the test book.

PART 1

Directions: For each question in this part, you will hear four statements about a picture in your test book. When you hear the statements, you must select the one statement that best describes what you see in the picture. Then find the number of the question on your answer sheet and mark your answer. The statements will not be printed in your test book and will be spoken only one time.

Statement (B), "The man is working at a desk," is the best description of the picture, so you should select answer (B) and mark it on your answer sheet.

MP3 듣기 

1.

2.

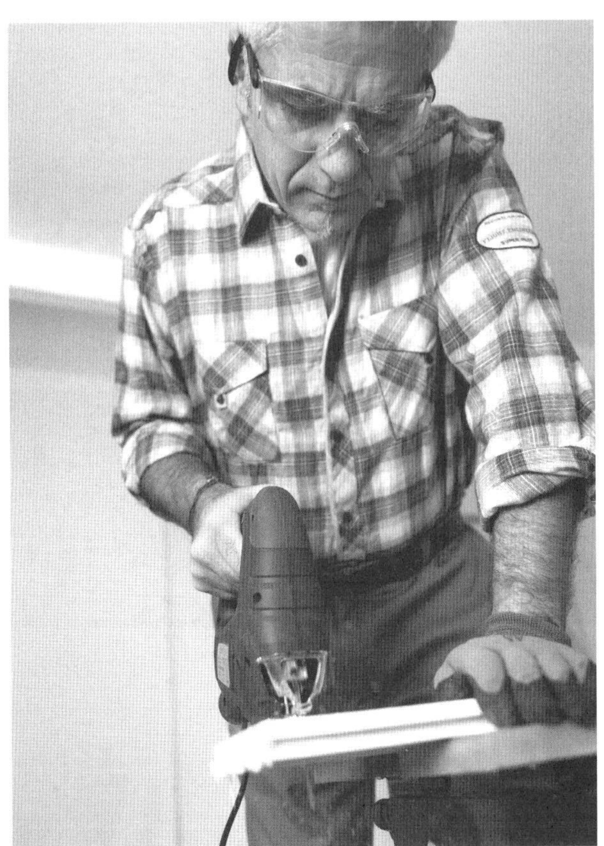

GO ON TO THE NEXT PAGE

3.

4.

5.

6.

GO ON TO THE NEXT PAGE

PART 2

Directions: You will hear a question or statement and three responses spoken in English. They will not be printed in your test book and will be spoken only one time. Select the best response to the question or statement and mark the letter (A), (B), or (C) on your answer sheet.

7. Mark your answer on your answer sheet.

8. Mark your answer on your answer sheet.

9. Mark your answer on your answer sheet.

10. Mark your answer on your answer sheet.

11. Mark your answer on your answer sheet.

12. Mark your answer on your answer sheet.

13. Mark your answer on your answer sheet.

14. Mark your answer on your answer sheet.

15. Mark your answer on your answer sheet.

16. Mark your answer on your answer sheet.

17. Mark your answer on your answer sheet.

18. Mark your answer on your answer sheet.

19. Mark your answer on your answer sheet.

20. Mark your answer on your answer sheet.

21. Mark your answer on your answer sheet.

22. Mark your answer on your answer sheet.

23. Mark your answer on your answer sheet.

24. Mark your answer on your answer sheet.

25. Mark your answer on your answer sheet.

26. Mark your answer on your answer sheet.

27. Mark your answer on your answer sheet.

28. Mark your answer on your answer sheet.

29. Mark your answer on your answer sheet.

30. Mark your answer on your answer sheet.

31. Mark your answer on your answer sheet.

PART 3

Directions: You will hear some conversations between two or more people. You will be asked to answer three questions about what the speakers say in each conversation. Select the best response to each question and mark the letter (A), (B), (C), or (D) on your answer sheet. The conversations will not be printed in your test book and will be spoken only one time.

32. What does the man want to do?

(A) Take the woman out for lunch
(B) Postpone his appointment with a dentist
(C) Move out of the town tomorrow
(D) Go to a dental clinic on short notice

33. What does the man ask the woman for?

(A) A dental record
(B) A recommendation
(C) A ride to the dentist
(D) A phone number

34. What does the woman offer to do?

(A) Contact a neighbor
(B) Go to a dental clinic
(C) Print a city map
(D) Book a different seat

---

35. Who most likely is the man?

(A) A taxi driver
(B) A ticket agent
(C) A market clerk
(D) A delivery man

36. Where does the woman want to go?

(A) To an airport
(B) To a bus station
(C) To a car race
(D) To a railroad station

37. What does the man tell the woman?

(A) The station is under construction.
(B) Her watch is broken.
(C) The ride will take some time.
(D) His work shift is over.

38. What are the speakers talking about?

(A) A speech
(B) A farewell party
(C) An accounting policy
(D) A compulsory meeting

39. What does the man say about the event?

(A) The registration is mandatory.
(B) There was a problem with the first location.
(C) Tickets must be purchased ahead of time.
(D) The speaker is going to be changed.

40. What will the woman probably do next?

(A) Set up a new appointment
(B) Email the presenter about the change
(C) Inform her coworkers of the change
(D) Delay the presentation to next week

---

41. What does the man mention about the dentist's office?

(A) He works there.
(B) He found his wallet there.
(C) He had a check-up there today.
(D) It is located on Andrew Street.

42. What does the man imply when he says, "Yes! What a relief"?

(A) He can make a reservation for dinner.
(B) A new subway line will start operating.
(C) He can make it to the dental clinic on time.
(D) He is glad to hear that his wallet has been found.

43. What does the woman suggest the man do?

(A) Contact a restaurant
(B) Visit the woman's workplace
(C) Purchase a new wallet
(D) Order more business cards

GO ON TO THE NEXT PAGE

44. Who most likely is the man?

(A) A tenant
(B) A home builder
(C) A designer
(D) A real estate agent

45. What does the woman say about the apartment?

(A) It is fully furnished.
(B) It is conveniently located.
(C) The rent is reasonable.
(D) The living room needs repairs.

46. What does the woman mean when she says, "That's more than I was hoping to spend"?

(A) The apartment is unnecessarily large.
(B) She has spent a lot of money on furniture.
(C) The rent is more expensive than she expected.
(D) She does not have time to think.

---

47. What are the speakers mainly discussing?

(A) A research budget
(B) A consumer campaign
(C) A managerial promotion
(D) A marketing survey

48. What do the men suggest?

(A) Extending a deadline
(B) Shortening a form
(C) Conducting longer interviews
(D) Emphasizing particular points

49. What does the woman decide to do?

(A) Alter the schedule for a meeting
(B) Find a way to satisfy customers
(C) Make a few revisions to a document
(D) Relay some feedback

50. What kind of business does the woman run?

(A) A catering firm
(B) A swimming school
(C) A clothing firm
(D) An advertising company

51. What does the woman hope will happen?

(A) That advertising will bring more trade
(B) That she will relocate her office
(C) That she joins a leisure center
(D) That additional employees will be hired

52. What does the man offer to do?

(A) Contact his friends
(B) Distribute some brochures
(C) Recommend the woman's business
(D) Learn how to swim

---

53. Who does the woman say she has to meet with?

(A) A new employer
(B) A transport supplier
(C) A catering firm
(D) A convention venue

54. What event are the speakers preparing for?

(A) A press reception
(B) An anniversary celebration
(C) A drive through facility
(D) A community event

55. How is the event being publicized?

(A) By promoting it online
(B) By handing out leaflets
(C) By calling potential customers
(D) By promoting it on television

56. What does the woman ask the man to do?

(A) Review her work
(B) Draft a report
(C) Release some records
(D) Update a Web site

57. What kind of organization do the speakers work for?

(A) A newspaper
(B) A banking firm
(C) A marketing company
(D) A software company

58. What does the woman mean when she says, "who can blame them"?

(A) Customers did not cause the problem.
(B) Customers' confusion was expected.
(C) Customers are likely to make some complaints.
(D) Customers' behavior is understandable.

---

59. What item are the speakers discussing?

(A) A mobile phone
(B) A child seat
(C) A television
(D) A watch

60. What does the woman suggest?

(A) Reviewing an advertising strategy
(B) Canceling production
(C) Delaying a consumer survey
(D) Altering a product design

61. What topic does the man say he will bring up at the meeting?

(A) A request for funding
(B) More time for research
(C) A changed schedule
(D) An alternative product

62. What are the speakers mainly discussing?

(A) A job opportunity
(B) A program reformat
(C) A work agenda
(D) An office layout

63. What problem does the woman mention?

(A) The work area is isolated.
(B) She is moving to Nairobi.
(C) Renovations are too expensive.
(D) The radio is noisy.

64. What will the woman probably do next?

(A) Transfer her office
(B) Listen to the radio
(C) Use specialist equipment
(D) Speak to management

GO ON TO THE NEXT PAGE

Southtown Fitness Club	
Class	Trainer
Power Yoga	Jessica
Spinning	Tim
Cardio Dance	James
Boxing	Jonathan

The Great Kings Sale SAVE 50% OFF EVERYTHING IN THE SHOWROOM!		
	Regular Price	Sale Price
Diamond Necklace	$500	$250
Ruby Necklace	$300	$150

65. Why is the woman at the fitness club?

(A) To cancel a membership
(B) To provide some feedback
(C) To learn about exercise classes
(D) To participate in a competition

66. Why does the woman prefer private lessons?

(A) She has worked at the gym before.
(B) There is no wait for exercise machines.
(C) Her work schedule is quite irregular.
(D) She is highly motivated to work out regularly.

67. Look at the graphic. Which trainer does the woman want to learn from?

(A) Jessica
(B) Tim
(C) James
(D) Jonathan

68. What was advertised in the newspaper?

(A) A fashion show
(B) A job opening
(C) A musical performance
(D) A half-off sale

69. What is the purpose of the woman's visit to Brussels?

(A) To attend a conference
(B) To purchase some jewelry
(C) To open a business
(D) To write an article

70. Look at the graphic. How much will the woman pay for a necklace?

(A) $150
(B) $250
(C) $300
(D) $500

PART 4

Directions: You will hear some talks given by a single speaker. You will be asked to answer three questions about what the speaker says in each talk. Select the best response to each question and mark the letter (A), (B), (C), or (D) on your answer sheet. The talks will not be printed in your test book and will be spoken only one time.

71. Who most likely is the listener?

(A) A fitness trainer
(B) A leisure center owner
(C) A bank loan officer
(D) A leasing agent

72. What is the speaker inquiring about?

(A) Joining a leisure center
(B) Renting parking spaces
(C) Renewing a contract
(D) Reducing a payment

73. What does the speaker ask the listener to do?

(A) Provide price information
(B) Check the security
(C) Review an application
(D) Employ a personal trainer

---

74. What is the talk mainly about?

(A) Entrance improvements
(B) Security upgrades
(C) Work availability
(D) A training timetable

75. According to the speaker, what will take place on Monday?

(A) A stock take will begin.
(B) The holiday season will start.
(C) The theme park will be closed.
(D) New rides will be announced.

76. What must employees do on Saturday?

(A) Ensure visitors have their tickets
(B) Update their emergency training
(C) Have their photos taken
(D) Review an instruction manual

77. Where does the speaker most likely work?

(A) At a catering company
(B) At a printing studio
(C) At a cake shop
(D) At a hotel

78. What does the speaker say about the order?

(A) It has already been cancelled.
(B) It is partially approved.
(C) An ingredient is out of stock.
(D) A price has changed.

79. What does the speaker ask the listener to do?

(A) Contact via email
(B) Taste a range of food
(C) Make a credit card payment
(D) Arrange another caterer

---

80. Who most likely are the listeners?

(A) Sales representatives
(B) Store customers
(C) Marketing staff
(D) Magazine reporters

81. What does the speaker mean when she says, "It is all because of everyone here"?

(A) Employees have developed a new product.
(B) Employees have organized tonight's event.
(C) Employees are able to multi-task.
(D) Employees have helped the company succeed.

82. What will the company do on December 1?

(A) Celebrate an anniversary
(B) Launch a new product
(C) Conduct a marketing survey
(D) Open a branch overseas

GO ON TO THE NEXT PAGE

83. Who is the message intended for?

(A) Online shoppers
(B) Internet users
(C) Call center representatives
(D) Travel agency customers

84. According to the speaker, why is there a wait?

(A) There is a backlog of calls.
(B) A telephone system has failed.
(C) A flight has been delayed.
(D) The payment system is faulty.

85. What will likely happen by nine o'clock tonight?

(A) Telephone help will be available.
(B) Normal flight schedules will resume.
(C) A computer system will be restored.
(D) A call center will close.

86. What is the news report mainly about?

(A) A desert construction project
(B) The relocation of the production facility
(C) Occupancy of a production factory
(D) Economic projections for a country

87. Why are residents concerned?

(A) Some businesses may go under.
(B) Urban pollution may increase.
(C) Streets may become overcrowded.
(D) Property values may decline.

88. What does the mayor say residents should wait for?

(A) Architectural drawings to be posted
(B) A regional decision to be made
(C) Updated employment figures to be released
(D) Road improvements to commence

89. What is the main purpose of the talk?

(A) To describe a nature tour
(B) To give directions to a tower
(C) To recommend a travel agency
(D) To introduce a speaker

90. What are listeners not allowed to do?

(A) Take photographs
(B) Swim in some areas
(C) Explore the site alone
(D) Use cell phones

91. Why does the speaker say, "So, please watch your step"?

(A) To encourage them to enjoy the beautiful view
(B) To ask them to wear a life vest
(C) To tell them to look around the falls
(D) To warn them not to slip

92. What was announced yesterday?

(A) A protest is going to be held.
(B) A proposal has been approved.
(C) A new business has opened.
(D) A construction project has been completed.

93. What can be understood from the report?

(A) Construction has already started.
(B) The tax will be increased next month.
(C) Many residents are against the project.
(D) The shopping mall will be torn down.

94. What did the Mayor of Akron mean when he said, "This project will be a boon to our city"?

(A) The tax increase will be worth it.
(B) The development will generate more income.
(C) The construction will cost a lot of money.
(D) The land should remain as open space.

Workshop Program	
Presenter	Time
Jack Huston	10:00 ~ 10:50
Emily Tennant	11:00 ~ 11:50
Lunch	12:00 ~ 13:50
Ryan Lee	14:00 ~ 14:50
Melissa Leo	15:00 ~ 15:50

95. What kind of event is taking place?

(A) An annual conference
(B) A television show
(C) A cooking competition
(D) An awards ceremony

96. What is the problem?

(A) A flight is fully booked.
(B) A venue has been changed.
(C) A presenter will arrive late.
(D) A food festival has been canceled.

97. Look at the graphic. According to the revised schedule, who will be the day's first speaker?

(A) Mr. Huston
(B) Ms. Tennant
(C) Mr. Lee
(D) Ms. Leo

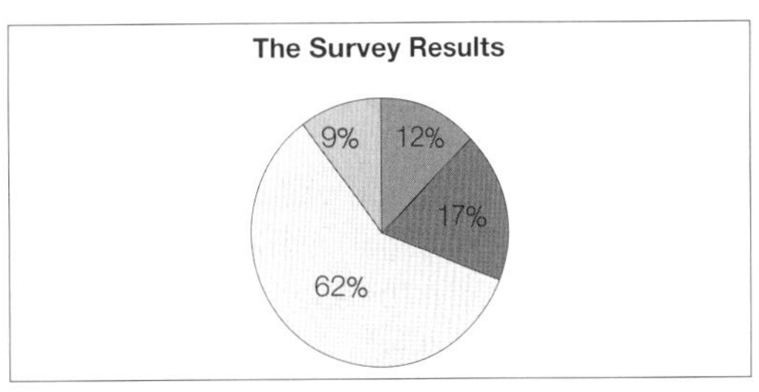

98. What merchandise does the speaker's company sell?

(A) Home appliances
(B) Motor vehicles
(C) Office equipment
(D) Cleaning products

99. What does the speaker say about the market research group?

(A) They designed new products.
(B) They put together a product manual.
(C) They researched a competing brand.
(D) They conducted a customer survey.

100. Look at the graphic. Which survey item accounts for 62 percent?

(A) Customer reviews
(B) Product quality
(C) Free shipping
(D) Competitive prices

This is the end of the Listening test. Turn to Part 5 in your test book.

GO ON TO THE NEXT PAGE

READING TEST

In the Reading test, you will read a variety of texts and answer several different types of reading comprehension questions. The entire Reading test will last 75 minutes. There are three parts, and directions are given for each part. You are encouraged to answer as many questions as possible within the time allowed.

You must mark your answers on the separate answer sheet. Do not write your answers in your test book.

PART 5

Directions: A word or phrase is missing in each of the sentences below. Four answer choices are given below each sentence. Select the best answer to complete the sentence. Then mark the letter (A), (B), (C), or (D) on your answer sheet.

101. Eden Hardware Shop ------- longer accepts credit cards as payment for goods.

(A) seldom
(B) any
(C) none
(D) no

102. Mr. Dooley's report reveals what appears ------- the early phases of a resurrection for the building industry.

(A) be
(B) been
(C) to be
(D) being

103. There are many ------- to becoming part of the Sharpshooting Club, such as being entered in its directory.

(A) advantages
(B) successes
(C) principles
(D) renewals

104. Reedus and Sons, Inc. has been hired to begin ------- of the new Auto Shop building on Ruby Road.

(A) application
(B) distribution
(C) construction
(D) distraction

105. Please verify that everyone expected at the conference this afternoon has been provided with copies of the ------- from Ms. Howell.

(A) contractors
(B) contracts
(C) contracting
(D) contracted

106. According to Trenton's commercial code, the units that will be constructed on Rocker Ave. must be more than five meters -------.

(A) apart
(B) beyond
(C) between
(D) far

107. ------- responsibility Mr. Singer has as head of security is to preserve network confidentiality.

(A) Other
(B) One another
(C) Another
(D) The others

108. In response to consumer feedback, Downey Decorators, Inc. has changed its Ocean Blue interior gloss paint to a ------- lighter shade.

(A) slightest
(B) slightly
(C) slighter
(D) slight

109. The IT department requires workers to change their passwords ------- six months.

(A) along
(B) even
(C) only
(D) every

110. The safety officer will arrive at 8:00 AM to carry out the annual ------- of the premises.

(A) inspection
(B) value
(C) opinion
(D) condition

111. If you have not yet submitted your personal details to your supervisor, please do ------- by the end of the month.

(A) them
(B) those
(C) one
(D) so

112. Faulty products must be ------- with the initial sales receipt in order for consumers to receive a refund or exchange.

(A) repaired
(B) advertised
(C) returned
(D) substituted

113. ------- a rise in wholesale costs, Judy's Fast Foods plans to raise prices for fried goods.

(A) As soon as
(B) In order that
(C) Even if
(D) Due to

114. James Singer, who holds a degree in tax law, is ideally ------- for the position of company tax consultant.

(A) suiting
(B) suited
(C) suitor
(D) suit

115. Kempt Textiles is planning to buy the premises that ------- housed Rubix Computers.

(A) once
(B) ever
(C) more
(D) since

116. ------- fans of the Missy Margaret crime novels should note that the fifth book in the series will be published on June 8.

(A) Devote
(B) Devotion
(C) Devoted
(D) Devoting

117. The new Novantas forklift truck is gaining popularity on the market, mainly because of its -------.

(A) affordable
(B) affordability
(C) afford
(D) afforded

118. Please hand your travel insurance documents to Mr. Kerber at least three days before your intended -------.

(A) efficiency
(B) exception
(C) departure
(D) progression

119. Every piece of Magson furniture is fully ------- before it is delivered.

(A) assembled
(B) established
(C) ordered
(D) designed

120. ------- for oven repair services is subject to change depending on repairs required.

(A) Having priced
(B) Pricing
(C) Priced
(D) To price

GO ON TO THE NEXT PAGE

121. Given the fact that the sun is shining today, the Lord's Cricket Match organizers expect that today's attendance will ------- yesterday's.

(A) surpass
(B) surpassingly
(C) surpassing
(D) surpassed

122. From July 21, monthly passes ------- weekly passes for admission to the Sellyton Swimming Pool can be purchased from the Web site.

(A) as well as
(B) owing to
(C) by the time
(D) so that

123. Many employees ------- in the painting shop have been reporting unsafe practices in the past three months.

(A) are working
(B) work
(C) have worked
(D) working

124. Dr. Magini identified an ------- large tumor that required surgery from the hospital's advanced cancer unit.

(A) outwardly
(B) unusually
(C) insecurely
(D) easily

125. Azure Fishing strives to make customer input ------- to its product development effort.

(A) moderate
(B) actual
(C) diligent
(D) central

126. Please review the guideline manual prior to ------- the water purifier.

(A) installing
(B) install
(C) installation
(D) installed

127. Alexandra Bakery creates cakes ------- clients in a variety of different designs.

(A) for
(B) by
(C) off
(D) as

128. Electrical store profits from domestic sales continue to see steady -------.

(A) grows
(B) grow
(C) grown
(D) growth

129. Ms. Mingalis expressed her desire that trainees attend ------- the training session on Thursday and the workshop on Friday.

(A) both
(B) so
(C) either
(D) neither

130. Albertson International produces many ------- treatments for your medical complaints.

(A) difference
(B) different
(C) differently
(D) differs

PART 6

Directions: Read the texts that follow. A word, phrase, or sentence is missing in parts of each text. Four answer choices for each question are given below the text. Select the best answer to complete the text. Then mark the letter (A), (B), (C), or (D) on your answer sheet.

Questions 131-134 refer to the following e-mail.

To: Zach Braff <zachbraff@uptonhotel.com>
From: Kristen Bell <kristenbell@kos.com>
Subject: Banquet hall

Hi, Mr. Braff. My name is Kristen Bell, and I am writing this e-mail regarding the banquet hall. I was wondering ------- **131.** the banquet hall in your hotel is available on December 9.

I'm ------- **132.** for a room that can accommodate up to 200 people for a retirement party we're holding for our president in the evening, from about 7 P.M. until 10 P.M. We would need at least 50 tables and 200 chairs. .------- **133.** The devices that we rent should be versatile enough to show clear graphics without any problems.

Could you get back to me no more than 5 days before the event, on December 4? My office number is 555-7890. I ------- **134.** forward to hearing from you soon.

131. (A) where
(B) if
(C) when
(D) how

132. (A) looking
(B) seeking
(C) selecting
(D) hoping

133. (A) Thank you for taking care of this matter for me.
(B) Also, we would like to rent equipment including beam projectors.
(C) They are not large enough to accommodate the people.
(D) Alternatively, you can reserve a larger table.

134. (A) look
(B) will have looked
(C) was looking
(D) have been looking

GO ON TO THE NEXT PAGE

Questions 135-138 refer to the following advertisement.

Are you suffering from a serious language barrier while you work or study? Then, come to ANC Language Institute. Here are some exclusive benefits we -------.
135.

First, all Internet users can access us at any time with any computer whether you are at your workstation or at home. Second, our education material delivered to you is of the highest standard.

-------, our professional instructors are all licensed and they have at least 10 years of teaching experience. Finally, we are scheduled to open an introductory Chinese course next month for the first time in this area.
136.

This class will ------- 2 times a week for 6 months. -------. For more information, please call our customer service desk at 555-9086.
137. **138.**

135. (A) offered
(B) had offered
(C) can offer
(D) are offered

136. (A) Besides
(B) And then
(C) Therefore
(D) Consequently

137. (A) meet
(B) teach
(C) schedule
(D) commence

138. (A) The intensive course will be better to learn various language skills at once.
(B) Advanced-level students will be eligible to join the free discussion club.
(C) If you sign up for the class by the end of this week, we will offer a 20% discount.
(D) Because of the scheduling conflict, it will be hard to change the instructor.

Questions 139-142 refer to the following e-mail.

To: Dave Franco <davefranco@msm.com>
From: Rebecca Spence <rebeccaspence@seattleweekly.com>
Date: July 15
Subject: Subscription Status

Hi, Mr. Franco. I am Rebecca Spence from *Seattle Weekly*. I'm writing this e-mail to let you know that your subscription to our newspaper will end on July 31. If you renew the subscription ------- **139.** this month, we will give you a 30% discount. This special offer is made to express our appreciation for your loyal ------- **140.** over the past 10 years.

Also, we noticed that you've been paying your subscription fee by check. ------- **141.**. If you find it more convenient to pay online by credit card, please do so.

To get more information, do not hesitate to visit our Web site at www.seattleweekly.com or you can call us at 555-7780 if you have further questions. Take advantage of these great ------- **142.**, and we hope to continue doing business with you.

139. (A) at
(B) on
(C) within
(D) after

140. (A) patronage
(B) patron
(C) patrons
(D) patronizing

141. (A) You will be given an additional 20% off during the period.
(B) I'd like to inform you that we offer an extra 5% off on all online payments.
(C) We are very sorry that this service has been discontinued.
(D) It is impossible to change your shipping address once your item has been shipped.

142. (A) deals
(B) positions
(C) markets
(D) selections

GO ON TO THE NEXT PAGE

Questions 143-146 refer to the following letter.

Drew Powell
112 Insa-dong
Jongno-gu, Seoul 12005

Dear Mr. Powell:

We acknowledge -------
143. of your application for the position of manager of our sales department, and sincerely appreciate your interest in our company. -------.
144.

Therefore, it may take longer for us to review each application and select candidates -------
145. qualifications seem to meet our needs.

We hope to fill this position by June 30. If you have not heard anything from us by this date, please -------
146. that the position has been filled.

Thank you for your interest in Garcia International, Ltd.

Sincerely,

Jane Adams
Personnel Director

143. (A) receives
(B) receiving
(C) receipt
(D) receiver

144. (A) As you are on a shortlist of 10 candidates, you will be eligible for the final interview.
(B) Please send some samples related to your work to one of our managers.
(C) We have chosen you because of your strong work ethic and excellent strategies.
(D) We have had tremendous response to our job posting.

145. (A) whose
(B) which
(C) whom
(D) what

146. (A) note
(B) assume
(C) ensure
(D) request

PART 7

Directions: In this part you will read a selection of texts, such as magazine and newspaper articles, e-mails, and instant messages. Each text or set of texts is followed by several questions. Select the best answer for each question and mark the letter (A), (B), (C), or (D) on your answer sheet.

Questions 147-148 refer to the following invitation.

The University of SAC
Senate of College Councils Undergraduate Research Committee

The Second Annual
RESEARCH RECEPTION

To honor excellence in undergraduate research
featuring special guest speaker Professor Douglas M. Berman

Thursday, November 29th, 2019

10:00 A.M. Cocktail Reception, 11:00 A.M. Award Ceremony
Randell Hall

Cocktail Attire
PLEASE RSVP TO research_committee@mail.com BY TUESDAY, NOVEMBER 19

147. How often is the event held?

(A) Once a day
(B) Once a week
(C) Once a month
(D) Once a year

148. What is indicated about the research reception?

(A) It is held for the first time in the campus.
(B) It has a set of rule for what you can wear.
(C) It offers a cocktail reception after the ceremony.
(D) It features doctoral programs and researchers.

GO ON TO THE NEXT PAGE

Questions 149-150 refer to the following text message chain.

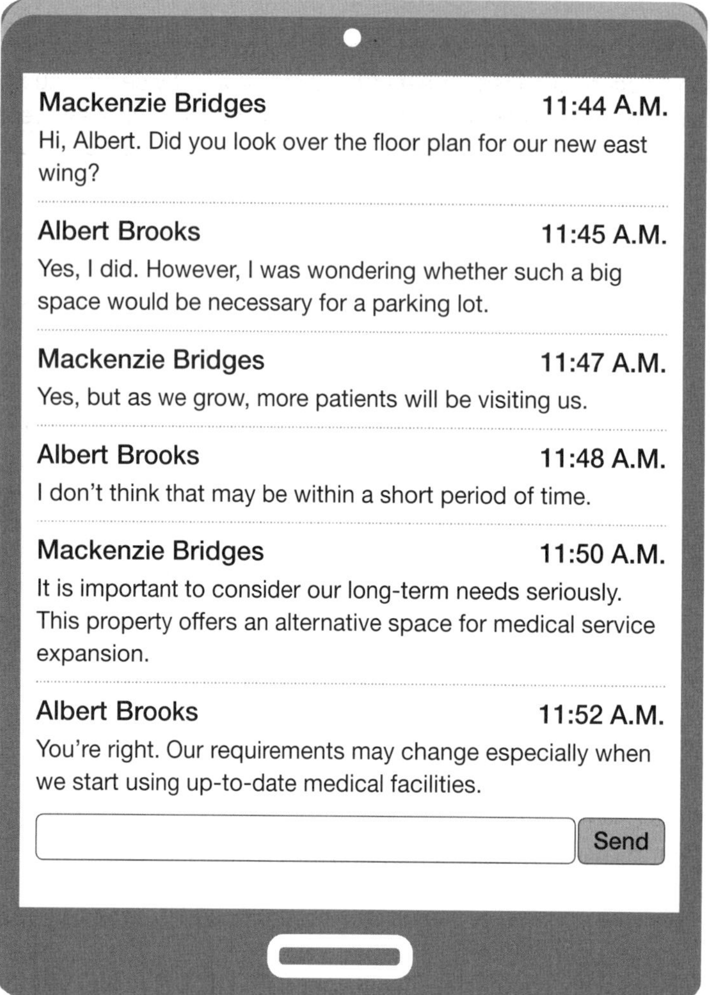

Mackenzie Bridges **11:44 A.M.**
Hi, Albert. Did you look over the floor plan for our new east wing?

Albert Brooks **11:45 A.M.**
Yes, I did. However, I was wondering whether such a big space would be necessary for a parking lot.

Mackenzie Bridges **11:47 A.M.**
Yes, but as we grow, more patients will be visiting us.

Albert Brooks **11:48 A.M.**
I don't think that may be within a short period of time.

Mackenzie Bridges **11:50 A.M.**
It is important to consider our long-term needs seriously. This property offers an alternative space for medical service expansion.

Albert Brooks **11:52 A.M.**
You're right. Our requirements may change especially when we start using up-to-date medical facilities.

Send

149. At what kind of business does Ms. Bridges most likely work?

(A) A hospital
(B) A construction company
(C) A real estate agency
(D) A local manufacturer

150. At 11:52 A.M., what does Mr. Brooks most likely mean when he writes, "You're right"?

(A) Medical equipment should be rented.
(B) A new service will be too expensive.
(C) The property may suit the future needs.
(D) The building needs structural renovations.

Questions 151-152 refer to the following advertisement.

Exclusive End of Year Sale

- Monday through Thursday! Come on over to, Skeeters!

Save up to 50% off on Warm up for Winter such as outerwear, hoodies, and sweaters.
Be the first to own the best selection of winter clothes while supplies last!

Visit our retail stores for savings at your convenience:
Rose Terrace, Pearl Harbor, and Broken Arrow

All buyers, please keep in mind;

- Footwear and Accessories are NOT included in the sales event.
- Our retail stores will be open from 9:00 A.M. to10:00 P.M. during the end of the year sales.

Regular store hours are 10:00 A.M. to 6:00 P.M.

Skeeters

151. What is indicated about the End of Year Sale?

(A) It will take place every year.
(B) It will continue until further notice.
(C) It will comprise all season items.
(D) It will extend its business hours during the sale period.

152. What is NOT included in sale items?

(A) Jackets
(B) Gloves
(C) Hoodies
(D) Sweaters

GO ON TO THE NEXT PAGE

Questions 153-154 refer to the following notice.

Employee Cafeteria Staff

Attention all staff of Pinnacle Corporation cafeteria. Safety is our top priority. Always follow these basic rules to practice good working habits at all times. Pay attention to what you are doing in the kitchen because one little mistake can cause serious injury.

- Store all sharp utensils in a drawer.
- Wear tidy clothes and keep long hair tied back. Clothes shouldn't be loose for they may get caught in objects and cause problems.
- Don't let temperature-sensitive foods sit out in the kitchen. They will get spoiled very quickly.
- Wash your hands with soap before handling food and after handling meat or poultry. Hands are full of bacteria.
- Locate the fire extinguisher and learn how to use it in case of emergency. You can't waste any time reading the instruction manual during a fire.

Safety checks will be conducted by Greg Naquin or Patty Lubin on a weekly basis without prior notice. Always be on your guard!

Any questions or concerns regarding these safety procedures may be directed to:

Shaina Guevara, Department of Safety
Pinnacle Corporation, 12542 Rosslare Dr.
Houston, TX 77066

153. Who is the notice intended for?

(A) Cafeteria users
(B) Kitchen staff
(C) Janitorial workers
(D) Safety department

154. What is the purpose of the notice?

(A) To announce a new dress code
(B) To instruct how to use a fire extinguisher
(C) To outline new safety requirements
(D) To regulate a safer environment

Questions 155-157 refer to the following e-mail.

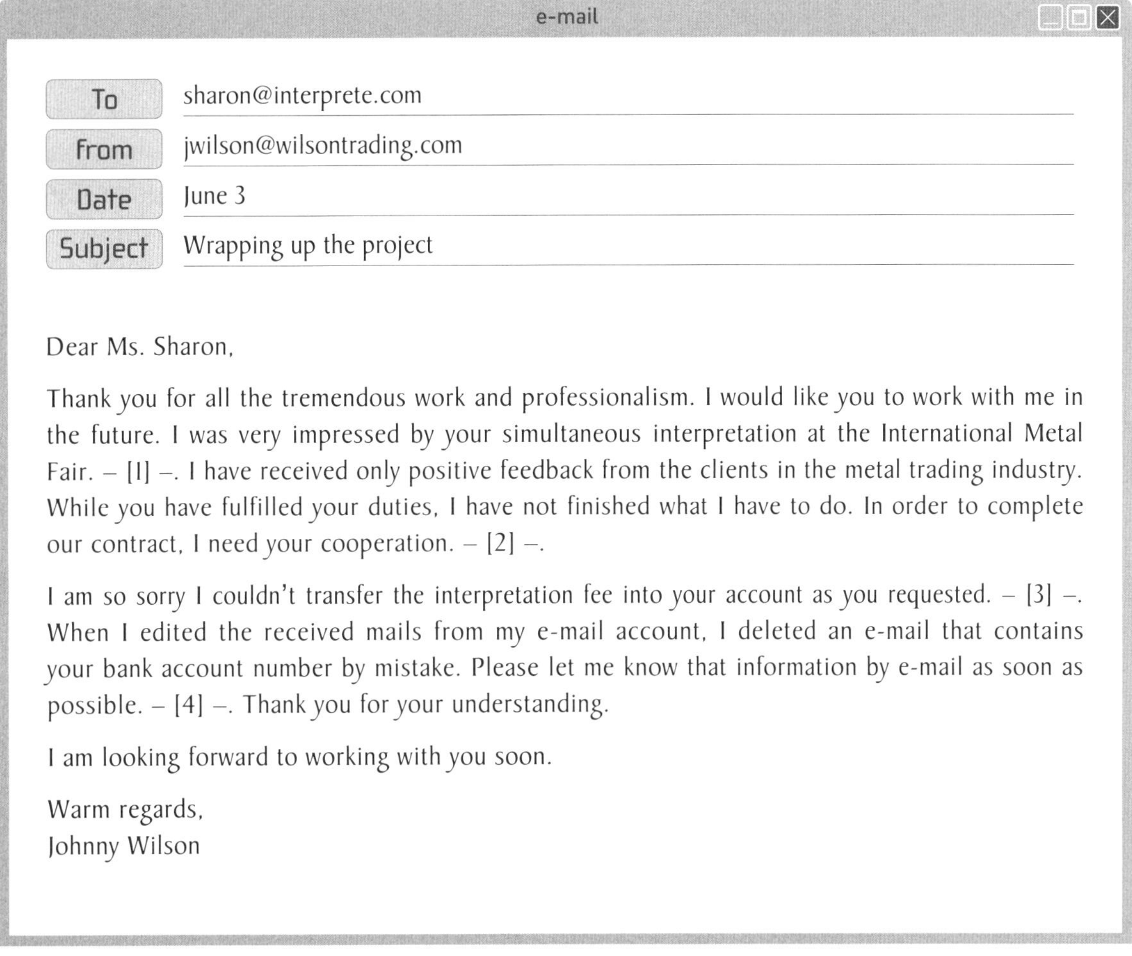

e-mail

To	sharon@interprete.com
From	jwilson@wilsontrading.com
Date	June 3
Subject	Wrapping up the project

Dear Ms. Sharon,

Thank you for all the tremendous work and professionalism. I would like you to work with me in the future. I was very impressed by your simultaneous interpretation at the International Metal Fair. – [1] –. I have received only positive feedback from the clients in the metal trading industry. While you have fulfilled your duties, I have not finished what I have to do. In order to complete our contract, I need your cooperation. – [2] –.

I am so sorry I couldn't transfer the interpretation fee into your account as you requested. – [3] –. When I edited the received mails from my e-mail account, I deleted an e-mail that contains your bank account number by mistake. Please let me know that information by e-mail as soon as possible. – [4] –. Thank you for your understanding.

I am looking forward to working with you soon.

Warm regards,
Johnny Wilson

155. What kind of company does Johnny Wilson most likely work for?

(A) A financial organization
(B) An interpretation agency
(C) A metal trading company
(D) An e-mail service provider

156. What is Ms. Sharon asked to do after receiving the e-mail?

(A) Open a bank account
(B) Request a remittance transfer
(C) Delete all e-mails from Mr. Wilson
(D) Offer her account information online

157. In which of the positions marked [1], [2], [3], and [4] does the following sentence best belong?

"Once I receive it, I will immediately remit your fee into your account."

(A) [1]
(B) [2]
(C) [3]
(D) [4]

GO ON TO THE NEXT PAGE

Questions 158-160 refer to the following advertisement.

JOB OPENING IN MONTREAL

Our moderately sized private school in Montreal, Canada has an opening for an English teacher beginning in July. You will be teaching elementary and middle-school students, using our tried-and-true curriculum. Your salary will be $1,800 per month, which is well above the average for such positions. You will teach 30 hours per week from 2 until 8 PM, Monday through Friday. You will be provided with a furnished apartment just 10 minutes from our school. We are looking for a native English speaker, keeping in mind that Montreal is a city where French is mostly used.

To be hired here, you must have at least a bachelor's degree (in any field) from an accredited university. If you have teaching experience, that is a plus but it is not absolutely necessary. You must be able to prove that you do not have a criminal background, however.

All of the other teachers at our school are friendly and willing to help you "learn the ropes." Sometimes we have teachers combine in a classroom, which facilitates our students' learning of English. We carefully screen our students, so you can be assured no loud or belligerent kids will disrupt your educational efforts.

Contact Jean Francois at 82-2-555-3371.

158. What is the purpose of this advertisement?

(A) To publicize the school to students throughout Canada
(B) To recruit overseas students to the academy
(C) To assure the importance of English
(D) To hire a foreigner to teach at an English academy

159. When does the teachers' work day begin?

(A) 10 A.M.
(B) Noon
(C) 2 P.M.
(D) 8 P.M.

160. What is indicated about the students?

(A) They are willing to help teachers.
(B) They have no interest whatsoever in learning English.
(C) They are obedient and respectful of the teachers.
(D) They come from French immigrants to Canada.

Questions 161-164 refer to the following online chat discussion.

Helen Foy [2:15 P.M.]	Thanks for participating in the discussion. I would like to share some information about how the preparation for the event is going. Tom, is there something new?
Tom Sturridge [2:16 P.M.]	Yes, I have good news. The local Chamber of Commerce finally allowed us to hold the job fair
Gina Rodriguez [2:17 P.M.]	How amazing!
Seth Green [2:18 P.M.]	That's great news! I was worried about it.
Tom Sturridge [2:19 P.M.]	I informed them that we planned to give local companies priorities to participate in the event. That convinced them.
Helen Foy [2:20 P.M.]	Oh, great! Any other news?
Gina Rodriguez [2:21 P.M.]	DailyGood Industries has already agreed to set up 5 booths at the fair. I am also making several calls to other local companies. I will try to have responses from other entries by Thursday.
Seth Green [2:22 P.M.]	I'm still getting more suitable lecturers for workshops we are planning in the event. Daniel Webber has tentatively agreed to lead a lecture, "5 ways to have a better conversation."
Helen Foy [2:23 P.M.]	That would be great. I know that he is a famous professional in this field.

Send

161. What are the writers discussing?

(A) A local company
(B) An exposition
(C) A lecture
(D) A public institution

162. At 2:18 P.M., what does Mr. Green most likely mean when he writes, "I was worried about it"?

(A) He did not think the proposal would be approved.
(B) He did not think the institution would attend the event.
(C) He thought the meeting would be canceled.
(D) He thought the local entrepreneur would be left out.

163. What is Ms. Rodriguez expecting?

(A) A notice about a permit
(B) A response from a lecturer
(C) Changes in the plan
(D) Replies from several businesses

164. Who most likely is Mr. Webber?

(A) A new official
(B) A speaker
(C) An event organizer
(D) A panelist

GO ON TO THE NEXT PAGE

Questions 165-167 refer to the following information.

READER'S TREASURE ISLAND

3116 Birch Street
Indianapolis, IN 46268

Do you love to read? What are you waiting for?
Register as a member at Reader's Treasure Island and
enjoy award-winning novels at an amazing price!

We feature mysteries, science fiction, and fantasies you will be addicted to, starting with the ever popular children's series, *Real Dream! Real Adventure!* to superior writing achievements by mystery novelists Marvin Bensen, Grant Mattox, and Keli Keller.

Privileges for a Reader's Treasure Island Member:

- Purchase books with a discount of up to 60% off the regular price
- Enjoy thousands of books in our store and Web site
- Gain access exclusively to the member's Web site at anytime

On top of that, our members will receive free weekly newsletters. Each newsletter will contain new releases, sales of the week, as well as book reviews from our editors. The requirement to maintain the membership is to purchase at least one book every month.

Join and Enjoy Reader's Treasure Island at www.treasurebook.com.

165. What is NOT a stated product of Reader's Treasure Island?

(A) Fantasies
(B) Mysteries
(C) References
(D) Science Fictions

166. What is a benefit of Reader's Treasure Island membership?

(A) Free overnight shipping
(B) Exclusively discounted prices
(C) Children's books rental service
(D) Access to the library's database

167. To keep their membership, what are members required to do?

(A) Work with a team of editors
(B) Write a newly released book review
(C) Subscribe to a newsletter every week
(D) Purchase a book every month at least

Questions 168-171 refer to the following article.

The Daily Economist

SLU Steels Quarterly Financial Report

London (April 19) — Luke Fisher, the CFO of SLU Steels, reported today that the firm's earnings for the year's first quarter have preceded last year's earning rate by 7%. This is a shocking outcome considering the current state of the market. – [1] –. Mr. Fisher has also applied the company's balance sheet showing the graph of the red arrow slowly but steadily going up. This result is an expected result from the alliance of SLU Steels with Rockport Steels (USA) last December. – [2] –. By creating a closer alliance, the two companies aim to strengthen their business of supplying high-grade products to automakers and shipbuilders.

Mr. Fisher told the press that SLU Steels will seek other ways to keep the red arrow from coming down. SLU Steels has been a driving force in England's economic growth since the 1970s as a key supplier of basic industries. – [3] –. It has gone beyond strengthening the basis, and is now going a step further with its focus shifted to new technology development for the purpose of leading the rapidly changing global steel industry.

Mr. Fisher declared that for the next few years, the company will concentrate mainly on technology and product diversification. There are only a few steelmakers in the world, including SLU Steels, but that doesn't mean the competition is any weaker than in other markets. – [4] –. Mr. Fisher mentioned that SLU Steels still seeks the top spot in the steel industry and will pull up the nation's economy.

168. What is the purpose of this article?

(A) To state the firm's financial performance
(B) To announce a merger
(C) To introduce the firm's new product
(D) To accuse a firm for an illegal act

169. In which of the positions marked [1], [2], [3], and [4] does the following sentence best belong?

"Both companies have made a deal to buy additional shares in each other to counterbalance challenges stemming from consolidation in the steel industry."

(A) [1]
(B) [2]
(C) [3]
(D) [4]

170. What has boosted the growth of SLU Steels?

(A) Development of a new material
(B) Increase in market share
(C) Good investment in stocks
(D) Union with another company

171. What is NOT suggested about SLU Steels?

(A) Its earning rate is going up.
(B) It plans to respond to changes in the industry.
(C) It is now the most powerful steel company in the world.
(D) It has taken a leading role in economic growth since the 1970s.

GO ON TO THE NEXT PAGE

Questions 172-175 refer to the following website.

HIGH END LOGISTICS

HEL Global | Express | Resource Center | **Customer Service FAQs**

- **Express Customer Service FAQs**
  HEL has always been committed to customer service, providing the highest level of service and reliability to our customers.

1. How do I find your location?
To find our stores, please click here www.highendlogistics.com/storelocator or call us at 1-800-555-2050. We have over 1,000 locations to provide customers with unbeatable prices and trustworthy personalized services in North America, Europe, and Asia. In addition, our stores stock all standard and specialized packing materials and supplies and have everything you need to ship your packages such as 300 sizes of shipping boxes, packing paper, bubble wrap, padded envelopes and mailing tubes.

2. Can you pick up my package from my home or office?
Yes, we provide a pickup service within and outside normal hours. To have your shipment picked up at your place, you have to schedule your pickup. Please click here www.highendlogistics.com/pickups to confirm that our pickup service is available in your area and then make an appointment for pickup. You can request our same day pickup. If you have any questions about locations or arrangements for pickup, please contact 1-800-555-2032.

3. How do I track my shipment?
With your tracking number, you can simply view the progress of your delivery with our carrier at our Web site. Please click here www.highendlogistics.com/track, and then enter your tracking number in the 'Track and Confirm' box and press enter. This will allow you to view the tracking information for your package. You can find your tracking number on the confirmation e-mail that you received when you placed the order.

4. How do I make a loss or damage claim?
If, for any reason, your shipment failed to arrive, please contact our customer service with an accurate description of the goods and their packaging as soon as possible. We will make every effort to help locate your shipment.

172. Who would be most interested in this information?

(A) Customers
(B) Post collectors
(C) Shipping vendors
(D) Mail carriers

173. What should you do first in order to use the pickup service?

(A) Call the customer service
(B) Request a pickup online
(C) Change a delivery date
(D) Wait for a HEL courier

174. What item is NOT available at the HEL store locations?

(A) Bubble wrap rolls
(B) Sealing tape
(C) Various mailing tubes
(D) Packing paper

175. What are customers asked to provide when reporting a lost or damaged claim?

(A) The value of the package
(B) Customer's personal information
(C) Tracking information for the package
(D) Detailed information about the package

GO ON TO THE NEXT PAGE

Questions 176-180 refer to the following letters.

April 2

India Carlos
Riverbank House
2 Swan Lane
London, EC4R 3BF

Dear Ms. Carlos,
I am contacting you to audition for the lead role in *Men of Steel* as advertised in the June 20 edition of *The Stage*. I am currently the lead actor in the performance of *Giants Causeway* at the Empire Theater in Leeds, which has been running for three years. I was offered the role as soon as I graduated from the London School of Acting.

Both at the London School of Acting and the Empire Theater, I was given the chance to exhibit my talents as a singer/dancer and my portfolio demonstrates my versatility. I have also been studying directing skills. Two months ago, I was featured in *Walking the Boards*, one of the most influential performing arts magazines. I have enclosed my résumé and a DVD of my performances. If you require any further information or examples of my talent, I can provide it. I am looking forward to hearing from you.

Sincerely,
Amina Alvarez
Amina Alvarez

April 8

Amina Alvarez
62 Kew Bridge Road
London, W4 3AF

Dear Ms. Alvarez,
I received and read your audition letter, and having looked at your résumé (particularly your experience in musicals) we are very interested in meeting you. We would like to offer you an audition for the lead role here at Riverbank House. Please contact us for an appointment for Tuesday, May 30. Also, if you could please send us a DVD of your performances by May 21, I would appreciate it. Although you said you had enclosed it, it was not included in the package you sent.

Sincerely,
India Carlos
India Carlos
Director of Human Resources

176. What does Riverbank House most likely specialize in?

(A) Dancing
(B) Directing
(C) Acting
(D) Publishing

177. When did Ms. Alvarez finish her education?

(A) Last week
(B) Last month
(C) One year ago
(D) Three years ago

178. What recognition did Ms. Alvarez recently receive for her work?

(A) She was the subject of a magazine article.
(B) She won a lead role at London School of Acting.
(C) She was promoted to a senior position in her company.
(D) She was asked to speak at an important conference in her field.

179. When does Ms. Carlos want to hold an interview with Ms. Alvarez?

(A) On May 14
(B) On May 17
(C) On May 21
(D) On May 30

180. What has Ms. Carlos received from Ms. Alvarez?

(A) A DVD
(B) A résumé
(C) A portfolio
(D) A copy of an article

GO ON TO THE NEXT PAGE

Questions 181-185 refer to the following memo and form.

To	All department managers
From	Ylong Batiste
Date	April 8
Subject	Information sessions

The Human Resources Department has devised a series of training sessions to educate employees who have been with the organization for less than 3 months in the practices of other departments here at Soames Department Store. All trainees in your team who were employed on or after December 31 will by now have received an itinerary for the sessions. As managers, you must ensure those employees attend the sessions, which will be run by managers from other departments. We also need feedback from the sessions, so inform your staff that they are required to complete a form after the last session they attend. Forms will be handed out after each session and should be returned within a week to Inge Johannis, Room 22, Jag Building.

Please see the full itinerary below. All sessions will be held on the second floor in the board room of the Dwaine Lodge. Lunch will be provided at each session.

Department	Presenter	Date and Time
Sales	Hamir Khan	July 10, 11:15 A.M. – 12:00 P.M.
Catering	Kyle Jacks	July 17, 10:45 A.M. – 11:30 A.M.
Product Development	Marise Lord	August 20, 11:15 A.M. – 12:00 P.M.
Marketing	Carl Everton	August 29, 10:45 A.M. – 11:30 A.M.

Thank you.

Ylong Batiste
Manager
Human Resources

Information Sessions Feedback Form

Employee Name: *Andre Bouchon*

Which sessions did you attend?

_✔_ Sales _✔_ Catering _✔_ Product Development ____ Marketing

Which session did you find most effective and why?

I liked the fact that the presenter of the product development session allowed us to test new ideas on new products to take home. It was a positive way to learn about what happens in that department.

How could the sessions be improved?

Three of my colleagues and I had to leave early from the July 17 session; my manager holds a stock take that begins at 11:15 every Wednesday. I think it would help if the human resources department would check with the department heads when scheduling future sessions.

181. Why was the memo written?

(A) To explain why a seminar has been relocated
(B) To invite managers to give presentations
(C) To introduce a new policy for interviewing prospective candidates
(D) To request that managers provide a reminder to staff members

182. What is true about all of the sessions?

(A) Managers must nominate candidates.
(B) Employees who attend them will receive a meal.
(C) They begin at 12:15 P.M.
(D) Trainees must fill in a questionnaire before they attend.

183. What is suggested about Andre Bouchon?

(A) His office is in the Jag Building.
(B) His manager is Hamir Khan.
(C) He works in the catering department of Soames Department Store.
(D) He has been employed by Soames for less than three months.

184. Who allowed testing during a session?

(A) Hamir Khan
(B) Kyle Jacks
(C) Marise Lord
(D) Carl Everton

185. What session did Andre Bouchon have to leave early?

(A) Catering
(B) Sales
(C) Product Development
(D) Marketing

GO ON TO THE NEXT PAGE

Questions 186-190 refer to the following e-mail, memo, and guideline.

To	Madeleine Harris <mharris@apex.com>
From	Samuel Joslin <sjoslin@apex.com>
Date	March 25
Subject	E-mail Usage

Dear Madeleine:

I believe that it is time to remind the employees of our company's protocol for the use of e-mail. While I do trust that the employees use e-mail properly most of the time, I also think that e-mails are not only used for business.

So as to refresh the memories of our original staff members and enlighten new employees, an announcement of the e-mail protocol is necessary. Apex Co. acknowledges that the use of e-mail is an essential tool for business. However, misuse of this tool can have a negative impact upon the reputation of the business.

While I want to make sure our staff members have a clear understanding of what kind of e-mail is appropriate or not, I do not want them to feel that they are being strictly regulated. So I would appreciate it if you would make a memo for the staff members to see on my behalf. Please complete it as soon as possible, and I hope the policy will be announced by the end of the month.

Thanks in advance.

Samuel Joslin
Apex Co.

Memo

Dear staff members,

This is about our current e-mail use policy. Please take time to read and familiarize yourself with the protocol for e-mail usage, for our company's safety and yours.

Do not misunderstand this memo as a warning. Use of e-mail is affirmatively permitted and supported wherever such use holds the goals and objectives for the benefit of the business. However, we have a policy that we would like all employees to be aware of. Therefore, you should download guidelines for the policy on our Web site, display them on your desk and keep checking them.

Madeleine Harris

E-mail Use Policy

Make sure that your e-mails:

- follow the current legislation
- are used in a tolerable manner
- are not misused

Unacceptable usage

1. Being in possession or spreading of images, text or materials that have the possibility of being illegal
2. Using e-mail and Internet for personal business
3. Using passwords or mailboxes that are not permitted
4. Violating copyright
5. Undertaking deliberate activities that can squander staff work or networked resources
6. Sending out unsolicited commercial or advertising material
7. Personal attacks or threats by sending offensive, discriminatory or abusive text

Monitoring

Please be aware that the company's e-mail resources are provided only for business purposes. Therefore, the company has the right to examine and inspect any data recorded in the system. In order to carry out this policy, Apex Co. also holds the right to use monitoring software to look into the use and content of e-mails. Such monitoring is for legitimate purposes only and will be implemented in accordance with a process agreed to by employees.

186. According to the e-mail, what does Mr. Joslin want Ms. Harris to do?

(A) Send out guidelines
(B) Find software that monitors e-mails
(C) Make a proposal for a policy
(D) Monitor compliance with a policy

187. In the guideline, the word "legitimate" in paragraph 3, line 4, is closest in meaning to

(A) particular
(B) reasonable
(C) common
(D) primary

188. What is indicated about the e-mail use policy?

(A) It was attached to the memo sent by Ms. Harris.
(B) It needs to be updated.
(C) Attachments will be limited to a certain volume.
(D) It was probably announced at the end of March.

189. What is NOT considered a violation of e-mail use?

(A) Using e-mail for employees' personal purpose
(B) Sending racist text
(C) Spreading illegal images
(D) Exchanging files between coworkers

190. What is mentioned about e-mail monitoring?

(A) The company will perform a monthly inspection.
(B) The company has the authority to monitor e-mails.
(C) The inspection process will be done by an outside agency.
(D) An employee with inappropriate data will be fired.

Questions 191-195 refer to the following memo, information, and e-mail.

To: Fiesta Spa
From: Jessica Green, Paradise Town Inc.
Date: December 7

Paradise Town Inc. is delighted to announce that our acquisition of Fiesta Spa has been finalized. We have already taken over the management and are now fully responsible for everything related to Fiesta Spa. We very much look forward to continuing a productive business relationship with all of our members. If you need some help, you can contact representatives listed on an enclosed sheet.

The following is a list of contacts for the significant people within our company:

Personnel Department

Human resources manager, Ms. Stella Stone <stellastone@paradisetown.com>

Service Maintenance

Maintenance supervisor, Mr. Nolan Dean <n_dean@paradisetown.com>

Facility Maintenance

Facility service coordinator, Mr. Lucas Barnes <lucasrepairs@paradisetown.com>

Technical Maintenance

Technical service coordinator, Mr. Dylan West <techdylan@paradisetown.com>

Office Management

Office operations manager, Ms. Jessica Green <green@paradisetown.com>

Paradise Town Inc.

555-6756

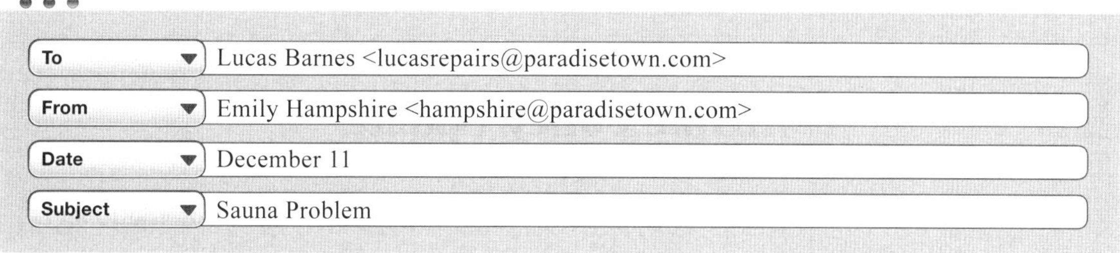

To: Lucas Barnes <lucasrepairs@paradisetown.com>
From: Emily Hampshire <hampshire@paradisetown.com>
Date: December 11
Subject: Sauna Problem

Hello. My name is Emily Hampshire, and I work at the front desk at the Japanese garden spa section of Fiesta Spa. Lately I have been receiving complaints about one of the saunas in the spa. The customers have said that the temperature is not high enough but the humidity is too dense. I have checked the sauna, and the actual temperature doesn't go above 60 degrees Celsius, while the indicated temperature is 77 degrees Celsius. Also, one of the ventilating fans has stopped. I think that this is the cause of the density problem. The sauna is closed for now but it needs to be fixed fast because it is an essential facility for the spa. Please let me know when it can be fixed.

Sincerely,
Emily Hampshire

191. What kind of business is Paradise Town Incorporated in?

(A) It trains professional massage therapists.
(B) It provides consulting to companies.
(C) It introduces suitable people to open positions.
(D) It manages spa facilities.

192. What is stated in the memo?

(A) Fiesta Spa will be raising its membership fees.
(B) Individuals of expertise may be contacted for aid.
(C) Fiesta Spa will be put up for auction.
(D) Workforce reduction will be carried out soon.

193. Which department is Ms. Hampshire contacting?

(A) Facility Maintenance
(B) Personnel Department
(C) Office Management
(D) Technical Maintenance

194. Why did Ms. Hampshire write the e-mail?

(A) To apply for a job
(B) To inquire about the user charge for the spa
(C) To report a problem
(D) To conduct an inspection

195. In the e-mail, the word "dense" in paragraph 1, line 4, is closest in meaning to

(A) light
(B) rough
(C) thick
(D) loose

GO ON TO THE NEXT PAGE

Questions 196-200 refer to the following information, review, and e-mail.

Airline Policy Update

Pan Pacific Air has initiated a change in its checked-baggage policy for international flights effective immediately. Specifically, the checked baggage allowance per international traveler has been increased from one piece of luggage to two pieces. Additionally, the weight limit for each bag has been raised from 20 to 25 kilograms, and the penalty for overweight bags has been lowered from $100 to $50 per bag. The charge for each additional checked bag above the two-piece allowance, however, remains $25 per bag for up to four additional bags. Please note that these changes do not affect our domestic flight policies in any way—the same policy of one free bag, a 20-kilogram limit and a $100 penalty for overweight bags currently remains in effect. If you have questions, please address them to a staff member at our check-in counter.

Thank you.

Flyin.com Airline Passenger Online Review

I recently took advantage of one of Pan Pacific Air's new direct flights, flying from Hong Kong to my hometown of Chicago. Overall, the flight experience was satisfactory. PPA exists somewhere between a budget airline and a standard international carrier—its prices are low, and you get what you pay for. I was quite pleased, however, to discover that I would not be charged for my second checked bag. Apparently this is a new change, and it's a very welcome one.

However, a friend who recently flew from LA to New York on PPA informed me that their old one-bag policy remains in effect for domestic flights, which I find very disappointing. I hope the airline considers expanding their new baggage policy to cover all of their flights.

To: Bill Paxton <paxton@jazzco.com>
From: Steven Luke <luke @ppa.com>
Date: December 10
Subject: Your Review

Thank you for taking the time to review your recent flight with Pan Pacific Air on the Flyin.com Web site. We're happy to hear that you're as excited as we are about our new, traveler-friendly baggage policy. The consumer response has been overwhelmingly positive, which is extremely gratifying. As for your suggestion regarding expanding the policy to our domestic flights, I'm sorry to say we are unable to do so due to restrictions imposed by the Federal Aviation Administration. However, we will be cutting the overweight baggage penalty for domestic passengers by 25% starting in 2020. We will also continue to search for ways to raise the quality of our domestic service to the level that our international customers have come to expect.

Sincerely,

Steven Luke
Pan Pacific Airlines

196. How many bags can each passenger now check for free on international flights?

(A) One
(B) Two
(C) Three
(D) Four

197. What is Mr. Paxton's general opinion of the airline?

(A) It is cheap but treats its passengers poorly.
(B) It is better than most international airlines.
(C) It is a good value considering its low prices.
(D) It is fast and convenient but overpriced.

198. In the e-mail, the word "gratifying" in paragraph 1, line 4, is closest in meaning to

(A) satisfying
(B) frightening
(C) embarrassing
(D) startling

199. How much money did Mr. Paxton save due to the new policy?

(A) $25
(B) $50
(C) $75
(D) $100

200. What will the overweight bag penalty for domestic passengers be in 2020?

(A) Nothing
(B) $10
(C) $50
(D) $75

Stop! This is the end of the test. If you finish before time is called, you may go back to Parts 5, 6, and 7 and check your work.

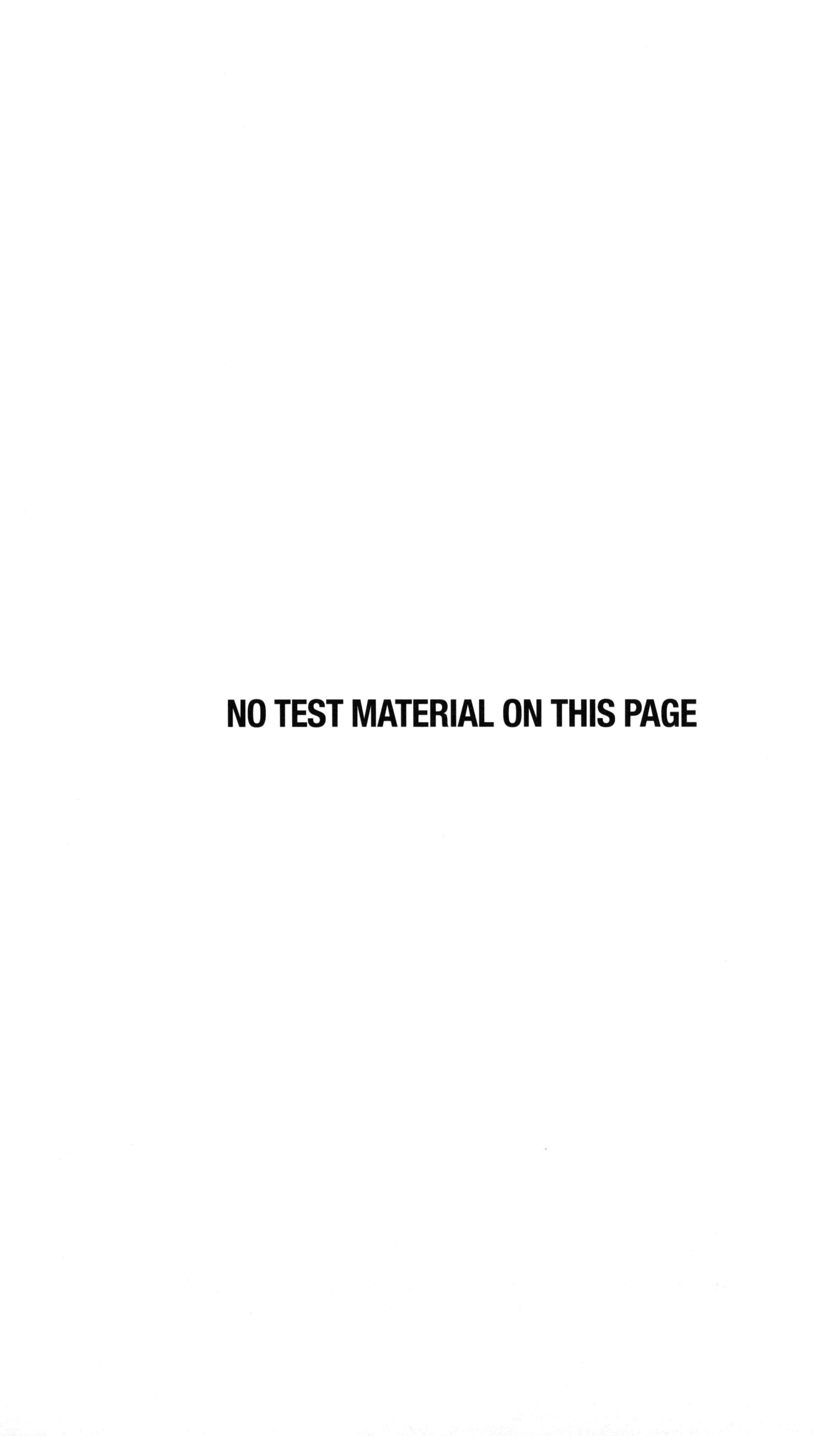

NO TEST MATERIAL ON THIS PAGE

ANSWER SHEET

수험번호						

Actual Test 1

성명	한글	
	한자	
	영자	

좌석번호
Ⓐ Ⓑ Ⓒ Ⓓ Ⓔ ① ② ③ ④ ⑤ ⑥ ⑦

응시일자 : 년 월 일

LISTENING (Part I~IV)

NO.	A	B	C	D	NO.	A	B	C	D	NO.	A	B	C	D	NO.	A	B	C	D	NO.	A	B	C	D
1	Ⓐ	Ⓑ	Ⓒ	Ⓓ	21	Ⓐ	Ⓑ	Ⓒ		41	Ⓐ	Ⓑ	Ⓒ	Ⓓ	61	Ⓐ	Ⓑ	Ⓒ	Ⓓ	81	Ⓐ	Ⓑ	Ⓒ	Ⓓ
2	Ⓐ	Ⓑ	Ⓒ	Ⓓ	22	Ⓐ	Ⓑ	Ⓒ		42	Ⓐ	Ⓑ	Ⓒ	Ⓓ	62	Ⓐ	Ⓑ	Ⓒ	Ⓓ	82	Ⓐ	Ⓑ	Ⓒ	Ⓓ
3	Ⓐ	Ⓑ	Ⓒ	Ⓓ	23	Ⓐ	Ⓑ	Ⓒ		43	Ⓐ	Ⓑ	Ⓒ	Ⓓ	63	Ⓐ	Ⓑ	Ⓒ	Ⓓ	83	Ⓐ	Ⓑ	Ⓒ	Ⓓ
4	Ⓐ	Ⓑ	Ⓒ	Ⓓ	24	Ⓐ	Ⓑ	Ⓒ		44	Ⓐ	Ⓑ	Ⓒ	Ⓓ	64	Ⓐ	Ⓑ	Ⓒ	Ⓓ	84	Ⓐ	Ⓑ	Ⓒ	Ⓓ
5	Ⓐ	Ⓑ	Ⓒ	Ⓓ	25	Ⓐ	Ⓑ	Ⓒ		45	Ⓐ	Ⓑ	Ⓒ	Ⓓ	65	Ⓐ	Ⓑ	Ⓒ	Ⓓ	85	Ⓐ	Ⓑ	Ⓒ	Ⓓ
6	Ⓐ	Ⓑ	Ⓒ	Ⓓ	26	Ⓐ	Ⓑ	Ⓒ		46	Ⓐ	Ⓑ	Ⓒ	Ⓓ	66	Ⓐ	Ⓑ	Ⓒ	Ⓓ	86	Ⓐ	Ⓑ	Ⓒ	Ⓓ
7	Ⓐ	Ⓑ	Ⓒ		27	Ⓐ	Ⓑ	Ⓒ		47	Ⓐ	Ⓑ	Ⓒ	Ⓓ	67	Ⓐ	Ⓑ	Ⓒ	Ⓓ	87	Ⓐ	Ⓑ	Ⓒ	Ⓓ
8	Ⓐ	Ⓑ	Ⓒ		28	Ⓐ	Ⓑ	Ⓒ		48	Ⓐ	Ⓑ	Ⓒ	Ⓓ	68	Ⓐ	Ⓑ	Ⓒ	Ⓓ	88	Ⓐ	Ⓑ	Ⓒ	Ⓓ
9	Ⓐ	Ⓑ	Ⓒ		29	Ⓐ	Ⓑ	Ⓒ		49	Ⓐ	Ⓑ	Ⓒ	Ⓓ	69	Ⓐ	Ⓑ	Ⓒ	Ⓓ	89	Ⓐ	Ⓑ	Ⓒ	Ⓓ
10	Ⓐ	Ⓑ	Ⓒ		30	Ⓐ	Ⓑ	Ⓒ		50	Ⓐ	Ⓑ	Ⓒ	Ⓓ	70	Ⓐ	Ⓑ	Ⓒ	Ⓓ	90	Ⓐ	Ⓑ	Ⓒ	Ⓓ
11	Ⓐ	Ⓑ	Ⓒ		31	Ⓐ	Ⓑ	Ⓒ		51	Ⓐ	Ⓑ	Ⓒ	Ⓓ	71	Ⓐ	Ⓑ	Ⓒ	Ⓓ	91	Ⓐ	Ⓑ	Ⓒ	Ⓓ
12	Ⓐ	Ⓑ	Ⓒ		32	Ⓐ	Ⓑ	Ⓒ	Ⓓ	52	Ⓐ	Ⓑ	Ⓒ	Ⓓ	72	Ⓐ	Ⓑ	Ⓒ	Ⓓ	92	Ⓐ	Ⓑ	Ⓒ	Ⓓ
13	Ⓐ	Ⓑ	Ⓒ		33	Ⓐ	Ⓑ	Ⓒ	Ⓓ	53	Ⓐ	Ⓑ	Ⓒ	Ⓓ	73	Ⓐ	Ⓑ	Ⓒ	Ⓓ	93	Ⓐ	Ⓑ	Ⓒ	Ⓓ
14	Ⓐ	Ⓑ	Ⓒ		34	Ⓐ	Ⓑ	Ⓒ	Ⓓ	54	Ⓐ	Ⓑ	Ⓒ	Ⓓ	74	Ⓐ	Ⓑ	Ⓒ	Ⓓ	94	Ⓐ	Ⓑ	Ⓒ	Ⓓ
15	Ⓐ	Ⓑ	Ⓒ		35	Ⓐ	Ⓑ	Ⓒ	Ⓓ	55	Ⓐ	Ⓑ	Ⓒ	Ⓓ	75	Ⓐ	Ⓑ	Ⓒ	Ⓓ	95	Ⓐ	Ⓑ	Ⓒ	Ⓓ
16	Ⓐ	Ⓑ	Ⓒ		36	Ⓐ	Ⓑ	Ⓒ	Ⓓ	56	Ⓐ	Ⓑ	Ⓒ	Ⓓ	76	Ⓐ	Ⓑ	Ⓒ	Ⓓ	96	Ⓐ	Ⓑ	Ⓒ	Ⓓ
17	Ⓐ	Ⓑ	Ⓒ		37	Ⓐ	Ⓑ	Ⓒ	Ⓓ	57	Ⓐ	Ⓑ	Ⓒ	Ⓓ	77	Ⓐ	Ⓑ	Ⓒ	Ⓓ	97	Ⓐ	Ⓑ	Ⓒ	Ⓓ
18	Ⓐ	Ⓑ	Ⓒ		38	Ⓐ	Ⓑ	Ⓒ	Ⓓ	58	Ⓐ	Ⓑ	Ⓒ	Ⓓ	78	Ⓐ	Ⓑ	Ⓒ	Ⓓ	98	Ⓐ	Ⓑ	Ⓒ	Ⓓ
19	Ⓐ	Ⓑ	Ⓒ		39	Ⓐ	Ⓑ	Ⓒ	Ⓓ	59	Ⓐ	Ⓑ	Ⓒ	Ⓓ	79	Ⓐ	Ⓑ	Ⓒ	Ⓓ	99	Ⓐ	Ⓑ	Ⓒ	Ⓓ
20	Ⓐ	Ⓑ	Ⓒ		40	Ⓐ	Ⓑ	Ⓒ	Ⓓ	60	Ⓐ	Ⓑ	Ⓒ	Ⓓ	80	Ⓐ	Ⓑ	Ⓒ	Ⓓ	100	Ⓐ	Ⓑ	Ⓒ	Ⓓ

READING (Part V~VII)

NO.	A	B	C	D	NO.	A	B	C	D	NO.	A	B	C	D	NO.	A	B	C	D	NO.	A	B	C	D
101	Ⓐ	Ⓑ	Ⓒ	Ⓓ	121	Ⓐ	Ⓑ	Ⓒ	Ⓓ	141	Ⓐ	Ⓑ	Ⓒ	Ⓓ	161	Ⓐ	Ⓑ	Ⓒ	Ⓓ	181	Ⓐ	Ⓑ	Ⓒ	Ⓓ
102	Ⓐ	Ⓑ	Ⓒ	Ⓓ	122	Ⓐ	Ⓑ	Ⓒ	Ⓓ	142	Ⓐ	Ⓑ	Ⓒ	Ⓓ	162	Ⓐ	Ⓑ	Ⓒ	Ⓓ	182	Ⓐ	Ⓑ	Ⓒ	Ⓓ
103	Ⓐ	Ⓑ	Ⓒ	Ⓓ	123	Ⓐ	Ⓑ	Ⓒ	Ⓓ	143	Ⓐ	Ⓑ	Ⓒ	Ⓓ	163	Ⓐ	Ⓑ	Ⓒ	Ⓓ	183	Ⓐ	Ⓑ	Ⓒ	Ⓓ
104	Ⓐ	Ⓑ	Ⓒ	Ⓓ	124	Ⓐ	Ⓑ	Ⓒ	Ⓓ	144	Ⓐ	Ⓑ	Ⓒ	Ⓓ	164	Ⓐ	Ⓑ	Ⓒ	Ⓓ	184	Ⓐ	Ⓑ	Ⓒ	Ⓓ
105	Ⓐ	Ⓑ	Ⓒ	Ⓓ	125	Ⓐ	Ⓑ	Ⓒ	Ⓓ	145	Ⓐ	Ⓑ	Ⓒ	Ⓓ	165	Ⓐ	Ⓑ	Ⓒ	Ⓓ	185	Ⓐ	Ⓑ	Ⓒ	Ⓓ
106	Ⓐ	Ⓑ	Ⓒ	Ⓓ	126	Ⓐ	Ⓑ	Ⓒ	Ⓓ	146	Ⓐ	Ⓑ	Ⓒ	Ⓓ	166	Ⓐ	Ⓑ	Ⓒ	Ⓓ	186	Ⓐ	Ⓑ	Ⓒ	Ⓓ
107	Ⓐ	Ⓑ	Ⓒ	Ⓓ	127	Ⓐ	Ⓑ	Ⓒ	Ⓓ	147	Ⓐ	Ⓑ	Ⓒ	Ⓓ	167	Ⓐ	Ⓑ	Ⓒ	Ⓓ	187	Ⓐ	Ⓑ	Ⓒ	Ⓓ
108	Ⓐ	Ⓑ	Ⓒ	Ⓓ	128	Ⓐ	Ⓑ	Ⓒ	Ⓓ	148	Ⓐ	Ⓑ	Ⓒ	Ⓓ	168	Ⓐ	Ⓑ	Ⓒ	Ⓓ	188	Ⓐ	Ⓑ	Ⓒ	Ⓓ
109	Ⓐ	Ⓑ	Ⓒ	Ⓓ	129	Ⓐ	Ⓑ	Ⓒ	Ⓓ	149	Ⓐ	Ⓑ	Ⓒ	Ⓓ	169	Ⓐ	Ⓑ	Ⓒ	Ⓓ	189	Ⓐ	Ⓑ	Ⓒ	Ⓓ
110	Ⓐ	Ⓑ	Ⓒ	Ⓓ	130	Ⓐ	Ⓑ	Ⓒ	Ⓓ	150	Ⓐ	Ⓑ	Ⓒ	Ⓓ	170	Ⓐ	Ⓑ	Ⓒ	Ⓓ	190	Ⓐ	Ⓑ	Ⓒ	Ⓓ
111	Ⓐ	Ⓑ	Ⓒ	Ⓓ	131	Ⓐ	Ⓑ	Ⓒ	Ⓓ	151	Ⓐ	Ⓑ	Ⓒ	Ⓓ	171	Ⓐ	Ⓑ	Ⓒ	Ⓓ	191	Ⓐ	Ⓑ	Ⓒ	Ⓓ
112	Ⓐ	Ⓑ	Ⓒ	Ⓓ	132	Ⓐ	Ⓑ	Ⓒ	Ⓓ	152	Ⓐ	Ⓑ	Ⓒ	Ⓓ	172	Ⓐ	Ⓑ	Ⓒ	Ⓓ	192	Ⓐ	Ⓑ	Ⓒ	Ⓓ
113	Ⓐ	Ⓑ	Ⓒ	Ⓓ	133	Ⓐ	Ⓑ	Ⓒ	Ⓓ	153	Ⓐ	Ⓑ	Ⓒ	Ⓓ	173	Ⓐ	Ⓑ	Ⓒ	Ⓓ	193	Ⓐ	Ⓑ	Ⓒ	Ⓓ
114	Ⓐ	Ⓑ	Ⓒ	Ⓓ	134	Ⓐ	Ⓑ	Ⓒ	Ⓓ	154	Ⓐ	Ⓑ	Ⓒ	Ⓓ	174	Ⓐ	Ⓑ	Ⓒ	Ⓓ	194	Ⓐ	Ⓑ	Ⓒ	Ⓓ
115	Ⓐ	Ⓑ	Ⓒ	Ⓓ	135	Ⓐ	Ⓑ	Ⓒ	Ⓓ	155	Ⓐ	Ⓑ	Ⓒ	Ⓓ	175	Ⓐ	Ⓑ	Ⓒ	Ⓓ	195	Ⓐ	Ⓑ	Ⓒ	Ⓓ
116	Ⓐ	Ⓑ	Ⓒ	Ⓓ	136	Ⓐ	Ⓑ	Ⓒ	Ⓓ	156	Ⓐ	Ⓑ	Ⓒ	Ⓓ	176	Ⓐ	Ⓑ	Ⓒ	Ⓓ	196	Ⓐ	Ⓑ	Ⓒ	Ⓓ
117	Ⓐ	Ⓑ	Ⓒ	Ⓓ	137	Ⓐ	Ⓑ	Ⓒ	Ⓓ	157	Ⓐ	Ⓑ	Ⓒ	Ⓓ	177	Ⓐ	Ⓑ	Ⓒ	Ⓓ	197	Ⓐ	Ⓑ	Ⓒ	Ⓓ
118	Ⓐ	Ⓑ	Ⓒ	Ⓓ	138	Ⓐ	Ⓑ	Ⓒ	Ⓓ	158	Ⓐ	Ⓑ	Ⓒ	Ⓓ	178	Ⓐ	Ⓑ	Ⓒ	Ⓓ	198	Ⓐ	Ⓑ	Ⓒ	Ⓓ
119	Ⓐ	Ⓑ	Ⓒ	Ⓓ	139	Ⓐ	Ⓑ	Ⓒ	Ⓓ	159	Ⓐ	Ⓑ	Ⓒ	Ⓓ	179	Ⓐ	Ⓑ	Ⓒ	Ⓓ	199	Ⓐ	Ⓑ	Ⓒ	Ⓓ
120	Ⓐ	Ⓑ	Ⓒ	Ⓓ	140	Ⓐ	Ⓑ	Ⓒ	Ⓓ	160	Ⓐ	Ⓑ	Ⓒ	Ⓓ	180	Ⓐ	Ⓑ	Ⓒ	Ⓓ	200	Ⓐ	Ⓑ	Ⓒ	Ⓓ

1. 사용 필기구 : 컴퓨터용 연필(연필을 제외한 사인펜, 볼펜 등은 사용 절대 불가)
2. 잘못된 필기구 사용과 〈보기〉의 올바른 표기 이외의 잘못된 표기로 한 경우에는 당 위원회의 OMR기기가 판독한 결과에 따르며 그 결과는 본인 책임입니다. 1개의 정답만 골라 아래의 올바른 표기대로 정확히 표기하여야 합니다.
   〈보기〉 올바른 표기 : ● 잘못된 표기 : ⊘ ⊗ ◍
3. 답안지는 컴퓨터로 처리되므로 훼손하시면 안 되며, 상단의 타이밍마크(▌▌▌▌)부분을 찢거나, 낙서 등을 하면 본인에게 불이익이 발생할 수 있습니다.
4. 감독관의 확인이 없거나 시험 종료 후에 답안 작성을 계속할 경우 시험 무효 처리됩니다.

*서약 내용을 읽으시고 확인란에 반드시 서명하십시오.

서 약	확 인
본인은 TOEIC 시험 문제의 일부 또는 전부를 유출하거나 어떠한 형태로든 타인에게 누설 공개하지 않을 것이며 인터넷 또는 인쇄물 등을 이용해 유포하거나 참고 자료로 활용하지 않을 것입니다. 또한 TOEIC 시험 부정 행위 처리 규정을 준수할 것을 서약합니다.	

ANSWER SHEET

Actual **Test 2**

수험번호						

성명	한글	
	한자	
	영자	

좌석번호
Ⓐ Ⓑ Ⓒ Ⓓ Ⓔ ① ② ③ ④ ⑤ ⑥ ⑦

응시일자 : 　　년　　월　　일

LISTENING (Part I~IV)

NO.	ANSWER				NO.	ANSWER				NO.	ANSWER				NO.	ANSWER				NO.	ANSWER			
	A	B	C	D		A	B	C	D		A	B	C	D		A	B	C	D		A	B	C	D
1	Ⓐ	Ⓑ	Ⓒ	Ⓓ	21	Ⓐ	Ⓑ	Ⓒ		41	Ⓐ	Ⓑ	Ⓒ	Ⓓ	61	Ⓐ	Ⓑ	Ⓒ	Ⓓ	81	Ⓐ	Ⓑ	Ⓒ	Ⓓ
2	Ⓐ	Ⓑ	Ⓒ	Ⓓ	22	Ⓐ	Ⓑ	Ⓒ		42	Ⓐ	Ⓑ	Ⓒ	Ⓓ	62	Ⓐ	Ⓑ	Ⓒ	Ⓓ	82	Ⓐ	Ⓑ	Ⓒ	Ⓓ
3	Ⓐ	Ⓑ	Ⓒ	Ⓓ	23	Ⓐ	Ⓑ	Ⓒ		43	Ⓐ	Ⓑ	Ⓒ	Ⓓ	63	Ⓐ	Ⓑ	Ⓒ	Ⓓ	83	Ⓐ	Ⓑ	Ⓒ	Ⓓ
4	Ⓐ	Ⓑ	Ⓒ	Ⓓ	24	Ⓐ	Ⓑ	Ⓒ		44	Ⓐ	Ⓑ	Ⓒ	Ⓓ	64	Ⓐ	Ⓑ	Ⓒ	Ⓓ	84	Ⓐ	Ⓑ	Ⓒ	Ⓓ
5	Ⓐ	Ⓑ	Ⓒ	Ⓓ	25	Ⓐ	Ⓑ	Ⓒ		45	Ⓐ	Ⓑ	Ⓒ	Ⓓ	65	Ⓐ	Ⓑ	Ⓒ	Ⓓ	85	Ⓐ	Ⓑ	Ⓒ	Ⓓ
6	Ⓐ	Ⓑ	Ⓒ	Ⓓ	26	Ⓐ	Ⓑ	Ⓒ		46	Ⓐ	Ⓑ	Ⓒ	Ⓓ	66	Ⓐ	Ⓑ	Ⓒ	Ⓓ	86	Ⓐ	Ⓑ	Ⓒ	Ⓓ
7	Ⓐ	Ⓑ	Ⓒ		27	Ⓐ	Ⓑ	Ⓒ		47	Ⓐ	Ⓑ	Ⓒ	Ⓓ	67	Ⓐ	Ⓑ	Ⓒ	Ⓓ	87	Ⓐ	Ⓑ	Ⓒ	Ⓓ
8	Ⓐ	Ⓑ	Ⓒ		28	Ⓐ	Ⓑ	Ⓒ		48	Ⓐ	Ⓑ	Ⓒ	Ⓓ	68	Ⓐ	Ⓑ	Ⓒ	Ⓓ	88	Ⓐ	Ⓑ	Ⓒ	Ⓓ
9	Ⓐ	Ⓑ	Ⓒ		29	Ⓐ	Ⓑ	Ⓒ		49	Ⓐ	Ⓑ	Ⓒ	Ⓓ	69	Ⓐ	Ⓑ	Ⓒ	Ⓓ	89	Ⓐ	Ⓑ	Ⓒ	Ⓓ
10	Ⓐ	Ⓑ	Ⓒ		30	Ⓐ	Ⓑ	Ⓒ		50	Ⓐ	Ⓑ	Ⓒ	Ⓓ	70	Ⓐ	Ⓑ	Ⓒ	Ⓓ	90	Ⓐ	Ⓑ	Ⓒ	Ⓓ
11	Ⓐ	Ⓑ	Ⓒ		31	Ⓐ	Ⓑ	Ⓒ		51	Ⓐ	Ⓑ	Ⓒ	Ⓓ	71	Ⓐ	Ⓑ	Ⓒ	Ⓓ	91	Ⓐ	Ⓑ	Ⓒ	Ⓓ
12	Ⓐ	Ⓑ	Ⓒ		32	Ⓐ	Ⓑ	Ⓒ	Ⓓ	52	Ⓐ	Ⓑ	Ⓒ	Ⓓ	72	Ⓐ	Ⓑ	Ⓒ	Ⓓ	92	Ⓐ	Ⓑ	Ⓒ	Ⓓ
13	Ⓐ	Ⓑ	Ⓒ		33	Ⓐ	Ⓑ	Ⓒ	Ⓓ	53	Ⓐ	Ⓑ	Ⓒ	Ⓓ	73	Ⓐ	Ⓑ	Ⓒ	Ⓓ	93	Ⓐ	Ⓑ	Ⓒ	Ⓓ
14	Ⓐ	Ⓑ	Ⓒ		34	Ⓐ	Ⓑ	Ⓒ	Ⓓ	54	Ⓐ	Ⓑ	Ⓒ	Ⓓ	74	Ⓐ	Ⓑ	Ⓒ	Ⓓ	94	Ⓐ	Ⓑ	Ⓒ	Ⓓ
15	Ⓐ	Ⓑ	Ⓒ		35	Ⓐ	Ⓑ	Ⓒ	Ⓓ	55	Ⓐ	Ⓑ	Ⓒ	Ⓓ	75	Ⓐ	Ⓑ	Ⓒ	Ⓓ	95	Ⓐ	Ⓑ	Ⓒ	Ⓓ
16	Ⓐ	Ⓑ	Ⓒ		36	Ⓐ	Ⓑ	Ⓒ	Ⓓ	56	Ⓐ	Ⓑ	Ⓒ	Ⓓ	76	Ⓐ	Ⓑ	Ⓒ	Ⓓ	96	Ⓐ	Ⓑ	Ⓒ	Ⓓ
17	Ⓐ	Ⓑ	Ⓒ		37	Ⓐ	Ⓑ	Ⓒ	Ⓓ	57	Ⓐ	Ⓑ	Ⓒ	Ⓓ	77	Ⓐ	Ⓑ	Ⓒ	Ⓓ	97	Ⓐ	Ⓑ	Ⓒ	Ⓓ
18	Ⓐ	Ⓑ	Ⓒ		38	Ⓐ	Ⓑ	Ⓒ	Ⓓ	58	Ⓐ	Ⓑ	Ⓒ	Ⓓ	78	Ⓐ	Ⓑ	Ⓒ	Ⓓ	98	Ⓐ	Ⓑ	Ⓒ	Ⓓ
19	Ⓐ	Ⓑ	Ⓒ		39	Ⓐ	Ⓑ	Ⓒ	Ⓓ	59	Ⓐ	Ⓑ	Ⓒ	Ⓓ	79	Ⓐ	Ⓑ	Ⓒ	Ⓓ	99	Ⓐ	Ⓑ	Ⓒ	Ⓓ
20	Ⓐ	Ⓑ	Ⓒ		40	Ⓐ	Ⓑ	Ⓒ	Ⓓ	60	Ⓐ	Ⓑ	Ⓒ	Ⓓ	80	Ⓐ	Ⓑ	Ⓒ	Ⓓ	100	Ⓐ	Ⓑ	Ⓒ	Ⓓ

READING (Part V~VII)

NO.	ANSWER				NO.	ANSWER				NO.	ANSWER				NO.	ANSWER				NO.	ANSWER			
	A	B	C	D		A	B	C	D		A	B	C	D		A	B	C	D		A	B	C	D
101	Ⓐ	Ⓑ	Ⓒ	Ⓓ	121	Ⓐ	Ⓑ	Ⓒ	Ⓓ	141	Ⓐ	Ⓑ	Ⓒ	Ⓓ	161	Ⓐ	Ⓑ	Ⓒ	Ⓓ	181	Ⓐ	Ⓑ	Ⓒ	Ⓓ
102	Ⓐ	Ⓑ	Ⓒ	Ⓓ	122	Ⓐ	Ⓑ	Ⓒ	Ⓓ	142	Ⓐ	Ⓑ	Ⓒ	Ⓓ	162	Ⓐ	Ⓑ	Ⓒ	Ⓓ	182	Ⓐ	Ⓑ	Ⓒ	Ⓓ
103	Ⓐ	Ⓑ	Ⓒ	Ⓓ	123	Ⓐ	Ⓑ	Ⓒ	Ⓓ	143	Ⓐ	Ⓑ	Ⓒ	Ⓓ	163	Ⓐ	Ⓑ	Ⓒ	Ⓓ	183	Ⓐ	Ⓑ	Ⓒ	Ⓓ
104	Ⓐ	Ⓑ	Ⓒ	Ⓓ	124	Ⓐ	Ⓑ	Ⓒ	Ⓓ	144	Ⓐ	Ⓑ	Ⓒ	Ⓓ	164	Ⓐ	Ⓑ	Ⓒ	Ⓓ	184	Ⓐ	Ⓑ	Ⓒ	Ⓓ
105	Ⓐ	Ⓑ	Ⓒ	Ⓓ	125	Ⓐ	Ⓑ	Ⓒ	Ⓓ	145	Ⓐ	Ⓑ	Ⓒ	Ⓓ	165	Ⓐ	Ⓑ	Ⓒ	Ⓓ	185	Ⓐ	Ⓑ	Ⓒ	Ⓓ
106	Ⓐ	Ⓑ	Ⓒ	Ⓓ	126	Ⓐ	Ⓑ	Ⓒ	Ⓓ	146	Ⓐ	Ⓑ	Ⓒ	Ⓓ	166	Ⓐ	Ⓑ	Ⓒ	Ⓓ	186	Ⓐ	Ⓑ	Ⓒ	Ⓓ
107	Ⓐ	Ⓑ	Ⓒ	Ⓓ	127	Ⓐ	Ⓑ	Ⓒ	Ⓓ	147	Ⓐ	Ⓑ	Ⓒ	Ⓓ	167	Ⓐ	Ⓑ	Ⓒ	Ⓓ	187	Ⓐ	Ⓑ	Ⓒ	Ⓓ
108	Ⓐ	Ⓑ	Ⓒ	Ⓓ	128	Ⓐ	Ⓑ	Ⓒ	Ⓓ	148	Ⓐ	Ⓑ	Ⓒ	Ⓓ	168	Ⓐ	Ⓑ	Ⓒ	Ⓓ	188	Ⓐ	Ⓑ	Ⓒ	Ⓓ
109	Ⓐ	Ⓑ	Ⓒ	Ⓓ	129	Ⓐ	Ⓑ	Ⓒ	Ⓓ	149	Ⓐ	Ⓑ	Ⓒ	Ⓓ	169	Ⓐ	Ⓑ	Ⓒ	Ⓓ	189	Ⓐ	Ⓑ	Ⓒ	Ⓓ
110	Ⓐ	Ⓑ	Ⓒ	Ⓓ	130	Ⓐ	Ⓑ	Ⓒ	Ⓓ	150	Ⓐ	Ⓑ	Ⓒ	Ⓓ	170	Ⓐ	Ⓑ	Ⓒ	Ⓓ	190	Ⓐ	Ⓑ	Ⓒ	Ⓓ
111	Ⓐ	Ⓑ	Ⓒ	Ⓓ	131	Ⓐ	Ⓑ	Ⓒ	Ⓓ	151	Ⓐ	Ⓑ	Ⓒ	Ⓓ	171	Ⓐ	Ⓑ	Ⓒ	Ⓓ	191	Ⓐ	Ⓑ	Ⓒ	Ⓓ
112	Ⓐ	Ⓑ	Ⓒ	Ⓓ	132	Ⓐ	Ⓑ	Ⓒ	Ⓓ	152	Ⓐ	Ⓑ	Ⓒ	Ⓓ	172	Ⓐ	Ⓑ	Ⓒ	Ⓓ	192	Ⓐ	Ⓑ	Ⓒ	Ⓓ
113	Ⓐ	Ⓑ	Ⓒ	Ⓓ	133	Ⓐ	Ⓑ	Ⓒ	Ⓓ	153	Ⓐ	Ⓑ	Ⓒ	Ⓓ	173	Ⓐ	Ⓑ	Ⓒ	Ⓓ	193	Ⓐ	Ⓑ	Ⓒ	Ⓓ
114	Ⓐ	Ⓑ	Ⓒ	Ⓓ	134	Ⓐ	Ⓑ	Ⓒ	Ⓓ	154	Ⓐ	Ⓑ	Ⓒ	Ⓓ	174	Ⓐ	Ⓑ	Ⓒ	Ⓓ	194	Ⓐ	Ⓑ	Ⓒ	Ⓓ
115	Ⓐ	Ⓑ	Ⓒ	Ⓓ	135	Ⓐ	Ⓑ	Ⓒ	Ⓓ	155	Ⓐ	Ⓑ	Ⓒ	Ⓓ	175	Ⓐ	Ⓑ	Ⓒ	Ⓓ	195	Ⓐ	Ⓑ	Ⓒ	Ⓓ
116	Ⓐ	Ⓑ	Ⓒ	Ⓓ	136	Ⓐ	Ⓑ	Ⓒ	Ⓓ	156	Ⓐ	Ⓑ	Ⓒ	Ⓓ	176	Ⓐ	Ⓑ	Ⓒ	Ⓓ	196	Ⓐ	Ⓑ	Ⓒ	Ⓓ
117	Ⓐ	Ⓑ	Ⓒ	Ⓓ	137	Ⓐ	Ⓑ	Ⓒ	Ⓓ	157	Ⓐ	Ⓑ	Ⓒ	Ⓓ	177	Ⓐ	Ⓑ	Ⓒ	Ⓓ	197	Ⓐ	Ⓑ	Ⓒ	Ⓓ
118	Ⓐ	Ⓑ	Ⓒ	Ⓓ	138	Ⓐ	Ⓑ	Ⓒ	Ⓓ	158	Ⓐ	Ⓑ	Ⓒ	Ⓓ	178	Ⓐ	Ⓑ	Ⓒ	Ⓓ	198	Ⓐ	Ⓑ	Ⓒ	Ⓓ
119	Ⓐ	Ⓑ	Ⓒ	Ⓓ	139	Ⓐ	Ⓑ	Ⓒ	Ⓓ	159	Ⓐ	Ⓑ	Ⓒ	Ⓓ	179	Ⓐ	Ⓑ	Ⓒ	Ⓓ	199	Ⓐ	Ⓑ	Ⓒ	Ⓓ
120	Ⓐ	Ⓑ	Ⓒ	Ⓓ	140	Ⓐ	Ⓑ	Ⓒ	Ⓓ	160	Ⓐ	Ⓑ	Ⓒ	Ⓓ	180	Ⓐ	Ⓑ	Ⓒ	Ⓓ	200	Ⓐ	Ⓑ	Ⓒ	Ⓓ

1. 사용 필기구 : 컴퓨터용 연필(연필을 제외한 사인펜, 볼펜 등은 사용 절대 불가)
2. 잘못된 필기구 사용과 〈보기〉의 올바른 표기 이외의 잘못된 표기로 한 경우에는 당 위원회의 OMR기기가 판독한 결과에 따르며 그 결과는 본인 책임입니다. 1개의 정답만 골라 아래의 올바른 표기대로 정확히 표기하여야 합니다.
   〈보기〉 올바른 표기 : ●　　잘못된 표기 : ✔ ⊗ ◍
3. 답안지는 컴퓨터로 처리되므로 훼손하시면 안 되며, 상단의 타이밍마크(▌▌▌▌)부분을 찢거나, 낙서 등을 하면 본인에게 불이익이 발생할 수 있습니다.
4. 감독관의 확인이 없거나 시험 종료 후에 답안 작성을 계속할 경우 시험 무효 처리됩니다.

*서약 내용을 읽으시고 확인란에 반드시 서명하십시오.

서　약	확 인
본인은 TOEIC 시험 문제의 일부 또는 전부를 유출하거나 어떠한 형태로든 타인에게 누설 공개하지 않을 것이며 인터넷 또는 인쇄물 등을 이용해 유포하거나 참고 자료로 활용하지 않을 것입니다. 또한 TOEIC 시험 부정 행위 처리 규정을 준수할 것을 서약합니다.	

ANSWER SHEET

수험번호						

Actual **Test 3**

성명	한글	
	한자	
	영자	

좌석번호
Ⓐ Ⓑ Ⓒ Ⓓ Ⓔ
① ② ③ ④ ⑤ ⑥ ⑦

응시일자 : 년 월 일

LISTENING (Part I~IV)

NO.	A	B	C	D	NO.	A	B	C	D	NO.	A	B	C	D	NO.	A	B	C	D	NO.	A	B	C	D
1	Ⓐ	Ⓑ	Ⓒ	Ⓓ	21	Ⓐ	Ⓑ	Ⓒ		41	Ⓐ	Ⓑ	Ⓒ	Ⓓ	61	Ⓐ	Ⓑ	Ⓒ	Ⓓ	81	Ⓐ	Ⓑ	Ⓒ	Ⓓ
2	Ⓐ	Ⓑ	Ⓒ	Ⓓ	22	Ⓐ	Ⓑ	Ⓒ		42	Ⓐ	Ⓑ	Ⓒ	Ⓓ	62	Ⓐ	Ⓑ	Ⓒ	Ⓓ	82	Ⓐ	Ⓑ	Ⓒ	Ⓓ
3	Ⓐ	Ⓑ	Ⓒ	Ⓓ	23	Ⓐ	Ⓑ	Ⓒ		43	Ⓐ	Ⓑ	Ⓒ	Ⓓ	63	Ⓐ	Ⓑ	Ⓒ	Ⓓ	83	Ⓐ	Ⓑ	Ⓒ	Ⓓ
4	Ⓐ	Ⓑ	Ⓒ	Ⓓ	24	Ⓐ	Ⓑ	Ⓒ		44	Ⓐ	Ⓑ	Ⓒ	Ⓓ	64	Ⓐ	Ⓑ	Ⓒ	Ⓓ	84	Ⓐ	Ⓑ	Ⓒ	Ⓓ
5	Ⓐ	Ⓑ	Ⓒ	Ⓓ	25	Ⓐ	Ⓑ	Ⓒ		45	Ⓐ	Ⓑ	Ⓒ	Ⓓ	65	Ⓐ	Ⓑ	Ⓒ	Ⓓ	85	Ⓐ	Ⓑ	Ⓒ	Ⓓ
6	Ⓐ	Ⓑ	Ⓒ	Ⓓ	26	Ⓐ	Ⓑ	Ⓒ		46	Ⓐ	Ⓑ	Ⓒ	Ⓓ	66	Ⓐ	Ⓑ	Ⓒ	Ⓓ	86	Ⓐ	Ⓑ	Ⓒ	Ⓓ
7	Ⓐ	Ⓑ	Ⓒ		27	Ⓐ	Ⓑ	Ⓒ		47	Ⓐ	Ⓑ	Ⓒ	Ⓓ	67	Ⓐ	Ⓑ	Ⓒ	Ⓓ	87	Ⓐ	Ⓑ	Ⓒ	Ⓓ
8	Ⓐ	Ⓑ	Ⓒ		28	Ⓐ	Ⓑ	Ⓒ		48	Ⓐ	Ⓑ	Ⓒ	Ⓓ	68	Ⓐ	Ⓑ	Ⓒ	Ⓓ	88	Ⓐ	Ⓑ	Ⓒ	Ⓓ
9	Ⓐ	Ⓑ	Ⓒ		29	Ⓐ	Ⓑ	Ⓒ		49	Ⓐ	Ⓑ	Ⓒ	Ⓓ	69	Ⓐ	Ⓑ	Ⓒ	Ⓓ	89	Ⓐ	Ⓑ	Ⓒ	Ⓓ
10	Ⓐ	Ⓑ	Ⓒ		30	Ⓐ	Ⓑ	Ⓒ		50	Ⓐ	Ⓑ	Ⓒ	Ⓓ	70	Ⓐ	Ⓑ	Ⓒ	Ⓓ	90	Ⓐ	Ⓑ	Ⓒ	Ⓓ
11	Ⓐ	Ⓑ	Ⓒ		31	Ⓐ	Ⓑ	Ⓒ		51	Ⓐ	Ⓑ	Ⓒ	Ⓓ	71	Ⓐ	Ⓑ	Ⓒ	Ⓓ	91	Ⓐ	Ⓑ	Ⓒ	Ⓓ
12	Ⓐ	Ⓑ	Ⓒ		32	Ⓐ	Ⓑ	Ⓒ	Ⓓ	52	Ⓐ	Ⓑ	Ⓒ	Ⓓ	72	Ⓐ	Ⓑ	Ⓒ	Ⓓ	92	Ⓐ	Ⓑ	Ⓒ	Ⓓ
13	Ⓐ	Ⓑ	Ⓒ		33	Ⓐ	Ⓑ	Ⓒ	Ⓓ	53	Ⓐ	Ⓑ	Ⓒ	Ⓓ	73	Ⓐ	Ⓑ	Ⓒ	Ⓓ	93	Ⓐ	Ⓑ	Ⓒ	Ⓓ
14	Ⓐ	Ⓑ	Ⓒ		34	Ⓐ	Ⓑ	Ⓒ	Ⓓ	54	Ⓐ	Ⓑ	Ⓒ	Ⓓ	74	Ⓐ	Ⓑ	Ⓒ	Ⓓ	94	Ⓐ	Ⓑ	Ⓒ	Ⓓ
15	Ⓐ	Ⓑ	Ⓒ		35	Ⓐ	Ⓑ	Ⓒ	Ⓓ	55	Ⓐ	Ⓑ	Ⓒ	Ⓓ	75	Ⓐ	Ⓑ	Ⓒ	Ⓓ	95	Ⓐ	Ⓑ	Ⓒ	Ⓓ
16	Ⓐ	Ⓑ	Ⓒ		36	Ⓐ	Ⓑ	Ⓒ	Ⓓ	56	Ⓐ	Ⓑ	Ⓒ	Ⓓ	76	Ⓐ	Ⓑ	Ⓒ	Ⓓ	96	Ⓐ	Ⓑ	Ⓒ	Ⓓ
17	Ⓐ	Ⓑ	Ⓒ		37	Ⓐ	Ⓑ	Ⓒ	Ⓓ	57	Ⓐ	Ⓑ	Ⓒ	Ⓓ	77	Ⓐ	Ⓑ	Ⓒ	Ⓓ	97	Ⓐ	Ⓑ	Ⓒ	Ⓓ
18	Ⓐ	Ⓑ	Ⓒ		38	Ⓐ	Ⓑ	Ⓒ	Ⓓ	58	Ⓐ	Ⓑ	Ⓒ	Ⓓ	78	Ⓐ	Ⓑ	Ⓒ	Ⓓ	98	Ⓐ	Ⓑ	Ⓒ	Ⓓ
19	Ⓐ	Ⓑ	Ⓒ		39	Ⓐ	Ⓑ	Ⓒ	Ⓓ	59	Ⓐ	Ⓑ	Ⓒ	Ⓓ	79	Ⓐ	Ⓑ	Ⓒ	Ⓓ	99	Ⓐ	Ⓑ	Ⓒ	Ⓓ
20	Ⓐ	Ⓑ	Ⓒ		40	Ⓐ	Ⓑ	Ⓒ	Ⓓ	60	Ⓐ	Ⓑ	Ⓒ	Ⓓ	80	Ⓐ	Ⓑ	Ⓒ	Ⓓ	100	Ⓐ	Ⓑ	Ⓒ	Ⓓ

READING (Part V~VII)

NO.	A	B	C	D	NO.	A	B	C	D	NO.	A	B	C	D	NO.	A	B	C	D	NO.	A	B	C	D
101	Ⓐ	Ⓑ	Ⓒ	Ⓓ	121	Ⓐ	Ⓑ	Ⓒ	Ⓓ	141	Ⓐ	Ⓑ	Ⓒ	Ⓓ	161	Ⓐ	Ⓑ	Ⓒ	Ⓓ	181	Ⓐ	Ⓑ	Ⓒ	Ⓓ
102	Ⓐ	Ⓑ	Ⓒ	Ⓓ	122	Ⓐ	Ⓑ	Ⓒ	Ⓓ	142	Ⓐ	Ⓑ	Ⓒ	Ⓓ	162	Ⓐ	Ⓑ	Ⓒ	Ⓓ	182	Ⓐ	Ⓑ	Ⓒ	Ⓓ
103	Ⓐ	Ⓑ	Ⓒ	Ⓓ	123	Ⓐ	Ⓑ	Ⓒ	Ⓓ	143	Ⓐ	Ⓑ	Ⓒ	Ⓓ	163	Ⓐ	Ⓑ	Ⓒ	Ⓓ	183	Ⓐ	Ⓑ	Ⓒ	Ⓓ
104	Ⓐ	Ⓑ	Ⓒ	Ⓓ	124	Ⓐ	Ⓑ	Ⓒ	Ⓓ	144	Ⓐ	Ⓑ	Ⓒ	Ⓓ	164	Ⓐ	Ⓑ	Ⓒ	Ⓓ	184	Ⓐ	Ⓑ	Ⓒ	Ⓓ
105	Ⓐ	Ⓑ	Ⓒ	Ⓓ	125	Ⓐ	Ⓑ	Ⓒ	Ⓓ	145	Ⓐ	Ⓑ	Ⓒ	Ⓓ	165	Ⓐ	Ⓑ	Ⓒ	Ⓓ	185	Ⓐ	Ⓑ	Ⓒ	Ⓓ
106	Ⓐ	Ⓑ	Ⓒ	Ⓓ	126	Ⓐ	Ⓑ	Ⓒ	Ⓓ	146	Ⓐ	Ⓑ	Ⓒ	Ⓓ	166	Ⓐ	Ⓑ	Ⓒ	Ⓓ	186	Ⓐ	Ⓑ	Ⓒ	Ⓓ
107	Ⓐ	Ⓑ	Ⓒ	Ⓓ	127	Ⓐ	Ⓑ	Ⓒ	Ⓓ	147	Ⓐ	Ⓑ	Ⓒ	Ⓓ	167	Ⓐ	Ⓑ	Ⓒ	Ⓓ	187	Ⓐ	Ⓑ	Ⓒ	Ⓓ
108	Ⓐ	Ⓑ	Ⓒ	Ⓓ	128	Ⓐ	Ⓑ	Ⓒ	Ⓓ	148	Ⓐ	Ⓑ	Ⓒ	Ⓓ	168	Ⓐ	Ⓑ	Ⓒ	Ⓓ	188	Ⓐ	Ⓑ	Ⓒ	Ⓓ
109	Ⓐ	Ⓑ	Ⓒ	Ⓓ	129	Ⓐ	Ⓑ	Ⓒ	Ⓓ	149	Ⓐ	Ⓑ	Ⓒ	Ⓓ	169	Ⓐ	Ⓑ	Ⓒ	Ⓓ	189	Ⓐ	Ⓑ	Ⓒ	Ⓓ
110	Ⓐ	Ⓑ	Ⓒ	Ⓓ	130	Ⓐ	Ⓑ	Ⓒ	Ⓓ	150	Ⓐ	Ⓑ	Ⓒ	Ⓓ	170	Ⓐ	Ⓑ	Ⓒ	Ⓓ	190	Ⓐ	Ⓑ	Ⓒ	Ⓓ
111	Ⓐ	Ⓑ	Ⓒ	Ⓓ	131	Ⓐ	Ⓑ	Ⓒ	Ⓓ	151	Ⓐ	Ⓑ	Ⓒ	Ⓓ	171	Ⓐ	Ⓑ	Ⓒ	Ⓓ	191	Ⓐ	Ⓑ	Ⓒ	Ⓓ
112	Ⓐ	Ⓑ	Ⓒ	Ⓓ	132	Ⓐ	Ⓑ	Ⓒ	Ⓓ	152	Ⓐ	Ⓑ	Ⓒ	Ⓓ	172	Ⓐ	Ⓑ	Ⓒ	Ⓓ	192	Ⓐ	Ⓑ	Ⓒ	Ⓓ
113	Ⓐ	Ⓑ	Ⓒ	Ⓓ	133	Ⓐ	Ⓑ	Ⓒ	Ⓓ	153	Ⓐ	Ⓑ	Ⓒ	Ⓓ	173	Ⓐ	Ⓑ	Ⓒ	Ⓓ	193	Ⓐ	Ⓑ	Ⓒ	Ⓓ
114	Ⓐ	Ⓑ	Ⓒ	Ⓓ	134	Ⓐ	Ⓑ	Ⓒ	Ⓓ	154	Ⓐ	Ⓑ	Ⓒ	Ⓓ	174	Ⓐ	Ⓑ	Ⓒ	Ⓓ	194	Ⓐ	Ⓑ	Ⓒ	Ⓓ
115	Ⓐ	Ⓑ	Ⓒ	Ⓓ	135	Ⓐ	Ⓑ	Ⓒ	Ⓓ	155	Ⓐ	Ⓑ	Ⓒ	Ⓓ	175	Ⓐ	Ⓑ	Ⓒ	Ⓓ	195	Ⓐ	Ⓑ	Ⓒ	Ⓓ
116	Ⓐ	Ⓑ	Ⓒ	Ⓓ	136	Ⓐ	Ⓑ	Ⓒ	Ⓓ	156	Ⓐ	Ⓑ	Ⓒ	Ⓓ	176	Ⓐ	Ⓑ	Ⓒ	Ⓓ	196	Ⓐ	Ⓑ	Ⓒ	Ⓓ
117	Ⓐ	Ⓑ	Ⓒ	Ⓓ	137	Ⓐ	Ⓑ	Ⓒ	Ⓓ	157	Ⓐ	Ⓑ	Ⓒ	Ⓓ	177	Ⓐ	Ⓑ	Ⓒ	Ⓓ	197	Ⓐ	Ⓑ	Ⓒ	Ⓓ
118	Ⓐ	Ⓑ	Ⓒ	Ⓓ	138	Ⓐ	Ⓑ	Ⓒ	Ⓓ	158	Ⓐ	Ⓑ	Ⓒ	Ⓓ	178	Ⓐ	Ⓑ	Ⓒ	Ⓓ	198	Ⓐ	Ⓑ	Ⓒ	Ⓓ
119	Ⓐ	Ⓑ	Ⓒ	Ⓓ	139	Ⓐ	Ⓑ	Ⓒ	Ⓓ	159	Ⓐ	Ⓑ	Ⓒ	Ⓓ	179	Ⓐ	Ⓑ	Ⓒ	Ⓓ	199	Ⓐ	Ⓑ	Ⓒ	Ⓓ
120	Ⓐ	Ⓑ	Ⓒ	Ⓓ	140	Ⓐ	Ⓑ	Ⓒ	Ⓓ	160	Ⓐ	Ⓑ	Ⓒ	Ⓓ	180	Ⓐ	Ⓑ	Ⓒ	Ⓓ	200	Ⓐ	Ⓑ	Ⓒ	Ⓓ

1. 사용 필기구 : 컴퓨터용 연필(연필을 제외한 사인펜, 볼펜 등은 사용 절대 불가)
2. 잘못된 필기구 사용과 〈보기〉의 올바른 표기 이외의 잘못된 표기로 한 경우에는 당 위원회의 OMR기기가 판독한 결과에 따르며 그 결과는 본인 책임입니다. 1개의 정답만 골라 아래의 올바른 표기대로 정확히 표기하여야 합니다.
   〈보기〉 올바른 표기 : ● 잘못된 표기 : ✓ ✗ ◍
3. 답안지는 컴퓨터로 처리되므로 훼손하시면 안 되며, 상단의 타이밍마크(❙❙❙❙)부분을 찢거나, 낙서 등을 하면 본인에게 불이익이 발생할 수 있습니다.
4. 감독관의 확인이 없거나 시험 종료 후에 답안 작성을 계속할 경우 시험 무효 처리됩니다.

*서약 내용을 읽으시고 확인란에 반드시 서명하십시오.

서 약	확 인
본인은 TOEIC 시험 문제의 일부 또는 전부를 유출하거나 어떠한 형태로든 타인에게 누설 공개하지 않을 것이며 인터넷 또는 인쇄물 등을 이용해 유포하거나 참고 자료로 활용하지 않을 것입니다. 또한 TOEIC 시험 부정 행위 처리 규정을 준수할 것을 서약합니다.	

TOEIC® 점수 환산표

정답수	Listening Comprehension	정답수	Reading Comprehension
96-100	480-495	96-100	460-495
91-95	435-490	91-95	410-475
86-90	395-450	86-90	380-430
81-85	355-415	81-85	355-400
76-80	325-375	76-80	325-375
71-75	295-340	71-75	295-345
66-70	265-315	66-70	265-315
61-65	240-285	61-65	235-285
56-60	215-260	56-60	205-255
51-55	190-235	51-55	175-225
46-50	160-210	46-50	150-195
41-45	135-180	41-45	120-170
36-40	110-155	36-40	100-140
31-35	85-130	31-35	75-120
26-30	70-105	26-30	55-100
21-25	50-90	21-25	40-80
16-20	35-75	16-20	30-65
11-15	20-55	11-15	20-50
6-10	15-40	6-10	15-35
1-5	5-20	1-5	5-20
0	5	0	5

나혼자 끝내는 新토익 FINAL 실전 모의고사 3회분

지은이 넥서스토익연구소
펴낸이 임상진
펴낸곳 (주)넥서스

출판신고 1992년 4월 3일 제311-2002-2호
10880 경기도 파주시 지목로 5
Tel (02)330-5500 Fax (02)330-5555

ISBN 979-11-6165-640-3 13740

가격은 뒤표지에 있습니다.
잘못 만들어진 책은 구입처에서 바꾸어 드립니다.

이 도서의 국립중앙도서관 출판예정도서목록(CIP)은
서지정보유통지원시스템 홈페이지(http://seoji.nl.go.kr)와
국가자료공동목록시스템(http://www.nl.go.kr/kolisnet)에서 이용하실 수
있습니다.
(CIP제어번호 : CIP2019022664)

www.nexusbook.com

나혼자 끝내는 新 토익

FINAL 실전 모의고사 3회분

新토익 실전 모의고사 3회분 + 정답/스크립트 해석/해설 제공 + 실전용·복습용 2종 MP3

MP3 듣기
정답 자동 채점

★ 실제 시험지 형태 그대로, 신토익 실전 모의고사 3회분 수록

★ 문제의 키워드를 단숨에 파악하는 알짜 해석·해설

★ 실전용 · 복습용 버전의 2종 MP3 무료 다운로드 >> QR코드 & 홈페이지 다운로드

★ 문제풀이 후 바로 채점할 수 있는 자동 채점 방식 제공 >> QR코드

★ 신토익 빈출 어휘 리스트 제공 >> www.nexusbook.com

스크립트+
정답 및 해설

나혼자 끝내는 新 토익

FINAL 실전 모의고사

3회분

新토익 실전 모의고사 3회분 + 정답/스크립트 해석/해설 제공 + 실전용·복습용 2종 MP3

넥서스

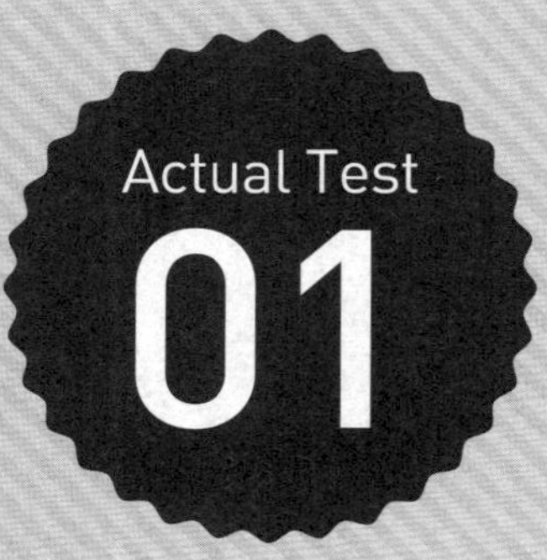

Listening Comprehension

PART 1

1 (C)	2 (D)	3 (D)	4 (B)	5 (B)	6 (C)				

PART 2

7 (C)	8 (B)	9 (B)	10 (C)	11 (A)	12 (B)	13 (B)	14 (C)	15 (B)	16 (B)
17 (C)	18 (C)	19 (C)	20 (C)	21 (C)	22 (A)	23 (B)	24 (B)	25 (C)	26 (A)
27 (C)	28 (B)	29 (C)	30 (C)	31 (C)					

PART 3

32 (B)	33 (B)	34 (C)	35 (C)	36 (D)	37 (B)	38 (D)	39 (D)	40 (B)	41 (D)
42 (B)	43 (A)	44 (B)	45 (C)	46 (C)	47 (B)	48 (D)	49 (D)	50 (D)	51 (B)
52 (A)	53 (D)	54 (B)	55 (A)	56 (B)	57 (D)	58 (B)	59 (A)	60 (A)	61 (A)
62 (D)	63 (C)	64 (C)	65 (C)	66 (A)	67 (B)	68 (B)	69 (A)	70 (D)	

PART 4

71 (A)	72 (D)	73 (A)	74 (B)	75 (B)	76 (B)	77 (A)	78 (D)	79 (D)	80 (C)
81 (B)	82 (A)	83 (B)	84 (A)	85 (D)	86 (D)	87 (D)	88 (A)	89 (C)	90 (C)
91 (A)	92 (D)	93 (B)	94 (B)	95 (A)	96 (C)	97 (C)	98 (A)	99 (C)	100 (C)

Reading Comprehension

PART 5

101 (D)	102 (A)	103 (B)	104 (A)	105 (B)	106 (A)	107 (A)	108 (A)	109 (B)	110 (C)
111 (B)	112 (A)	113 (C)	114 (D)	115 (A)	116 (C)	117 (D)	118 (C)	119 (B)	120 (C)
121 (A)	122 (B)	123 (C)	124 (A)	125 (C)	126 (D)	127 (B)	128 (D)	129 (A)	130 (A)

PART 6

131 (A)	132 (B)	133 (A)	134 (D)	135 (A)	136 (D)	137 (A)	138 (D)	139 (B)	140 (A)
141 (C)	142 (C)	143 (D)	144 (A)	145 (A)	146 (B)				

PART 7

147 (B)	148 (A)	149 (A)	150 (C)	151 (A)	152 (A)	153 (C)	154 (B)	155 (C)	156 (A)
157 (A)	158 (A)	159 (A)	160 (C)	161 (B)	162 (A)	163 (C)	164 (D)	165 (A)	166 (B)
167 (A)	168 (B)	169 (B)	170 (A)	171 (B)	172 (A)	173 (B)	174 (D)	175 (C)	176 (C)
177 (A)	178 (D)	179 (D)	180 (A)	181 (D)	182 (D)	183 (A)	184 (C)	185 (B)	186 (D)
187 (B)	188 (D)	189 (B)	190 (A)	191 (C)	192 (B)	193 (D)	194 (B)	195 (B)	196 (D)
197 (D)	198 (B)	199 (C)	200 (D)						

Part 1

1 미M
(A) A man is loading some bricks onto a cart.
(B) A man is cutting the grass alongside a road.
(C) A man is using a shovel to move some dirt.
(D) A man is driving a car into a garage.

(A) 한 남자가 카트에 벽돌을 싣고 있다.
(B) 한 남자가 도로를 따라 풀을 자르고 있다.
(C) 한 남자가 삽을 이용해서 흙을 옮기고 있다.
(D) 한 남자가 차를 차고로 이동시키고 있다.

alongside ~을 따라　dirt 흙　garage 차고

2 영W
(A) A shopkeeper is organizing a display.
(B) One of the men is distributing documents.
(C) One of the women is putting merchandise on a shelf.
(D) One of the women is carrying a handbag.

(A) 가게 주인이 진열장을 정리하고 있다.
(B) 한 남자가 서류를 나눠 주고 있다.
(C) 한 여자가 선반에 상품을 올려두고 있다.
(D) 한 여자가 핸드백을 들고 있다.

shopkeeper 가게 주인　distribute 나누어 주다　merchandise 상품

3 미W
(A) Some workers are cleaning the floor.
(B) Some people are entering a shop.
(C) Some cups are being filled.
(D) Some chairs are arranged around tables.

(A) 몇몇 직원이 바닥을 청소하고 있다.
(B) 몇몇 사람이 가게에 들어가고 있다.
(C) 몇몇 컵이 채워지고 있다.
(D) 테이블 주위로 의자가 놓여 있다.

arrange 정리하다, 배열하다

4 영W
(A) A woman is handing a dish to a customer.
(B) A woman is working behind the counter.
(C) A man is making a purchase in an outdoor café.
(D) A man is pointing at something on the board.

(A) 한 여자가 손님에게 접시를 건네주고 있다.
(B) 한 여자가 계산대 뒤에서 일하고 있다.
(C) 한 남자가 야외 카페에서 구매를 하고 있다.
(D) 한 남자가 칠판에 있는 무언가를 향해 손가락으로 가리키고 있다.

hand 건네다　counter 계산대　make a purchase 구매하다　outdoor 야외의　point at ~을 향해 손가락으로 가리키다

5 미W
(A) People are lined up to enter a garden.
(B) People are skating in a city park.
(C) Some people are competing in a race.
(D) Leaves have fallen onto the ground.

(A) 사람들이 정원에 들어가기 위해 줄을 서 있다.
(B) 사람들이 도시 공원에서 스케이트를 타고 있다.
(C) 몇몇 사람들이 시합에서 경쟁하고 있다.
(D) 낙엽이 땅에 떨어져 있다.

line up 줄 서다　compete 겨루다, 경쟁하다　race 경주

6 미M
(A) An employee is assembling some shelves.
(B) Some workers are unloading a shipment of boxes.
(C) Some boxes are stacked in a warehouse.
(D) Some suitcases are being wrapped in plastic.

(A) 한 직원이 선반을 조립하고 있다.
(B) 몇몇 직원들이 박스를 내리고 있다.
(C) 몇몇 박스가 창고에 쌓여 있다.
(D) 몇몇 가방이 비닐로 포장되고 있다.

assemble 조립하다　shipment 적하물　stack 쌓다　wrap 포장하다

Part 2

7 미M 미W
What would you prefer to drink?
(A) I think so, as well.
(B) I like it very much.
(C) Some tea, please.

당신은 무엇을 마시고 싶은가요?
(A) 저 또한 그렇게 생각합니다.
(B) 저는 그것이 매우 좋아요.
(C) 차를 주세요.

as well 또한, 역시

8 미M 영W
Where can I get a large scheduler for my desk?
(A) I think she is quite organized.
(B) Look in the store closet.
(C) How much did you pay?

제 책상에 놓을 큰 수첩을 어디에서 구할 수 있을까요?
(A) 그녀는 꽤 체계적인 사람 같아요.
(B) 매장 벽장을 찾아보세요.
(C) 얼마나 지불했나요?

scheduler 할 일을 적는 수첩　closet 벽장

9 미W 영W
Have we authorized Therese's expense form yet?
(A) Yes, she can.
(B) Has she sent it to us?
(C) Three should be sufficient.

우린 아직 테레즈의 비용 지출서를 재가하지 않았죠?
(A) 네, 그녀는 할 수 있어요.
(B) 그녀가 우리에게 그것을 보냈나요?
(C) 셋이면 충분할 거예요.

authorize 재가하다　expense form 비용 지출서　sufficient 충분한

10 미M 영W
Has Mr. Takei approved the plans or are they still being reviewed?
(A) It's out of paper.
(B) I met some of them.
(C) He still has them.

타케이 씨가 계획을 승인했나요, 아니면 아직 검토 중인가요?
(A) 용지가 떨어졌어요.
(B) 저는 그들 중 몇 명을 만났어요.
(C) 그는 아직 그것들을 갖고 있어요.

approve 승인하다　be out of ~이 없는

11 미M 미W
The science department is on this level, isn't it?
(A) Yes, I can show you where.
(B) I'm looking for my phone.
(C) No, she isn't the scientist.

과학 부서는 2층에 있죠, 그렇지 않나요?
(A) 네, 제가 어디인지 알려 드릴게요.
(B) 저는 제 전화기를 찾고 있어요.
(C) 아니요, 그녀는 과학자가 아니에요.

level 층

12 영W 미W
When did Hans purchase the piano?
(A) At a music convention.
(B) Last month, I think.
(C) His colleague's performance.

한스가 언제 피아노를 샀나요?
(A) 음악 대회에서요.
(B) 지난달일 거예요.
(C) 그의 동료의 공연이요.

convention 컨벤션; 대회　colleague 동료　performance 공연

13 미M 영W
When does your flight leave?
(A) He's already left.

(B) At 5:50.
(C) To Alabama.

당신의 비행 편은 언제 떠나나요?
(A) 그는 벌써 떠났어요.
(B) 5시 50분에요.
(C) 알라바마로요.
flight 비행 편

14 I can book the hotel room today if you'd like.
미M (A) I really appreciated it.
영W (B) Yes, many times before.
(C) Okay, if you have time.

원하신다면, 제가 오늘 호텔 객실을 예약할 수 있습니다.
(A) 매우 감사했습니다.
(B) 네, 이전에 여러 번이요.
(C) 네, 시간이 된다면 그렇게 해 주세요.
book 예약하다 appreciate 고맙게 여기다, 존중하다

15 Are you renovating the sports center?
영W (A) Very much, thank you.
미M (B) It should be completed in April.
(C) Just a few sports events.

당신이 스포츠 센터를 리모델링하고 있나요?
(A) 매우 그렇습니다, 감사합니다.
(B) 그건 4월에 끝날 거예요.
(C) 몇 개의 스포츠 행사들만요.
renovate 개조[보수]하다

16 Why isn't there a photocopier in this office?
미M (A) It's not difficult. I will demonstrate.
영W (B) Actually, there's one in reception.
(C) She pressed the blue switch.

왜 이 사무실에는 복사기가 없나요?
(A) 어렵지 않습니다. 제가 시연해 볼게요.
(B) 사실, 접수처에 하나 있어요.
(C) 그녀가 파란 스위치를 눌렀어요.
photocopier 복사기 demonstrate 시연하다

17 When did the sports academy first open?
미M (A) Buffalo, Chicago.
미W (B) It's his favorite game.
(C) In 1962, I think.

그 스포츠 학교는 언제 처음 문을 열었나요?
(A) 시카고 버펄로요.
(B) 그가 가장 좋아하는 게임이에요.
(C) 1962년으로 알고 있어요.
academy (특수 분야의) 학교

18 Where did the marketing convention take place?
미W (A) The third week of June.
미M (B) He arrived late at the port.
(C) It was held in Marbella.

마케팅 컨벤션은 어디에서 개최되었나요?
(A) 6월 셋째 주요.
(B) 그는 항구에 늦게 도착했습니다.
(C) 마벨라에서 개최되었습니다.
take place 개최되다[일어나다] port 항구

19 Which date did Ms. Anker choose for the general assembly?
미M
영W (A) At 11:55 A.M.
(B) No, she didn't.
(C) Next Thursday.

앙케르 씨는 총회를 위해 어느 날짜를 골랐나요?
(A) 오전 11시 55분에요.
(B) 아니요, 그녀는 하지 않았어요.
(C) 다음 주 목요일이요.
general assembly 총회

20 Where did you put the packages with the extra files?
미W (A) That's a good idea.
미M (B) About twelve pounds.
(C) In the stockroom.

여분의 파일들이 들어 있는 소포를 어디에 두었나요?
(A) 좋은 생각이에요.
(B) 12파운드 정도 됩니다.
(C) 물품 보관소에요.
package 봉투; 상자 stockroom 물품 보관소

21 How many journalists will be attending the event?
영W (A) After the display.
미W (B) In three days.
(C) At least twenty.

행사에 몇 명의 기자들이 참석할 건가요?
(A) 전시 후에요.
(B) 3일 내에요.
(C) 적어도 20명이요.
journalist 기자 display 전시회, 전시

22 What time do you usually get to the office?
영W (A) Between 7:30 and 8.
미M (B) I normally take the bus.
(C) I only started two months ago.

당신은 보통 몇 시에 사무실에 도착하나요?
(A) 7시 반에서 8시 사이에요.
(B) 저는 보통 버스를 탑니다.
(C) 저는 단지 2개월 전에 시작했어요.
normally 보통은, 보통 때는

23 When should we leave for the wedding?
영W (A) In the Green Elm room.
미M (B) How about three o'clock?
(C) We're shut for the holiday.

우리는 언제 결혼식에 출발해야 하나요?
(A) 그린 엘름 방에서요.
(B) 3시는 어때요?
(C) 우리는 휴일로 인해 쉽니다.
shut 닫다, 닫히다

24 How often do you hold open days?
미M (A) Since last winter.
영W (B) About twice a year.
(C) All the workers.

개관일을 얼마나 자주 갖나요?
(A) 작년 겨울부터요.
(B) 1년에 두 번 정도예요.
(C) 모든 직원들이요.
open days 공개일, 개관일 pass 건네주다

25 Is the hospital nearby or is it far away?
미W (A) They open early.
미M (B) He's in the surgery.
(C) It's just by the park.

그 병원은 근처에 있나요, 아니면 멀리 있나요?
(A) 그들은 일찍 문을 엽니다.
(B) 그는 수술실에 있어요.
(C) 공원 바로 옆에 있어요.
far away 멀리 surgery 수술(실)

26 This wall is shorter than the specification.
미M (A) Then I'll have to add to it.
미W (B) The *Wall Street Journal*.
(C) It's towards the middle of the day.

이 벽은 설명서에 나와 있는 것보다 짧아요.
(A) 그렇다면 제가 거기에 추가해야겠네요.
(B) 〈월 스트리트 저널〉입니다.
(C) 한낮으로 가고 있네요.

specification 안내서, 사양   middle of the day 대낮

27 Where was his last exhibition held?
미W (A) In early May.
영W (B) Some of his recent artwork.
(C) In a gallery.

그의 마지막 전시회가 어디에서 개최되었나요?
(A) 5월 초에요.
(B) 그의 최근 미술품들 몇 점입니다.
(C) 화랑에서요.

exhibition 전시, 전시회   artwork 미술품   gallery 화랑

28 What was the price of the present?
미W (A) It was for a leaving party.
미M (B) About 200 dollars.
(C) At the store across the walkway.

그 선물은 얼마였나요?
(A) 그것은 송별회를 위해서였어요.
(B) 약 200달러요.
(C) 통로의 건너편 가게에서요.

leaving party 송별회, 작별 파티   walkway 통로

29 When should we start renovating the exterior of the
미M building?
미W (A) That's what I believed.
(B) Sign it on the back.
(C) How about on Monday?

우리는 언제 그 건물의 외관 개조를 시작해야 할까요?
(A) 그게 제가 생각한 거예요.
(B) 뒤에 사인해 주세요.
(C) 월요일은 어때요?

renovate 개조하다, 보수하다   exterior 외관

30 I couldn't find any photocopier ink.
영W (A) The bank is in the high street.
미M (B) Some large envelopes.
(C) There is more in the stock room.

저는 복사기 잉크를 하나도 찾을 수 없어요.
(A) 그 은행은 시내 중심가에 있어요.
(B) 대봉투 몇 장이요.
(C) 창고에 더 있어요.

photocopier 복사기   high street 시내 중심가   envelope 봉투   stock room 물품 보관소, 창고

31 You ordered a projector for the session, didn't you?
미W (A) It's out of stock.
미M (B) No, we've met previously.
(C) First thing this morning.

당신은 교육을 위해 영사기를 주문했어요, 그렇지 않았나요?
(A) 그건 품절이에요.
(B) 아니요, 우리는 전에 만났어요.
(C) 오늘 아침 제일 처음으로 했어요.

projector 영사기   session (특정한 활동을 위한) 시간[기간]   out of stock 품절이 되어

Part 3

Questions 32-35 refer to the following conversation. 미W 미M

W Have you heard about the new restaurant which is across from our office?
M No. What about it?
W I haven't been there yet, but some of our coworkers said that the food is splendid. Also, they serve a lot of fusion dishes. So I was thinking of having a farewell party for Ms. Erring tomorrow at that place. Do you think 5 P.M. would be good for everyone?
M How about an hour later? Half of the department will be in a meeting tomorrow, and that may end after 5 P.M.

여 사무실 건너 새 레스토랑 얘기 들으셨어요?
남 아니요. 무슨 이야기인데요?
여 저도 아직 못 갔는데 직원들이 그러는데 음식이 정말 괜찮대요. 또 여러 가지 퓨전 요리도 많대요. 그래서 내일 어링 씨 송별회를 거기서 할까 생각 중이었어요. 다들 5시 괜찮겠죠?
남 한 시간 후는 어떠세요? 팀 절반이 내일 회의에 있을 거고 5시 넘어서 끝날 것 같아요.

coworker 동료   splendid 정말 좋은, 훌륭한   fusion 결합   farewell party 송별회   department 팀   luxurious 고급스러운   within walking distance 걸어갈 수 있는 범위 내의

32 What is mentioned about the new restaurant?
(A) It has a luxurious interior.
(B) It is within walking distance.
(C) It opened yesterday.
(D) It serves Italian food.

새로운 레스토랑에 관해 언급한 것은?
(A) 고급스러운 인테리어를 갖추고 있다.
(B) 걸어갈 수 있는 거리이다.
(C) 어제 오픈했다.
(D) 이탈리아 음식을 제공한다.

33 What will take place tomorrow?
(A) An opening ceremony
(B) A farewell banquet
(C) An interview for a position
(D) A company picnic

내일 일어날 일은?
(A) 개장식
(B) 송별회
(C) 구직 면접
(D) 회사 야유회

34 What time does the man suggest for the party?
(A) At 4:00 P.M.
(B) At 5:00 P.M.
(C) At 6:00 P.M.
(D) At 7:00 P.M.

남자가 파티를 하자고 제안한 시간은?
(A) 오후 4시
(B) 오후 5시
(C) 오후 6시
(D) 오후 7시

Questions 35-37 refer to the following conversation. 영W 미M

W Dr. Chen, I heard that your research team had succeeded in developing a new fabric. It's all over the newspapers. Congrats!

M Thank you. Well, for the past three years, my research team worked over 12 hours a day to develop a new fabric that can withstand bad weather. Not only is it waterproof but it's light and thin. So it should be used to make hiking clothes, for one.

W Sounds great. You will definitely get many calls from businesses. When do you think it will be available on the market?

M We will sign the manufacturing agreements next month, but the public won't see them in stores for at least a year.

여 첸 박사님, 당신의 연구팀이 새로운 옷감 개발에 성공했다고 들었습니다. 모든 신문에 실렸던데요. 축하해요!

남 고마워요. 지난 3년간 제 연구팀은 악천후에 견딜 수 있는 새로운 옷감을 개발하느라 하루에 거의 12시간씩 근무했어요. 그 옷감은 방수가 될 뿐만 아니라 가볍고 얇아요. 그래서 예를 들면 등산복 같은 옷을 만드는 데 쓰일 수 있을 겁니다.

여 멋지네요. 관련 기업으로부터 분명히 전화를 많이 받으시겠네요. 시장에는 언제 출시될 것 같나요?

남 우리는 다음 달 제조 계약서에 서명할 거예요. 하지만 시중에는 최소 1년 뒤에나 볼 수 있을 겁니다.

succeed in ~에 성공하다 fabric 옷감 withstand 견디다 waterproof 방수의 light 가벼운 available 이용 가능한 agreement 계약서, 합의

35 Who is the man?
(A) A reporter
(B) A clothing designer
(C) A researcher
(D) A store owner

남자는 누구인가?
(A) 기자
(B) 의류 디자이너
(C) 연구원
(D) 매장 주인

36 What is NOT a characteristic of the fabric being mentioned?
(A) It is light.
(B) It is waterproof.
(C) It is thin.
(D) It is warm.

언급된 옷감의 특징이 아닌 것은?
(A) 가볍다.
(B) 방수가 된다.
(C) 얇다.
(D) 따뜻하다.

37 When does the man say will the fabric be ready for sale?
(A) In a month
(B) In one year
(C) In two years
(D) In three years

남자는 옷감이 언제 판매될 것이라고 하는가?
(A) 1달 뒤
(B) 1년 뒤
(C) 2년 뒤
(D) 3년 뒤

Questions 38-40 refer to the following conversation. 미M 미W

M Good afternoon, Genie Cable customer service. This is Steve speaking. How can I help you?

W Hello. I recently purchased your cable service, premium package. I read the instructions and did as they say but I think some of the channels that are included in the premium package are blocked.

M I think I can help you with that. The channels are being blocked because of the child-proof function. Go to the channel you wish to see and then press the small red button on the end of the remote control. The screen will ask you to put in a secret code number. Simply insert your secret code number. Then the block will be gone.

W Let me try. Yes, I can see the channel. Thank you so much for your help.

남 안녕하세요. 지니 케이블 고객 센터입니다. 저는 스티브입니다. 무엇을 도와 드릴까요?

여 안녕하세요. 최근에 그 회사 케이블 서비스를 이용했어요. 프리미엄 패키지요. 설명서를 읽었고 나온 대로 했는데 프리미엄 채널에 포함된 몇 개 채널이 안 나오네요.

남 제가 도와 드릴게요. 그 채널들은 아동 시청 보호를 위해 차단되고 있습니다. 보고 싶으신 채널로 가서 리모컨 끝에 있는 작은 빨간 버튼을 누르세요. 그러면 화면에서 비밀번호를 입력하라고 할 겁니다. 간단하게 비밀번호를 입력하세요. 그럼 차단이 해제될 겁니다.

여 그렇게 해 볼게요. 네, 채널이 보이네요. 도와주셔서 감사합니다.

recently 최근에 purchase 구입하다 premium 고급의 block 차단하다 child-proof 아동 보호 장치 function 기능 secret code number 비밀번호 insert 삽입하다 incorrectly 부정확하게 spill 엎지르다

38 What are the speakers discussing?
(A) Changing the type of service
(B) Registering a secret code number
(C) Cancelling cable services
(D) Unblocking channels

화자들이 얘기하는 것은?
(A) 서비스 종류 변경
(B) 비밀번호 등록
(C) 케이블 서비스 취소
(D) 채널 차단 해제

39 What was the woman's problem?
(A) She forgot her secret code number.
(B) She found too many violent channels.
(C) The repairman didn't come on time.
(D) She couldn't see some of the channels.

여자의 문제는 무엇이었나?
(A) 비밀번호를 잊어버렸다.
(B) 너무 많은 폭력 채널을 찾았다.
(C) 수리 기사가 제때 오지 않았다.
(D) 채널 일부를 볼 수 없었다.

40 According to the man, what was the reason for the woman's problem?
(A) The cable was inserted incorrectly.
(B) Some channels require a secret code number.
(C) Her child spilled juice on the cable box.
(D) The instruction book had several pages missing.

남자에 의하면 여자의 문제의 원인은?

(A) 케이블이 잘못 꽂혔다.
(B) 몇몇 채널은 비밀번호가 필요하다.
(C) 아이들이 케이블 박스에 주스를 엎질렀다.
(D) 사용 설명서의 몇 페이지가 빠졌다.

Questions 41-43 refer to the following conversation. 미M 영W

M Ms. Roberts, I have one final question before we finish the interview. What makes you think that you are the strongest candidate for our international sales division?
W Well, I have 3 years of field experience in sales and I enjoy working with other people. In addition, I am fluent in Japanese and Chinese, which I believe will be an asset to your department.
M Good. I was looking for someone who can work in our Singapore office. Do you mind working overseas?
W **Not at all.** In fact, I lived in Singapore before and I loved it there.

남 로버츠 씨, 면접을 끝내기 전에 마지막 질문이 하나 있습니다. 당신이 우리 해외 영업부를 위한 가장 강력한 후보자라고 생각할 수 있는 점은 무엇인가요?
여 음, 저는 영업 분야에서 3년간의 경력이 있고 다른 사람들과 함께 일하는 것을 즐깁니다. 그뿐만 아니라, 제가 일본어와 중국어에 유창하다는 점은 당신의 부서에 자산이 될 것이라고 믿습니다.
남 좋습니다. 우리 싱가포르 사무실에서 일할 수 있는 누군가를 찾고 있었어요. 당신은 해외에서 일하는 것은 꺼리십니까?
여 **천만에요.** 실은, 전에 싱가포르에서 살았었고 그곳을 좋아했었습니다.

final question 최종 질문 candidate 후보자 field experience 현장 경험, 경력 in addition 게다가, 그뿐만 아니라 fluent 유창한 asset 자산, 재산 mind 꺼리다, 싫어하다 work overseas 해외에서 일하다

41 What are the speakers mainly discussing?
(A) An employee evaluation
(B) A foreign country
(C) A sales strategy
(D) A job opportunity
화자들은 주로 무엇에 대해 이야기하는가?
(A) 직원 평가
(B) 다른 나라
(C) 영업 전략
(D) 취업 기회

42 Who most likely is the woman?
(A) A business owner
(B) A potential employee
(C) A language instructor
(D) A travel agent
여자는 누구일 것 같은가?
(A) 업체 사장
(B) 잠재 직원
(C) 어학 강사
(D) 여행사 직원

43 What does the woman imply when she says, "Not at all"?
(A) She wants to work abroad.
(B) She has not signed the contract.
(C) She does not speak a foreign language.
(D) She wants to attend a sales meeting.
여자가 "천만에요"라고 말한 의도는 무엇인가?
(A) 그녀는 해외에서 일하고 싶어 한다.
(B) 그녀는 계약서에 서명하지 않았다.
(C) 그녀는 외국어를 하지 못한다.
(D) 그녀는 세일즈 미팅에 참석하기 원한다.

Questions 44-46 refer to the following conversation with three speakers. 미W 미M 영W

W1 David, what did you think about Shawn Gomez, the candidate we met this afternoon?
M I think he is one of the promising candidates so far but he may be overqualified for this position. You know, he managed more than a hundred employees in his last position.
W2 You make a good point. Speaking of which, why don't we recommend him for the managerial position in Tokyo? He wouldn't be overqualified for that, right?
W1 Oh, you're right, Selena. Plus, the Tokyo office wants to fill the position right away because the construction of our new research facility will begin in a week.
M I just wonder if he is willing to relocate to another country immediately.
W2 Why don't I call him to discuss the position? If he is interested, I'll arrange a phone interview with the Tokyo office.

여1 데이비드, 오늘 오후에 면접 본 숀 고메즈 씨에 대해 어떻게 생각했나요?
남 현재까지 가장 유망한 지원자 중 한 명이라고 생각하지만 이 직위에는 지나치게 경력이 좋은 것 같아요. 아시다시피 그는 마지막 직장에서 수백 명의 직원들을 관리했잖아요.
여2 좋은 지적이에요. 얘기가 나와서 말인데, 그를 도쿄의 매니저 직에 추천하는 것은 어떨까요? 그 직위에는 경력이 지나치지 않을 거예요, 그렇죠?
여1 오, 당신 말이 맞아요, 셀레나. 게다가 새로운 연구 시설의 공사가 일주일 후면 시작되기 때문에 도쿄 사무실은 그 공석을 빨리 채우고 싶어해요.
남 전 다만 그가 해외로 당장 전근하기를 원할지 모르겠어요.
여2 제가 그것에 대해서 그와 상의를 해 볼까요? 관심 있어 하면, 도쿄 사무실과 전화 인터뷰를 마련해 볼게요.

candidate 지원자 overqualified 필요 이상의 자격을 갖춘 fill a position 공석을 채우다

44 What does the man say about Shawn Gomez?
(A) He has lived in a foreign country.
(B) He has more experience than required.

(C) He does not want to travel often.
(D) He applied for several positions.

숀 고메즈에 대해서 남자는 뭐라고 말하는가?
(A) 그는 해외에 살아본 적이 있다.
(B) 그는 요구한 것보다 더 경력이 많다.
(C) 그는 자주 출장 가기를 원치 않는다.
(D) 그는 여러 직위에 지원하였다.

45 What does Selena suggest doing?
(A) Building a new shopping center overseas
(B) Relocating the company's headquarters
(C) Recommending a candidate for another position
(D) Advertising job openings in a newspaper

셀레나는 무엇을 할 것을 제안하는가?
(A) 해외에 새로운 쇼핑센터를 짓는 것
(B) 회사의 본사를 이전하는 것
(C) 다른 직위에 지원자를 추천하는 것
(D) 신문에 일자리 광고를 내는 것

46 What will happen in Tokyo in a week?
(A) A computer system will be upgraded.
(B) A phone interview will be conducted.
(C) A construction project will begin.
(D) An annual event will be held.

일주일 후에 도쿄에서 무슨 일을 있을 것인가?
(A) 컴퓨터 시스템이 업그레이드될 것이다.
(B) 전화 인터뷰가 진행될 것이다.
(C) 공사 프로젝트가 시작될 것이다.
(D) 연례 행사가 열릴 것이다.

Questions 47-49 refer to the following conversation. 미W 미M

W Did you hear about the delay from the supplier? He said that the glass panels we ordered won't be delivered until next Tuesday because of a strike.

M That's not good. We promised Ms. Theron to finish the front door of her house by the end of March. I'm worried because this delay might cause us to fall behind schedule.

W How about asking Ms. Theron to allow us more time to finish the work?

M Okay, let me speak to her about it.

여 공급업체로부터 지연에 관하여 들으셨나요? 우리가 주문한 유리 패널이 파업 때문에 다음 주 화요일이 되어야 배달될 것이라고 하더군요.

남 좋지 않네요. 우리가 테론 씨에게 집 현관 작업을 3월 말까지 마치겠다고 약속했잖아요. 이 지연으로 인해 일정보다 늦게 될까 걱정이 됩니다.

여 테론 씨에게 작업을 완료할 시간을 더 요청하는 건 어떨까요?

남 좋아요. 제가 그녀와 이야기해 보겠습니다.

delay 지연, 연기 glass panel 유리 패널 strike 파업 behind schedule 일정보다 뒤처진

47 Who most likely are the speakers?
(A) Building inspectors
(B) Home builders
(C) Personnel employees
(D) Professional gardeners

화자들은 누구일 것 같은가?
(A) 건물 조사관
(B) 주택 건축업자
(C) 인사부 직원
(D) 전문 정원사

48 What does the man mean when he says, "That's not good"?
(A) A budget might not be approved.
(B) Some materials are out of stock.
(C) Heavy rains are forecast.
(D) A project might not be finished on time.

남자가 "좋지 않네요"라고 말한 의미는 무엇인가?
(A) 예산이 승인되지 않을지도 모른다.
(B) 일부 자재의 재고가 없다.
(C) 호우가 예보되어 있다.
(D) 프로젝트가 제때 끝나지 않을 수 있다.

49 What do the speakers decide to do?
(A) Cancel an order
(B) Purchase from another supplier
(C) Hire more workers
(D) Contact a client

화자들은 무엇을 하기로 결정하는가?
(A) 주문 취소하기
(B) 다른 공급자에게서 구입하기
(C) 인부 더 고용하기
(D) 고객에게 연락하기

Questions 50-52 refer to the following conversation. 미M 미W

M Philippa, I've been checking the comments that our restaurant patrons have posted over the past two months. There are many constructive comments about our menu choices. But we've got some criticism about the ingredients we use.

W Really? I'm a little taken aback. We spent a fair amount of time choosing high quality ingredients for our food.

M Well, it's not the quality they were bothered about. They would just prefer that the items were sourced organically from recognized farms.

W Oh, that would fit in with our existing environmentally-friendly procedures. Could you do some investigating and source another supplier?

남 필리파, 저는 레스토랑 단골손님이 지난 두 달 동안 게시한 평들을 확인하고 있었어요. 메뉴 선택에 관한 건설적인 평들이 많아요. 하지만 우리가 사용하는 재료에 관해서는 비판을 좀 받았어요.

여 정말인가요? 그것 참 놀랍네요. 우리는 음식에 사용되는 품질 좋은 재료를 고르기 위해 상당히 많은 시간을 보내잖아요.

남 음, 그들이 신경 쓰는 게 품질이 아니었어요. 단지 상품이 잘 알려진 농장에서 유기 재배로 공급되는 것을 선호했던 거였어요.

여 오, 그건 기존의 친환경적 절차와 잘 어울리네요. 당신이 조사를 해서 다른 공급업체를 찾아 주시겠어요?

comment 평 patron 단골손님; 후원자 post 게시하다 constructive 건설적인 criticism 비판 ingredient 재료 be taken aback 깜짝 놀라

다 fair 상당한 be bothered ~을 중요하게 여기다, 개의하다 source (특정한 곳에서 무엇을) 얻다, 공급자를 찾다 organically 유기 재배로; 유기적으로 fit in with ~와 어울리다 existing 기존의, 현존하는 procedure 공정 investigate 조사하다 butcher's 정육점 distribute 배부하다

50 What kind of business do the speakers work for?

(A) A butcher's
(B) A farm
(C) A laboratory
(D) A restaurant

화자들은 어떤 종류의 회사에서 일하는가?

(A) 정육점
(B) 농장
(C) 연구실
(D)레스토랑

51 What are customers concerned about?

(A) The pricing of some dishes
(B) The ingredients in the food
(C) The cleanliness of the restaurant
(D) The hours of opening

손님들은 무엇을 걱정하는가?

(A) 일부 요리의 가격
(B)음식의 재료
(C) 레스토랑의 청결
(D) 영업시간

52 What does the woman ask the man to do?

(A) Search for a new supplier
(B) Open a new branch
(C) Design a new menu
(D) Distribute a survey

여자는 남자에게 무엇을 하라고 요구하는가?

(A)새로운 공급업체 검색하기
(B) 새 분점 개장하기
(C) 새 메뉴 만들기
(D) 조사 발부하기

Questions 53-55 refer to the following conversation. 영W 미M

W I am grateful for your making the effort to meet me, Mr. Carlisle. I understand that you're operating a very profitable factory here, but of course that's why I believe my energy company can help.

M Yes, our production growth is expanding rapidly. In fact, my motive for requesting this meeting is because we're spending too much to run our production facilities. I'd like to find ways to lessen that cost.

W Well, energy management is one of our specialties. I propose we begin by analyzing your production procedures to find out where energy excess is generated. Then we will look for solutions to reduce some of the usage or even change the times of operation.

여 저를 만나려고 애써 주신 것에 대해 감사드립니다, 칼라일 씨. 제가 알기로 당신은 이곳에서 매우 수익률이 높은 공장을 운영하고 있고, 그 때문에 저의 에너지 회사가 도울 수 있다고 생각합니다.

남 네, 저희 생산율이 급격히 확장되고 있습니다. 사실, 이 회의를 요청한 동기는 저희가 생산 시설을 운영하는 데에 비용을 너무 많이 소비하고 있기 때문입니다. 그 비용을 줄이는 방법을 찾고 싶어서요.

여 음, 에너지 관리는 저희의 전문입니다. 에너지 과소비가 어디에서 발생하는지 알아내기 위해 생산 공정의 분석부터 시작할 것을 제안합니다. 그 다음 우리는 일부 이용을 줄이거나 심지어 운영 시간을 바꾸는 해결책을 찾을 것입니다.

grateful 고마워하는, 감사하는 make an effort 노력하다, 애쓰다 profitable 수익성이 있는; 유익한 rapidly 급격히 motive 동기, 이유 run 운영하다 production facility 생산 시설 lessen 줄이다 energy management 에너지 관리 specialty 전문, 전공; 장기 propose 제안하다 analyze 분석하다 procedure 절차, 수순 excess 과잉 generate 발생시키다, 만들어내다 usage 이용 costly 돈이 많이 드는 demolish 철거하다

53 Where most likely does the man work?

(A) At an energy station
(B) At a training company
(C) At an advertising firm
(D) At a manufacturing plant

남자는 어디에서 일할 것 같은가?

(A) 에너지 충전소
(B) 교육 회사
(C) 광고 회사
(D)제조 공장

54 Why does the man say he requested a consultation?

(A) Some members of staff need retraining.
(B) An expense has become too costly.
(C) A building needs to be demolished.
(D) Some equipment needs to be replaced.

남자는 왜 상담을 요청했다고 말하는가?

(A) 직원들 중 일부는 재교육이 필요하다.
(B)비용이 너무 높아졌다.
(C) 건물이 철거되어야 한다.
(D) 일부 장비가 교체되어야 한다.

55 What does the woman suggest doing first?

(A) Analyzing a process
(B) Relocating to a different plant
(C) Moving some manufacturing equipment
(D) Creating a budget

여자가 처음에 제안하는 것은?

(A)과정 분석
(B) 다른 공장으로 이전
(C) 제조 장비 옮기기
(D) 예산 세우기

Questions 56-58 refer to the following conversation. 미W 미M

W Hey, Brad, I'm glad you're finally here. I can't access the Internet, and I have an e-mail I need to send by 3 o'clock. Could you please help me out?

M No problem. Let me have a look. Ah, you're connected to the wrong network. You have to use the one named "real-time-connection."

W **Is that all?** It kept asking for a password, and I couldn't figure out why, since the office computers all connect automatically. How can I fix it?

M Do you see this icon? Click on that, and then click on "real-time-connection." That's all you should do. You're now online.

여 브래드, 드디어 당신을 찾았군요. 3시까지 보내야 할 이메일이 있는데 인터넷에 연결이 안 됩니다. 좀 도와주시겠어요?

남 그럼요. 한번 볼게요. 아, 잘못된 네트워크에 연결했네요. "실시간 접속"이라는 이름을 사용해야 해요.

여 **그것 뿐이에요?** 계속 비밀번호를 묻는데 도저히 왜 그런 것인지 알 수가 없었어요. 사무실 컴퓨터는 모두 자동으로 연결되잖아요. 어떻게 고쳐야 하나요?

남 이 아이콘 보이죠? 그걸 누른 다음에 "실시간 접속"을 눌러 보세요. 그렇게만 하면 되요. 이제 연결되었어요.

access 접속하다 figure out 생각해내다, 알아내다 automatically 자동적으로

56 What is the man asked to do?
(A) Provide a new password
(B) Assist with getting online
(C) Help writing an e-mail
(D) Analyze some data

남자는 무엇을 요청받고 있는가?
(A) 새로운 비밀번호를 제공하는 것
(B) 인터넷 접속을 도와주는 것
(C) 이메일 작성을 돕는 것
(D) 몇몇 자료를 분석하는 것

57 What was the problem?
(A) The computer was broken.
(B) The e-mail address was wrong.
(C) The password had been changed.
(D) The connection was wrong.

무엇이 문제였는가?
(A) 컴퓨터가 고장 났다.
(B) 이메일 주소가 잘못되었다.
(C) 비밀번호가 바뀌었다.
(D) 연결이 잘못되었다.

58 Why does the woman say, "Is that all"?
(A) She found an e-mail address.
(B) She understood the problem.
(C) She fixed the laptop.
(D) She had to restart the computer.

여자가 "그것 뿐이에요?"라고 말한 이유는 무엇인가?
(A) 이메일 주소를 찾았다.
(B) 문제점을 이해했다.
(C) 노트북을 수리했다.
(D) 컴퓨터를 다시 시작해야 한다.

Questions 59-61 refer to the following conversation. 미M 미W

M Hello, this is Nayan Patel calling. I rented an industrial tool from your store two weeks ago and yesterday I received an e-mail message from one of your staff telling me that I have to pay a 20 pound excess. I think there's an error.

W Well, let me see. I just accessed your account, and it seems that the power drill was returned without the drill accessories. We charge a 20 pound replacement fee if the drill parts are not returned with the item.

M But I'm sure I put them in. I placed all the accessories in the original box which was checked when I gave the tool back.

W Okay, well I'm not saying you didn't, sir. But I don't have the authority to cancel the fee, only a manager can do that. So let me ask my supervisor to sort it out for you.

남 안녕하세요, 나얀 파텔입니다. 2주 전에 당신의 매장에서 산업 도구를 빌렸는데, 어제 당신의 직원들 중 한 명에게서 20파운드의 초과 요금을 내야 한다는 이메일을 받았습니다. 제 생각엔 실수가 있었던 것 같습니다.

여 음, 한번 확인해 보죠. 방금 당신의 계정에 접속했는데, 전기 드릴이 드릴 부속품 없이 반환되었던 것으로 보이네요. 저희는 드릴 부속품이 제품과 함께 반환되지 않으면 대체 비용으로 20파운드를 청구합니다.

남 하지만 전 그것들을 같이 넣었다고 확신합니다. 도구를 돌려줄 때 확인했던 원래의 상자에 모든 부속품들을 넣었습니다.

여 알겠습니다. 당신이 그러지 않았다고 말하는 것은 아니에요. 하지만 저는 그 비용을 취소할 권한이 없고, 오직 관리자가 할 수 있어요. 그러니 관리자에게 이 문제를 해결하도록 요청해 보겠습니다.

rent 빌리다; 고용하다 industrial tool 산업 도구 excess 초과량[액] access 접근하다, 접속하다 account 계정; 계좌 power drill 전기 드릴 accessory 부속품 replacement 교체, 대체 fee 비용 place 놓다 give back 돌려주다 authority 권한 supervisor 감독관, 관리자 sort out 해결하다 invoice 송장 component 요소, 부품 authorization 허가, 인가 waive 포기하다

59 Why is the man calling?
(A) He thinks an excess charge is wrong.
(B) He did not receive an invoice.
(C) Some drill parts are missing.
(D) He wants a newer component.

남자가 전화를 하고 있는 이유는?
(A) 그는 추가 요금 청구가 잘못되었다고 생각한다.
(B) 그는 송장을 받지 못했다.
(C) 몇몇 드릴 부품들이 분실되었다.
(D) 그는 더 새로운 부품을 원한다.

60 What does the woman say is missing?
(A) Some tool components
(B) A credit card authorization
(C) Correct contact details
(D) The original packaging

여자는 무엇이 분실되었다고 말하는가?
(A) 어떤 도구의 부품
(B) 신용 카드의 승인
(C) 올바른 연락 정보
(D) 원래의 포장

61 What does the woman say her supervisor can do?
(A) Waive a fee
(B) Locate a replacement
(C) Change a booking
(D) Review a product

여자는 그녀의 관리자가 무엇을 해 줄 수 있다고 말하는가?
(A) 요금 취소하기
(B) 교체 상품 찾기
(C) 예약 변경하기
(D) 제품 검토하기

Questions 62-64 refer to the following conversation. 영W 미M

W Wayne, Jenx Chemicals just emailed an urgent request for changes to the synthetic rubber manufacturing equipment. We have to dispatch their revised product machinery by midday on Monday. That's in 3 days. I trust we can come to the factory to work extra hours over the weekend.
M I can work overtime, but I already have other plans in the daytime over the weekend. Could I work late in the evenings, instead?
W No problem. I'll organize the security team to open the factory from 7 P.M. every evening over the weekend so that engineers can work late.

여 웨인, 젱스 화학 회사가 합성 고무 제조 장비의 변경을 긴급 요청하는 이메일을 보내 왔어요. 우리는 월요일 오전까지 그들의 수정된 기기 제품을 보내야 합니다. 그건 3일 후입니다. 우리가 잔업을 하기 위해 주말에 공장에 올 수 있다고 믿어요.
남 저는 잔업을 할 수는 있지만, 주말 동안 낮에는 이미 다른 계획이 있어요. 대신 저녁에 일해도 될까요?
여 문제없습니다. 엔지니어들이 늦게 일을 할 수 있도록 매일 저녁 오후 7시에 공장문을 열어 두는 보안팀을 준비시킬게요.

chemicals 화학약품 urgent 긴급한 synthetic 합성한, 인조의 rubber 고무 manufacturing equipment 제조 장비 dispatch 보내다, 발송하다 revised 수정된 machinery 기기 midday 오전 work extra hours 잔업을 하다 work overtime 시간 외 근무를 하다, 잔업을 하다 commitment 약속

62 According to the woman, what has Jenx Chemicals requested?
(A) A reduced price
(B) An extended deadline
(C) An emergency meeting
(D) A revised product

여자에 따르면, 젱스 화학 회사는 무엇을 요청했는가?
(A) 할인된 가격
(B) 연장된 마감일
(C) 긴급회의
(D) 수정된 제품

63 What problem does the man mention?
(A) His team is not available.
(B) He does not have the required skills.
(C) He has prior commitments.
(D) The factory is closed.

남자가 언급한 문제점은?
(A) 그의 팀은 시간이 되지 않는다.
(B) 필요한 기술이 없다.
(C) 선약이 있다.
(D) 공장이 문을 닫았다.

64 What does the woman say she will arrange?
(A) New equipment for workers
(B) Free transport for employees
(C) Access to work areas
(D) Training for temporary workers

여자는 무엇을 준비하겠다고 말하는가?
(A) 작업자들을 위한 새로운 장비
(B) 직원들을 위한 무료 교통수단
(C) 작업 구역으로의 접근
(D) 임시 직원들을 위한 교육

Questions 65-67 refer to the following conversation and chart. 미W 미M

Sales of Flooring Materials

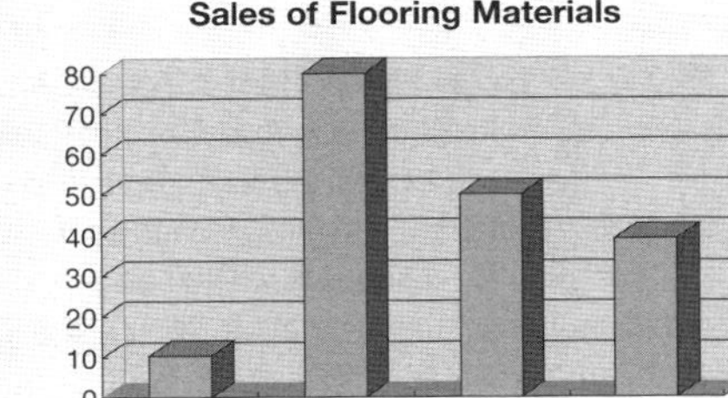

W Thank you for coming, Bruce. Did you bring the chart of last month's sales?
M Yes, here's a copy. As you can see, hardwood flooring is the best-selling material in our store. So I think we should start selling other types of wood flooring, such as bamboo.
W Bamboo flooring? I don't know much about it. Do you think our customers will like it?
M Definitely. It is much like hardwood flooring, which has proved to be popular, and it is an eco-friendly option. So I think many people will buy it.
W Okay, Let's try selling bamboo flooring. By the way, this material has been a bad seller for the last 6 months. What do you think is the problem?
M Well, I'm not sure. I just assume that many people are looking for something new for their homes these days.
W Could you conduct a survey to find out why this material is not selling well?

바닥재 판매

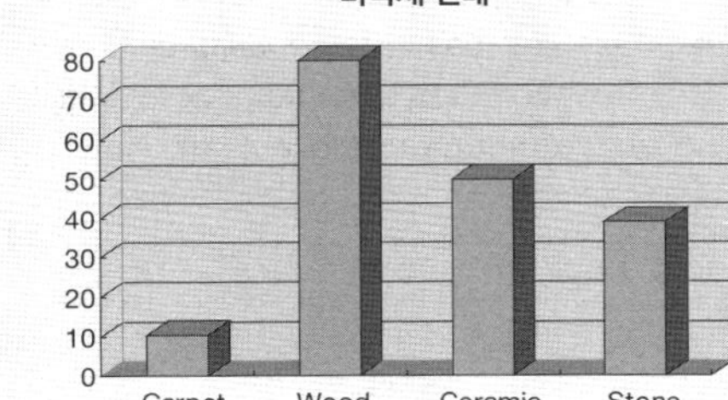

여 와 주셔서 감사합니다, 브루스. 지난달 판매 차트는 가져 오셨나요?
남 네, 여기 한 부 있습니다. 보시다시피, 우리 가게에서 제일 잘 팔리는 재질은 강화 나무 바닥입니다. 그래서 대나무와 같은 다른 종류의 나무 바닥재의 판매를 시작하는 게 좋을 것 같아요
여 대나무 바닥재요? 전 그것에 대해서는 잘 몰라서요. 우리 고객들이 좋아할까요?
남 당연합니다. 이미 인기가 증명된 강화 나무 바닥재와 비슷하면서 친환경적 제품입니다. 그래서 많은 사람들이 구매할 것 같습니다.
여 좋아요. 대나무 바닥재를 팔아 보도록 하죠. 그나저나 이 재질은 지난 6개월 동안 판매가 저조하군요. 뭐가 문제인가요?
남 음, 잘 모르겠습니다. 제 추측으로는 많은 사람들이 최근에는 집에 놓을 뭔가 새로운 것을 원하는 것 같습니다.
여 이 제품이 왜 잘 안 팔리는지 고객 설문 조사를 진행해 주시겠어요?

hardwood flooring 강화 나무 바닥재 bamboo 대나무 eco-friendly 친환경적인 a bad seller 잘 안 팔리는 제품 conduct a survey 설문 조사를 하다

65 Which material is the best seller in the store?
(A) Carpet
(B) Bamboo
(C) Hardwood
(D) Ceramic

어떤 재질이 이 가게에서 가장 잘 팔리는가?
(A) 카페트
(B) 대나무
(C) 강화 나무
(D) 세라믹

66 Look at the graphic. Which material will the man investigate?
(A) Carpet
(B) Wood
(C) Ceramic
(D) Stone

시각 정보를 보시오. 남자는 어떤 재질을 조사할 것인가?
(A) 카펫
(B) 나무
(C) 세라믹
(D) 돌

67 What does the man mention about bamboo flooring?
(A) It is easy to clean.
(B) It is environmentally friendly.
(C) It is affordable.
(D) It is durable.

대나무 바닥재에 대해서 남자는 무엇을 언급하는가?
(A) 청소가 쉽다.
(B) 친환경적이다.
(C) 가격이 적절하다.
(D) 내구성이 좋다.

Questions 68-70 refer to the following conversation and table.
미M 영W

MENU		
Item	Tray for 20	Each Additional Tray
Greek Salad	$100	$50
BBQ Tacos	$200	$150

M So, how are the preparations for the office party going? It's in three days from now.
W Well, everything is set except for the catering order. I emailed everybody in our department, requesting RSVP by the 21st, which was yesterday. However, only half of them have replied so far. 20 people have confirmed they will be attending so I just placed a catering order for one tray of Greek salad and one tray of BBQ tacos, which will cost us $300 in total.
M Oh, but I'm sure there will be more than 30 of us at the party. Why don't you order another tray of BBQ tacos?
W Okay. We can actually get a discount on the second tray. I'll call the caterer to add the item to our order and ask for a revised price estimate.

메뉴		
품목	20인분 트레이	추가 트레이
그리스식 샐러드	100달러	50달러
BBQ 타코	200달러	150달러

남 그래서 사무실 파티 준비는 어떻게 진행이 되고 있나요? 이제 3일 밖에 남지 않았어요.
여 음, 출장 뷔페 주문 외에는 모두 준비가 되었습니다. 부서 사람들 모두에게 어제인 21일까지 참석 여부를 알려 달라는 이메일을 보냈습니다. 그렇지만 현재까지 절반만 답장을 주었어요. 20명이 참석을 확인해 주었기 때문에 그리스식 샐러드 트레이 하나와 BBQ 타코 트레이 하나를 주문하였고 총 300달러가 들 예정입니다
남 아, 그런데 파티에는 30명 이상은 확실히 올 거예요. BBQ 타코 트레이를 하나 더 주문하는 게 어떨까요?
여 알겠습니다. 실은 두 번째 트레이는 할인을 받을 수 있어요. 지금 업체에 전화해서 그 품목을 추가하고 수정된 가격 견적서를 요청하겠습니다.

reply 답장하다 confirm 확인하다 tray 쟁반 revised 수정된

estimate 견적서

68 What problem does the woman mention?
(A) A rain shower is forecast.
(B) Not many people have replied.
(C) A supplier has raised its prices.
(D) A restaurant does not accept reservations.

여자는 어떤 문제점을 언급하는가?
(A) 소나기가 예보되었다.
(B) 많은 사람들이 답을 하지 않았다.
(C) 공급업체가 가격을 올렸다.
(D) 레스토랑이 예약을 받지 않는다.

69 What will the woman probably do next?
(A) Contact a catering company
(B) Pay a bill
(C) Call a party planner
(D) Cancel an event

여자는 다음에 무엇을 할 것 같은가?
(A) 출장 뷔페 업체에 연락하기
(B) 청구서의 돈을 지불하기
(C) 파티 플래너에게 전화하기
(D) 이벤트 취소하기

70 Look at the graphic. How much is it for the entire catering order?
(A) $100
(B) $200
(C) $300
(D) $450

시각 정보를 보시오. 전체 출장 뷔페 주문은 얼마인가?
(A) 100달러
(B) 200달러
(C) 300달러
(D) 450달러

Part 4

Questions 71-73 refer to the following excerpt from a meeting. 미W

And to conclude, as I'm sure you are aware, the organization has begun an energy saving scheme. Every member of staff should ensure that all lights are switched off when the office is vacant or in the hours of daylight. Our maintenance manager, Peter Bow, has stated that if we all adhere to this rule, we can save the organization up to 15,000 dollars every six months in energy and material costs.

마무리 짓자면, 당신은 이미 알고 있으리라 확신하지만, 회사는 에너지 절약 정책을 시작했습니다. 모든 직원들은 사무실이 비어 있거나 시간이 대낮일 때, 모든 사무실 불의 스위치가 꺼져 있는지 확실히 해야 합니다. 우리의 유지 보수 관리자인 피터 보우는 우리가 이 규칙을 엄수하면, 회사의 에너지 비용과 자재 비용을 6개월마다 최대 15,000달러까지 절약할 수 있다고 말했습니다.

conclude 마치다, 끝내다 aware 알고 있다, 인지하고 있다 energy saving 에너지 절약 ensure 확실히 하다 switch off 스위치를 끄다 vacant 비어 있는 daylight 대낮 state 말하다, 언급하다 adhere to the rule 규칙을 엄수하다, 법을 준수하다 material 자재, 재료 conserve 아끼다, 아껴 쓰다 accountant 회계사 administrator 관리자 expenditure 지출, 경비

71 What are listeners encouraged to do?
(A) Conserve energy
(B) Work in daylight
(C) Share office space
(D) Reduce the cost of living

청자들은 무엇을 하도록 권장되는가?
(A) 에너지 아껴 쓰기
(B) 대낮에 일하기
(C) 사무실 공간 공유하기
(D) 생활비 줄이기

72 Who is Peter Bow?
(A) A lighting expert
(B) An accountant
(C) An office administrator
(D) A maintenance manager

피터 보우는 누구인가?
(A) 조명 기사
(B) 회계사
(C) 사무 관리자
(D) 유지 보수 관리자

73 According to the speaker, why is the change being made?
(A) To reduce energy expenditure
(B) To promote recycling practices
(C) To help employees
(D) To recruit staff

화자에 따르면, 변화가 일어나는 이유는?
(A) 에너지 경비를 줄이기 위해
(B) 재활용 실천을 홍보하기 위해
(C) 직원들을 돕기 위해
(D) 직원을 모집하기 위해

Questions 74-76 refer to the following advertisement. 미M

This fall, science researchers at the Slumberland Corporation are seeking participants to take part in a survey about the negative aspects of too much sleep. Head researcher, Dr. Asim Choudhry, says that for three months, volunteers will be asked to sleep for a minimum of twelve hours a day. During this time, participants will also be expected to live at the Corporation's company housing where researchers can monitor their progress. If you're interested in taking part, you can go to www.slumberland.com to take an online test and submit an application form.

이번 가을, 슬럼버랜드 사의 학술 연구원들은 지나치게 많은 수면의 부정적인 측면에 관한 설문조사에 참여할 분들을 찾고 있습니다. 수석 연구원인 아심 쵸드리 박사는 3개월 동안 지원자들이 하루에 최소 12시간을 자도록 요구받을 것이라고 말합니다. 또한, 이 시기 동안 참여자들은 연구원들이 그들의 진행 과정을 감시할 수 있는 회사의 사택에서 생활할 것이 요구될 것입니다. 만약 당신이 참여하는 것에 관심이 있다면, 당신은 온라인 시험을 치르고 지원서를 제출하기 위해 www.slumberland.com으로 가시면 됩니다.

science researcher 과학 연구원, 학술 연구원 corporation 기업 seek 찾다 participant 참여자 take part in ~에 참여하다 survey 설문조사 aspect 측면 head researcher 수석 연구원 company house 사택 monitor 감시하다 progress 진행과정 take a test 시험을 치르다 application form 지원서 insomnia 불면증 suitability test 적성검사 in person 직접

74 What is the topic of the study?
(A) How to beat insomnia
(B) The health effects of sleep patterns
(C) Better ways to exercise
(D) Sleeping in a strange environment

연구의 주제는?
(A) 불면증을 이겨내는 방법
(B) 수면 패턴의 건강 효과
(C) 더 좋은 운동 방법
(D) 낯선 환경에서 수면하기

75 How long will the study last?
(A) For 2 months
(B) For 3 months
(C) For 6 months
(D) For a year

연구는 얼마나 지속될 것인가?
(A) 2개월
(B) 3개월
(C) 6개월
(D) 1년

76 What will volunteers be required to do according to the passage?
(A) Take a suitability test at the university
(B) Reside much of their time at the center
(C) Submit an application form in person
(D) Monitor their own progress through surveys

지문에 따르면 지원자들은 무엇을 하도록 요구받는가?
(A) 대학에서 적성검사 받기
(B) 센터에서 많은 시간 거주하기
(C) 지원서 직접 제출하기
(D) 설문을 통해 각자의 진행 과정 감독하기

Questions 77-79 refer to the following telephone message. (영W)

Hi, Mr. Chang. This is Akai Junipe from the customer resource department at Preston. I note that you messaged us with your worries about our possible takeover by General Vehicle emporium. I just wanted to let you know that your car leasing agreement will not alter even if we merge with GV in future. Until this happens, all week long we will be answering all questions about the matter on our online forum. I hope you get the opportunity to check it out. Thank you for your call. We appreciate your concern.

안녕하세요, 창 씨. 저는 프레스턴 고객 자원부의 아카이 쥬니페입니다. 귀하께서 제너럴 비히클 상점에 의한 가능성 있는 인수에 관한 우려를 메시지로 남긴 것으로 알고 있습니다. 저는 다만 우리가 미래에 GV와 합병을 한다 하더라도 당신의 자동차 임대 계약은 변경 사항이 없을 것이라고 알려 드리고 싶었습니다. 이와 같은 사항이 발생할 때까지, 일주일 내내 우리는 저희 온라인 포럼의 문제에 관한 모든 질문에 답변할 것입니다. 확인해 주시기 바랍니다. 전화 주셔서 감사합니다. 귀하의 관심에 감사합니다.

note 주목하다, 유의하다; 알아차리다 takeover 인수하다 general 일반적인 emporium 큰 상점 leasing agreement 임대[임차] 계약 alter 변하다, 변경하다 merge 합병하다 in future 미래에, 앞날에 forum 포럼, (토론의) 장 check out 확인하다 appreciate 고마워하다 concern 우려, 염려 allay 가라앉히다 fleet 무리 pharmaceutical 제약의

77 What is the purpose of the message?
(A) To allay a customer's worries
(B) To confirm a shipment address
(C) To advertise a fleet of cars
(D) To announce a company change

메시지의 목적은?
(A) 손님의 우려를 진정시키기 위해
(B) 배송지를 확인하기 위해
(C) 한 집단의 차들을 홍보하기 위해
(D) 회사의 변경 사항을 발표하기 위해

78 What kind of company is Preston?
(A) A construction firm
(B) An Internet provider
(C) A pharmaceutical company
(D) A car rental service

프레스턴은 어떤 종류의 회사인가?
(A) 건설회사
(B) 인터넷 제공업체
(C) 제약 회사
(D) 자동차 대여 서비스

79 According to the speaker, what will Preston do this week?
(A) Merge with a competitor
(B) Open a new branch
(C) Send a letter to customers
(D) Answer questions on a Web site

화자에 따르면, 프레스턴은 이번 주에 무엇을 할 것인가?
(A) 경쟁업체와 합병
(B) 새 지사 개장
(C) 고객들에게 편지 보내기
(D) 웹 사이트의 질문에 답변하기

Questions 80-82 refer to the following excerpt from a meeting. 미M

First, I'd like to talk about the new recycling policies. We've recently changed recycling companies to Ever Green Recycling Inc. With the previous company we had to use 5 different bins, and many of you did not appreciate the fact that those bins were taking up a lot of office space. **But it's going to be different with the new company.** Now, you can put all the recyclable materials into one container. But please make sure you put only recyclable materials into the bin. If you're not sure whether or not a material can be recycled, please check the list of recyclable materials, which is posted on the wall in the lobby.

첫 번째로 저는 새로운 재활용 방침에 대해서 이야기하고 싶습니다. 우리는 최근에 재활용 업체를 에버 그린 리사이클링으로 바꾸었습니다. 이전 회사와는 5개의 다른 재활용 용기를 이용해야 했었고, 여러분 중 다수가 그 용기들이 사무실 공간을 많이 차지한다는 점에 대해서 좋아하지 않았습니다. **그러나 새 회사에서는 다를 것입니다.** 이제 한 개의 통에 모든 재활용이 가능한 물건을 넣을 수 있게 되었습니다. 반드시 재활용이 가능한 물건만 용기 안에 넣어 주세요. 어떤 물건이 재활용 가능한 것인지 확실하지 않은 경우, 로비의 벽에 붙어 있는 공지에서 재활용 가능 물품의 명단을 확인해 주십시오.

recycling procedures 재활용 절차 previous 이전의 bin 용기, 통 take up (공간을) 차지하다 container 용기, 통 material 물질, 재질, 물건 recyclable 재활용 할 수 있는

80 What change has the company recently made?
(A) It has adopted a strict recycling policy.
(B) It has moved to a more spacious office.
(C) It has replaced a service provider.
(D) It has hired additional employees.

회사는 최근에 무엇을 변경했는가?
(A) 엄격한 재활용 정책을 채택했다.
(B) 더 넓은 사무실로 이전했다.
(C) 서비스 제공 업체를 교체했다.
(D) 추가 직원을 고용했다.

81 What does the speaker mean when he says, "But it's going to be different with the new company"?
(A) Uncomfortable furniture will be replaced.
(B) Problems regarding insufficient office space will be resolved.
(C) The company will purchase new office equipment.
(D) Employees will not need to do paperwork.

화자가 "그러나 새 회사에서는 다를 것입니다"라고 말한 의미는 무엇인가?
(A) 불편한 가구가 교체될 것이다.
(B) 부족한 사무실 공간에 관한 문제점이 해결될 것이다.
(C) 회사는 새 사무 기기를 구매할 것이다.
(D) 직원들은 문서 업무를 할 필요가 없을 것이다.

82 What are listeners encouraged to do?
(A) Read a list
(B) E-mail a supplier
(C) Conserve paper
(D) Work overtime

청자들은 무엇을 하라고 권고되는가?
(A) 목록 읽기
(B) 공급자에게 이메일 보내기
(C) 종이 아껴 쓰기
(D) 시간 외 근무하기

Questions 83-85 refer to the following talk. 영W

I want to simplify a few issues about the company's discount rules. Your discount will be applied only if the goods are reduced for resale. So if you are interested in an item, always remember to get approval from your manager at the latest 3 days after the goods are returned. Then, if your item is available, it will be your responsibility to sort out all paperwork. If you don't provide proof of the item being returned to your manager, the company won't allow you a discount.

저는 회사의 할인 정책에 관한 몇몇 사안을 간소화하고 싶습니다. 귀하의 할인은 상품이 재판매로 할인되었을 때에만 적용될 것입니다. 그러니 상품에 관심이 있다면, 상품이 반품된 후로 늦어도 3일이 지나기 전까지 관리자에게 승인받는 것을 기억하세요. 그 다음, 만약 상품이 이용 가능하다면 모든 서류 작업을 정리하는 것은 당신의 책임입니다. 만약 귀하가 관리자에게 상품 반품 증거를 제공하지 못하면, 회사는 할인을 허용하지 않을 것입니다.

simplify 간소화하다, 간단하게 만들다 goods 상품 resale 재판매 approval 승인, 허가 at the latest 늦어도 sort out 정리하다 paperwork 서류 작업 clarify 명확하게 하다 achievement 업적, 성취 clarify 명확히 하다 revise 수정하다 recruitment 채용 up front 선불로

83 What is the purpose of the talk?
(A) To clarify weekly sales achievements
(B) To explain a company policy
(C) To revise budget plans
(D) To describe the recruitment process

담화의 목적은?
(A) 주간 판매 성과를 밝히기 위해
(B) 사내 정책을 설명하기 위해
(C) 예산 계획을 수정하기 위해
(D) 채용 모집 과정을 설명하기 위해

84 What are employees reminded to do in advance?
(A) Prepare necessary paperwork
(B) Request customer approval
(C) Pay for items up front
(D) Check the cost of items

직원들이 미리 하도록 상기되는 것은?
(A) 필요한 서류 작업 준비하기
(B) 고객의 승인 요청하기
(C) 상품값 선불하기
(D) 상품들의 가격 확인하기

85 What are employees asked to provide?
(A) Expense application forms
(B) Contact information
(C) Copies of receipts
(D) Proof of returned items

직원들은 무엇을 제공하도록 요구받는가?
(A) 비용 신청서
(B) 연락처
(C) 영수증 사본
(D) 반품 상품의 증거

Questions 86-88 refer to the following announcement. 미W

If you are in the vicinity of the Shipman Theater tomorrow, make sure to drop by to see the International Garden Festival. This year's focus is on "Gardens of The Future", by well-known Swiss landscape architect, Jean Paul Glisson, who has designed the main feature in the display. His creation is expected to be the most viewed attraction. In a 200 meter long garden space, he has revolutionized the use of traditional materials. Utilizing glass cloches and plastic decking rather than timber, his garden displays two differing outdoor options and visitors are invited to vote for which one they prefer.

만약 여러분이 내일 시프먼 극장 근처에 계시면, 국제 정원 축제에 들러 보도록 하세요. 올해의 초점은 전시회에서 주요 특집을 제작한, 유명한 스위스 조경사인 장 폴 글리슨에 의한 〈미래의 정원〉입니다. 그의 작품은 가장 많이 관람될 것으로 예상됩니다. 200미터 길이의 긴 정원 공간에서, 그는 전통적인 자재의 사용에 대변혁을 일으켰습니다. 유리로 만들어진 종 모양 식물 덮개와 목재가 아닌 플라스틱 마룻장을 이용한 그의 정원은 서로 다른 두 가지 야외 선택권을 보여 주며, 방문객들은 그들이 어느 쪽을 선호하는지 투표하도록 초대받습니다.

vicinity 근처, 부근 well-known 잘 알려진, 유명한 landscape architect 조경사 feature 특집; 특징 display 전시회; 전시하다, 보여 주다 creation 창작물, 작품 attraction (사람을 끄는) 명소, 명물 revolutionize 혁신을 일으키다 material 자재, 자료 utilize 활용하다 cloche (어린 식물 보호용으로 씌우는) 종 모양 덮개 decking 마룻장 timber 목재 differing 상이한, 다른 vote 투표하다 architectural 건축의 enthusiast 열광적인 팬 official 공무원 preference 선호

86 What is the theme of the exhibition?
(A) Modern architectural technology
(B) Use of traditional materials
(C) Plastic manufacturing in Switzerland
(D) Gardens of the future

전시회의 테마는?
(A) 현대 건축 기술
(B) 전통 재료의 사용
(C) 스위스의 플라스틱 제조업
(D) 미래의 정원

87 Who is Jean Paul Glisson?
(A) An outdoor enthusiast
(B) An architect
(C) An exhibition official
(D) A landscape architect

장 폴 글리슨은 누구인가?
(A) 야외 활동파
(B) 건축가
(C) 전시회 관리인
(D) 조경사

88 What are visitors invited to do?
(A) Indicate a preference
(B) Take a brochure
(C) Ask for an estimate
(D) Take photographs

방문객들은 무엇을 하라고 요청받는가?
(A) 선호도 밝히기
(B) 책자 받기
(C) 견적 요청하기
(D) 사진 찍기

Questions 89-91 refer to the following telephone message. 미M

Hi, Frank! This is Aaron. I'm calling because I have a favor to ask of you. Our department is planning a training workshop on the new accounting software for all of our accounting members on Monday. They need to learn how to build spreadsheets and charts using the software. Originally Katey was going to lead the session, but she in the hospital now from a car accident. So I'd really like you to take her place. I know it's on short notice, but you know the program better than anyone else. Please call me back and let me know if you can do it. In the meantime, I'll email you a copy of the training agenda. So you have an idea as to which of the software's capabilities to focus on during the training. Thank you.

안녕하세요, 프랭크! 아론입니다. 부탁할 게 있어서 전화드립니다. 저희 부서는 월요일에 회계부서 직원들을 위해서 새로운 회계 소프트웨어에 관한 교육 워크숍을 진행하려고 합니다. 그들은 소프트웨어를 이용해서 스프레드시트와 도표 만드는 방법을 배워야 하거든요. 원래는, 케이티가 세션을 진행하려고 했으나 자동차 사고로 인해 병원에 입원을 했어요. 그래서 당신이 그녀의 자리를 대신해주길 바랍니다. 갑작스럽다는 것은 알지만, 당신이 누구보다도 그 프로그램에 대해서 더 잘 알고 있어서요. 그렇게 하실 수 있는지 저에게 답신 전화를 주세요. 그동안 교육 목록을 이메일로 보내겠습니다. 교육 중에 어떤 소프트웨어 기능에 집중해야 할지 알 수 있을 것입니다. 감사합니다.

originally 원래 take one's place ~의 자리를 대신하다 short notice 촉박한 통보 in the meantime 그동안에 as to ~에 관해서 capability 기능

89 What is the topic of the training session?
(A) Online references
(B) Web design
(C) Computer software
(D) Home building

교육의 주제는 무엇인가?
(A) 온라인 참고 자료
(B) 웹 디자인
(C) 컴퓨터 소프트웨어
(D) 주택 건설

90 What does the speaker mean when he says, "So I'd really like you to take her place"?
(A) There was a computer malfunction.
(B) Some equipment needs to be installed.
(C) He wants the listener to lead a workshop.
(D) The listener needs to meet a deadline.

화자가 "그래서 당신이 그녀의 자리를 대신해주길 바랍니다"라고 말한 의미는 무엇인가?
(A) 컴퓨터 오작동이 있다.
(B) 장비가 설치되어야 한다.
(C) 청자가 워크숍을 진행하기를 원한다.
(D) 청자는 마감을 맞춰야 한다.

91 What will the caller probably do next?
(A) Send an agenda
(B) Visit a hospital
(C) Plan an event
(D) Call tech support

전화를 건 사람은 다음에 무엇을 할 것 같은가?
(A) 목록 보내기
(B) 병원 방문하기
(C) 행사 기획하기
(D) 기술 지원팀에 전화하기

Questions 92-94 refer to the following message and schedule.
미W

Meeting Schedule	
Kali Hawk	10:00 A.M.
Hank Harris	11:00 A.M.
Alexandra Park	1:00 P.M.
Shawn Smith	2:00 P.M.

Hi, it is Alexandra Park. Congratulations on your promotion, Shawn. We're really looking forward to having you on our production development team. You've probably had a chance to look at the meeting schedule I sent to you by now. But there have been some changes made to it. Originally, Kali Hawk's presentation was scheduled for 10 in the morning and Hank's presentation for 11 A.M. However, they've both agreed to push back their presentations to the afternoon so that I can give you an update on the products we're currently developing in the morning first. After that, I'll introduce you to the team and you can say a few words before lunch. After the lunch break, Kali will present our next product launch at 1 o'clock. And Hank's presentation will follow after that. If you have any questions, please call me at any time. I'll see you on Monday.

회의 일정	
칼리 호크	오전 10시
행크 해리스	오전 11시
알렉산드라 파크	오후 1시
숀 스미스	오후 2시

안녕하세요, 저는 알렉산드라 파크입니다. 승진을 축하합니다, 숀. 저희 상품 개발팀에 합류하게 되어서 정말 기대가 됩니다. 지금쯤이면 제가 보내드린 미팅 스케줄을 보셨을 것 같습니다. 그런데 몇 가지 변경 사항이 생겼습니다. 원래는 칼리 호크의 발표가 오전 10시에 잡혀 있었고 행크의 발표가 11시였습니다. 그러나, 그들 둘 다 오후로 발표를 미뤄주기로 합의를 했어요, 제가 아침에 먼저 우리가 작업 중인 상품들에 대해 보고를 해드릴 수 있도록요. 그 이후에, 제가 당신을 팀원들에게 소개할 것이고 점심 전에 짧게 한 말씀 해주시면 됩니다. 점심 시간 후에, 칼리가 1시에 다음 상품 출시에 대해 발표를 할 것이고 행크의 발표가 그 뒤를 따를 것입니다. 질문이 있으시면, 저에게 언제든 전화 주세요. 월요일에 뵙겠습니다.

congratulations on ~을 축하하다 look forward to ~을 기대하다 have a chance to ~할 기회를 갖다 originally 원래는 push back ~을 미루다 product launch 상품 출시

92 Why is the speaker congratulating Shawn?
(A) He has won an award.
(B) He has met a deadline.
(C) He has developed a new product.
(D) He has been promoted at work.

화자는 왜 숀에게 축하를 하는가?
(A) 그는 상을 받았다.
(B) 그는 마감을 맞췄다.
(C) 그는 신상품을 개발했다.
(D) 그는 직장에서 승진되었다.

93 Look at the graphic. According to the revised schedule, who will give a presentation at 2 P.M. on Monday?
(A) Kali Hawk
(B) Hank Harris
(C) Alexandra Park
(D) Shawn Smith

시각 정보를 보시오. 바뀐 스케줄에 따르면 누가 월요일 오후 2시에 발표를 할 것인가?
(A) 칼리 호크
(B) 행크 해리스
(C) 알렉산드라 파크
(D) 숀 스미스

94 What is the topic of Kali's presentation?
(A) A marketing strategy
(B) A product launch
(C) A new advertisement
(D) A product budget

칼리의 발표 주제는 무엇인가?
(A) 마케팅 전략
(B) 상품 출시
(C) 새 광고
(D) 상품 예산

Questions 95-97 refer to the following talk and directory. 영W

Employee Directory	
Name	Extension
Winona Brown	09
Kathryn Newton	19
Annette Heaton	21
Mckenna Grace	45

Hello, Brad. This is Winona Brown calling from the payroll department. I've read your e-mail concerning travel reimbursement. You wanted to know when you're going to get reimbursed for your travel expenses. In order for me to process a reimbursement payment, I need approval from Annette Heaton in accounting. She usually takes care of expense reports and approves the payment as long as there are no problems. So I suggest that you contact Ms. Heaton to see if there are any discrepancies between your expense report and the receipts you submitted. I think she will give you a better explanation than I can provide. You can find her extension number in the employee directory.

직원 전화번호부	
이름	내선 번호
위노나 브라운	09
캐서린 뉴튼	19
아넷 히튼	21
매케나 그레이스	45

안녕하세요 브래드, 저는 급여 정산 부서의 위노나 브라운입니다. 출장비 환급과 관련한 당신의 이메일을 읽었어요. 출장비 환급을 언제 받게 되는지 알고 싶어 하셨죠. 제가 환급금을 처리해 드리기 위해서는 회계부서의 아넷 히튼 씨로부터의 승인이 필요합니다. 그녀가 비용 보고서 업무를 담당하고 문제가 없는 한 지불을 승인해 줍니다. 그러니 당신이 제출한 비용 보고서와 영수증 사이에 불일치하는 것이 있는지 히튼 씨에게 연락해 보실 것을 권고드립니다. 그녀가 저보다는 더 자세한 설명을 해 줄 겁니다. 직원 전화번호부에서 그녀의 내선번호를 찾을 수 있을 겁니다.

payroll department 급여 정산 부서 get reimbursed 환급받다 reimbursement 환급 travel expenses 출장 경비 approval 승인 discrepancy 불일치 receipt 영수증 extension 내선 번호

95 What is the main purpose of the message?
(A) To respond to an inquiry
(B) To request a document
(C) To explain a new policy
(D) To provide contact information

메시지의 주된 목적은 무엇인가?
(A) 문의에 답하려고
(B) 서류를 요청하려고
(C) 새로운 정책을 설명하려고
(D) 연락처를 제공하려고

96 What is mentioned about Annette Heaton?
(A) She is on a business trip.
(B) She runs her own business.
(C) She reviews expense reports.
(D) She works in the payroll department.

아넷 히튼에 대해서 언급된 것은 무엇인가?
(A) 출장 중이다.
(B) 본인의 사업체를 이끈다.
(C) 비용 보고서를 검토한다.
(D) 급여 정산 부서에서 일한다.

97 Look at the graphic. Which extension will the listener probably dial?
(A) 09
(B) 19
(C) 21
(D) 45

시각 정보를 보시오. 청자는 어떤 내선번호로 전화할 것인가?
(A) 09
(B) 19
(C) 21
(D) 45

Questions 98-100 refer to the following talk and chart. 미M

Thank you for attending our first official meeting since I took on the role of sales director at our Company. I'm glad that I have the opportunity to meet you all today. But first, we need to focus on the task at hand. Our last quarter's sales were the lowest ever. And as you can see from the chart, our major competitor ranked first with the largest market share at 40% for the first time last quarter and our company's market share was the second largest. In order to regain our No. 1 soft drink company title, I think we should release our new line of flavored Mojito earlier than scheduled. Originally, they weren't scheduled to come on the market until June 10th. But with increased productivity, we'll be able to move up the release date to May 20th. So everybody, let's do everything we can to make the launch a success.

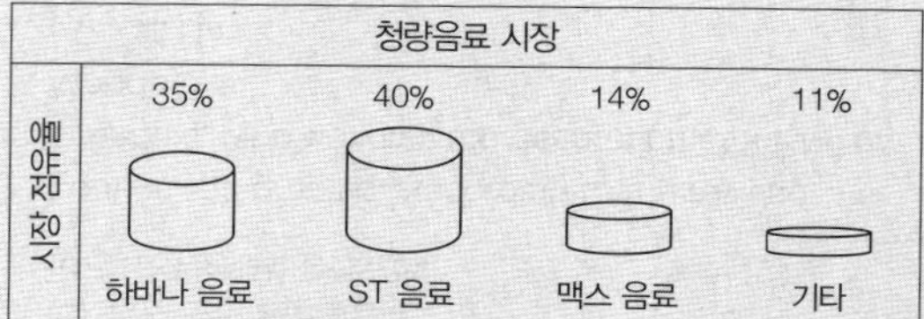

제가 우리 회사에서 영업 부서장을 맡은 후 첫 공식 회의에 참석해 주셔서 감사합니다. 오늘 여러분 모두를 만나게 되어 기쁩니다. 그러나 우선, 당장 급한 업무에 집중할 필요가 있습니다. 지난 분기의 판매는 지금까지 중에서 가장 낮았습니다. 그리고 차트에서 보시다시피, 주요 경쟁사는 지난 분기에 최초로 40퍼센트라는 시장 점유율로 1위를 차지하였고 우리의 시장 점유율은 2위였습니다. 다시 우리의 1위 청량음료 회사라는 타이틀을 되찾기 위해서는, 신상품인 모히토를 예정보다 일찍 출시하는 것이 좋을 것 같습니다. 원래는 6월 10일이 되어야 시장에 나올 예정이었지만 생산력 증가와 함께, 5월 20일로 출시 날짜를 앞당길 수 있을 것 같습니다. 자 여러분, 성공적인 출시를 위해 모든 노력을 기울입시다.

official 공식적인 take on (일, 책임 등을) 맡다 task 업무 at hand 가까운, 급한 competitor 경쟁자, 경쟁사 rank first 1위를 차지하다 market share 시장 점유율 for the first time 최초로 increased productivity 증가된 생산력 move up 앞당기다 release date 출시 날짜 launch 출시

98 Which department does the speaker work in?
(A) Sales
(B) Personnel
(C) Advertising
(D) Product development

화자는 어떤 부서에서 일하는가?
(A) 영업
(B) 인사
(C) 광고
(D) 상품 개발

99 Look at the graphic. How much market share did the man's company have last quarter?
(A) 9%
(B) 16%
(C) 35%
(D) 40%

시각 정보를 보시오. 남자의 회사는 지난 분기에 얼마의 시장 점유율을 보였는가?
(A) 9퍼센트
(B) 16퍼센트
(C) 35퍼센트
(D) 40퍼센트

100 According to the speaker, what will happen on May 20th?
(A) A merger will take place.
(B) The division head will get a promotion.
(C) A new product will be introduced.
(D) Employees will submit proposals.

화자에 따르면, 5월 20일에 무슨 일이 일어날 것인가?
(A) 합병이 일어날 것이다.
(B) 부서장이 승진될 것이다.
(C) 신제품이 소개될 것이다.
(D) 직원들이 제안서를 제출할 것이다.

Part 5

101 **해설** 숫자 앞에 오면서 more와 함께 쓰여 '~ 이상'이라고 쓰는 것은 (D)이다. more than과 같은 의미로 over를 쓸 수 있다. 참고로 숫자 앞에 와서 '거의, 대략'의 의미로 쓰이는 부사에는 nearly, almost, approximately, around, about, roughly가 있고, '최소[대]한, 적어도'라는 의미로 쓰이는 표현은 at least, a minimum[maximum] of 등이 있다.

수술이 3개월 이상 지연된 환자들은 보상을 받을 권리가 있다.

operation 수술 be entitled to ~할 권리가 있다 compensation 보상

102 **해설** 명사 어휘 문제로 문맥상 '이 이메일을 ~하는 즉시 당신이 참석할 수 있는지 알려 주세요'에서 가장 적절한 명사는 (A)이다. 〈upon+명사〉는 '~하자마자, 즉시'라는 의미이다. appear는 동사이므로 명사 자리에 올 수 없다.

이 이메일을 수신하는 즉시 당신이 참석할 수 있는지 제게 알려 주세요.

upon ~하는 즉시 receipt 수령 entry 출전, 참가

103 **해설** 분사구문 문제로 before가 전치사 혹은 부사절 접속사라서 뒤에 올 수 있는 것은 -ing, pp 또는 문장인데 뒤에 목적어가 있으므로 (B)가 정답이다. 과거분사 left는 뒤에 목적어를 쓸 수 없고, leave는 동사이므로 주어 없이 before 뒤에 올 수 없다.

호텔을 떠나기 전, 모든 열쇠를 접수처에 반납해 주세요.

reception 접수처; 연회, 환영회

104 **해설** 빈칸에 들어갈 알맞은 형태를 고르는 문제로 〈be p.p.〉 뒤에 올 수 있는 것은 동사를 수식하는 부사이므로 (A)가 정답이다. successful은 형용사, succeeded는 분사 혹은 동사, success는 명사이므로 동사를 수식할 수 없다.

루이즈 다메즈의 꼼꼼한 작업 덕분에 그 프로젝트는 지연 없이 예산 내에서 성공적으로 완료되었다.

thanks to ~덕에 meticulous 세심한, 꼼꼼한 budget 예산

105 **해설** 선택지를 통해 알맞은 명사를 고르는 문제임을 알 수 있다. 문맥상 '추가된 것, 부가물'이라는 의미의 (B)가 가장 적절하다.

캠피언 휴양지 호텔 리스트는 어느 기관에서든지 환영받는 부가물이 될 것이다.

retreat 휴가 welcome 환영받는 establishment 기관, 시설 output 생산량, 산출량 response 반응 treatment 치료; 대우

106 **해설** 대명사 문제로 give는 4형식 구조로 쓸 수 있는 동사로 a list of the new roster가 직접 목적어이고, 그 앞의 빈칸은 직접 목적어 자리이다. which는 명사절 접속사 혹은 관계대명사이므로 적절하지 않고, themselves는 재귀 대명사로 재귀 대명사가 목적어 자리에 오려면 의미상 주어와 일치해야 하는데 명령문은 일반적으로 주어 you가 생략된 것이므로 문맥상 적절하지 않다. anyone은 부정이나 의문문에 쓰이므로 제외된다. 따라서 (A)가 정답이다.

모두에게 다음 주 근무 당번표 리스트를 주세요.

roster (근무) 당번표

107 **해설** 선택지가 모두 부사이므로 부사 어휘 문제임을 알 수 있다. 어휘 문제는 해석을 통해 가장 자연스러운 어휘를 골라야 하며, 여기서는 문맥상 (A)가 가장 적절하다.

작은 결점에 뒤이어, 중앙 사무실의 새로운 냉방 기구가 드디어 주문되고 설치되었다.

following ~ 후에; ~을 뒤따라 minor 작은, 사소한 commission 의뢰하다, 주문하다 rarely 드물게, 좀처럼 ~하지 않는 immensely 엄청나게, 대단히

108 **해설** 빈칸 앞에 소유격(His)과 형용사(good)가 있기 때문에 빈칸은 명사 자리이다. 문맥상 그의 훌륭한 주의력(his good attention)이 적절하므로 (A)가 정답이다. attendant는 '시중드는 사람, 수행원, 안내원'으로 쓰인다.

그의 세부 사항에 대한 주의력 덕분에 작지만 잠재적으로 위험한 제품 디자인의 결함을 알아차릴 수 있었다.

potentially 가능성 있게, 잠재적으로

109 **해설** 날짜 앞에 쓰여 '~까지는 시행되지 않을 것이다'라는 의미로 활용되는 (B)가 가장 적절하다. during은 날짜가 아닌 기간과 함께 쓰이므로 적절하지 않다.

연봉 삭감이 지난달에 발표되었지만 4월 2일 전까지는 시행되지 않을 것이다.

cutback 삭감, 감축 announce 발표하다 come into effect 시행되다, 발효되다

110 **해설** 형용사 어휘 문제로 문맥상 container를 꾸며 주는 표현으로 가장 자연스러운 선택지는 (C)이다. 참고로 comply with(규칙 등을 준수하다)와 유사한 표현으로 conform to, observe, follow가 있다.

출장 요리업 규정을 따르기 위해, 음식은 승인받은 밀폐되고 깨끗한 용기에 보관되어야 한다.

comply with (법 · 명령 등을) 따르다, 준수하다 catering 출장 요리업 legislation 제정법, 규정 airtight 밀폐된 container 용기 honorable 명예로운 positive 확실한; 긍정적인 approved 승인받은

111 **해설** 빈칸부터 saw까지는 say의 목적어 역할을 해야 하므로 명사절을 이끄는 복합 관계대명사 (B)가 정답이다. whatever는 명사절 접속사 혹은 부사절 접속사 두 가지 모두 사용되며, 뒤에 불완전한 절을 받을 수 있다.

목격자들은 그들에게 그 정보가 얼마나 사소해 보이는지 상관없이, 그들이 본 것은 어떤 것이라도 말하도록 강력히 권고받았다.

eyewitness 목격자 urge ~하도록 충고하다, 설득하려 하다 regardless of ~와 상관없이 trivial 사소한

112 **해설** 부사절 접속사 vs. 전치사 문제로 빈칸 뒤에 명사(determination)가 있고 빈칸은 전치사 자리이므로 (A)가 정답이다. so that, whereas, because는 모두 부사절 접속사로 뒤에 완전한 절이나 분사가 와야 하므로 정답이 될 수 없다. due to와 같은 의미의 전치사 owing to, because of, on account of도 알아 둔다.

셀레나 아메드가 마케팅 책임자로 승진한 것은 영국 보수당이 성공하게 만들려는 그녀의 의지 덕택이었다.

rise (더 나은 위치 · 계급 등으로) 오르다 determination 의지 Conservative Party 영국 보수당

113 **해설** be동사 뒤의 보어 자리로 명사와 형용사가 올 수 있다. 현재분사 recognizing과 형용사 recognizable이 정답의 가능성이 있으나 recognizing은 보어 역할은 할 수 있지만 뒤에 목적어도 없고 문맥상 적절하지 않다. 따라서 정답은 (C)이다. recognize는 동사, recognizably는 부사로 보어 역할을 할 수 없다.

루인 모리슨의 예술적 스타일은 단순한 색상을 폭넓게 사용하는 것으로 알아볼 수 있다.

artistic 예술적인 extensive 광범위한, 폭넓은 recognize 알아보다, 구분하다 recognizable 알아볼 수 있는

114 **해설** 조동사(will)와 동사원형(affect) 사이는 동사를 수식하는 부사 자리이므로 (D)가 정답이다. favoring은 분사나 동명사, favored는 동사나 분사, favorable은 형용사이므로 모두 동사를 수식할 수 없다.

회사 합병은 기업에 이로운 영향을 끼칠 것이고, 남아프리카 시장으로의 새로운 진출을 제공할 것이다.

merger 합병 inroad 진출 favor 호의를 보이다; 호의 favorable 이로운 favorably 이롭게

115 **해설** 명사 어휘 문제로 해석을 통해 가장 적합한 어휘를 고른다. 문맥상 세차와 광택제 사용을 통해 향상시킬 수 있는 것은 '외관'이므로 가장 적절한 선택지는 (A)이다.

당신의 오래된 자동차의 외관을 향상시키는 가장 간단한 방법은 정기적으로 세차를 하고, 도장면에 왁스 광택제를 사용하는 것이다.

enhance 향상시키다 automobile 자동차 polish 광택제 paintwork 페인트칠 appearance 외관 improvement 향상, 개선 instruction 설명, 지시

116 **해설** 한정사 문제로 빈칸 뒤에 가산 단수 명사(washing machine)가 있으므로 some과 few는 정답에서 제외된다. some은 가산 복수나 불가산 명사 앞, few는 가산 복수 앞에 쓸 수 있다. 문맥상 '지금까지 나와 있는 어떤 세탁기 중'이 적절하므로 (C)가 정답이다. each(각각)는 문맥상 적절하지 않고 any가 긍정문에 쓰이면 '어떤 ~라도'의 의미로 쓸 수 있다는 것을 알아 둔다.

웍슬리 가전에서 현재까지 나와 있는 어떤 세탁기 중에서도 가장 높은 에너지 효율 순위를 가진 세탁기인 투스핀을 자랑스럽게 출시합니다.

appliance 가전제품 launch 출시하다 energy efficiency 에너지 효율 rating 순위 to date 지금까지, 오늘에 이르기까지

117 **해설** 동사(has been introducing) 뒤의 목적어 자리로 명사가 정답이다. 빈칸 뒤 관계절의 동사가 are이므로 복수 명사 (D)가 정답이다. to measure, measuring은 관계절의 수식을 받을 수 없으며 뒤에 목적어도 없다. 주격 관계대명사 뒤에 오는 동사의 수는 수식을 받는 선행사에 맞춘다는 것을 알아 둔다.

지난 일 년간 윈터 가든스 크리에이티브 위원회는 그 지역 내의 다른 기관들과 양립할 수 있는 조치들을 소개해 오고 있다.

compatible 양립 가능한; 호환 가능한 region 지역 measure 조치(정책); 단위

118 **해설** 문맥상 '새로운 조각상 건립을 위해서'가 가장 적절하므로 (C)가 정답이다. towards는 '~에 드는 비용의 일부로서'란 의미로 쓸 수 있다는 것을 알아 둔다.

앤사 시민 문화 회관은 그들의 연례 자선 바자회에서 모은 돈을 새로운 조각상의 건립 비용의 일부로 기부할 것이다.

community center 시민 문화 회관 donate 기부하다, 기증하다 annual 연례의 charity 자선 erection 건립, 설치 statue 조각상

119 **해설** 전치사(for)와 명사(renovations) 사이에 올 수 있는 것은 명사를 수식하는 형용사이므로 (B)가 정답이다. 동사 structuralize, 부사 structurally, 명사 structure는 명사를 수식할 수 없다.

뉴 스트리트 브리지가 구조적인 수리를 위해 폐쇄되는 동안, 첼튼햄의 통근자들은 퀸 스트리트로 우회하게 될 것입니다.

renovation 개조, 보수, 수리 commuter 통근자 redirect (다른 주소 · 방향으로) 다시 보내다 structuralize 구조화하다 structural 구조적인

120 **해설** 동사 어휘 문제로 문맥상 특정 행사가 '수천 명의 사람들을 ~다'에 들어갈 가장 적절한 어휘는 (C)이다.

투어링 액터스 로드쇼는 매년 여러 도시를 방문하면서 수천 명의 사람들을 끌어들인다.

roadshow 순회 공개 방송, (기업 · 정당의) 순회 홍보 행사 explore 탐험하다, 답사하다 attract 유치하다, 매력을 끌다

121 **해설** as 이하의 내용을 통해 정답을 추론할 수 있다. 청소되는 동안에 이용할 수 없다고 했으므로 '일시적으로' 이용할 수 없다는 (A)가 가장 자연스럽다.

콘크리트 바닥 표면이 청소되는 동안, 지하 주차장은 일시적으로 주민들이 이용할 수 없을 것이다.

underground 지하 unavailable 이용 불가능한 resident 주민 surface 표면 temporarily 일시적으로 previously 이전에 constructively 건설적으로 stylishly 현대식으로

122 **해설** 빈칸은 동사(offers)와 명사(solutions) 사이에 위치해 있으며, 명사 앞에서 명사를 수식하는 형용사 (B)가 정답이다. innovate는 동사, innovatively는 부사로 명사를 수식할 수 없다.

MJ 컨설팅은 노트북 컴퓨터의 보안 위협을 방지하는 혁신적인 해결책을 제공한다.

solution 해결 방안, 해결책 combat (좋지 않은 일의 발생이나 악화를) 방지하다 security threat 보안 위협 laptop 노트북 컴퓨터

123 **해설** 명사 어휘 문제로 해석을 통해 정답을 고른다. 빈칸 앞에 two가 있으므로 단수형인 precaution과 emergency는 적절하지 않고, 문맥상 '동료를 동반해야 한다'가 자연스러우므로 (C)가 알맞다.

소방관들은 잠재적으로 위험한 건물에 들어갈 때에는 두 명의 동료를 동반해야 한다.

fire fighter 소방관 accompany 동반하다, 동행하다 potentially 잠재적으로 precaution 예방조치 colleague 동료 personnel 인사부; (조직 · 군대의) 인원

124 **해설** 빈칸이 명사 앞에 위치하므로 명사구나 전치사구 앞에 와서 이를 강조하는 역할을 하는 부사 (A)가 정답이다. moreover는 접속부사, but은 등위 접속사, unless는 부사절 접속사로 명사구를 강조할 수 없다.

그 직책은 복잡한 수치들을 회의에서 보여 주어야 하므로, 폭넓은 파워포인트 경험이 있는 지원자들만 고려될 것이다.

complex 복잡한 figure 수치 candidate 후보자, 지원자 extensive 폭넓은

125 **해설** 관사 a와 전치사 in 사이는 명사 자리이므로 분사나 동명사 형태의 corresponding과 동사 correspond는 답에서 제외된다. 명사 correspondence와 correspondent 중에서 문맥상 (C)가 자연스럽다.

그녀의 최신 방송에서, 수상 발표자였던 그레이스 안잠은 테헤란에서 기자의 일상을 보내고 있다.

broadcast 방송, 보도 award-winning 수상한 presenter 발표자 correspondence 서신, 편지 corresponding 해당되는, 부합하는 correspondent 기자, 특파원 correspond 응답하다

126 **해설** 부사 어휘 문제로 문맥상 '다음 부로 승격되었다'라는 내용과 가장 잘 어울리는 부사는 (D)이다.

리그 성적에서 지속적으로 높은 위치에 있어서, 샤클리 유나이티드는 사우스 웨스트 리그에서 다음 부로 승격되었다.

league table 성적표, 실적 일람표 promote 촉진하다; 승진시키다 division (축구의 리그를 구성하는) 부 reluctantly 마지못해, 꺼려해서 potentially 잠재적으로 evenly 고르게, 균등하게

127 **해설** 빈칸 뒤에 명사(training programs)가 있으므로 빈칸은 명사를 수식하는 형용사 자리이다. cooperate가 자동사이므로 cooperated는 형용사 역할을 할 수 없다. 따라서 정답은 형용사 (B)이다. cooperate는 동사, cooperatively는 부사로 형용사 역할을 할 수 없다.

새로 인수한 회사인 스미슨 주식회사와의 관계를 강화하기 위해, 경영진은 협동 조합식의 훈련 프로그램을 권하고 있다.

cement 접합시키다; A와 B를 결속시키다 newly-acquired 새로 획득한 management 경영진 cooperative 협력의; 협동 조합식의 cooperate 협력하다

128 **해설** 선택지가 모두 명사이므로 알맞은 명사 어휘를 고르는 문제이다. 문맥상 '재활용 습관'이 자연스러우므로 (D)가 가장 적절하다. practice가 '실행'이 나닌 '관습, 습관'의 의미로도 쓰이는 것을 알아 둔다.

최근 설문조사가 재활용 습관이 식사하는 사람들에게 중요하다는 것을 보여 주기 때문에, 재활용 포장재는 레스토랑 내에서 일상적인 광경이 되어 가고 있다.

reusable 재활용 가능한 packaging 포장; 포장재 sight 광경; 시야 diner 식사하는 손님 composition 구성 요소들; 구성; 작곡 creation 창조

129 **해설** all employees ~ holiday는 완전한 문장이므로 빈칸부터 profitability까지는 수식 역할을 한다. 빈칸 뒤에 명사(expectations)가 있으므로 수동 형태를 만드는 To be와 Being은 답에서 제외된다. Having과 To have 중 문맥상 '매출과 수익성 면에서 회사의 기대치를 뛰어 넘었기 때문에'가 자연스러우므로 (A)가 정답이다. to부정사가 문장 맨 앞에서 수식 역할을 할 때 '~하기 위해서'라고 해석되므로 문맥상 적절하지 않다. 참고로 분사구문에서 부사절 접속사는 생략될 수 있고 이 경우 문맥에 적절한 접속사를 대입하여 해석한다.

매출과 수익성 면에서 회사의 기대치를 뛰어넘었기 때문에, 로스사이드사 재무 부서의 모든 직원들은 하루의 추가 휴가를 받았다.

exceed 초과하다, 초월하다 expectation 기대 in terms of ~ 면에서 turnover 매출량, 매출액 profitability 수익성 financial department 재무 부서 award 수여하다

130 **해설** 명사 어휘 문제로 문맥상 '현지 극장의 무료입장에 대한 자격이 있다'가 가장 자연스러우므로 정답은 (A)이다.

햄튼 병원의 특수아들은 현지 극장에 무료로 입장할 자격이 있다.

be entitled to ~할 권리[자격]가 있는 local 현지의, 지역의

Part 6

[131-134]

수신: 전 직원
발신: 루크 페리
날짜: 5월 21일

휴가 시즌이 다가오면서, 직원 안내서 5페이지에 나와 있는 선물에 관한 회사 방침에 대해 여러분 모두에게 다시 한 번 알려 드릴 기회를 갖고자 합니다. 직업적 (131) 청렴함을 장려하기 위해 모든 직원들은 선물을 받는 것이 금지됩니다.

이 방침 (132) 하에서, '선물'은 다른 소매업체, 고객, 잠재적 근로자, 또는 코노브 프로덕츠와 사업상 관계에 있는 사람들로부터 받은 것으로 정의됩니다. (133) 선물 물품의 범위는 작은 홍보 제품부터 공연 티켓, 고급 제품까지를 말합니다. 상품권이나 무료 샘플과 같은 다른 혜택들도 역시 선물에 포함됩니다. 직원들은 소매업체들과 다른 고객들에게 이 방침에 대해 숙지시킬 (134) 책임이 있습니다.

감사합니다.

루크 페리
대외 관계 부서장, SH 프로덕츠

promote 촉진하다, 장려하다 define 정의하다 prospective 잠재적인 integrity 고결, 성실, 청렴 intuition 직감 enactment 제정 sensitivity 민감함 regardless of ~와 상관없이 range ~에 미치다, 걸치다 recipient 수령인, 수취인

131 선물을 받는 것이 금지된다고 했으므로 직업적 '청렴함'에 대해 장려하는 내용임을 알 수 있다. 따라서 (A) integrity(청렴함, 도덕성)가 정답이다.
정답_(A)

132 뒤의 명사 policy와 어울려야 하며, 문맥상 '이 방침 하에서 선물이 정의된다'는 의미가 적절하다. 규정, 법, 방침 등의 앞에는 전치사 under(~하에)가 오므로 (B)가 정답이다.
정답_(B)

133 (A) 선물 물품의 범위는 작은 홍보 제품부터 공연 티켓, 고급 제품까지를 말합니다.
(B) 그와 같은 경우, 전 직원은 그들이 받은 것을 상사에게 보고해야 합니다.
(C) 하지만 받은 사람이 누구인지를 알아내는 것은 종종 매우 힘든 일입니다.
(D) 대신에, 여러분은 그들에게 감사 편지를 쓰실 수 있습니다.

문맥상 가장 적절한 문장을 고르는 문제이다. 빈칸 앞에서 선물의 정의에 대해서 이야기하고 있고 뒤에서는 상품권이나 무료 샘플도 역시 선물에 포함된다고 했다. 따라서 빈칸에는 선물의 범위에 대한 내용이 오는 것이 적절하므로 (A)가 정답이다.
정답_(A)

134 여기서 hold는 보어와 함께 '(사람, 물건 등을) 어떠한 상태로 두다'라는 의미이다. 원래는 hold employees accountable for(직원들이 ~에 책임을 지도록 만들다)라는 표현에서 수동태가 된 문장이다. 따라서 빈칸에는 형용사 (D) accountable이 와야 한다.
정답_(D)

[135-138]

새 휴가 방침

최근 몇 번의 이사회 회의에서 우리의 135 기존의 휴가 방침을 바꿔야 한다는 필요성이 계속해서 제기되었습니다. 현재는 12개월 이상 파트타임과 풀타임으로 일한 직원들만이 휴가 요청서를 136 제출할 수 있습니다. 137 하지만 회사는 이제 최소 3개월간 일했을 경우 휴가 요청서를 받을 것입니다. 이 수정된 방침은 8월 1일부터 효력이 생깁니다. 게다가, 추가 이틀간의 유급휴가를 개인적 사유로 매년 사용하실 수 있습니다. 138 이는 당신의 팀장의 승인이 있을 경우에만 허용될 것입니다.

be eligible to ~할 자격이 있다 **take effect** 시행되다 **confirm** 확인하다 **fulfill** 이행하다, 충족시키다 **ensure** 보장하다, 확실히 하다 **submit** 제출하다 **however** 하지만 **besides** 게다가 **otherwise** 그렇지 않으면 **namely** 즉, 다시 말해

135 〈소유격 대명사(our)+빈칸+명사(vacation policy)〉의 구조로 빈칸에는 명사를 수식하는 형용사가 와야 한다. 형용사의 역할을 할 수 있는 분사 (A), (C) 중에서 exist는 자동사이므로 분사가 형용사의 역할을 할 경우 현재분사만 가능하다. 따라서 (A) existing이 정답이다.
정답_(A)

136 12개월 이상 일한 직원들만 휴가 요청서를 '제출할' 수 있다는 뜻이 적절하므로 (D) submit(제출하다)이 정답이다.
정답_(D)

137 앞뒤 문장의 의미 관계를 자연스럽게 연결해 줄 수 있는 접속부사를 고르는 문제이다. 앞 문장에서는 현재는 12개월 이상 근무한 직원들의 경우에만 휴가 요청서를 제출할 수 있다고 하고, 뒤 문장에서는 최소 3개월 근무했다면 휴가 요청서를 제출할 수 있다는 내용으로 보아 역접의 관계를 나타내는 (A) however(그러나, 하지만)가 정답이다.
정답_(A)

138 (A) 우리는 당신이 우리와 계속 거래를 해주시기를 바랍니다.
(B) 이번 달 이사회 회의는 오전 11시에 시작합니다.
(C) 정규직 직원들은 내부 승진을 지원할 자격이 있습니다.
(D) 이는 당신의 팀장 승인이 있을 경우에만 허용될 것입니다.

문맥상 가장 적절한 문장을 고르는 문제이다. 바로 앞 문장에서 유급 휴가를 이틀 더 사용할 수 있다는 문장이 있는 것으로 보아 이 내용을 This로 받아 '이것'은 팀장의 승인을 받을 경우에만 허용될 수 있다는 (D)의 내용이 이어지는 것이 적절하다.
정답_(D)

[139-142]

수신: 하퍼 인터내셔널 전 직원
발신: 노아 하프스터, 행정 매니저

코로나도 다리 근처에 아파트 단지를 건설하겠다는 정부의 결정에 반대하는 시위가 오늘 오후 6시 아담 애비뉴에서 예정되어 있습니다.

하퍼 인터내셔널 맞은편에 있는 아담 애비뉴에 3천명 이상의 사람들이 시위에 참석할 것입니다. 139 예방 조치로서, 상임 경영진은 직원들을 오늘 오후 5시 30분까지 퇴근시키기로 결정했습니다. 140 조기 퇴근이 직원들이 혼잡을 피하는 데 도움이 될 것이라 생각합니다. 퇴근 전, 전화나 이메일로 당신의 직속 상사에게 반드시 141 연락을 취하십시오.

시간 당 급여를 받는 직원들은 퇴근할 때 평소처럼 퇴근 시간을 기록하셔야 합니다.

모든 부서장은 시간 당 급여를 받는 직원들의 차질 없는 급여 수령을 보장하기 위해 시간 기록 승인을 검토하고 142 완료할 수 있도록 적절한 조정을 해야 합니다.

노아 하프스터

protest 시위, 항의 **measure** 대책, 조치 **adjustment** 적응, 조정 **careful** 신중한 **precautionary** 조심의, 예방의 **replaceable** 바꿀 수 있는 **immovable** 움직일 수 없는 **congestion** 혼잡, 정체

139 회사 맞은편에서 시위가 있으니, 조기 퇴근 결정을 '예방' 조치로 내렸다는 내용이 자연스러우므로 (B) precautionary(예방의)가 정답이다.
정답_(B)

140 (A) 조기 퇴근이 직원들이 혼잡을 피하는 데 도움이 될 것이라 생각합니다.
(B) 아파트 단지는 안전의 이유로 보수공사가 이루어질 필요가 있습니다.
(C) 경영진은 두 번째 인터뷰 전에 각각의 지원서를 검토할 것입니다.
(D) 혼잡시간 동안, 여러분은 건물 근처 길가에 차를 주차하실 수 있습니다.

문맥상 가장 적절한 문장을 고르는 문제이다. 앞에서 시위 때문에 직원들을 5시 30분에 퇴근시키기로 결정했다는 내용이 있으므로 '조기 퇴근이 직원들이 혼잡을 피하는 데 도움이 될 것이라 생각한다'는 (A)의 내용이 뒤에 이어지는 것이 적절하다.
정답_(A)

141 〈make sure + to부정사〉는 '반드시 ~하다'의 구조로 빈칸에는 to부정사 (C) to contact가 정답이다.
정답_(C)

142 등위 접속사 and를 사이에 두고 빈칸은 앞의 to부정사와 병치를 이루고 있으므로, to부정사가 와야 하지만 중복되는 to는 생략할 수 있으므로 동사원형 (C) complete가 정답이다.
정답_(C)

[143-146]

수신: 라이언 예르던
발신: 고객 서비스 센터
날짜: 6월 4일
제목: 주문

저희 온라인 상점에서 식탁을 구입해 주셔서 감사합니다. 귀하께서는 세일 기간에 제품을 구매하셨기 때문에 143 운송 중 파손된 것이 아니라면 환불이나 교환이 불가능합니다.

저희의 트럭 배달 서비스는 고객 여러분이 주문품을 손상되지 않도록 받아보시는 것을 144 보장하는 데 있어 자긍심을 갖고 있습니다.

145 유감스럽게도, 가끔 문제가 발생하기도 합니다. 제품 사용 후, 제품이 귀하의 기대에 미치지 못한다면, 저희가 해결할 수 있도록 문제가 무엇인지 알려주시기 바랍니다. 귀하의 146 의견을 언제나 감사하게 생각합니다.

다시 한 번 저희 상점을 이용해 주셔서 감사합니다.

주노 템플, 고객 서비스 직원

undamaged 손상을 입지 않은 **meet expectations** 기대에 미치다 **usage** 사용, 용법 **display** 전시 **payment** 지급 **transit** 운송, 운반 **assembly** 조립 **donation** 기부 **invitation** 초대 **transaction** 거래

143 빈칸 앞에 전치사 in이 왔고 다음에 '트럭 배달 서비스에 자긍심을 갖고 있다'는 뒤 문장의 내용으로 보아 '운송'에 자신이 있으니 운송 중 파손된 것이 아니라면 환불이나 교환이 불가능하다는 의미가 선행하는 것이 적절하다. 따라서 (D) transit(운송)이 정답이다.
정답_(D)

144 'ensure that ~: ~를 확실히 하다'의 구조로 앞에 전치사 on이 있기 때문에 동명사인 (A) ensuring이 정답이다.
정답_(A)

145 (A) 유감스럽게도, 가끔 문제가 발생하기도 합니다.
(B) 당신의 선호하는 배송 옵션을 선택하셔야 합니다.
(C) 포함된 조립 설명서가 매우 혼동됩니다.
(D) 저희의 고객 서비스 센터는 매일 24시간 근무합니다.

문맥상 가장 적절한 문장을 고르는 문제이다. 앞뒤 문장에서 단서를 찾아야 한다. 앞 문장에서는 손상되지 않은 완전한 상태로 제품을 배송하는 것에 자긍심이 있다는 내용이 선행하고, 뒤 문장에서는 제품이 기대에 미치지 못하면 알려달라는 내용이 이어지고 있다. 그러므로 배송에 자신이 있으나 문제가 드물게 발생을 할 수 있으니 만족하지 못할 경우 알려달라는 내용으로 이어지는 것이 자연스럽다. 따라서 (A)가 정답이다.
정답_(A)

146 명사 어휘 문제이다. 앞 문장에서 문제를 개선할 수 있도록 무엇이 문제인지 알려달라는 내용이 있는 것으로 보아 고객의 '의견(feedback)'에 감사한다는 내용이 이어져야 적절하다. 따라서 (B) feedback(의견)이 정답이다.
정답_(B)

[147-148]

징기스

피아자 플레이스 9 • 아메르테 베이 • 뉴질랜드

1월 3일

질리안 네이마 씨
플렉켄 드라이브, 민스터 로드 112
웰링턴, 뉴질랜드

네이마 씨께,

징기스 의류점 클럽의 엘리트 회원이 되신 것을 축하합니다. 이 새 카드는 점포나 웹 사이트에서 구매한 모든 상품에 대해 20퍼센트 할인을 제공합니다. 여기에는 모든 여성 의류, 남성 의류, 아동 상품을 포함합니다. 또한 독점적인 거래에 대한 세부 정보도 보내 드립니다. 징기스 클럽의 회원들은 매 시즌 초에 소개되는 신상품을 독점적으로 처음 보실 수 있습니다. 특정 상품들에 대해 30퍼센트까지 놀라운 할인을 받을 수 있습니다.

클럽 회원으로서 귀하께서는 자동 청구 서비스 혜택도 받을 수 있는데, 지불하셔야 하는 금액을 매달 은행 계좌에서 빠져나가도록 하실 수 있습니다. 물론, 우편을 통한 수표 또는 신용 카드로 지불하셔도 됩니다. 귀하의 회원 활성화를 위해 www.genghis.com.nz/activate에 방문하시거나 555-0154로 전화 주시고, 오늘부터 절약을 시작하세요!

조지 헤르난데즈
고객 서비스부

elite member 정예 회원 grant 주다, 수여하다 viewing 구경, 감상 automatic 자동의 activate 활성화하다

147 편지의 대상은?
(A) 헬스클럽 회원
(B) 의류점 손님
(C) 고객 서비스 직원
(D) 신용 카드 회사 직원

148 클럽 회원들이 받는 혜택은?
(A) 징기스 청구서를 자동으로 결제할 수 있다.
(B) 20개 품목 구매 후에 현금 보너스를 받는다.
(C) 매달 새로운 카드를 받는다.
(D) 웹 사이트에서 회원 전용 코너에 접근할 수 있다.

[149-150]

앨리샤 위트 **오전 11:23**
로스 씨, 테일러 인더스트리스의 사장인 러셀 씨에게 막 전화 왔습니다. 그는 자신의 회사를 위한 광고사를 찾던 중에 내일 오후 3시에 여기에 오고 싶다고 했습니다.

팀 로스 **오전 11:25**
좋은 소식이네요! 테일러 인더스트리스는 규모가 커서 우리의 최상의 사업 파트너가 될 것 같습니다. 그러면, 그를 위해서 가장 좋은 회의실로 예약해 주실래요? 회의실 407호가 제일 좋을 겁니다.

앨리샤 위트 **오전 11:26**
네, 제가 해봤는데, 다른 누군가가 이미 3시에 그곳을 예약했더라고요.

팀 로스 **오전 11:26**
정말요? 제가 확인해 볼게요.

팀 로스 **오전 11:28**
당신 말이 맞네요. 디아즈 씨가 예약했네요. 그가 607호 회의실을 쓸 수 있으면 좋을 텐데요.

앨리샤 위트 **오전 11:29**
그건 괜찮을 거예요. 제가 그에게 변경할 수 있을지 물어볼게요.

huge 거대한 book 예약하다 reserve 예약하다 conference room 회의실

149 로스 씨와 위트 씨가 일하는 곳은 어디인가?
(A) 법률 회사
(B) 출판사
(C) 연예 기획사
(D) 광고 회사

150 오전 11시 29분에, 위트 씨가 "그건 괜찮을 거예요"라고 쓴 의미는 무엇인가?
(A) 그녀는 자기 동료에게 전화할 필요가 있다.
(B) 그녀는 로스 씨가 그 장소를 예약하길 원한다.
(C) 그녀는 디아즈 씨가 그 변화를 받아들이길 원한다.
(D) 그녀는 회의의 일정을 변경할 필요가 있다.

[151-153]

헬싱키 기차 승객들을 위한 공지

오슬로 철로 일부의 표면 작업과 수리 작업 때문에 7월 3일에서 7월 17일까지 기차 운행이 원활하지 못할 것입니다. 여행객들은 이 기간 동안 대체 가능한 이동 수단을 마련하셔야 합니다. 정상적인 기차 운행은 7월 17일 이후에 재개될 것으로 예상됩니다.

	경로	출발	날짜
34	이타바일라 – 비푸리 행	매 시간	일정대로 운행
36	란시바일라 – 메인스트러스 행	매 시간	7월 6일 ~ 7월 9일: 운행하지 않음
37	에스푸 – 반타 행	매 시간	7월 3일 ~ 7월 8일: 운행하지 않음
45	카우니아이엔 – 투르크 행	30분마다	일정대로 운행
51	탈린 – 사포 행	매 시간	7월 11일 ~ 7월 15일: 운행하지 않음
58	헬싱키 – 오슬로 행	매 시간	7월 13일 ~ 7월 17일: 운행하지 않음

출발과 경로 정보는 정기 일정표를 참조해 주세요.

추가 정보를 위해 www.helsinkitrains.org을 방문하시거나 info@helsinkitrains.org로 이메일을 보내 주세요.

surface restructuring 표면 재구조 작업 track 노선 severely 심하게 disrupt 중단하다, 방해하다 urge 촉구하다 alternative 대안의 arrangement 준비 normal 평상시의 resume 다시 시작하다 refer to ~을 참조하다 regular 정상적인, 정기적인 route 길, 경로 temporary 일시적인 renovation 수리 undergo 겪다 maintenance 유지 보수 frequently 자주

151 공지는 무엇에 관한 것인가?
(A) 기차 운행의 일시적인 변경
(B) 새 여행 경로의 추가
(C) 일부 오래된 열차의 개조
(D) 기차 여행의 비용 인상

152 공지에 따르면 유지 보수를 하는 노선은?
(A) 오슬로 철로
(B) 사포 철로
(C) 탈린 철로
(D) 투르크 철로

153 가장 자주 운행하는 것으로 일정이 잡힌 기차는?

(A) 34번 기차
(B) 36번 기차
(C) 45번 기차
(D) 58번 기차

[154-155]

이동 및 관리

화분에 심어진 관목과 식물을 다른 장소로 옮길 때, 손상 없이 새 장소에서 잘 자라게 하기 위해 특별 관리가 필수적입니다. 식물의 위나 몸통을 들어 올리는 것은 뿌리를 상하게 할 수 있으므로, 식물을 운반할 때는 화분 채로 운반하세요. 구매하신 식물의 정확한 유형별 관리를 위해 전단에 있는 물 주는 방법대로 따라 하세요. 이 전단은 무료이고, 계산 창구 근처에서 찾으실 수 있습니다.

potted 화분에 심어진 shrub 관목 vital 필수인 injury 부상 flourish 잘 자라다 habitat 거주지 trunk 몸통 complimentary 무료인 checkout register 계산 창구 packet 꾸러미

154 정보는 주로 누구를 대상으로 하는가?

(A) 용기 판매자
(B) 식물 구매자
(C) 안전 상담가
(D) 점포 관리자

155 비용 없이 이용 가능한 것은?

(A) 배달
(B) 상자
(C) 서면 설명서
(D) 씨앗 봉투

[156-157]

제이즈 보석점
테스만 가 22
네덜란드

제이즈 보석점이 점포 이전 세일을 합니다.
네덜란드의 가장 독점적인 보석점이 더 넓은 장소(루 프란세스 361)로 이전합니다. 그리고 이를 기념하기 위해 상점의 모든 재고를 통틀어 대대적인 할인을 합니다.

모든 보석류는 50퍼센트 이상 할인됩니다.
이 광고지를 지참하시면 판매가의 10퍼센트를 추가로 할인 받을 수 있습니다.

서두르세요! 세일은 3월 12일에 끝납니다.
현재 위치: 테스만 스트리트 22
새 위치: 루 프란세스 361, 4월 22일 개점

현재 위치와 새 위치로 찾아오시는 길 안내를 위해 온라인으로 방문해 주시거나 (+44) 555-2281로 전화 주세요.

jewelry 보석류 exclusive 독점적인 mark the occasion 행사를 기념하다 massive 거대한 reduction 할인 stock 재고 further 추가의 direction 길 안내 premise 건물, 점포 go out of business 폐점하다

156 제이즈 보석점에 관해 언급된 것은?

(A) 점포 건물을 옮긴다.
(B) 매월 할인을 한다.
(C) 폐점할 것이다.
(D) 남성용 장신구를 전문으로 한다.

157 광고에 언급된 것은?

(A) 개점 전에 할인이 끝날 것이다.
(B) 제이즈 보석점은 다음 해 해외로 확장할 것이다.
(C) 할인되지 않는 물건에만 10퍼센트 할인이 적용된다.
(D) 더 많은 쇼핑객들이 온라인으로 제이드 보석점에서 구매할 것이다.

[158-159]

케펜 제약 회사

1월 28일

오반게 씨께,

1월 21일에 케펜 제약 회사의 연구 보조원 직책에 관련한 귀하의 편지를 받았습니다. 구인 광고에 언급되었듯, 저희는 완료된 지원서만 1월 14일까지 받고 있었습니다. 적격인 지원자들의 기준이 매우 높았기에 다른 지원자에게 일자리를 제안했습니다. 그러나 저는 귀하의 이력서를 매우 인상 깊게 보았고 파일로 보관하고 있다는 점을 알아주십시오. 특히 마일로 실험실 인턴으로서의 귀하의 현재 직책에 특히 매료되었는데, 저도 그곳에서 일을 시작했기 때문입니다.

케펜 제약 회사에 대한 귀하의 관심에 다시 한 번 감사드립니다. 가까운 시일 내에 또 다른 연구 보조원 공석이 있을 경우 연락을 드리겠습니다.

애디슨 모리스
선임 연구원

pharmaceuticals 제약 회사 regarding ~와 관련한 position 직책 research assistant 연구 보조원 job advertisement 취업 광고 qualified 자격이 있는 candidate 후보자 impressive 인상 깊은 fascinated 매료된 current 현재 opening 공석 in the near future 가까운 시일 내에 vacant 결원의 confirm 확인하다 decline 거절하다 lack 부족

158 편지가 쓰인 이유는?

(A) 공석인 직책이 충원된 것을 설명하기 위해
(B) 면접의 세부 사항을 확인하기 위해
(C) 인턴의 책무를 설명하기 위해
(D) 갱신된 이력서를 요청하기 위해

159 오반게 씨에 관해 언급된 것은?

(A) 그는 현재 직업이 있다.
(B) 그의 지원서는 경험 부족으로 거절되었다.
(C) 그는 책임 연구원 자리에 지원하고 있다.
(D) 그의 업무 경력은 관련이 없다.

[160-162]

포레스트 글레이드 갤러리

5월 18일 일요일에 매년 열리는 유기농 식품과 식물 판매에 함께 하세요. 지역의 정원 센터에서 기부한 대량의 꽃이 있습니다. 모든 수익은 갤러리의 강좌와 전시회의 지원에 사용됩니다. 갤러리 입장은 판매 기간 동안 무료입니다.

포레스트 글레이드 갤러리는 고인이 된 화가이자 도예가인 에른스트 스타인버그의 가족에 의해 25년 전에 설립되었습니다. 갤러리는 유명한 예술가들의 다양한 작품뿐만 아니라 에른스트 스타인버그의 여정에서 수집된 물품과 도기들을 소장하고 있습니다. 아름답게 조경이 된 정원에는 분수대와 다양한 산책로를 따라 세워진 그림 같은 조각상이 있습니다.

갤러리의 기념품 가게는 식물 판매 기간 동안 구매 물건에 15퍼센트의 할인을 제공합니다. 갤러리 운영 시간은 월요일에서 금요일까지, 오전 10시부터 오후 5시 30분까지입니다. 주말 운영 시간은 오전 11시부터 오후 4시까지입니다. (현재 진행 중인 전시회는 앨리샤 머튼의 〈풍경〉을 포함하고, 5월 내내 갤러리 운영 시간 동안 대중에게 공개됩니다.) 더 많은 정보를 위해 www.forestgladegallery.org를 방문해 주세요.

organic food 유기농 식품 floral 꽃의 exhibit 전시회 admission 입장(료) late 고인이 된 ceramicist 도예가 house 소장하다 outstanding 뛰어난 artifact 인공물 pottery 도자기 renowned 유명한 landscaped 조경이 된 water fountain 분수대 picturesque 그림 같은, 생생한 sculpture 조각상 walking path 산책로 fundraising 기금 모금

160 무엇이 광고되고 있는가?
(A) 에른스트 스타인버그 씨의 강의
(B) 도자기 판매
(C) 기금 모금 판매
(D) 개점 축하식

161 포레스트 글레이드 갤러리에 관해 언급된 것은?
(A) 전시회를 재조정하고 있다.
(B) 한 예술가의 가족에 의해 설립되었다.
(C) 도예에 관한 수업을 제공한다.
(D) 최근에 조경되었다.

162 5월 18일에 포레스트 글레이드 갤러리에서 예정된 일이 아닌 것은?
(A) 갤러리는 오후 9시까지 열 것이다.
(B) 도자기류가 전시될 것이다.
(C) 갤러리의 기념품 가게에서 할인이 있을 것이다.
(D) 갤러리 입장료는 무료일 것이다.

[163-166]

제이슨 리 [오후 4:31]	안녕하세요. 구조조정 발표 이후 여러분 지사의 직원 의견에 대해 말씀해 주길 바랍니다.
브리 제임스 [오후 4:33]	처음 발표가 난 직후에는 힘들어 했었는데, 점차 안정되어 가는 것처럼 보였습니다. 그들은 추후의 변화에 대해 자세히 주시하고 있습니다.
메리 고긴 [오후 4:34]	여기 직원들은 구조조정으로 일부 인사 이동과 대량 해고를 수반할 것이라고 예상합니다. 심각한 경기 침체 때문에 직원들은 앞으로 발생할지도 모르는 변화에 대해 걱정하고 있습니다.
크리스 메시나 [오후 4:35]	저는 저의 직원들에게 이 문제에 대해 무언가를 말하는 게 조심스럽습니다. 추가적인 정보 없이는 그들에게 말해 줄 게 없습니다.
제이슨 리 [오후 4:36]	우리는 그것을 한창 작업 중입니다. 5월 부장 회의를 거쳐 대략적인 결정이 난 후에 여러분과 더 자세히 상의하도록 하겠습니다.
메리 고긴 [오후 4:37]	6월에 우리 사무실 일부가 이삿짐으로 가득 찰지도 모르겠네요. 만감이 교차합니다.
제이슨 리 [오후 4:38]	구조조정이 끝날 때까지 여러분의 협조가 매우 절실합니다. 그 외에 다른 질문이 있으시면, 편하게 저에게 연락해 주세요.

branch 지사, 지점 announcement 발표 restructuring 구조조정 uncomfortable 불편한, 유쾌하지 않은 gradually 점차 keep a close eye on ~에 자세히 주시하다 involve 수반하다 arrangement 조정, 배치 massive 대량의 layoff 해고 severe 혹독한 recession 경기 침체 roughly 대략 be filled with ~로 가득 차다 have mixed feeling 만감이 교차하다

163 리 씨가 메시지를 보낸 이유는 무엇인가?
(A) 회의 일정을 잡기 위해서
(B) 가능한 계획을 발표하기 위해서
(C) 직원의 의견을 알아내기 위해서
(D) 사무실 이전 일정을 확정하기 위해서

164 오후 4시 36분에 리 씨가 "우리는 그것을 한창 작업 중입니다."라고 쓴 의미는 무엇인가?
(A) 업무 시간이 상당히 연장되었다.
(B) 여러 사무실이 곧 문을 닫게 될 것이다.
(C) 그는 대표이사들을 정기적으로 만난다.
(D) 경영진들이 더욱 자세한 정보를 모으는 중이다.

165 지사들은 언제 최신 정보를 얻게 될 것인가?
(A) 5월에
(B) 6월에
(C) 7월에
(D) 8월에

166 지사장들은 무엇을 하도록 요구되는가?
(A) 새로운 직원을 고용하기
(B) 언제든 질문하기
(C) 새로운 신분증을 제공하기
(D) 사무 장비를 주문하기

[167-170]

짐 토마스
980 앨름 가
덴버, 콜로라도 80247

토마스 씨에게,

저는 콜로라도 노바 공장에 도착할 날짜를 예약해 두었습니다. -[1]-. 10월 24일 월요일 오후 4시에 덴버 국제공항에 도착할 예정입니다. 귀하는 제가 묵을 장소에 대해 걱정하지 않으셔도 됩니다. 그 지역의 홀리데이 모텔에 방을 예약했습니다.

저는 공장 현장을 직접 다녀 보기를 학수고대하고 있습니다. 또한, 직원 건강 기록과 안전 기록을 보는 것에 관심이 있습니다. -[2]-. 우리는 내년 초부터 시작해서 작업장의 새로운 안전 프로그램을 시행할 예정입니다. 저는 또한, 공장의 새로운 형광등 제품군을 볼 생각에 들떠 있습니다. -[3]-. 저는 이것이 국가가 발전함에 따라 내년에 해외에 열리게 될 새로운 시장을 위한 굉장한 제품이라고 믿고 있습니다.

항상 그렇듯, 저는 당신을 다시 볼 것을 학수고대하고 있습니다. 24일에 뵙시다. -[4]-.

아서 클라크

arrival 도착 look forward to ~하기를 학수고대하다 instigate 실시하게 하다 fluorescent light 형광등 be in need of ~이 필요하다

167 편지의 주제는 무엇인가?
(A) 클라크 씨의 콜로라도 노바 공장 방문
(B) 클라크 씨의 본사 방문
(C) 형광등의 새로운 생산
(D) 해외로 열리는 새로운 시장

168 회사는 내년 초에 무엇을 할 것인가?
(A) 건강 기록을 확인한다.
(B) 작업장에서 안전 프로그램을 시작한다.
(C) 형광등을 생산한다.
(D) 일부 직원을 해고한다.

169 [1], [2], [3], [4]로 표시된 곳 중 다음 문장의 위치로 가장 적절한 곳은 어디인가?

"본사에서 작업장의 안전을 개선해야 한다는 우려가 있었습니다."

(A) [1]
(B) [2]
(C) [3]
(D) [4]

170 편지에서 언급되지 않은 것은 무엇인가?

(A) 클라크 씨가 얼마 동안 머무를 예정인지
(B) 클라크 씨가 언제 도착할 예정인지
(C) 해외로 열리는 새로운 시장
(D) 클라크 씨가 어디에 머물 예정인지

[171-175]

5월 14일

루이 친
티엔 사
쓰촨 지방 1005
중국 00354

친 씨께,

사무실의 광대역과 전화 서비스를 위해 수이탄 서비스를 신청해 주셔서 감사합니다. 5월 17일 오전 9시에 기사가 서비스를 연결할 수 있도록 준비했습니다. 편리하신 시간이기를 바랍니다. -[1]-.

계약 조항에는 24개월 동안 광대역과 전화 서비스를 제공한다고 언급되어 있습니다. 설치비는 30달러이고 서비스 비용은 매달 25달러입니다. 설치비는 따로 청구될 것입니다. -[2]-. 2년 후에는 매달 40달러가 청구됩니다. 계약 기간이 끝나기 전에 취소하시면, 계약 위반으로 간주되며 75달러의 벌금이 발생합니다. 계약서 사본이 동봉되었습니다. -[3]-.

매달 말에 청구서를 받으시면 자동 이체 또는 직불 이체를 통해 14일 이내에 지불하셔야 합니다. 계신 곳에서 가장 가까운 수이탄 서비스 지점은 하이 스트리트의 상하이 은행 반대편인 캔톤 스트리트 992번지입니다. -[4]-. 거래에 감사드립니다.

라씨 비렌테
수이탄 경리 부장

subscribe to ~에 가입하다 broadband 광대역 terms 조항 installation 설치 fixed rate 정가 bill 청구하다 separately 별도로 charge 청구하다 breach 위반 incur 초래하다 penalty 벌금 enclose 동봉하다 transfer 이체 direct debit 자동 이체 in person 직접

171 친 씨가 인터넷 연결을 설치할 곳은?

(A) 그의 가게
(B)그의 사무실
(C) 그의 집
(D) 그의 카페

172 [1], [2], [3], [4]로 표시된 곳 중 다음 문장의 위치로 가장 적절한 곳은 어디인가?

"그날 기사가 설치 작업이 많기 때문에 전날 일정 확인을 위해 연락 주십시오."

(A) [1]
(B) [2]
(C) [3]
(D) [4]

173 2년의 서비스 후, 친 씨는 매달 얼마를 낼 것으로 예상되는가?

(A) 30달러
(B)40달러
(C)75달러
(D) 100달러

174 편지에 따르면 친 씨가 추가 청구를 받을 수 있는 이유는?

(A) 그의 계좌의 비밀번호를 분실한 것 때문에
(B) 정확하지 않은 지불 정보를 제출한 것 때문에
(C) 자동 이체를 취소한 것 때문에
(D)그의 서비스 계약을 위반한 것 때문에

175 친 씨는 첫 수이탄 서비스 요금을 언제까지 내야 하는가?

(A) 5월 10일
(B) 5월 14일
(C)6월 14일
(D) 6월 31일

[176-180]

10월 2일

안와 싱
덴햄 사
뭄바이 스트리트 41
페쉬와 지역
델리, 인도

싱 씨께,

애비콤 사는 귀사의 모든 포장재, 산업 폐기물, 다른 쓰레기를 책임지고 재활용하는 것에 전념합니다. 저희는 비용을 낮추고 경쟁력 있는 서비스를 위한 광범위한 네트워크와 효율적인 기술을 갖추고 있습니다. 저희 회사는 3개국의 창고를 두고 대규모의 폐기물을 지속적으로 처리하는 수단을 보유하고 있습니다.

인도 최대 규모의 재활용 회사 중 한 곳을 책임지는 경리 담당자로서, 저희는 귀사가 어디에서 무엇을 재활용하는지에 관심을 갖고 있습니다. 재활용 가능 폐기물을 처리하는 안내서로 동봉한 애비콤 사의 브로슈어를 한번 봐주시기 바랍니다. 저희의 품질에 관한 추가 정보를 위해 브로슈어에 있는 다른 회사들의 추천글들을 확인해 보시기 바랍니다. 특별한 요구사항이 있으시면 제게 연락해 주십시오. 원하시면 델리 사무실의 해리 차이 씨와 이야기하세요.

쿠마 바히
경리 부장
동봉

발신: 안와 싱 <asingh@denham.in>
수신: 찰스 웨스트<cwest@fxincorporated.com>
제목: 애비콤
날짜: 10월 10일

저는 델리에 있는 덴햄 사의 시설 관리자입니다. 저희는 산업 폐기물과 포장재를 재활용하기 위해 애비콤 사와 제휴하는 것을 생각 중입니다. 애비콤 사와 이야기를 나누기 전에 당신의 의견을 듣고 싶습니다.

귀사는 다양한 국제 공장들로부터 나오는 산업 폐기물을 수거하기 위해 애비콤 사를 이용한다고 알고 있습니다. 저는 특히 마사우아에 있는 귀사의 시설에 관심이 있습니다. 애비콤 사는 그곳에서 수거된 폐기물을 라잔에 있는 처리 공장으로 수송하는데, 저희의 폐기물도 그곳으로 보내질 것입니다. 애비콤 사가 자재를 제시간에 수거하는지, 수거에 관해 믿을 만한지 알고 싶습니다. 추가 정보를 주시면 감사하겠습니다.

안와 싱
델리 사무소 시설 관리자

be committed to ~에 전념하다 responsibly 책임감 있게 packaging 포장재 industrial waste 산업 폐기물 disposable 쓰레기 extensive

아주 넓은, 많은 competitive 경쟁력을 가진 depot 창고 continuous 지속적인 dispose 버리다 recyclable 재활용 가능한 testimonial 추천의 글 look to ~을 생각하다 partner with ~와 제휴하다 processing plant 처리 공장 regulation 규제 reliability 신뢰도

176 편지의 목적은?
(A) 단골 고객에게 할인을 제공하기 위해
(B) 새 환경 규제를 설명하기 위해
(C) 재활용 서비스를 홍보하기 위해
(D) 산업 장비의 상표를 추천하기 위해

177 편지에 따르면 애비콤 사는 어떻게 경쟁력을 유지하는가?
(A) 최신식 시설을 운영한다.
(B) 값싼 배송 방식을 사용한다.
(C) 제품을 익일로 배송한다.
(D) 쓰레기를 새 제품으로 재활용한다.

178 애비콤 사의 지역 직원은 누구일 것 같은가?
(A) 안와 싱
(B) 쿠마 바히
(C) 찰스 웨스트
(D) 해리 차이

179 싱 씨는 웨스트 씨의 연락 정보를 어디에서 받았을 것 같은가?
(A) 인도 기업 네트워크에서
(B) 차이 씨의 동료로부터
(C) 애비콤 사의 웹 사이트에서
(D) 애비콤 사의 추천 목록에서

180 싱 씨가 애비콤 사에 관해 걱정하는 것은?
(A) 서비스의 신뢰도
(B) 추가될 수 있는 여분의 비용
(C) 해외 배송 운영
(D) 사업을 해 온 기간

[181-185]

수신: 마리아 나마즈
발신: 카렌 존스
날짜: 2월 7일
제목: 마틴스 스포츠 교육

저는 마틴스 스포츠의 직원들을 위한 교육을 준비하고 있으며, 엠랜드 호텔을 이용하려고 고려 중입니다. 귀사에서 지난달 제 동료인 심스 씨를 위해 비공개 파티를 열었죠. 그는 당신의 호텔이 제공한 장소와 탁월한 서비스에 깊은 인상을 받았다고 했어요.
마틴스 스포츠 교육 행사는 3월 22일에 열릴 예정이고, 2시간 동안 작은 회의실이 필요합니다. 최소 20명의 인원이 참석할 것으로 예상되고, 오전 9시에 시작했으면 합니다. 대다수의 사람들이 하룻밤 묵을 숙박 시설이 필요할 것 같아요. 참석자를 위한 아침 식사도 필요하므로, 식사가 포함된 아침 패키지의 견적을 알려 주실 수 있나요? 발표를 위해 컴퓨터 액세스 포인트와 오버헤드 프로젝터, 큰 화면이 필요하고요.

미리 감사드리며
카렌 존스

수신: 카렌 존스
발신: 마리아 나마즈
날짜: 2월 8일
제목: 회신: 마틴스 스포츠 교육
첨부: 메뉴
귀사의 교육 행사를 담당하게 된다면 기쁠 것입니다. 저희는 인터넷 접속이 가능한 4가지 회의 시설을 제공합니다.

플래티넘 옵션 – 90달러/1인당, 8시간까지 지속되는 온종일 회의.
조식, 중식, 석식, 시청각 장비와 손님을 위한 무료 주차 서비스 포함.
골드 옵션 – 60달러/1인당, 8시간까지 지속되는 온종일 회의.
조식, 중식, 시청각 장비와 무료 주차 포함.
실버 옵션 – 60달러/1인당, 4시간까지 지속되는 반나절 회의.
중식, 시청각 장비와 무료 주차 포함.
브론즈 옵션 – 40달러/1인당, 4시간까지 지속되는 반나절 회의.
조식, 시청각 장비와 무료 주차 포함.

이메일에 메뉴를 첨부했습니다. 다른 정보를 원하시면 알려 주세요.
마리아 나마즈

private party 비공개 파티 quote 견적을 내다; 견적서 overhead projector 위에 달려 있는 영사기 in advance 미리 equipped 장비를 갖춘 full-day 하루 동안의 last 지속하다 audiovisual equipment 시청각 장비 complimentary 무료 valet service 주차 서비스 correct 바로잡다 registration form 신청서

181 첫 번째 이메일의 목적은?
(A) 파티 초대장을 보내기 위해
(B) 신청서의 실수를 바로잡기 위해
(C) 예약 날짜를 확인하기 위해
(D) 회의의 옵션에 관해 문의하기 위해

182 세미나에 관해 알 수 있는 것은?
(A) 아침에 영화가 상영될 것이다.
(B) 참가자들은 다양한 산업에 종사한다.
(C) 원래 다른 장소로 일정이 잡혔었다.
(D) 발표가 있을 것이다.

183 나마즈 씨에 관해 언급된 것은?
(A) 존스 씨의 동료에 의해 추천되었다.
(B) 최근에 엠랜드 호텔에서 일하기 시작했다.
(C) 이전에 마틴스 스포츠에서 일했었다.
(D) 엠랜드 호텔의 음식 제공 메뉴를 고안했다.

184 회의 패키지의 특징으로 언급되지 않은 것은?
(A) 호텔 손님을 위한 무료 주차
(B) 회의실의 인터넷 접속
(C) 참가자들을 위한 객실 요금 할인
(D) 회의실을 위한 시청각 장비

185 어느 패키지가 마틴스 스포츠의 요구를 가장 충족시키는가?
(A) 골드 옵션
(B) 브론즈 옵션
(C) 실버 옵션
(D) 플래티넘 옵션

[186-190]

수신: 모든 지점장
발신: GLN 은행, 본사
날짜: 3월 3일
제목: 그린 카드 출시 준비

그린 카드는 우리 은행의 가장 최신 신용 카드 서비스 중의 하나입니다. 이는 이번 달 16일부터 시장에 출시될 것입니다.

그렇기에, 모든 은행 직원들은 그린 카드와 관련된 계약 조건들을 다 숙지하여야 합니다. 비록 이 세부 사항들이 아직 마련되지 않았지만, 내일 아침까지는 모든 최종적인 관련 정보를 확인할 수 있을 것입니다.

더불어, 모든 지점장은 그린 카드 제품에 대한 평가 보고서를 제품 출시 한 달 후에 제출해야만 합니다.

그린 카드

계약 조건

* 모든 은행 직원들은 그린 카드 제품에 관련된 계약 조건을 충분히 이해하고 있어야 합니다.

1) 고객은 최초 예금 100달러를 가지고 있어야 합니다.
2) 고객은 신청서를 작성해야 합니다.
3) 제품 수혜자는 반드시 최소 한 달에 5,000달러의 수입이 있어야 합니다.
4) 카드 수령인은 반드시 아래와 같은 신분증을 제시해야 합니다:
   - 사원증, 운전면허증, 여권

* 서비스 가입에 관심이 있는 고객들은 위에 언급된 조항들에 대해 충분히 인지되어 있어야 합니다.

수신: 전 직원들
발신: GLN 은행, 시애틀 지점
날짜: 4월 20일
제목: 그린 카드 업데이트

주의: 참고를 위해 이 메시지의 복사본을 보관하세요. 그린 카드 출시 이후, 다음과 같은 문제들이 있었습니다:

1. 카드가 작동하지 않거나 주요 시스템에 등록되지 않아 고객들이 불평함.
2. 미성년자들이 운전면허증을 가지고 카드를 요청함. (주의: 운전면허증은 16세에 취득할 수 있습니다. 하지만 신용 카드는 20세 미만의 고객에게 발급될 수 없습니다.)

우리가 지난달에 얻은 값진 교훈이 미래에 더 나은 계획을 세우는 데 도움이 될 것입니다. 우리는 더 철저해야 하고 같은 실수를 반복해서는 안 됩니다. 그리하여 그린 카드 제품에 대한 세미나를 하려고 합니다. 이 교육이 고객에게 더 높은 질의 서비스를 제공할 수 있는 바탕이 되기를 바랍니다.

제프리 도노반
시애틀 지점

launching 출시 personnel 직원 terms and conditions 계약 조건 specific 세부 사항 furthermore 더욱이 be obligated to ~할 의무가 있다 aware 알고 있는 initial 초기의 deposit 예치금 beneficiary 수혜자 income 수입 recipient 수령인 secure 확보하다 inoperative 효력이 없는 minor 미성년자 thorough 철저한 foundation 토대, 기초 assessment 평가 brainstorm 생각해내다, 떠올리다 affiliating company 가맹점

186 메모의 목적은 무엇인가?
(A) 직원들에게 새로운 카드 제품을 판매하라고 말하려고
(B) 그린 카드에 대한 의견을 요청하려고
(C) 새로운 제품에 대한 고객의 반응을 물으려고
(D) 모든 지점장에게 가까운 미래의 계획에 대해 알리려고

187 지점장들에게 요구되는 것은 무엇인가?
(A) 현장에서 고객들에게 새로운 제품을 판매하기
(B) 새로운 제품에 대한 평가를 제출하기
(C) 이번 달까지 카드 디자인 브레인스토밍하기
(D) 더 많은 가맹점 모으기

188 그린 카드 제품을 받으려는 고객에게 요구되는 것이 아닌 것은 무엇인가?
(A) 신분증 제시
(B) 최초 예금
(C) 정기적 소득
(D) 부동산 자산

189 다음 중 제품 출시에 관해 밝혀지지 않은 것은 무엇인가?
(A) 몇몇 카드가 작동하지 않았다.
(B) 제품은 4월 초에 출시되었다.
(C) 제품 출시 후 워크숍이 예정되어 있다.
(D) 미성년자들이 카드를 요구했다.

190 도노반 씨가 제안하는 것은 무엇인가?
(A) 직원들이 교육에 참여하는 것
(B) 영업 직원의 수를 늘리는 것
(C) 은행 마감 시간을 조정하는 것
(D) 직원들이 가능한 한 많은 경험을 하는 것

[191-195]

블루 테이블 음식 제공 서비스

다음 행사 때는 걱정하지 마시고 블루 테이블 음식 제공 서비스를 통해 우아하게 차려진 고급 요리를 준비해 보세요.

저희는 다음과 같은 서비스를 제공합니다:
- 준비부터 청소까지, 풀서비스 음식 제공 서비스
- 다양한 메뉴 선택권
- 훈련된 예절 바른 서비스 직원들
- 다양한 식기류
- 장식 전문가

대규모의 행사를 계획한다면, 동봉된 특별 쿠폰을 사용할 수 있습니다. 제한된 기간 내에 놀라운 혜택을 누려 보세요.

궁금하신 사항이 있으시면 555-6524으로 전화를 주시거나, 555-6527로 팩스를 보내 주시거나, 웹 사이트 www.bluetable.com을 방문해 주시기 바랍니다.

블루 테이블 음식 제공 서비스

특별 할인 쿠폰

우리는 당신에게 최상의 완벽한 서비스를 제공하고 있습니다!
아래에 있는 쿠폰을 잘라 필요에 따라 자유롭게 사용하세요.

200분 이상을 모실 수 있는 행사를 위한 요금의 20% 할인 7월 1일 ~ 8월 31일	300분 이상을 모실 수 있는 행사를 위한 요금의 30% 할인 7월 1일 ~ 8월 31일

수신: 블루 테이블 음식 제공 서비스
발신: 에바 테넌트
날짜: 6월 20일
제목: 음식 주문 예상 가격

저는 제 직원들과 그들의 가족을 위해 7월 4일 야유회를 개최하려고 합니다. 제 직원들은 100명이고 그들이 가족을 데리고 오면 220~250명 정도 될 것입니다. 바비큐나 조그만 샌드위치 그리고 손으로 집어 먹을 만한 음식같이 간단하고 전형적인 독립 기념일 메뉴들이면 좋겠습니다.

정식으로 서비스를 요청하기 전에 제가 계획하고 있는 행사의 대략적인 가격과 메뉴 선택권들을 알고 싶습니다. 그리고 제 손님이 250명이 넘으면 25% 할인을 받을 수 있나요?

제 휴대전화 014-555-0987로 연락 주셔서 알려 주세요.

감사합니다.
에바 테넌트

catering 출장 음식 서비스업 aside 제쳐놓고 gourmet 미식가를 위한 delicate 섬세한 presentation 제시, 보여주는 방식 expert 숙달된 coordinator 진행자 courteous 예의 바른 tableware 식탁용 식기류 specialist 전문가 huge 대규모의 incredible 놀라운 cut out 자르다 rate 요금 estimate 견적 outing 야유회 formal 정식의 approximate 대략적인 abundant 풍성한

191 블루 테이블 음식 제공 서비스에서 제공하지 않는 것은 무엇인가?
(A) 장식 전문가
(B) 다양한 식기류의 선택
(C) 예절 교육 서비스
(D) 풍부한 메뉴 선택권

192 전단지에서 첫 번째 단락 두 번째 줄의 "delicate"와 의미상 가장 가까운 것은 무엇인가?
(A) 밝은
(B) 우아한
(C) 비싼
(D) 약한

193 테넌트 씨는 누구를 위해 행사를 계획하고 있는가?
(A) 친구들
(B) 고객들
(C) 조부모님
(D) 동료와 가족들

194 테넌트 씨는 행사에서 얼마만큼의 할인을 받을 수 있는가?
(A) 10%
(B) 20%
(C) 25%
(D) 30%

195 테넌트 씨는 블루 테이블 음식 제공 서비스로부터 어떻게 연락받고 싶어 하는가?
(A) 팩스로
(B) 전화로
(C) 그녀의 사무실을 방문해서
(D) 이메일로

[196-200]

수신: 폴 둘리 〈dooley@pr.net〉
발신: 마틴 도노반 〈donovan@chc.com〉
날짜: 12월 20일
주제: 제안된 일정

안녕하세요, 폴.

우리가 난관에 봉착한 것 같습니다. 우리는 맥키 주택 단지 개발에 대한 귀하가 제안한 건축 일정을 받았는데, 경영진은 이에 불만족스러워하고 있습니다. 우리 관리자인 숀 그레디 씨나 우리 프로젝트 조정자 중 한 분이 하루 정도 뒤에 귀하의 상사에게 정식으로 연락을 취할 것이지만, 저는 귀하에게 구체적인 문제들에 관한 주의를 드리려고 합니다.

첫 번째로는 배관과 배선 부품의 예정된 배송 날짜와 설치 시작 날짜 사이에 오랜 지연이 있습니다. 그들은 배송과 설치 시작 사이의 10일 동안에 잠재적인 기상 피해를 막을 어떤 저장고가 준비될 것인지를 알고 싶어 합니다. 두 번째는 프로젝트 중간에 끼어 있는 일주일의 휴식입니다. 그것은 이전에 언급된 바도 없으며 승인된 바도 없었습니다. 그리고 마지막으로 개장식을 6월 1일에 하기로 예정되어 있지만, 귀하의 건축 종료일은 더 늦게 잡혀 있습니다. 저는 우리가 몇몇 절충안을 찾을 수 있도록 귀사가 일정에 대해 탄력적으로 움직일 수 있기를 바랍니다.

마틴

2019년 12월 26일

제니퍼 위너
시애틀 주택 회사
61 화이트 크릭 레인

위너 씨에게,

맥키 주택 단지 개발에 관한 귀하의 12월 21일 자 편지에 대한 응답으로, 저는 다음의 해결책을 제시할 수 있습니다. 우선, 귀하의 6월 1일 개장식 계획을 받아들이는 것은 문제가 되지 않습니다. 저희가 최종 검사 과정을 6일에서 3일로 단축하면 될 문제입니다. 배관과 배선 부품에 대해서는 현장 저장 시설이 없습니다—사용 대기될 자재들은 단순히 방수포로 덮을 것입니다. 우리가 예정된 부품 설치 시작일인 5월 1일을 바꿀 수 없지만, 귀하가 허락한다면 우리는 배송 날짜를 변경할 수 있습니다. 마지막으로, 프로젝트 중간 휴식은 협상이 불가합니다. 그것은 노동조합 규정이며 콘크리트 토대가 마르고 굳어져야 할 시기에 맞춘 것입니다.

진심으로

제레미 피번
프리미엄 건설

맥키 주택 단지 개발 – 최종 건축 일정			
날짜	업무	날짜	업무
1/18 ~ 2/10	현장의 수평화와 준비	4/28	배관과 배선 부품 배송
2/10 ~ 2/20	토대를 위한 콘크리트 도포	5/1 ~ 5/15	배관과 배선 부품 설치
2/21 ~ 2/28	휴식 기간	5/16~ 5/28	내부와 외부 마무리 작업
3/1 ~ 4/30	건물 뼈대의 전체적인 건축	5/29 ~ 5/31	최종 검사

run into (곤경 등을) 만나다 snag (뜻하지 않은) 장애 coordinator 조정자 formally 정식으로 or so ~쯤[정도] heads-up 주의, 경고 plumbing 배관 (공사) wiring 배선 component 부품 storage 저장고 in place ~을 위한 준비가 되어 있는 weeklong 일주일에 걸친 approve 승인하다 opening ceremony 개장식 be meant to ~할 예정이다, ~하기로 되어 있다 occur 일어나다, 발생하다 flexible (시간을) 조정할 수 있는; 유연한 middle ground 절충안, 타협안 in response to ~에 응답하여 accommodate (요구 등을) 받아들이다 condense 단축[요약]하다 as for ~에 관해 on-site 현장에 materials 자재 waterproof 방수의 tarp 방수포 alter 바꾸다 in question 불확실한; 문제의 non-negotiable 협상할 수 없는 union 노동조합 mandated 규정된 coincide with 부합[일치]하다 foundation 토대, 하부 구조 set (시멘트 등이) 굳어지다, 응고하다 leveling 수평화, 균등화 application 도포, 바르기 frame (건물 등의) 뼈대 finishing touch 마무리 작업[손질]

196 이메일의 목적은 무엇인가?
(A) 일정 지연에 대해 사과하기
(B) 누군가에게 앞으로 있을 행사에 대해 알려 주기
(C) 잘못된 건설에 대해 불평하기
(D) 누군가에게 잠재적인 문제에 대해 주의 주기

197 제니퍼 위너 씨는 누구일 것 같은가?
(A) 마틴 도노반 씨의 관리자
(B) 숀 그레디 씨의 상사
(C) 건물 검사관
(D) 프로젝트 조정자

198 원래 일정에서 배관과 배선 부품 배송 날짜는?
(A) 4월 1일
(B) 4월 20일
(C) 5월 1일
(D) 5월 15일

199 피번 씨가 일주일간의 휴식에 대해 말한 것은 무엇인가?
(A) 짧아질 것이다.
(B) 미뤄질 것이다.
(C) 바꿀 수 없다.
(D) 이 프로젝트에는 적용되지 않는다.

200 원래 일정에서 마지막 건설 날짜는 언제였는가?
(A) 5월 28일
(B) 5월 29일
(C) 6월 1일
(D) 6월 3일

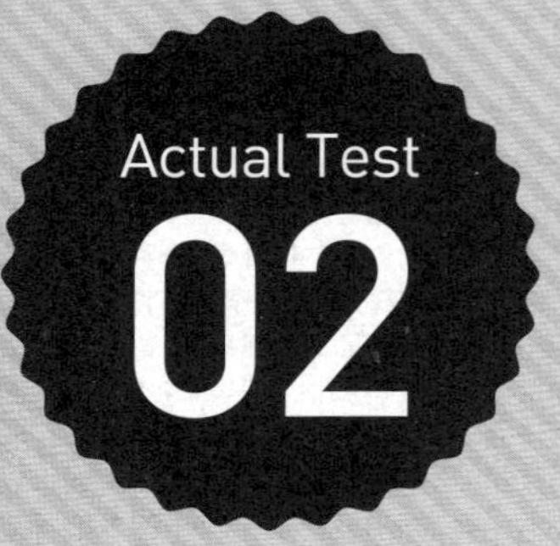

Listening Comprehension

PART 1

1 (B)	2 (C)	3 (B)	4 (B)	5 (A)	6 (A)				

PART 2

7 (C)	8 (C)	9 (A)	10 (B)	11 (A)	12 (C)	13 (B)	14 (C)	15 (C)	16 (B)
17 (B)	18 (B)	19 (A)	20 (C)	21 (C)	22 (A)	23 (A)	24 (B)	25 (C)	26 (A)
27 (C)	28 (B)	29 (A)	30 (B)	31 (B)					

PART 3

32 (C)	33 (A)	34 (D)	35 (C)	36 (C)	37 (A)	38 (C)	39 (A)	40 (D)	41 (C)
42 (A)	43 (D)	44 (A)	45 (B)	46 (C)	47 (A)	48 (C)	49 (B)	50 (B)	51 (A)
52 (D)	53 (D)	54 (A)	55 (B)	56 (B)	57 (D)	58 (C)	59 (A)	60 (A)	61 (D)
62 (D)	63 (A)	64 (B)	65 (D)	66 (D)	67 (D)	68 (A)	69 (A)	70 (D)	

PART 4

71 (A)	72 (A)	73 (A)	74 (D)	75 (C)	76 (A)	77 (C)	78 (C)	79 (B)	80 (B)
81 (C)	82 (A)	83 (A)	84 (D)	85 (C)	86 (C)	87 (A)	88 (A)	89 (C)	90 (A)
91 (C)	92 (B)	93 (C)	94 (C)	95 (B)	96 (A)	97 (C)	98 (C)	99 (A)	100 (B)

Reading Comprehension

PART 5

101 (D)	102 (D)	103 (C)	104 (B)	105 (B)	106 (D)	107 (A)	108 (D)	109 (B)	110 (C)
111 (A)	112 (D)	113 (B)	114 (A)	115 (C)	116 (B)	117 (A)	118 (A)	119 (D)	120 (A)
121 (B)	122 (D)	123 (B)	124 (A)	125 (A)	126 (C)	127 (A)	128 (A)	129 (C)	130 (C)

PART 6

131 (C)	132 (A)	133 (D)	134 (A)	135 (D)	136 (C)	137 (A)	138 (D)	139 (C)	140 (A)
141 (C)	142 (A)	143 (B)	144 (A)	145 (B)	146 (D)				

PART 7

147 (C)	148 (A)	149 (C)	150 (C)	151 (C)	152 (B)	153 (D)	154 (D)	155 (B)	156 (C)
157 (B)	158 (A)	159 (D)	160 (C)	161 (A)	162 (B)	163 (D)	164 (D)	165 (A)	166 (C)
167 (A)	168 (B)	169 (A)	170 (D)	171 (D)	172 (B)	173 (D)	174 (D)	175 (A)	176 (D)
177 (B)	178 (B)	179 (A)	180 (D)	181 (B)	182 (B)	183 (C)	184 (B)	185 (C)	186 (A)
187 (C)	188 (C)	189 (C)	190 (B)	191 (C)	192 (A)	193 (D)	194 (B)	195 (D)	196 (D)
197 (D)	198 (D)	199 (C)	200 (D)						

Part 1

1 미W
(A) Some sacks have been piled in the wheelbarrow.
(B) The man is emptying a bucket into a sack.
(C) Some bricks are being transported.
(D) The man is carrying a tray of fruits.

(A) 몇몇 자루들이 손수레에 쌓여 있다.
(B) 남자가 양동이를 자루에 비우고 있다.
(C) 벽돌들이 운송되고 있다.
(D) 남자가 과일이 든 쟁반을 나르고 있다.

sack 자루 pile 쌓다 wheelbarrow 손수레 bucket 양동이 brick 벽돌 tray 쟁반

2 미M
(A) Some people have gathered for a meeting.
(B) Some people are entering a building.
(C) A sign is hanging from the ceiling.
(D) An outdoor area is crowded with people.

(A) 몇몇 사람들이 회의를 하기 위해 모여 있다.
(B) 몇몇 사람들이 건물 안으로 들어가고 있다.
(C) 표지판이 천장에 걸려 있다.
(D) 야외 지역이 사람들로 붐비고 있다.

gather 모이다 ceiling 천장

3 호M
(A) One of the people is looking at the computer monitor.
(B) The people are reading a document.
(C) The people are placing folders in a cabinet.
(D) The woman is adjusting a picture frame on the wall.

(A) 사람들 중 한 명이 컴퓨터 화면을 보고 있다.
(B) 사람들이 서류를 읽고 있다.
(C) 사람들이 캐비닛에 서류철을 넣고 있다.
(D) 여자가 벽의 액자를 조정하고 있다.

document 서류 folder 폴더, 서류철 adjust 조정하다 picture frame 액자

4 미W
(A) Some people are installing music stands in rows.
(B) Some musicians are marching with instruments.
(C) Some people are passing under a bridge.
(D) Some flags are being lowered down the flagpoles.

(A) 몇몇 사람들이 줄지어 악보대를 정렬하고 있다.
(B) 몇몇 음악가들이 악기를 들고 행진하고 있다.
(C) 몇몇 사람들이 다리를 건너고 있다.
(D) 몇몇 깃발들이 깃대에서 내려지고 있다.

music stand 악보대 in rows 줄지어 march 행진하다 instrument 악기 lower 내리다 flagpole 깃대

5 미M
(A) There is a path through a park.
(B) Some bicycles are parked near a road.
(C) People are jogging along a walkway.
(D) Benches have been placed in a row.

(A) 공원을 가로지르는 길이 있다.
(B) 몇몇 자전거가 도로 근처에 세워져 있다.
(C) 사람들이 길을 따라 조깅을 하고 있다.
(D) 벤치가 일렬로 놓여 있다.

walkway 통로 in a row 일렬로

6 미W
(A) Reading material is on display.
(B) A cabinet is in the corner.
(C) Furniture is being removed from a room.
(D) A pillar is being painted.

(A) 읽을거리가 진열 중이다.
(B) 구석에 캐비닛이 하나 있다.
(C) 가구가 방에서 옮겨지고 있다.
(D) 기둥이 페인트칠되고 있다.

on display 진열된 pillar 기둥

Part 2

7 Where is the accounting department?
미W (A) It's empty.
미M (B) We have 10 employees.
(C) In Room 919.

회계 부서는 어디에 있나요?
(A) 아니요, 그건 비었어요.
(B) 우리는 직원이 10명 있습니다.
(C) 919호에요.

accounting department 회계 부서

8 When did you accept the position?
미M (A) She wanted those.
호M (B) In the cabinet.
(C) Two days ago.

당신은 언제 그 직책을 수락했나요?
(A) 그녀가 그것들을 원했어요.
(B) 보관장 안에요.
(C) 이틀 전에요.

position 직책

9 Should I remind Akram about his interview?
미W (A) No, I already mentioned it to him.
미M (B) Yes, he is one of the attorneys.
(C) Yes, I've been there previously.

아크람에게 그녀의 면접을 상기시켜야 할까요?
(A) 아니요, 제가 이미 그녀에게 언급했어요.
(B) 네, 그는 변호사 중 한 명입니다.
(C) 네, 전에 그곳에 갔습니다.

mention 언급하다, 말하다 previously 전에

10 Why was the seminar rescheduled?
미M (A) Board Room 6.
미W (B) Mr. King's absent.
(C) There's a long line.

왜 세미나 일정이 다시 잡혔나요?
(A) 중역 회의실 6호입니다.
(B) 킹 씨가 부재중이었기 때문입니다.
(C) 줄이 길어요.

reschedule 일정을 다시 잡다 board room 중역 회의실 absent 부재한, 결석한

11 Operating in shifts is highly productive, isn't it?
미M (A) Our manager believes it is.
미W (B) Yes, that's the official status.
(C) They're revealing the results tonight.

교대조로 운영하는 것은 매우 생산적이에요, 그렇지 않나요?
(A) 우리 관리자는 그렇다고 생각해요.
(B) 네, 그것이 공식적인 상황입니다.
(C) 그들은 오늘 밤 그 결과를 공개합니다.

shift 교대 근무(조) productive 생산적인 official 공식적인 status (진행 과정상의) 상황 reveal 공개하다

12 Why don't we break for lunch now?
미M (A) Yes, the brake is working fine.
미W (B) They serve really nice spaghetti.
(C) Sure and please ask Ms. Joan to join us.

지금 잠깐 쉬며 점심 먹는 게 어때요?
(A) 네, 브레이크는 제대로 작동합니다.
(B) 그들은 정말 맛있는 스파게티를 제공합니다.
(C) 물론이죠, 조앤 씨에게 우리랑 같이 가자고 물어보세요.

어휘 break 쉬다 brake (차의) 브레이크

13 Would you like to go out for fresh air?
미M (A) Yes, I would like to stay inside.
호M (B) No, I have to finish this by 2.
(C) By airmail, I think.

바람 쐬러 밖으로 나갈래요?
(A) 네, 저는 안에 있고 싶습니다.
(B)아니요, 이걸 2시까지 끝내야 해요.
(C) 항공 우편인 것 같아요.
어휘 go out 밖으로 나가다 airmail 항공 우편

14 Did you renew that contract last week?
미W (A) That's a great idea.
미M (B) Once in a while.
(C) Yes, on the 16th.

지난주 그 계약을 갱신하셨나요?
(A) 멋진 생각이네요.
(B) 아주 가끔이요
(C)네, 16일에요.
어휘 renew 갱신하다 once in a while 아주 가끔씩

15 To whom should I speak about the work schedule?
미M (A) The speaker will be here in a minute.
미W (B) Mr. Thompson is the keynote speaker.
(C) It's all in the memo on your desk.

근무 일정에 관해 누구에게 이야기해야 하나요?
(A) 그 연사는 곧 여기에 올 겁니다.
(B) 톰슨 씨가 기조연설자입니다.
(C)모두 다 책상에 있는 메모에 적혀 있습니다.
어휘 in a minute 곧 keynote 기조

16 Did you go to the weekly meeting yesterday?
호M (A) Yes, I am going to join.
미M (B) No, it was cancelled.
(C) Oh, are you ready to meet?

어제 주간 회의에 가셨어요?
(A) 네, 저도 합류하려고요.
(B)아니요, 취소됐어요.
(C) 아, 만날 준비가 되었나요?
어휘 weekly 주간의 cancel 취소하다

17 How long will you be away on vacation?
미W (A) In five days, he will come back.
미M (B) My boss hasn't approved it yet.
(C) I really had a good time there.

휴가는 얼마나 가실 겁니까?
(A) 5일 지나면 그는 돌아올 겁니다.
(B)제 상사가 아직 그것을 승인하지 않았습니다.
(C) 거기에서 정말 좋은 시간 보냈습니다.
어휘 be away 떠나 있다 approve 승인하다

18 Who will be driving you to your appointment?
호M (A) From the headquarters.
미M (B) My coworker's taking me.
(C) At 3 in the afternoon.

약속 자리에 누가 운전해서 당신을 데려다 주죠?
(A) 본사에서요
(B)제 동료가요.
(C) 오후 3시요
어휘 appointment 약속 headquarters 본사

19 Did you drop off the check at the bank?
미W (A) I thought Sam would do that for me.
미M (B) You should report to work every day.
(C) It's located right across our building.

은행에 수표 입금했어요?
(A)샘이 저 대신할 거라고 생각했어요.
(B) 매일 출근 보고를 하세요.
(C) 우리 건물 바로 맞은편에 있어요.
어휘 drop off 갖다 주다 report to work 출근 보고를 하다 locate 위치하다

20 Should we get permission before renting a car?
호M (A) No, I am a previous owner.
미M (B) Can you lend it to me?
(C) I will ask Mr. Tyron.

저희가 차를 빌리는 데 허가를 받아야 할까요?
(A) 아니요, 저는 예전 주인입니다.
(B) 저한테 빌려 주실 수 있어요?
(C)타이런 씨에게 물어볼게요.
어휘 rent 빌리다 previous 이전의 owner 주인

21 You are the new project leader, aren't you?
미W (A) Yes, the project is going as planned.
미M (B) I was told to leave the office by 1.
(C) Yes, as of today, I'm in charge.

당신이 새로운 공사 담당자죠, 그렇죠?
(A) 네, 그 공사는 계획대로 진행되고 있습니다.
(B) 1시까지 사무실을 떠나라고 들었습니다.
(C)네, 오늘부로 제가 책임자입니다.
어휘 as planned 계획대로 as of ~부터 be in charge 담당하다

22 Where did you buy a tuna sandwich?
미M (A) At the café across the road.
미W (B) Thanks, I've had enough.
(C) Wherever you want.

참치 샌드위치는 어디에서 샀어요?
(A)길 건너 카페요.
(B) 고마워요, 충분히 먹었어요.
(C) 당신이 원하는 곳 어디든.
어휘 tuna 치즈 wherever 어디든지

23 Where did you park the company vehicle?
미W (A) Mr. Hopkins took it for a regular inspection.
미M (B) The parking lot is going to raise the fee.
(C) It has been chosen the best car of the year.

회사 차량을 어디에 주차했나요?
(A)홉킨스 씨가 정기 검사 때문에 가지고 갔어요.
(B) 그 주차장은 요금을 올릴 겁니다.
(C) 그것은 올해의 최고의 차로 선정되었어요.
어휘 vehicle 차량 inspection 검사 raise 인상하다 fee 요금

24 Aren't those the keys to the laboratory?
호M (A) At the research laboratory.
미M (B) Yes, I've been looking for them all day.
(C) No, it takes up too much space.

저것 실험실 열쇠 아닌가요?
(A) 연구 실험실에서요.
(B)맞네요, 제가 하루 종일 찾고 있었어요.
(C) 아니요, 공간을 너무 많이 차지해요.
어휘 laboratory 실험실 take up 차지하다 space 공간

25 Who should I contact for the computer lesson?
미M (A) From Lesson 5, I think.
미W (B) Annual members are entitled to a 25% price reduction.
(C) I'm afraid they have recently closed that program.

컴퓨터 수업에 대해선 누구에게 연락해야 하나요?
(A) 5과부터인 것 같은데요.
(B) 연간 회원들은 25퍼센트 할인을 받습니다.
(C)최근에 그 프로그램이 최근에 중단된 것 같아요.
어휘 contact 연락하다 be entitled to ~을 받을 자격이 있다 price reduction 가격 인하

26 Could you tell me where I can find the extra tea cups?
미M (A) In the cupboard, over the sink.
미W (B) Just a little amount.
(C) I made it a day ago.

차 마시는 컵 남는 게 어디 있나요?
(A) 싱크대 위 찬장에 보세요.
(B) 아주 조금요.
(C) 하루 전에 만들었어요.

어휘 extra 여분의 cupboard 찬장 amount 양

27 To redeem your coupon, please follow the instructions.
미M (A) The coupon is valid until the end of the week.
호M (B) I deem the instructions to be necessary.
(C) I did it on the Internet just a while ago.

쿠폰을 사용하시려면 지시 사항을 따라 주세요.
(A) 그 쿠폰은 이번 주말까지 유효해요.
(B) 저는 지시 사항이 필요하다고 생각하는데요.
(C) 좀 전에 인터넷으로 했습니다.

어휘 redeem (쿠폰을) 현금처럼 쓰다 instruction 지시 사항 valid 유효한 deem ~라고 생각하다 just a while ago 좀 전에

28 Where does the bus to Cambridge stop?
미M (A) Every twenty minutes.
미W (B) Just around the corner.
(C) Can you give me a ride?

케임브리지로 가는 버스는 어디에 서나요?
(A) 20분마다요.
(B) 모퉁이 바로 돌면요.
(C) 저 좀 태워 주실 수 있나요?

어휘 give a ride 태워 주다

29 I'm looking for a ride to the conference hall.
미M (A) You can join us in our carpool.
호M (B) The hall can accommodate 200 people.
(C) It doesn't start until 2 in the afternoon.

회의장까지 갈 차편이 필요합니다.
(A) 저희와 차를 같이 타고 가시면 돼요.
(B) 그 홀은 200명을 수용할 수 있습니다.
(C) 오후 2시나 되어야 시작합니다.

어휘 ride 탈것 carpool 차를 함께 타다 accommodate 수용하다

30 That was the best movie I've seen in years.
미M (A) I'm getting better, thanks.
미W (B) I wonder why the reviews were so negative.
(C) For the next couple of years.

몇 년 만에 본 것 중 가장 좋은 영화였어요.
(A) 점점 좋아지고 있어요, 감사해요.
(B) 평이 왜 안 좋은지 궁금하네요.
(C) 다음 몇 년 동안이요.

어휘 review 후기, 평 negative 부정적인

31 Could we discuss the new product over dinner?
미W (A) A buffet will be served on that occasion.
미M (B) That would be a nice and relaxed setting.
(C) It was named after the hit product.

저녁 먹으면서 그 신제품에 대해 이야기할 수 있을까요?
(A) 뷔페가 그 행사를 위해 제공될 것입니다.
(B) 분위기가 편안하면서 괜찮겠네요.
(C) 히트 상품을 따라 이름을 붙였어요.

어휘 over ~하면서 occasion 행사 relaxed 편안한 setting 분위기 name 이름을 붙이다

Part 3

Questions 32-34 refer to the following conversation. 미M 미W

M Excuse me. Is this the room for the "Investment Technique 101" Seminar?
W Yes, it is. But you are here a bit too early. The seminar won't begin until 2 o'clock, and it's only 1 o'clock now. The room needs a bit more time to be ready. You can stay in the lounge down the hall.
M Oh, I think I mixed up the time the seminar was supposed to start. Is there a place I can get a cup of coffee while I wait?
W Coffee and some snacks have been prepared in the lounge. Just go straight down the hall.

남 실례합니다. 이 방이 '투자 기술 입문' 세미나 맞나요?
여 네, 맞아요. 좀 일찍 오셨네요. 세미나는 2시 되어야 시작하는데 지금 1시네요. 방이 준비되려면 시간이 좀 필요해요. 아래 라운지에 계셔도 됩니다.
남 세미나가 시작했다고 시간을 착각했네요. 기다리는 동안 커피 한 잔 마실 데가 있을까요?
여 라운지에서 커피와 간식이 제공됩니다. 홀 따라 계속 가세요.

investment 투자 technique 기술 101 입문의, 기초 과정의 mix up 혼동하다 correct 정확한

32 What time does the event start?
(A) At noon
(B) At 1 o'clock
(C) At 2 o'clock
(D) At 3 o'clock

행사 시작 시간은?
(A) 정오
(B) 오후 1시
(C) 오후 2시
(D) 오후 3시

33 What does the woman tell the man to do?
(A) Wait while the room is being prepared
(B) Buy some juice for the attendees
(C) Come back tomorrow
(D) Remember the correct time

여자가 남자에게 하라고 하는 것은?
(A) 방이 준비되는 동안 기다리기
(B) 참석자들에게 주스 사 주기
(C) 내일 다시 오기
(D) 정확한 시간 기억하기

34 What will the man do next?
(A) Find a café
(B) Give a lecture
(C) Clean the room
(D) Go to the lounge

남자가 다음에 할 일은?
(A) 카페 찾기
(B) 강의 제공
(C) 방 청소
(D) 라운지에 가기

Questions 35-37 refer to the following conversation. 미W 호M

W Hello, I'd like to purchase 5 tickets for admission to the Children's Science Center. Three for kids, two for adults. And I was wondering if you give student discounts.

M With a valid ID, it costs $4 per student and $10 per adult. So the total comes to $34 dollars. But if you are going to visit here often, I recommend you take a 1-year membership which costs $200.

W Is that right? Actually, this is the first time we're here. Could you tell me about it in detail?

M Certainly. It gives you lots of benefits like free admissions to all exhibits and a 10% discount on souvenirs.

여 안녕하세요. 어린이 과학 센터 입장권 5매 주세요. 어린이 3장, 어른 2장입니다. 학생은 할인이 가능한지 궁금하네요.

남 적절한 신분증이 있으시면 학생은 한 명당 4달러이고 어른은 10달러입니다. 총 합계는 34달러입니다. 그런데 자주 오실 거면, 200달러에 1년 연간 회원권을 구입하세요.

여 그래요? 사실 여기 처음이라 좀 더 자세하게 그것에 관해 말씀해 주실래요?

남 그럼요. 회원권을 구입하시면 모든 전시회 무료입장에 기념품을 10퍼센트 할인해 드립니다.

purchase 구입하다 admission 입장 valid 적절한 ID 신분증(=identification) comes to 총합계가 ~이다 in detail 자세히 benefit 혜택 exhibit 전시회 souvenir 기념품

35 Where are the speakers now?
(A) At a natural forest
(B) At an art museum
(C) At an educational institution
(D) At a gift shop

화자들은 지금 어디에 있는가?
(A) 자연림
(B) 미술관
(C) 교육 기관
(D) 선물 가게

36 What does the woman ask about?
(A) Business hours
(B) Group rates
(C) Discounts for students
(D) Prices of souvenirs

여자는 무엇에 관해 물어보는가?
(A) 영업시간
(B) 단체 요금
(C) 학생 할인
(D) 기념품 가격

37 What does the man suggest?
(A) Buying an annual ticket
(B) Visiting the special exhibit
(C) Shopping for souvenirs
(D) Coming early for admission

남자는 무엇을 제안하는가?
(A) 연간 회원권 구매
(B) 특별 전시회 관람
(C) 기념품 구입
(D) 일찍 입장하기

Questions 38-40 refer to the following conversation. 미W 미M

W Keith, Mr. Wilder from the Grand Department store just called. He seemed to be concerned that the extension of the parking lot is going a bit slow.

M I can see why he might think that. It usually takes a long time to do the foundation. After that, it's real quick. Also, I'm checking the schedule and everything is going as planned. I'm pretty sure that we'll be able to finish by the end of this month, which is the deadline.

W Should I call Mr. Wilder and let him know this?

M That's OK. I have to call him anyway to talk to him about some minor revisions.

여 키스, 그랜드 백화점 와일더 씨 전화 왔어요. 주차장 확장이 좀 늦어진다고 걱정하는 것 같던데요.

남 그분이 왜 그렇게 생각하는지 알 것 같아요. 기초 공사하는 데 보통 오래 걸리거든요. 그 후에는 정말 빨라요. 제가 일정을 확인하고 있고 모든 게 예정대로 진행되고 있어요. 우리가 마감 시한인 이번 달 말까지 분명히 끝낼 수 있을 겁니다.

여 와일더 씨에게 전화해서 이걸 알려 주셔야 할 것 같은데요?

남 좋아요. 제가 몇 가지 변경을 말씀드릴 게 있어서 어쨌든 그분과 통화해야 해요.

extension 확대, 증축 foundation 토대, 기초 as planned 예정대로 minor 사소한 revision 수정, 변경 express 표현하다 inquire 문의하다

38 Why did Mr. Wilder call?
(A) To change the deadline date
(B) To invite the woman to the store
(C) To express his concern about the construction
(D) To inquire about the materials

와일더 씨가 전화한 이유는?
(A) 마감일을 변경하기 위해
(B) 여자를 가게에 초대하기 위해
(C) 공사에 관한 자신의 염려를 표현하기 위해
(D) 자재에 관해 문의하기 위해

39 What does the man tell the woman?
(A) They can meet the due date.
(B) They need a larger space.
(C) They are over budget.
(D) They need an extra month.

남자가 여자에게 말한 것은?
(A) 그들이 마감일을 맞출 수 있다.
(B) 그들은 더 넓은 공간이 필요하다.
(C) 그들은 예산을 초과했다.
(D) 그들은 한 달이 더 필요하다.

40 What will the man do next?
(A) Stop building the foundation
(B) Repaint the department store
(C) Check the schedule
(D) Contact Mr. Wilder

남자가 다음에 할 일은?
(A) 기초 공사 중단
(B) 백화점에 다시 페인트칠하기
(C) 일정 확인
(D) 와일더 씨에게 연락

Questions 41-43 refer to the following conversation. 미W 호M

W Hey, Max. Is it true that the power went out at the Lloyd Factory yesterday? I'm worried because we have to send the customized coffee mugs to Salinas Products by tomorrow.

M Don't worry, Glenn. The Lloyd Factory had a blackout for a couple of hours yesterday, but it was after the order was already sent.

W I'm relieved to hear that. They're supposed to distribute the mugs with the company logo at the promotional event next week.

M Well, the shipment will arrive at Salinas Products by tomorrow at the latest. So I think everything will be fine.

여 저기요, 맥스. 어제 로이드 공장에 전기가 나갔었다는 게 사실인가요? 내일까지 살리나스 프로덕츠로 주문 제작된 머그컵을 보내줘야 해서 걱정이 되네요.

남 걱정 말아요, 글렌. 어제 두어 시간 정도 로이드 공장에서 정전이 되었지만, 그건 이미 그 주문품을 보낸 후였어요.

여 그 말을 들으니 안심이 되네요. 그들은 다음 주에 있을 홍보 행사에서 회사의 로고가 박힌 머그컵을 나눠주기로 되어 있거든요.

남 음, 배송은 늦어도 내일까지 살리나스 프로덕츠에 도착할 거예요. 그러니 다 잘될 것 같네요.

go out (전기 등이) 나가다 customized 주문 제작된 blackout 정전 distribute 나눠주다 promotional event 홍보 행사 shipment 선적

41 What are the speakers mainly discussing?
(A) The location of a promotional event
(B) The opening of a new factory
(C) The shipment of some goods
(D) The cause of a power failure

화자들은 무엇에 대해 주로 논의하는가?
(A) 홍보 행사의 장소
(B) 새 공장의 개장
(C) 상품의 배송
(D) 정전의 원인

42 What does the woman imply when she says, "I'm relieved to hear that"?
(A) She is happy that a delivery will arrive on time.
(B) She is satisfied with the quality of some products.
(C) She feels better after receiving treatment.
(D) She likes to hear other people's opinions.

여자가 "그 말을 들으니 안심이 되네요"라고 말한 의도는 무엇인가?
(A) 여자는 배송이 제때에 도착하리라는 것에 만족한다.
(B) 여자는 상품의 질에 만족한다.
(C) 여자는 치료를 받은 후에 몸이 나아졌다.
(D) 여자는 다른 사람들의 견해를 듣고 싶어한다.

43 According to the woman, what will happen next week?
(A) A factory tour
(B) A trade show
(C) A demonstration
(D) A promotional event

여자에 따르면, 다음 주에 무슨 일이 있을 것인가?
(A) 공장 견학
(B) 무역 박람회
(C) 시연
(D) 홍보 행사

Questions 44-46 refer to the following conversation. 미W 호M

W We have unloaded the last box from the truck, Mr. Pitt. My team members are unpacking the pads used to protect your electric appliances during the move.

M Thanks for all your hard work, Ms. Pearce. The move went smoothly as your team worked very efficiently.

W You're welcome. By the way, where would you like to put this last box? There's no label on it that says where it should go.

M I think some office supplies are in it. Can you put it in the storage room please?

여 피트 씨, 트럭에서 마지막 상자를 내렸습니다. 저의 팀원들이 지금 이사 중에 전자제품을 보호하기 위해 사용했던 패드를 풀고 있습니다.

남 열심히 일해 주셔서 감사합니다. 피어스 씨. 당신의 팀이 일을 효율적으로 해줘서 이사가 순조롭게 진행됐어요.

여 천만에요. 그나저나 이 마지막 박스는 어디에 둘까요? 어디에 놓으라는 라벨이 박스에 붙어 있지는 않네요.

남 그 안에 사무용품이 있을 거예요. 그 박스를 창고 안에 넣어 주시겠어요?

unload (짐을) 내리다 unpack (짐을) 풀다 move 이사 go smoothly 순조롭게 진행되다 label 라벨 storage room 창고, 비품실

44 Where does the woman most likely work?
(A) At a moving company
(B) At a financial firm
(C) At an office supply store
(D) At a property development company

여자는 어디에서 일할 것 같은가?
(A) 이삿짐 회사
(B) 금융 회사
(C) 사무용품 상점
(D) 자산 개발 회사

45 What does the man imply when he says, "Thanks for all your hard work, Ms. Pearce"?
(A) He has received a discount.
(B) He is satisfied with his office relocation.
(C) He wants the woman to try harder.
(D) A renovation project is ahead of schedule.

남자가 "열심히 일해주셔서 감사합니다, 피어스 씨"라고 말한 의도는 무엇인가?
(A) 그는 할인을 받았다.
(B) 그는 사무실 이전에 만족한다.
(C) 그는 여자가 좀 더 노력하기 원한다.
(D) 보수 프로젝트가 일정보다 빠르다.

46 What does the woman ask the man about?
(A) How to get to a meeting room
(B) The cost of a special service
(C) Where to place a container
(D) The name of a company

여자는 남자에게 무엇에 관해 묻는가?
(A) 회의실에 가는 방법
(B) 특별 서비스의 비용
(C) 용기를 놓을 장소
(D) 회사의 이름

Questions 47-49 refer to the following conversation with three speakers. 미M 미W 호M

M1 Did you guys hear the news? Beginning today, the Bloomville Bridge will be closed for repairs.

W Yes, I just read about it in the newspaper. Road crews will be closing one lane of the Bloomville Bridge to do maintenance work at 8 P.M. every night. But all the lanes will reopen by 7 A.M. the following morning.

M2 Then we don't have to worry about traffic during the morning commute. Do you know how long it will take, Paul?

M1 Yes. Unless it rains or snows, the work will be finished within a week.

W I'm worried about night time congestion though. It's going to be pretty backed up in the evening leaving the city, since vehicles in both directions will have to share the one open lane.

M2 I know. Maybe I should take a rain check on the movie tonight. I hate being stuck in traffic after a long day of work.

남1 여러분 뉴스 들으셨어요? 오늘부터 블룸빌 브릿지가 수리 때문에 폐쇄된다고 하네요.

여 네, 저도 신문에서 방금 읽었어요. 매일 밤 8시에 도로 작업자들이 블룸빌 브릿지의 차선 하나를 봉쇄하고 수리 작업을 한대요. 그러나 다음 날 아침 7시까지는 전 차선이 다시 열린다고 해요.

남2 그럼 아침 출근 때 교통 체증은 걱정할 필요 없겠네요. 그게 얼마나 걸릴지 알아요, 폴?

남1 네, 비나 눈이 오지 않으면 작업은 일주일 안에 끝날 거예요.

여 그런데 저는 저녁 교통 체증이 걱정되네요. 양쪽 차선 차량들이 열린 한 차선을 번갈아 이용해야 하니 저녁 시간에 도시를 빠져 나갈 때 꽤 막히겠어요.

남2 맞아요. 전 오늘 밤 영화는 다음으로 미뤄야겠어요. 하루 종일 일하고 막히는 차에 갇혀 있는 건 싫거든요.

road crew 도로 작업자 lane 차선 congestion 체증 be backed up (차량이) 막히다 take a rain check on 다음 기회로 미루다 be stuck in traffic 교통 체증에 갇히다

47 What is scheduled to begin today?
(A) Some repair work
(B) A sporting event
(C) Building renovations
(D) A new theater production

오늘 무엇이 시작될 예정인가?
(A) 보수 공사
(B) 스포츠 경기
(C) 건물 보수
(D) 새로운 무대 공연

48 According to Paul, what might delay the scheduled repairs?
(A) Labor costs
(B) Special events
(C) Changes in the weather
(D) Complaints from local residents

폴에 따르면, 무엇이 예정된 보수를 연기할 수 있는가?
(A) 특별 행사
(B) 노동 임금
(C) 날씨의 변화
(D) 지역 주민의 불평

49 Why is traffic congestion expected at night?
(A) Some road crews are off sick.
(B) A bridge is not fully open to traffic.
(C) Many people are attending an event.
(D) Several cars are involved in an accident.

왜 밤에 교통 체증이 예상되는가?
(A) 몇 명의 도로 작업자가 아파서 결근했다.
(B) 다리가 차량들에 완전히 열리지 않는다.
(C) 많은 사람들이 행사에 참석한다.
(D) 여러 차량이 사고에 휘말렸다.

Questions 50-52 refer to the following conversation. 미M 미W

M Emma, what do you know about the new audio software that the university is planning to install?

W Well, the software translates text into spoken words. It'll enable our students to listen to certain texts. But we can find out more at the meeting for the lecturers on Monday.

M Unfortunately, I can't make it. I'll be teaching at the high school on Monday. But I'd be interested to find out more. Could you bring back any available documents for me?

남 엠마, 대학이 설치하려고 계획 중인 새로운 오디오 소프트웨어에 관해 무엇을 알고 있나요?

여 음, 그 소프트웨어는 문자를 말로 바꿔줘요. 우리 학생들이 특정 문자들을 들을 수 있도록 해 줄 것입니다. 하지만 월요일에 있는 교수 회의에서 더 자세히 알아볼 수 있습니다.

남 안타깝게도, 저는 그 자리에 참석할 수 없어요. 월요일에 고등학교에서 수업이 있거든요. 하지만 더 알아보는 데는 관심이 있어요. 이용할 수 있는 아무 자료나 가져와 주실 수 있나요?

translate 번역하다, 통역하다; (다른 형태로) 바꾸다 text 문자 spoken word 말 enable 가능하게 하다 certain 특정한 lecturer 교수 unfortunately 불행히도, 안타깝게도 assess 평가하다 fitness 신체 단련, 건강

50 Where do the speakers work?
(A) At a library
(B) At a university
(C) At a software lab
(D) At a computer store

화자들은 어디에서 일하는가?
(A) 도서관
(B)대학
(C)소프트웨어 연구실
(D) 컴퓨터 매장

51 What does the new software do?
(A) It translates written text to spoken words.
(B) It assesses student fitness.
(C) It helps provide better feedback.
(D) It analyzes people's speech.

새로운 소프트웨어는 무엇을 하는가?
(A)쓰인 글자를 말로 바꾼다.

(B) 학생들의 건강 상태를 평가한다.
(C) 더 나은 피드백을 주는 데 도움을 준다.
(D) 사람의 말을 분석한다.

52 What does the man ask the woman to do?
(A) Write a summary
(B) Upgrade a computer
(C) Register for a workshop
(D) Bring back some information
남자가 여자에게 해 달라고 요청하는 것은?
(A) 요약본 쓰기
(B) 컴퓨터 업그레이드하기
(C) 워크숍 신청하기
(D) 일부 정보 가져다 주기

Questions 53-55 refer to the following conversation. 호M 미W

M You know, our newest wedding dress designs, particularly the new oriental styles, have interested a lot of customers from abroad. We've received inquiries from Malaysia, Belgium, and Africa.
W Yes, it's excellent news. But there are so many other designers on the market. If we really intend to expand our overseas customer base, we need an international agent to sell our product range.
M Yes, I agree. That's why I've already arranged a meeting with the Global Sales Agency to discuss this. They have an excellent overseas reputation and their headquarters are just in the next town.
남 있잖아요, 우리의 최신 웨딩드레스 디자인, 특히 새로운 동양 스타일은 해외에서 많은 고객들의 관심을 받았어요. 우리는 말레이시아, 벨기에, 아프리카에서 문의를 받았습니다.
여 네, 정말 좋은 소식이에요. 하지만 시장에는 너무나 많은 디자이너들이 있어요. 만약 우리가 정말 해외의 고객층을 확장하려 한다면, 우리는 우리 상품군을 판매할 국제 중개인이 필요해요.
남 네, 동의합니다. 그것이 이 문제를 논하기 위해 벌써 글로벌 세일즈 회사와의 회의를 준비한 이유입니다. 그들은 높은 해외 인지도를 가지고 있고, 본사는 바로 옆의 도시에 있습니다.

particularly 특히 oriental 동양적인 abroad 해외에서 inquiry 문의 intend to ~할 의향이다, ~할 작정이다 expand 확장하다 overseas 해외의 customer base 고객층 agent 대리인, 중개상 product range 상품군 reputation 명성, 인지도 headquarters 본사 trustee 이사, 신탁 관리자

53 Where do the speakers most likely work?
(A) At a relocation company
(B) At a clothing store
(C) At an international law firm
(D) At a design company
화자들은 어디에서 일할 것 같은가?
(A) 이사 업체
(B) 의류 매장
(C) 국제 법률 사무소
(D) 디자인 회사

54 What does the woman recommend doing?
(A) Recruiting an overseas agent
(B) Promoting designs online
(C) Publishing a brochure
(D) Hiring a domestic sales team
여자는 무엇을 하라고 추천하는가?
(A) 해외 중개인 채용
(B) 온라인으로 디자인 홍보
(C) 안내 책자 출판
(D) 국내 영업 팀 채용

55 What has the man done?
(A) Joined the board of trustees
(B) Arranged an appointment
(C) Prepared a portfolio
(D) Booked a flight
남자가 한 일은 무엇인가?
(A) 이사회에 참여
(B) 만날 약속 준비
(C) 포트폴리오 준비
(D) 비행편 예약

Questions 56-58 refer to the following conversation. 미W 미M

W Jason, I got your e-mail with the materials you've created for our presentation to the board of directors next week. You asked me to get back to you with my opinions. Do you have a moment now?
M Sure, Kathy. I've been looking forward to hearing from you.
W Well, for the most part, everything looks good. But I would recommend including some graphs.
M Oh, that sounds good. What type of graphs?
W I'll leave that to you. Whatever you think will make it easier to understand the figures we'll be reporting.
여 제이슨, 다음 주에 있을 이사회 보고를 위해 만든 자료가 담긴 당신의 이메일을 받았어요. 제 의견을 달라고 요청하셨는데, 지금 시간 있으세요?
남 그럼요, 캐시. 회신을 기다리고 있었어요.
여 거의 모든 부분이 좋아 보이긴 하지만 그래프를 포함시키는 걸 추천하고 싶네요.
남 아, 그거 좋겠네요. 어떤 종류의 그래프요?
여 그건 당신에게 맡길게요. 보고해야 할 수치들을 더 이해하기 쉽게 만들 수 있다면 무엇이든 생각해 보세요.

material 자료, 소재 board of directors 이사회 look forward to ~을 기대하다 figures 수치 length 길이 visual 시각적인 accompany 동행하다

56 What did the man ask the woman to do in his e-mail?
(A) Contact the board of directors
(B) Provide some feedback on his work
(C) Offer some presentation materials
(D) Confirm the length of a presentation
남자는 이메일에 여자에게 무엇을 하라고 요청했는가?
(A) 이사회에 연락하는 것
(B) 그의 작업에 대한 피드백을 제공하는 것
(C) 발표 자료를 제공하는 것
(D) 프레젠테이션의 길이를 확정하는 것

57 What does the woman mean when she says, "I'll leave that to you"?
(A) She plans to give an item to the man.
(B) She does not intend to stay for much longer.
(C) She will not accompany the man.
(D) She will allow the man to make a decision.

여자가 "그건 당신에게 맡길게요"라고 말한 의미는 무엇인가?
(A) 여자는 남자에게 제품을 줄 예정이다.
(B) 여자는 오래 머물 생각이 없다.
(C) 여자는 남자와 동행하지 않을 것이다.
(D) 여자는 남자가 결정을 내리도록 할 것이다.

58 What does the woman suggest?
(A) Contacting a coworker
(B) Increasing a budget
(C) Adding a visual aid
(D) Shortening a document

여자가 제안하는 것은 무엇인가?
(A) 동료에게 연락하는 것
(B) 예산을 증가시키는 것
(C) 시각 자료를 추가하는 것
(D) 문서를 축약하는 것

Questions 59-61 refer to the following conversation. 미W 호M

W So, from your application form, I understand you have extensive experience at design agencies in various countries. How did you hear about this job vacancy?
M A recruitment agency mentioned it. The company is Signup Agency. I've wanted to work for an international graphic design company and work on global accounts for a long time now. So I seized the opportunity.
W Yes, I know Signup. They find a lot of staff for us. Did they mention that if we hire you, we will pay your removal costs? Let me tell you more.

여 자, 당신의 지원서를 통해, 당신이 여러 나라의 디자인 회사에서 폭넓은 경력을 가진 것을 알고 있어요. 이 공석은 어떻게 알게 되었나요?
남 채용업체에서 알려 주었습니다. 그 회사는 사인업 에이전시입니다. 저는 오랜 시간 동안 국제적인 그래픽 디자인 회사에서 국제 고객과 일하고 싶었습니다. 그래서 이번 기회를 잡았고요.
여 네, 저도 사인업을 알아요. 거기에서 직원들을 많이 찾아 줍니다. 만약 저희가 당신을 채용하게 되면, 당신의 이사 비용을 내 줄 것이라고 말하던가요? 제가 더 말씀드릴게요.

extensive 폭넓은, 광범위한 job vacancy 일자리 공석 recruitment agency 인재 주선업체 agency 대행 회사 seize 잡다 removal cost 이사 비용

59 What industry do the speakers work in?
(A) Graphic design
(B) Television programming
(C) Global media
(D) Online advertising

화자들은 어떤 업계에서 일하는가?
(A) 그래픽 디자인
(B) 텔레비전 프로그래밍
(C) 국제 미디어
(D) 온라인 광고

60 How did the man find out about the job?
(A) From a recruitment agency
(B) From a corporate Web site
(C) From a newspaper advertisement
(D) From a colleague

남자는 그 일자리에 관해 어떻게 알게 되었는가?
(A) 인력 알선업체로부터
(B) 대기업 웹 사이트에서
(C) 신문 광고에서
(D) 동료로부터

61 What will the woman discuss next?
(A) Pension benefits
(B) Working hours
(C) Employment rights
(D) Relocation expenses

여자는 다음에 무엇을 이야기할 것인가?
(A) 연금 혜택
(B) 근무 시간
(C) 고용권
(D) 이사 비용

Questions 62-64 refer to the following conversation. 미M 미W

M Welcome to News 94's Local Businesses. I'm chatting this morning with Wanda Ryder, the designer of *Gold Top*, one of this year's most sought after video games. So Wanda, why don't you explain to our viewers how this concept for the game was invented?
W Well, when my nephew was growing up, he loved dreaming up make-believe places in his head but he'd get frustrated when he forgot details. So I got the idea of developing a fantasy world on the computer to which he could add different areas. I took the idea to Creative Gaming, a large computer firm in the city. And they agreed to fund further development.
M So they helped you get the product to market.
W Yes, without Creative Gaming's financial support, I could never have afforded to complete it. Well, we began at the bottom but now the game has a huge fan base running into the thousands.

남 뉴스 94의 로컬 비즈니스에 오신 것을 환영합니다. 저는 오늘 아침, 올해 가장 많은 사람들이 원하는 비디오 게임인 〈골드 탑〉의 디자이너, 완다 라이더와 이야기 나누고 있습니다. 완다, 게임의 이 개념이 어떻게 만들어진 건지 시청자들에게 설명해 주시겠어요?
여 글쎄요. 제 조카가 성장할 때 그 아이는 머릿속에 환상의 장소들을 꾸며내는 것을 좋아했지만 그가 세부 사항을 기억하지 못할 때 좌절하곤 했습니다. 그래서 저는 조카가 다른 지역을 추가할 수 있는 컴퓨터로 환상 속의 세계를 발달시키는 아이디어를 갖게 되었습니다. 저는 그 아이디어를 도시의 큰 컴퓨터 회사인 크리에이티브 게이밍에 가져갔고, 그들은 추후 개발에 재정 지원을 하겠다고 동의했습니다.
남 그래서 그들이 그 제품을 시장에 나오도록 도왔군요.
여 네, 크리에이티브 게이밍의 재정적 지원 없이는 절대 끝낼 수 없었을 것입니다. 음, 우리는 바닥에서 시작했지만, 이제 그 게임은 몇천 명에 이르는 거대한 팬층을 갖고 있습니다.

chat 담소를 나누다, 수다를 떨다 sought after 많은 사람들이 원하는, 수요가 많은 viewer 시청자 nephew 조카 dream up 생각해 내다 make-believe 꾸며낸, 환상의 frustrated 좌절하는 fantasy 환상 fund 자금을 대다 further 추후의 afford to ~할 여유가 있다, ~할 형편이 된다 begin at the bottom 바닥에서 시작하다 fan base 팬층 run into 이르다, 달하다 must-have 꼭 필요한 feature 특집 fair 박람회 distributor 배급[판매, 유통] 업자 convention 대규모 협의회 inexpensive 비싸지 않은

62 What are the speakers mainly discussing?
(A) A city funding project
(B) An educational program
(C) A must-have wooden toy
(D) A best-selling electronic game
화자들은 주로 무엇에 관해 이야기하는가?
(A) 도시 기금 프로젝트
(B) 학습 프로그램
(C) 꼭 필요한 목재 장난감
(D) 베스트셀러 비디오 게임

63 What gave the woman the idea for her product?
(A) Watching her nephew
(B) Talking with colleagues
(C) Reading a magazine feature
(D) Visiting a games fair
여자에게 그녀의 제품에 관한 아이디어를 준 것은?
(A) 그녀의 조카 관찰
(B) 동료들과의 대화
(C) 잡지의 특집 읽기
(D) 게임 박람회 방문

64 How was the woman able to launch her business?
(A) By requesting foreign distributors
(B) By using another company's funding
(C) By advertising at game conventions
(D) By hiring inexpensive labor
여자는 어떻게 그녀의 사업을 출시할 수 있었는가?
(A) 외국의 유통업체를 요청함으로써
(B) 다른 회사의 기금을 이용함으로써
(C) 게임 컨벤션에서 광고함으로써
(D) 값싼 노동력을 고용함으로써

Questions 65-67 refer to the following conversation and chart.
호M 미W

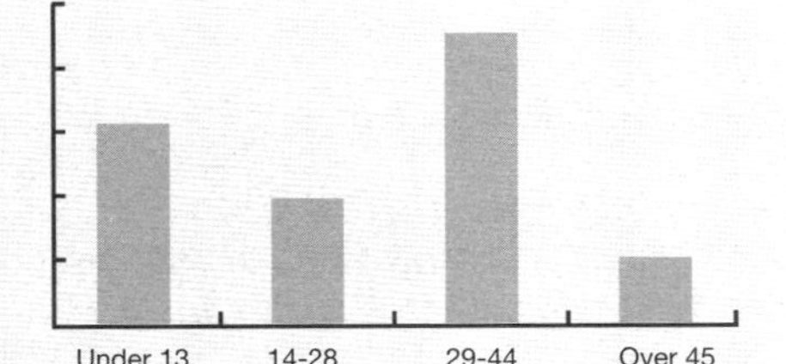

M Elisha, these are the results of a recent survey conducted at our community center. We gave a questionnaire to 500 of our members asking if they are satisfied with the programs we offer.
W Well, it is interesting to see how differently each age group responded to the services we offer. I see that this age group is the happiest of all.
M Yes, that group consists mostly of parents with young children. They feel that we offer a variety of programs for both adults and children and that is reflected in the survey result. As you can see, the second happiest group is the under-13 age group.
W I see. Is there any particular program they like the best?
M The Sunday morning football game is very popular.
W Right. On the other hand, this age group here is the least satisfied with our programs. What is the problem?
M Many of the members in that age group are interested in learning something new, like a foreign language or painting. So they want us to offer more classes.

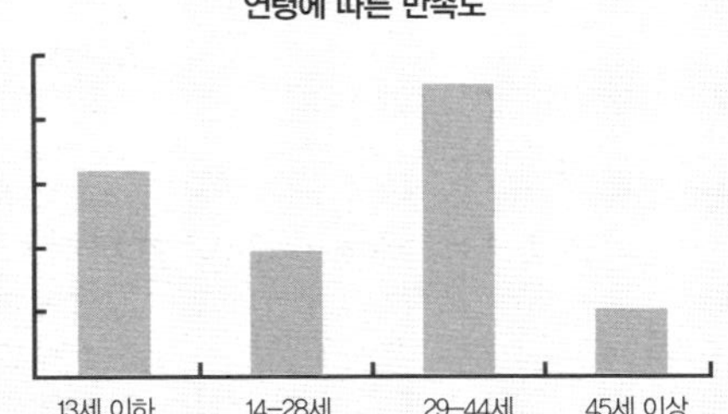

남 엘리샤, 여기 우리 커뮤니티 센터에서 설문 조사한 결과입니다. 회원 중에서 500명에게 설문지를 주었고 우리가 제공하는 프로그램에 대해서 만족하는지를 물었습니다.
여 음, 우리가 제공하는 서비스에 대해서 각 연령대가 다르게 응답한 것이 흥미롭네요. 이 연령대가 가장 만족한 그룹이군요.
남 네, 그 그룹은 대부분 어린 아이를 둔 부모들로 구성되어 있어요. 그들은 우리가 성인과 아이들 둘 다를 위한 다양한 프로그램을 제공한다고 느끼고 있고 이 부분이 설문 결과에 반영이 되었습니다. 보시다시피, 두 번째로 만족한 그룹이 13세 미만 연령대입니다.
여 그렇군요. 이들이 가장 좋아하는 특정한 프로그램이 있나요?
남 일요일 아침 축구 경기가 굉장히 인기가 좋아요.
여 그렇군요. 반면에, 여기 이 연령대 그룹은 우리 프로그램에 대해 가장 만족도가 낮네요. 무엇이 문제죠?
남 그 연령대의 많은 회원들은 외국어나 그림 같이 뭔가 새로운 것을 배우는 데 관심이 많습니다. 그래서 저희가 더 많은 수업을 제공하기 원하고 있어요.

questionnaire 설문지 be satisfied with ~에 만족하다 age group 연령대 consist of ~로 구성되다 a variety of 다양한 particular 특정한

65 Where do the speakers most likely work?
(A) At a fitness club
(B) At an art gallery
(C) At a graphic design firm
(D) At a community center
화자들은 어디에서 일할 것 같은가?
(A) 체육관
(B) 아트 갤러리
(C) 시각 디자인 회사
(D) 커뮤니티 센터

66 What are the speakers mainly discussing?
(A) A family membership
(B) Promoting a new program
(C) A schedule change
(D) The results of a recent survey

화자들은 주로 무엇에 대해 이야기하는가?
(A) 가족 멤버십
(B) 새 프로그램을 홍보하는 것
(C) 스케줄 변경
(D) 최근 설문 조사의 결과

67 Look at the graphic. Which age group wants the center to offer more classes?
(A) Under 13
(B) 14-28
(C) 29-44
(D) Over 45

시각 정보를 보시오. 어떤 연령대가 센터에서 더 많은 수업을 제공하길 원하는가?
(A) 13세 이하
(B) 14–28세
(C) 29–44세
(D) 45세 이상

Questions 68-70 refer to the following conversation and brochure.
미W 미M

City Sights of LA		
	Adult	Senior/Student
Half Day City Tour	$50	$25
Full Day City Tour	$120	$84

W Welcome to City Sights of LA. How can I help you?
M Hello. I'm here to get some information about sightseeing tours of the city. Do you offer single-day tours?
W Yes, we have two different types of day trips. Here, there's more information in this brochure. They both begin at 8 A.M., but the half-day tour goes only until lunchtime. The full-day tour includes a trip to the Natural History Museum and ends at 7 P.M.
M The full-day tour sounds great. Do you offer a discount for students? That would be even better!
W Yes, if you choose the full-day tour and present your student ID, you can get a 30 percent discount.
M I'll take a full-day ticket. Uh-oh, I didn't bring my ID with me. Can I still get the discounted price?
W I'm sorry but that's not possible.

뉴욕시 광광		
	성인	경로/학생
반일 시티 투어	50달러	25달러
종일 시티 투어	120달러	84달러

여 LA 관광에 오신 것을 환영합니다. 어떻게 도와 드릴까요?
남 안녕하세요. 도시 관광 투어에 대해 알아보려고요. 하루 투어도 제공하나요?
여 네, 두 종류의 하루 투어가 있습니다. 여기 이 안내 책자에 더 많은 정보가 있어요. 둘 다 아침 8시에 시작되지만 반일 투어는 점심 시간까지만 투어가 지속됩니다. 종일 투어는 자연사 박물관 견학까지 포함하여 저녁 7시에 끝이 납니다.
남 저는 종일 투어가 좋을 것 같네요. 학생은 할인을 해주시나요? 그러면 더 좋겠는데.
여 네, 종일 투어를 선택하시고 학생증을 제시하시면, 30퍼센트 할인을 받을 수 있어요.
남 종일 투어 티켓을 구입하겠습니다. 이런, 제가 신분증을 가져오지 않았네요. 그래도 할인을 받을 수 있을까요?
여 죄송하지만 그건 불가능합니다.

sightseeing tour 관광 투어 single-day tour 하루 투어 present 제시하다

68 What is the man asking about?
(A) A sightseeing tour
(B) A concert schedule
(C) A famous artist
(D) Directions to an attraction

남자는 무엇에 관하여 문의하는가?
(A) 관광 투어
(B) 콘서트 일정
(C) 유명한 예술가
(D) 관광 명소에 가는 길

69 According to the woman, what is included in the full-day city tour?
(A) A museum tour
(B) A seafood lunch
(C) A ferry ride
(D) A Broadway show

여자에 따르면, 종일 시티 투어에는 무엇이 포함되는가?
(A) 박물관 투어
(B) 해산물 점심
(C) 페리 탑승
(D) 브로드웨이 쇼

70 Look at the graphic. How much will the man pay for a tour?
(A) $25
(B) $50
(C) $84
(D) $120

시각 정보를 보시오. 남자는 투어에 얼마를 낼 것인가?
(A) 25달러
(B) 50달러
(C) 84달러
(D) 120달러

Part 4

Questions 71-73 refer to the following telephone message. 호M

Hi, Ms. Reinhard. This is Dan Lelong. I'm calling about the scheduled meeting we had planned for next Tuesday. I'm afraid my partner and I won't be attending after all. We've made the decision to postpone improving our garden because we had to attend to some crucial repairs to the house foundations. We were impressed with your landscape designs however. So we'll contact you when we have more money. You might get a call from my colleague Jeanette soon. She mentioned she was looking for a company to landscape her garden, too. So I gave her your number.

안녕하세요, 라인하르트 씨. 저는 단 르롱입니다. 저는 다음 주 화요일로 계획했던 회의 일정에 관해 전화했습니다. 제 파트너와 저는 결국 참석하지 못할 것 같습니다. 집의 토대에 중대한 수리를 처리해야 해서, 정원 리모델링을 미루기로 했거든요. 그러나 저희는 당신의 조경 디자인에 매우 감명받았습니다. 그래서 자금이 더 여유가 될 때 연락하겠습니다. 당신은 제 동료인 자넷에게 곧 전화를 받을 수도 있어요. 그녀도 그녀의 정원을 조경해 줄 회사를 찾고 있다고 했지요. 그래서 그녀에게 당신의 전화번호를 주었습니다.

scheduled 일정이 잡힌 after all 결국 postpone 미루다 attend to ~을 처리하다 crucial 중대한 foundation (건물의) 토대 impressed 감명받은 landscape 조경 query 문의 criticize 비판[비난]하다 initially 처음에

71 Why is the speaker calling?
(A) To cancel a meeting
(B) To ask for a quote
(C) To query a design
(D) To criticize a co-worker

화자는 왜 전화하고 있는가?
(A) 미팅을 취소하기 위해
(B) 견적을 요청하기 위해
(C) 디자인에 대한 질문하기 위해
(D) 동료를 비난하기 위해

72 What did the speaker initially want to remodel?
(A) The garden
(B) The kitchen
(C) The foundations
(D) The bedroom

화자가 처음에 리모델링을 하고 싶어 한 것은 무엇인가?
(A) 정원
(B) 부엌
(C) 토대
(D) 침실

73 Who did the speaker give Ms. Reinhard's phone number to?
(A) His colleague
(B) His partner
(C) A gardener
(D) A designer

화자는 누구에게 라인하르트 씨의 전화번호를 주었는가?
(A) 그의 동료
(B) 그의 파트너
(C) 정원사
(D) 디자이너

Questions 74-76 refer to the following broadcast. 미W

In this morning's regional business news, we'll be focusing on an embroidery factory that Nicholls Incorporated will open here at Henman Falls this summer. We will consult with business consultant Jin Sun, who will provide her analysis of the impact of the Nicholls' new factory on our regional economy and in particular how it will encourage valuable employment opportunities to this area. This special report will be broadcast at 10 A.M. following the weather forecast. So, be sure to stay tuned.

오늘 아침 지역 비즈니스 뉴스에서, 우리는 니콜스 주식회사가 이번 여름 이곳 헨맨 폴스에서 개장할 자수 공장에 조명해 보겠습니다. 니콜스의 새 공장이 우리 지역의 경제에 어떤 영향을 줄 것인지, 그리고 특히 어떻게 이 지역에 귀중한 취업 기회를 장려할 것인지 그 영향에 대한 분석을 제공할 비즈니스 상담가인 진선과 상의해 보겠습니다. 이 특별한 보도는 일기 예보가 끝나고 오전 10시에 방송될 것입니다. 그러니 고정해 주세요.

embroidery 자수 consult with ~와 상의하다 analysis 분석 economy 경제 in particular 특히 valuable 귀중한 employment opportunity 취업 기회 broadcast 방송하다 following ~을 뒤따라 weather forecast 일기 예보 stay tuned (라디오 · TV의 주파수에) 고정하다

74 What will happen in Henman Falls this summer?
(A) Community meetings will be held.
(B) The economy will be analyzed.
(C) A range of clothing will be introduced.
(D) A new factory will be opened.

이번 여름 헨맨 폴스에 무슨 일이 일어날 것인가?
(A) 주민 회의가 열릴 것이다.
(B) 경제가 분석될 것이다.
(C) 다양한 옷이 소개될 것이다.
(D) 새 공장이 문을 열 것이다.

75 Who is Jin Sun?
(A) A business owner
(B) A factory worker
(C) A business expert
(D) The president of a company

진선은 누구인가?
(A) 사업 소유주
(B) 공장 직원
(C) 비즈니스 전문가
(D) 회사 회장

76 What will Jin Sun discuss?
(A) Local job opportunities
(B) Increasing taxes
(C) Traffic delays
(D) Education costs

진선은 무엇을 이야기할 것인가?
(A) 지역 취업 기회
(B) 세금 인상
(C) 교통 정체
(D) 교육비

Questions 77-79 refer to the following telephone message. (미M)

Hello, Mr. Dansell. This is Roger Miller from the Student Real Estate Company. I'm checking to ensure that we're still planning to meet this evening at the Hanston University campus. There are five student houses for sale and I can show you each one of them. Before that, we can examine the purchase documents and I can reply to any queries you might have. Just to remind you, the car park of the main campus is being resurfaced, so I will park at the rear entrance by the gymnasium. Email if you have any questions.

안녕하세요, 단셀 씨. 저는 학생 부동산 회사의 로저 밀러입니다. 오늘 저녁에 핸스턴 대학 구내에서 만나기로 한 우리 계획이 여전한지 확실히 하기 위해 확인합니다. 학생 기숙사 5개가 매물로 나와 있고, 각각의 방을 당신에게 보여 줄 수 있습니다. 그 전에, 우리는 구매 서류를 검토하고 당신이 가질 수 있는 어떠한 문의에도 답변해 드릴 수 있습니다. 상기시키고자 말씀드리지만 메인 캠퍼스의 주차장은 재포장되고 있으므로 체육관의 후문에 주차를 하겠습니다. 질문이 있으면 이메일을 보내 주세요.

real estate 부동산 student houses 기숙사 examine 검토하다 resurface (도로 등에) 표면 처리를 다시 하다, 재포장하다 rear entrance 뒷문, 후문 gymnasium 체육관

77 Who most likely is the speaker?
(A) A student
(B) A car park attendant
(C) A real estate agent
(D) A lawyer

화자는 누구일 것 같은가?
(A) 학생
(B) 주차 요원
(C) 부동산 중개인
(D) 변호사

78 What is the purpose of the call?
(A) To query a transaction
(B) To undertake research
(C) To confirm an appointment
(D) To rent a vehicle

전화의 목적은 무엇인가?
(A) 거래에 대한 질문을 하기 위해
(B) 연구에 착수하기 위해
(C) 약속을 확인하기 위해
(D) 자동차를 대여하기 위해

79 Where will the speaker be waiting?
(A) At the main entrance
(B) At the rear entrance
(C) At the gymnasium
(D) At the house

화자는 어디에서 기다릴 것인가?
(A) 중앙 출입구
(B) 후문
(C) 체육관
(D) 집

Questions 80-82 refer to the following introduction. (호M)

Ladies and Gentlemen, welcome to the 19th Annual ICM Marketing Conference. I'm sure this three-day conference will give you the opportunity to advance your career and acquire new skills in marketing and advertising. Our first presenter is Dr. Jane Adams, a prominent marketing expert. Her talk today will focus on how to get your brand recognized by using a creative Web site and logo. She is going to explain a marketing strategy that will more effectively attract clients. Following her talk, there will be a question and answer session. So please hold your questions until the end. Now everyone, please give Dr. Adams a warm welcome.

신사 숙녀 여러분, 19번째 연례 ICM 마케팅 컨퍼런스에 오신 것을 환영합니다. 저는 3일간의 컨퍼런스가 여러분에게 마케팅 홍보 분야에서 경력을 발전시키고 새로운 기술을 획득할 수 있는 기회를 제공하리라 확실합니다. 첫 번째 발표자는 저명한 마케팅 전문가 중 한 분이신 제인 아담스 박사입니다. 오늘 연설은 창의적인 웹 사이트 및 로고를 사용해서 어떻게 여러분의 브랜드를 인식하게 만들 것인지에 대해 초점을 맞출 것입니다. 또한 고객을 효과적으로 끌어들일 수 있는 마케팅 전략에 대해 설명해 주실 겁니다. 연설 후에는 질의응답 시간이 있을 예정입니다. 그러니 그때까지 질문은 참아 주세요. 자 그럼 여러분, 아담스 박사를 따뜻하게 환영해 주세요.

opportunity to ~하는 기회 advance 발전시키다 acquire 획득하다 presenter 발표자 prominent 저명한 expert 전문가 focus on ~에 초점을 맞추다 recognize 인식하다 creative 창의적인 question and answer session 질의응답 시간 hold 보유하다, 가지고 있다

80 What kind of event is taking place?
(A) An opening ceremony
(B) An annual conference
(C) A company outing
(D) An awards dinner

어떤 종류의 행사가 일어나고 있는가?
(A) 개회식
(B) 연례 컨퍼런스
(C) 회사 야유회
(D) 시상식 만찬

81 What is Dr. Adams famous for?
(A) Receiving a prestigious award
(B) Having written a series of books
(C) Developing a successful marketing strategy
(D) Expanding her own business overseas

아담스 박사는 무엇으로 유명한가?
(A) 명망 있는 상을 받은 것
(B) 책 시리즈를 쓴 것
(C) 성공적인 마케팅 전략을 개발한 것
(D) 해외로 자신의 사업을 확장한 것

82 What does the speaker mean when he says, "So please hold your questions until the end"?
(A) The audience should not interrupt the speaker.
(B) The audience should not leave their seats.
(C) The audience should applaud the speaker.
(D) The audience should answer some questions.

남자가 "그러니 그때까지 질문은 참아 주세요"라고 말한 의미는 무엇인가?
(A) 청중은 연사를 중단시키지 않아야 한다.
(B) 청중은 자리를 뜨지 않아야 한다.
(C) 청중은 연사에게 박수를 보내야 한다.
(D) 청중은 질문에 대답해야 한다.

Questions 83-85 refer to the following talk. 미W

That's all for this week's cooking class. I hope that this workshop assists you to gain inspiration on ideas for providing nutritious and delicious récipes. Before you go, I'd be very grateful if you complete the blue sheet on the front of your workbook. It's a questionnaire. The answers you provide will help us to develop future récipes. When you have finished, I will be in the common room and I will be glad to discuss any questions about the topics we discussed in today's lesson. I will look forward to hearing your views. And thanks for coming!

이번 주의 요리 수업은 이것으로 마칩니다. 이번 워크숍이 당신이 영양가 있고 맛있는 요리법을 제공하는 아이디어에 관해 영감을 얻는 데 도움이 되었기를 바랍니다. 가기 전에, 당신의 작업 일지 앞의 푸른 용지를 작성해 주시면 매우 감사하겠습니다. 그것은 설문지입니다. 당신이 제공하는 답변은 우리가 추후 요리법들을 개발하는 데 도움이 될 것입니다. 완성하셨으면, 저는 휴게실에 있을 것이고 오늘 강좌에서 논한 주제들에 관해 어떤 질문이라도 기쁜 마음으로 상의해 드리겠습니다. 당신의 견해를 듣기를 기대하겠습니다. 와 주셔서 감사합니다!

inspiration 영감 nutritious 영양가 있는 sheet 종이, 용지 workbook 작업 일지 questionnaire 설문지 common room 휴게실 lesson 수업 view 견해 tutor 개인 지도 교사

83 What are the listeners attending?
(A) A cooking class
(B) A research group
(C) A marketing session
(D) A job interview
청자들은 무엇을 참석 중인가?
(A) 요리 수업
(B) 연구 그룹
(C) 마케팅 수업
(D) 취업 면접

84 What does the speaker ask the listeners to do?
(A) Ask questions
(B) Turn off appliances
(C) Clean up the area
(D) Fill in a form
화자는 청자들이 무엇을 하도록 요청하는가?
(A) 질문하기
(B) 가전제품 전원 끄기
(C) 구역 청소
(D) 양식 작성

85 Why are listeners directed to the common room?
(A) To taste some food
(B) To take refreshments
(C) To talk with the tutor
(D) To exchange contact info
청자들이 휴게실로 안내되는 이유는?
(A) 음식을 맛보기 위해
(B) 다과를 즐기기 위해
(C) 지도 교사와 대화하기 위해
(D) 연락처를 주고받기 위해

Questions 86-88 refer to the following announcement. 호M

Okay, I have one more statement before we finish this review. As you know, we're proactively seeking suitable material suppliers. Our production is increasing and there's been a growth in the demand for our facade cleaning services. To accommodate the increased workload, we'd like to affiliate with at least three new suppliers by the end of the quarter. We've placed an advertisement on a construction industry Web site but we require your help. Inform your friends and contacts that we are searching and please persuade suitable companies to apply. As a motivation, we are offering $500 reward, if you refer someone who can supply us with raw timber.

자, 저는 이 검토를 끝내기 전에 한 가지 더 진술할 것이 있습니다. 알다시피, 우리는 사전 대책을 위해 적합한 자재 공급업체를 찾고 있습니다. 생산은 증가하고 있고, 건물 외관 청소 서비스에 대한 수요 증가가 있었습니다. 증가된 작업량을 수용하기 위해, 이번 분기 말까지 적어도 3개의 새 공급업체와 제휴하고 싶습니다. 우리는 건설 산업 웹 사이트에 광고를 게재했지만, 당신의 도움이 필요합니다. 당신의 친구들과 지인들에게 우리가 검색 중인 것을 알리고, 적합한 회사들이 지원하도록 설득하세요. 동기 부여로, 만약 당신이 원목재를 공급할 수 있는 누군가를 소개해 주시면, 500달러를 보상으로 제공합니다.

statement 진술 proactively 사전 대책을 강구해 suitable 적합한 supplier 공급업체 facade (건물의) 정면, 표면 accommodate 수용하다 workload 업무량 affiliate 제휴하다 quarter 분기 place an advertisement 광고를 내다 construction 건설 contact 연줄(이 닿는 사람) persuade 설득하다 suitable 알맞은 motivation 동기 부여 reward 상금; 보상 refer 추천하다 raw timber 원목재 offload 없애다 make a referral 소개하다 recognition 인정

86 What is the company trying to do?
(A) Offload some timber
(B) Hire more employees
(C) Find new partners
(D) Improve customer service
회사는 무엇을 하려고 하는 중인가?
(A) 몇몇 목재 없애기
(B) 직원 더 고용하기
(C) 새 파트너 찾기
(D) 고객 서비스 개선하기

87 What are listeners asked to do?
(A) Make referrals
(B) Work extra shifts
(C) Recruit family members
(D) Fill in a survey
청자들은 무엇을 하라고 요청받는가?
(A) 소개하기
(B) 추가 교대조 근무하기
(C) 가족 구성원 모집하기
(D) 설문조사 작성하기

88 What incentive is mentioned?
(A) A financial bonus
(B) Extra vacation days
(C) Promotion at work
(D) Recognition on the company Web site
어떤 장려책이 언급되고 있는가?
(A) 재정적 보너스
(B) 추가 휴가일
(C) 직장 내 승진
(D) 사내 웹 사이트에서의 인정

Questions 89-91 refer to the following telephone message. (미W)

Hi, this is Rachel Bilson calling for Jake Johnson. Yesterday, we met at the seminar on effective communication skills. I think we must have accidentally taken each other's laptop computers since we both brought the same white KC laptop. Luckily I did find your business card with your office number. I'm actually preparing for a marketing presentation scheduled for tomorrow morning, and all the necessary information is on my laptop. So I really hope it is in your possession. I'd like to trade the computers today if possible. Could you please call me on my mobile as soon as you can? My number is 077-529-0023. Thank you.

안녕하세요, 저는 레이첼 빌슨이고 제이크 존슨에게 전화를 드립니다. 어제, 우리가 효율적인 의사소통 기술에 관한 세미나에서 만났었죠. 제 생각에는 우리 둘 다 똑같은 검정 KC 노트북을 갖고 있었는데 실수로 상대방의 노트북을 가져간 것 같아요. 다행히 저는 당신의 사무실 전화번호가 있는 명함을 찾아냈습니다. 실은 제가 내일 아침에 있을 마케팅 발표를 준비 중인데요, 제 노트북에 필요한 모든 정보가 다 들어 있습니다. 그래서 당신이 그걸 가지고 있길 정말 바랍니다. 가능하다면 컴퓨터를 오늘 교환하고 싶습니다. 저에게 최대한 빨리 휴대전화로 전화를 주시겠습니까? 제 번호는 077-555-0023입니다. 감사합니다.

effective communication skill 효과적인 의사소통 기술 accidentally 실수로, 우연히 business card 명함 in one's possession ~의 소유에 있다, ~가 지니고 있다 trade 교환하다

89 Where did the speaker meet Jake Johnson?
(A) At a trade fair
(B) At a business meeting
(C) At a seminar
(D) At a press conference

화자는 어디에서 제이크 존슨을 만났는가?
(A) 무역 박람회
(B) 사업상 회의
(C) 세미나
(D) 기자 회견

90 What is the purpose of the message?
(A) To exchange some devices
(B) To arrange for an event
(C) To make a complaint
(D) To apologize for being late

메시지의 목적은 무엇인가?
(A) 기기를 교환하려고
(B) 행사를 준비하려고
(C) 불만을 제기하려고
(D) 늦은 것에 대해 사과하려고

91 What does the speaker mean when she says, "So I really hope it is in your possession"?
(A) She would like to buy a new computer.
(B) She does not want to pay an extra fee.
(C) She hopes her computer hasn't gone missing.
(D) She wants to arrive at work on time.

화자가 "그래서 당신이 그걸 가지고 있길 정말 바랍니다"라고 말한 의미는 무엇인가?
(A) 여자는 새 컴퓨터를 사고 싶다.
(B) 여자는 추가 수수료를 내고 싶지 않다.
(C) 여자는 그녀의 컴퓨터가 없어지지 않았기를 바란다.
(D) 여자는 늦지 않게 회사에 도착하기 원한다.

Questions 92-94 refer to the following telephone message. (미M)

Hi. This is Jake Johnson. Two weeks ago, I hired your roofing company to replace my roof. It was fine at first, but ever since it rained really hard four days ago, it has been leaking. It really worries me because the rain water is still dripping through a crack in the ceiling. And even more rain is forecast for the weekend. I've already covered my PC and furniture with plastic sheets, but I'd like to get it fixed as soon as possible. Please return my call about when you can visit my house. My number is 555-1241. Thank you.

안녕하세요. 저는 제이크 존슨입니다. 2주 전에 귀하의 지붕 수리회사를 고용해서 지붕을 교체했습니다. 처음에는 괜찮았었지만, 4일 전에 비가 많이 온 이후로 물이 새고 있습니다. 빗물이 천장의 틈을 통해 아직도 뚝뚝 떨어지고 있어서 정말 걱정이 됩니다. 그리고 심지어 더 많은 비가 주말에 예보되어 있어요. 제가 이미 컴퓨터와 가구를 비닐 천으로 덮어 두었습니다만, 가능한 한 빨리 이걸 고치고 싶습니다. 언제 저희 집을 방문할 수 있을지 답신 전화해 주세요. 제 번호는 555-1241입니다. 감사합니다.

roofing company 지붕 수리 업체 replace 교체하다 at first 처음에는 leak (물 등이) 새다 drip 뚝뚝 떨어지다 crack (갈라진) 틈 ceiling 천장 plastic sheet 비닐 천 return one's call ~에게 답신 전화하다

92 What type of business is the speaker calling?
(A) A gardening company
(B) A roofing company
(C) An auto repair shop
(D) A home-improvement store

화자는 어떤 종류의 업체에 전화하고 있는가?
(A) 정원 관리 회사
(B) 지붕 수리 업체
(C) 차량 정비 업체
(D) 주거 개선용품 상점

93 What does the speaker mean when he says, "And even more rain is forecast for the weekend"?
(A) A repair person will be late.
(B) He cannot keep windows open.
(C) A problem will get worse.
(D) He will have to change his schedule.

화자가 "그리고 심지어 더 많은 비가 주말에 예보되어 있어요"라고 말한 의미는 무엇인가?
(A) 수리공이 늦을 것이다.
(B) 남자는 창문을 열어 둘 수 없다.
(C) 문제가 더 심각해질 것이다.
(D) 남자는 일정을 바꿔야만 할 것이다.

94 What does the speaker ask the listener to do?
(A) Visit his office
(B) Deliver some items to his home
(C) Call him back
(D) Give him a discount

화자는 청자에게 무엇을 해달하고 요청하는가?
(A) 그의 사무실 방문하기
(B) 그의 집으로 물품 배달하기
(C) 그에게 답신 전화하기
(D) 그에게 할인해 주기

Questions 95-97 refer to the following message and table. 미W

List of Catering Companies	
Company	Price Quote
1. Jude Catering	$2,500
2. O'Hara Catering	$5,000
3. Art of Catering	$6,000
4. Shawn Catering	$3,000

Thank you all for volunteering to help with the arrangements for the company's awards banquet. Firstly, the location has been decided. We're going to hold this year's event at the MK Convention Hall. Now we have to decide which catering company to hire. We have narrowed down the list to four caterers. Many of you probably know Jude Catering because we hired them for last year's event. Their prices were very reasonable but the quality of their food was not very satisfactory. This year I think we should try another caterer that offers better food and great service. This company's price seems high compared to the others, but it is known for its gourmet food and its well trained staff. Although it's our most expensive option, I think we should give this company a try.

출장 뷔페 업체 리스트	
회사	가격 견적
1. 주드 케이터링	2,500달러
2. 오하라 케이터링	5,000달러
3. 아트 오브 케이터링	6,000달러
4. 숀 케이터링	3,000달러

회사의 시상식 연회를 준비하는 데 도와주기로 자원해 주셔서 감사합니다. 첫째로 장소가 결정되었습니다. 우리는 올해의 행사를 MK 컨벤션홀에서 하기로 했습니다. 이제 어떤 출장 뷔페 업체를 고용할지 결정해야 합니다. 4개의 업체로 리스트를 줄여 놓았는데요. 많은 분들이 작년에 우리가 고용했었던 주드 케이터링은 아실 겁니다. 그들은 가격이 매우 좋았지만 음식의 질은 만족스럽지 못했습니다. 올해는 더 좋은 음식과 서비스를 제공하는 다른 업체를 시도해 보는 게 좋을 것 같습니다. 이 회사의 가격은 다른 회사들과 비교해서 높아 보이지만, 이곳은 고급 음식과 잘 훈련된 직원들로 유명합니다. 비록 가장 가격이 비싼 회사이지만, 이 회사를 한 번 써보는 게 좋을 것 같습니다.

volunteer 자원하다 narrow down 줄이다 satisfactory 만족스러운 gourmet food 고급 음식 give a try 시도해 보다

95 What event will the company hold?

(A) A retirement party
(B) An awards banquet
(C) A press conference
(D) An annual convention

회사는 무슨 행사를 열 것인가?

(A) 은퇴 파티
(B) 시상식 연회
(C) 기자 회견
(D) 연례 컨벤션

96 What does the speaker mention about Jude Catering?

(A) The food was not good.
(B) The service was excellent.
(C) The price was expensive.
(D) The employees are well trained.

화자는 주드 케이터링에 관하여 무엇을 언급하는가?

(A) 음식이 좋지 않았다.
(B) 서비스가 우수했다.
(C) 가격이 비쌌다.
(D) 직원들이 잘 훈련되었다.

97 Look at the graphic. Which company does the speaker want to hire?

(A) Jude Catering
(B) O'Hara Catering
(C) Art of Catering
(D) Shawn Catering

시각 정보를 보시오. 화자는 어떤 회사를 고용하기 원하는가?

(A) 주드 케이터링
(B) 오하라 케이터링
(C) 아트 오브 케이터링
(D) 숀 케이터링

Questions 98-100 refer to the following excerpt from a meeting and list. 호M

Best Sellers in science-fiction novel (April)
1. *Broken Stars* by Arron Shiver
2. *Life* by Sam Neill
3. *Unknown* by Ray Stevenson
4. *Orbit 2020* by Paul Schneider

This is our first marketing meeting since we published our new science-fiction novel, *Life*, a month ago. We've been promoting this book heavily and even author Sam Neill has appeared on several TV shows to talk about his new novel. So far the book has been selling very well nationwide and in fact it has become the second best seller in science-fiction novel. Arron Shiver's *Broken Stars* is the best-selling science-fiction novel of the month. But at the rate it's selling, I'm pretty sure our book will top the list next month. Also, we're teaming up with Gateway Bookstore to host a book signing and Meet-the-Author event. Clark and his team are in charge of organizing the events but there is a lot of work to be done. So if you have time to volunteer, please let Clark know by the end of the day. Thank you for your help.

공상과학 소설 분야 베스트셀러 (4월)
1. 브로큰 스타스(아론 쉬버 지음)
2. 라이프(샘 닐 지음)
3. 언노운(레이 스티븐슨 지음)
4. 오르빗 2020(폴 슈나이더 지음)

한 달 전에 새 공상과학 소설인 〈라이프〉를 출간한 이후 갖는 첫 번째 마케팅 회의입니다. 우리는 이 책을 크게 홍보해왔고 심지어 작가 샘 닐 씨도 여러 TV쇼에 본인의 책을 소개하기 위해서 출연했습니다. 현재까지 책은 전국적으로 매우 잘 팔리고 있고 스릴러 분야에서 2위를 했습니다. 아론 쉬버의 〈브로큰 스타스〉가 이달의 베스트 공상과학 소설이지만, 이 책이 팔리는 속도대로라면 다음 달에는 우리 책이 리스트에서 1위를 할 것이 틀림없습니다. 또한, 우리는 작가 사인회와 작가를 만나는 행사를 주최하기 위해서 게이트웨이 서점과 협력하여 일하게 됩니다. 클락과 그의 팀이 이 행사를 준비하는 책임을 맡고 있지만 끝내야 할 일이 매우 많습니다. 그러니 여러분 중 자원할 시간이 있는 분은 오늘까지 클락에게 알려주세요. 여러분의 도움에 감사합니다.

promote 홍보하다 author 작가 appear 출연하다 so far 현재까지 nationwide 전국적으로 top the list 리스트에서 1위에 오르다 team up with 팀을 이루다, 협력하다 book signing 작가 사인회

98 Where most likely does the speaker work?

(A) At a television station
(B) At a bookstore
(C) At a publishing firm
(D) At an advertising agency

화자는 어디에서 일할 것 같은가?

(A) 텔레비전 방송국
(B) 서점
(C) 출판사
(D) 광고 대행사

99 What are listeners asked to do?

(A) Help with some preparations
(B) Make travel arrangements
(C) Meet a project deadline
(D) Donate money to a charity

청자들은 무엇을 할 것을 요청 받는가?

(A) 준비 돕기
(B) 출장 준비하기
(C) 프로젝트 마감일 맞추기
(D) 자선 단체에 돈 기부하기

100 Look at the graphic. According to the speaker, which book will become the best seller in May?

(A) *Broken Stars*
(B) *Life*
(C) *Unknown*
(D) *Orbit 2020*

시각 정보를 보시오. 화자에 따르면, 5월에는 어떤 책이 베스트셀러가 될 것인가?

(A) 〈브로큰 스타스〉
(B) 〈라이프〉
(C) 〈언노운〉
(D) 〈오르빗 2020〉

Part 5

101 **해설** 관사(the)와 명사(cost approximation) 사이는 명사를 수식하는 형용사 자리이므로 (D)가 정답이다. originally는 부사, origin 명사로 형용사 역할을 할 수 없다.

프레토리아 로드 확장 계획을 위한 원래의 비용 근사치를 15퍼센트 늘려야 했다.

approximation 근사치 widen 넓히다 extend 늘리다; 연장하다 origin 기원 original 원래의

102 **해설** be expected to에서 to는 to부정사로 빈칸은 동사원형 자리이므로 (D)가 정답이다. be expected to do(~할 것이라고 예상되다)를 알아 둔다.

승객들은 표와 신분증 원본을 공항 접수처에 제시해야 한다.

authentic 진본인; 진짜인, 정확한 form 형태; 형식 identification 신분증 present 제시하다

103 **해설** rise는 자동사이므로 뒤에는 동사를 수식하는 부사 자리로 (C)가 정답이다. 증가·감소 의미의 동사들을 수식하는 다음의 부사를 알아 둔다. dramatically(극적으로), drastically(과감하게), tremendously(엄청나게), consistently(지속적으로), sharply(급격히), slightly(약간, 조금), gradually(서서히), considerably[significantly, substantially](상당히), noticeably[remarkably](현저히), constantly[continuously](끊임없이)

원자재의 수요가 급격히 올랐기 때문에, 치 라이 코팅스는 그들의 페인트의 권장 소매가를 인상했다.

raw material 원자재 recommend 권고[권장]하다 retail cost 소매값 sharpen 날카롭게 하다 sharpness 날카로움 sharply 날카롭게; 급격히

104 **해설** 빈칸은 관사(the)와 형용사(proposed) 뒤의 빈칸은 명사를 수식하는 형용사 자리로 착각하기 쉬우나 뒤의 arrangement와 함께 '좌석 배치'라는 의미의 복합 명사로 쓰이는 명사 (B)가 정답이다. 자주 출제되는 복합 명사를 꼭 암기해 둔다.

제시된 좌석 배치를 확인하시고 꼭 되어야 한다고 생각하는 변경 사항을 알려 주세요.

proposed 제안된 seating arrangement 좌석 배치 alteration 변화, 변경

105 **해설** 명사(playwrights) 앞은 명사를 수식하는 형용사 자리이므로 (B)가 정답이다. difference는 명사, differently는 부사로 형용사 자리에 쓸 수 없다.

7명의 다른 극작가들의 연극이 하이난 지역의 연례 예술 경연 대회에서 공연될 것이다.

play 연극 playwright 극작가 perform 공연하다 province 지역, 지방 competition 경쟁, 경연

106 **해설** 빈칸 뒤에 명사(book)가 왔으므로 빈칸은 명사를 수식하는 형용사 자리이다. 따라서 more recent와 most recent가 정답 후보인데 문맥상 '가장 최신작'이 적절하므로 최상급 (D)가 정답이다.

아키누오에 씨의 가장 최신작인 〈슬리핑 스루 투모로우〉는 12월 30일부터 페이퍼백으로 출판될 것이다.

publish 출판하다 paperback 페이퍼백(종이 한 장으로 표지를 장정한, 싸고 간편한 책)

107 **해설** 동사(has trebled) 사이에 빈칸이 왔으므로 빈칸은 동사를 수식하는 부사 자리이다. while은 부사절 접속사이고, until, after는 전치사와 부사절 접속사이므로 정답에서 제외된다. 따라서 부사 (A)가 정답이다.

지난해 유기 농업 방식을 선택한 이후로, 파슨 앤 보트맨즈 과수원은 그들의 이윤을 거의 3배로 늘렸다.

organic farming 유기 농업 option 선택권 orchard 과수원 treble 3배가 되다 profit margin 이윤 폭

108 **해설** 전치사(of)와 명사(applications) 사이는 명사를 수식하는 형용사 자리이므로 (D)가 정답이다. qualify는 동사, qualification은 명사이므로 명사를 수식할 수 없다. 전치사인 given, 부사절 접속사인 given that(~을 고려해 볼 때)도 알아 둔다.

그 직책에 대한 지원이 늘어나는 것을 고려해 볼 때, 바크하드 산업은 오직 가장 뛰어난 지원자만 면접을 볼 것이다.

given ~을 고려해 볼 때 application 지원 exceptional 이례적일 정도로 우수한, 특출한 candidate 후보 qualification 자격, 자격증

109 **해설** 명사 어휘 문제로 일자리와 관련된 어휘는 '급여'이므로 (B)가 가장 알맞다.

오딘 헤르모드 사의 채용 담당자는 장래의 직원들에게 일자리 제의를 할 때, 보통 급여 협상을 한다.

recruiting manager 채용 담당 관리자 negotiate 협상하다 prospective 유망한, 장래의 job offer 일자리 제의 revenue 수익

110 **해설** 부사 어휘 문제로 delicate와 가장 자연스럽게 이어지는 부사는 carefully이므로 (C)가 정답이다. 어휘 문제를 풀 때 빈칸 앞뒤의 단서를 잘 살펴 서로 어울리는 어휘를 고르는 것이 요령이다.

운송 중에 소포가 움직일 수 있으므로, 부서지기 쉬운 물건들은 조심스럽게 치워 주세요.

delicate 연약한, 여린, 부서지기 쉬운 transit 수송 relatively 상대적으로 powerlessly 무력하게, 효과 없이

111 **해설** 동사 has expanded 사이에 올 수 있는 것은 동사를 수식하는 부사이므로 (A)가 정답이다. substantiated는 동사의 과거나 과거분사, substance는 명사, substantial은 형용사로 동사를 수식할 수 없다.

바르셀로나 방송사는 자사 관할 지역을 상당히 확대했는데, 그곳은 이제 산트 안드레우와 레 코츠의 모든 곳까지 닿는다.

expand 확장하다 substantially 상당히, 많이 substantiate 입증하다 substance 물질 substantial 상당한, 크고 튼튼한

112 **해설** 동사 어휘 문제로 문맥상 '기차의 각 끝에 위치한 식당 칸에서 음식과 음료를 구매할 수 있다'가 가장 자연스러우므로 정답은 (D)이다.

로드리게즈 철도 승객들은 기차의 각 끝에 위치한 식당 칸에서 음식과 음료를 구매할 수 있다.

rail 철도 beverage 음료 refreshments 다과 carriage 열차, 수레 situate 위치하다 rear 끝

113 **해설** 지난 9개월 동안 예상보다 높은 수익을 거둔 지암파니도우 디자인의 확장에 대한 태도로 가장 적절한 것은 (B)이다.

지난 9개월 동안의 예상보다 높은 수익으로 인해 지암파니도우 디자인스는 당연하게도 그들의 확장에 대해 낙관적이다.

understandably 당연하게도, 당연히 expansion 확장 devoted 헌신적인 optimistic 낙관적인 impressive 인상적인 ample 충분한

114 **해설** 부사 어휘 문제로 문맥상 '쿠릴렌코 씨가 공장 매니저로 승진할 준비가 되었는지를 검증하기 위해서 그녀의 상사는 그녀의 생산량을 ~으로 감시해 왔다'에서 가장 적절한 것은 (A)이다.

쿠릴렌코 씨가 공장 관리자로의 승진할 준비가 되었는지 검증하기 위해 그녀의 상사가 일상적으로 그녀의 생산량을 감시해 왔다.

promotion 승진 monitor 감시하다 output 생산량 routinely 일상적으로 correctively 수정적으로 availably 쓸모 있게, 유효하게 approximately 거의

115 **해설** 동사 어휘 문제로 문맥상 '벌금이 ~된다'에 들어갈 가장 적절한 동사는 (C)이다.

벌금은 렌탈 계약서에 찍힌 날짜 이후에 반환된 제품에 대해 부과된다.

rental contract 대여 계약서 oblige 의무적으로 ~하다 summon 소환하다 impose 부과하다 dispense 나누어 주다

116 **해설** 대명사 문제로 빈칸은 provide의 목적어 자리이다. 따라서 she를 제외하고는 모두 정답 후보인데, provide A with B라는 구문에서 A에는 보통 사람이 오므로 hers는 제외되고 회사가 벨햄 씨에게 제공하는 것이므로 her와 herself 중 (B)가 적절하다.

벨햄 씨는 회사가 그녀에게 표를 제공하겠지만, 비즈니스석은 타지 않기로 결정했다.

decide against ~에 반대 결정을 하다 business class 항공기의 비즈니스석

117 **해설** 빈칸은 make의 목적어 역할을 하면서 뒤에 관계절(that ~ future)의 수식을 받는 명사 자리이므로 (A)가 정답이다. invest는 동사, invested는 동사 혹은 분사, investing는 동명사 혹은 분사로 적절하지 않다. 참고로 동명사는 관계절의 수식을 받지 않는다. 또한, 〈help+목적어+(to)+동사원형〉에서 목적어가 생략된 〈help+동사원형〉 형태도 기억하자.

브링햄 그룹은 그들의 고객이 안전한 미래를 제공할 투자를 하도록 도우려 한다.

make investment 투자를 하다

118 **해설** 동사 어휘 문제로 문맥상 '당신이 공개 연설하는 것을 도울 수 있다'가 가장 자연스러우므로 (A)가 정답이다.

저희의 훈련된 상담가들이 당신의 공개 연설을 도와 드립니다.

trained 훈련된, 단련된 speak in public 공개 연설을 하다, 대중 앞에서 연설을 하다

119 **해설** Bert Tong이 주어, said가 동사, 그 뒤 that ~ several times가 목적어인 절을 이루므로 빈칸 이후는 수식 역할을 한다. 빈칸 뒤에 submitting을 받으면서 수식할 수 있는 것은 전치사 혹은 부사절 접속사인데 문맥상 '연기자들에게 제출하기 전에'가 적절하므로 (D)가 정답이다.

신문 기사에서 수상 극작가인 버트 통은 완성된 대본을 연기자들에게 제출하기 전에 그의 첫 연극 줄거리의 결말을 여러 번 수정했다고 말했다

article 기사 award winning 수상한 playwright 극작가 ending 결말 plot 구성, 줄거리

120 **해설** 관계대명사 문제로 빈칸부터 party까지는 주어(Mr. Gonzalez)를 수식하고 있다. 명사 뒤에서 명사를 수식하면서 동사를 포함하고 있는 것은 관계절로, 빈칸 뒤에 동사가 나왔으므로 주격 관계대명사 중에서 사람을 선행사로 받고 콤마 뒤에 올 수 있는 것은 (A)이다. that은 콤마나 전치사 뒤에 쓸 수 없다.

은퇴식을 위해 요리를 했던 곤잘레스 씨가 내일 송장을 이메일로 보낼 것이다.

retirement party 은퇴식 invoice 송장

121 **해설** 부사 어휘 문제로 문맥상 '클라인 패션이 얼마나 빨리 손님을 잃었는지'가 가장 자연스러우므로 (B)가 정답이다.

재무 분석가는 클라인 패션이 얼마나 빨리 손님을 잃었는지에 대해 실망했다.

financial analyst 재무 분석가 tightly 단단히, 꽉

122 **해설** 부사 문제로 more와 함께 쓰면서 수 표현 앞에 와서 '~ 이상'이라는 의미로 쓰이는 (D)가 정답이다.

4월에, 그렌스워스 과수원은 3월에 판매한 농산물보다 두 배 이상 판매했다.

produce 농산물

123 **해설** 명사(brands) 앞은 명사를 수식하는 형용사 자리이므로 (B)가 정답이다. 〈had led+동사〉, 〈(to) lead+동사〉는 형용사 자리에 올 수 없다. to부정사가 명사를 수식할 때는 명사 뒤에 와야 한다.

프린스턴의 유리 용기는 더 나은 기술을 제공하고, 타 선두 브랜드들보다 오래간다.

leading 선두적인

124 **해설** 〈be p.p.〉를 수식하는 것은 부사이므로 (A)가 정답이다. nearest는 최상급, neared는 분사, nears는 동사이므로 부사 자리에 올 수 없다. 참고로 nearly는 숫자 앞에 와서 '거의, 대략'이라는 의미로 쓰이는데 같은 역할을 하는 단어로 almost, approximately, about, around, roughly 등이 있다.

바 뒤의 병들이 거의 없어졌을 때, 바의 직원은 더 주문해야 한다.

nearly 거의 near 가까운; 가까워지다

125 **해설** 동사 어휘 문제로 문맥상 '암드람의 웹 사이트를 통해 취득한 티켓들'이 가장 자연스러우므로 정답은 (A)이다.

암드람의 웹 사이트를 통해 취득한 입장권은 2달러 50센트의 추가 요금을 납부해야 한다.

liable to ~에게 변상해야 하는 surcharge 추가 요금 acquire 취득하다 value 소중하게 여기다 fine 벌금을 물다

126 **해설** 전치사 문제로 문맥상 '오늘까지 제출해야 한다'가 적절하므로 정답은 (C)이다. as는 전치사로 쓰이면 '~로서'라는 의미로 시점 명사와 함께 쓰이지 않고, along은 전치사로 '~을 따라서'라는 의미로 주로 along the road[the street, the river]로 쓰인다. so는 부사나 접속사이므로 전치사 자리에 쓸 수 없다.

브라운 씨에게 그의 2월 비용 보고서를 오늘까지 제출해야 한다는 것을 알려 주세요.

expense 비용

127 **해설** 명사 문제로 빈칸은 be동사 뒤에서 보어 역할을 하면서 관사(the)와 함께 쓰이는 명사 자리이므로 distributor(유통업체, 업자), distribution(유통)이 정답 후보인데 문맥상 '프리미엄 가전제품의 유일한 유통업체'가 적절하므로 (A)가 정답이다.

앤더슨 홀세일은 그린데일 지역 사회에서 프리미엄 가전제품의 유일한 유통업체이다.

wholesale 도매의 premium 아주 높은; 고급의 home appliance 가정용 기기 distributor 유통업자 distribution 유통

128 **해설** 부사 어휘 문제로 문맥상 '독점적으로 잡은'이 자연스러우므로 알맞은 선택지는 (A)이다.

르 창 카페는 현지의 강가에서 독점적으로 잡은 어류로 훌륭한 요리를 제공한다.

dish 요리 exclusively 독점적으로 fluently 유창하게 heavily 심하게, 아주 많이

129 **해설** 전치사 문제로 빈칸 이하에서 앞의 내용에 대한 이유를 말하고 있으므로 (C)가 가장 알맞다.

화재경보기가 정기 보수로 인해 다음 주 월요일 오전 7시에서 오후 6시 사이에 시험될 것입니다.

fire alarm 화재경보기 as for ~에 관하여 routine maintenance 정기 보수

130 **해설** 관사(a)와 명사(increase) 사이는 명사를 수식하는 형용사 자리이므로 (C)가 정답이다. 나머지는 뒤에 오는 명사 increase를 수식할 수 없다.

아스마 국제 대학의 연간 예산은 스포츠와 레저 관련 학과에 급격히 증가한 지출을 포함하고 있다.

annual budget 연간 예산 spending 지출, 소비 department 부서, 학과 sharpen 날카롭게 하다

Part 6

[131-134]

발신: 존 마가로
수신: 전 직원
날짜: 10월 20일
제목: 서버 점검

내일부터 시작되는 서버 점검으로 인하여 이메일 서비스가 잠정적으로 (131) 중단됨을 전 직원에게 알려 드립니다. 본 점검은 10월 30일까지 진행될 예정입니다. 점검 기간 동안에는 회사 이메일 계정에 접속이 불가능하기 때문에 고객 및 동료들과의 (132) 모든 연락은 귀하가 소유한 다른 이메일 계정을 통하여서만 가능합니다. (133) 본 점검은 광범위한 관리 작업들 중 마지막 절차입니다. 이전 작업은 사무실 전체에 경비 문을 달고 메인 로비에 감시 카메라를 설치하는 작업이었습니다. 이메일 서비스는 11월 1일부터 (134) 정상화 될 것입니다.

협조에 감사드립니다.

존 마가로, 기술지원부 부장

maintenance 보수, 정비 surveillance 감시 transition 변화 absence 부재 interruption 방해, 중단 identification 신분 증명 personnel 직원 extensive 광범위한 normal 정상, 보통 direction 지침, 안내, 방향 original 원형, 원본

131 형용사 temporary와 어울리는 명사를 고르는 문제이다. 빈칸 뒤에 service라는 단어가 있으므로 '서비스의 잠정, 일시적인 중단'이라는 의미가 가장 적절하다. 따라서 정답은 (C)이다.
정답_(C)

132 빈칸 뒤의 명사 contact를 수식하는 형용사를 고르는 문제이다. 먼저 대명사인 (C) others는 오답이며, (D) some은 가산 명사를 수식할 때 복수 명사를 주로 수식하므로 역시 오답이다. (A), (B) 중 앞 문장에 특별히 언급된 연락처가 없기 때문에, 앞의 내용을 받을 때 쓰는 지시형용사 (B) this를 오답으로 소거한다. 의미상 고객들의 연락, 연락처 등은 여러 개 있을 것이므로 복수의 의미를 갖지만 단수 명사를 수식하는 (A) every가 정답이다.
정답_(A)

133 (A) 보안 직원에게 당신의 신분증 배지를 보여주어야 합니다.
(B) 저희 회사는 최근에 주문 처리 과정을 개선하였습니다.
(C) 교육을 잘 받은 보수 관리 직원에 대한 수요가 증가해 왔습니다.
(D) 본 점검은 광범위한 관리 작업들 중 마지막 절차입니다.

문맥상 가장 적절한 문장을 고르는 문제이다. 빈칸 앞뒤에 위치한 문장을 통해 힌트를 얻어야 하는데, 빈칸 뒤로는 Previous works로 시작하는 문장으로 이전 작업들이 어떤 것이었는지 설명하는 내용이므로, 서버 점검이 관리 작업들 중 마지막 절차라는 내용의 (D)가 가장 적절하다.
정답_(D)

134 글은 서론과 결론이 일치하는 맥락을 보여야 좋은 연결이 된다. 글의 서론 부분에 잠정적인 이메일 서비스의 중단이라는 말이 있었으므로 하단 부분에는 서비스가 다시 정상적으로 운영되는 부분에 대해 언급하는 것이 적절하다. 따라서 정답은 (A) normal이다. normal은 형용사와 명사를 혼용하는 어휘이기 때문에 전치사 to 뒤에 충분히 들어갈 수 있는 품사이며 (D) original은 주로 형용사로 사용하며 시기적으로 맨 처음 것, 원래의 것을 의미하므로 오답이다.
정답_(A)

[135-138]

발신: 케이트 버튼 <burton@harper.com>
수신: 전 직원
제목: 릴레이 강의
날짜: 1월 8일

안녕하세요 여러분,

지난 직원 회의 때 이미 공지한대로 3월 릴레이 강의 (135) 특별 연사는 제시카 스팍스입니다. 스팍스 씨는 KS 사의 회장이며 가장 인기 있는 SF 작가 중 한 명입니다. 세 달 전 과학기술 컨퍼런스에서 저는 그녀의 강연을 들을 기회가 있었고, 저는 그녀의 프레젠테이션이 사람들을 깨우치는 매우 통찰력 있는 강의라는 (136) 느낌을 받았습니다. 그녀는 도쿄 미래 박람회에서 그녀의 신작인 〈미래에서 온 메시지〉에 대하여 프레젠테이션을 해 달라는 저희의 제안을 기꺼이 수락하였습니다. (137) 이번에는 평소보다 해외 지사에서 더 많은 참석자가 있을 것으로 예상됩니다. 그러므로 행사 최소 3주 전에 좌석 예약을 해주실 것을 추천합니다. 과거 어느 때보다 성공적인 행사가 될 것임을 (138) 확신합니다! 이 멋진 기회를 놓치지 마세요.

케이트 버튼

notify 통보하다, 알리다 conference 회의, 회담 enlightening 깨우치는 insightful 통찰력 있는 willingly 기꺼이 miss out 놓치다 turnout 참석자의 수 qualified 자격을 갖춘 confirmed 확인된 confident 확신하는

135 빈칸 앞에 정관사 the가 있고 뒤에는 명사가 있으므로 빈칸에는 명사를 수식하는 형용사가 와야 한다. 형용사의 역할을 할 수 있는 분사인 (B), (D) 중에서 골라야 하는데 featured는 형용사로 '주연의, 특별한'이라는 의미로 사람을 수식하는 역할을 한다. a featured actor(주연배우)처럼 featured가 speaker를 수식해서 '주요 연설자, 특별 연사'라는 의미가 된다. 따라서 정답은 (D)이다.
정답_(D)

136 동사의 시제를 묻는 문제이다. 빈칸 바로 앞에서 세 달 전 컨퍼런스에서 제시카 스팍스의 연설을 들었다는 과거시제가 오고, 그 컨퍼런스에서 그녀의 발표가 통찰력 있다고 생각했다고 했으므로 역시 과거시제가 와야 한다.

따라서 정답은 (C)이다.
정답_(C)

137 (A) 이번에는 평소보다 해외 지사에서 더 많은 참석자가 있을 것으로 예상됩니다.
(B) 각 발표는 30분을 초과해서는 안 됩니다.
(C) 참가 작가 목록은 회사 웹 사이트에서 확인할 수 있습니다.
(D) 매우 성공적인 행사를 개최하게 되어 대단히 영광이었습니다.

문맥상 가장 적절한 문장을 고르는 문제이다. 빈칸 앞뒤 문장으로 미루어 선택해야 하는데, 바로 뒤 문장에서 '적어도 행사 3주 전에 좌석을 예약해 줄 것을 추천한다'는 내용으로 보아 평소보다 참석자 수가 많을 것으로 예상된다는 (A)의 내용이 들어가야 자연스럽다.
정답_(A)

138 형용사 어휘 문제이다. 빈칸 뒤에서 '이번 행사가 그 어느 때보다도 더 성공적일 것이다'라는 것으로 보아 '성공적일 것이라고 확신한다'는 내용이 되어야 적절하다. 따라서 (D) confident가 정답이다. (A) possible은 가주어 it과 함께 사용되어 〈It is possible to부정사〉의 구조로 사용된다.
정답_(D)

[139-142]

세입자들은 주의해 주세요!

139 아시다시피 저희와의 임대 계약이 4월 1일에 종료가 됩니다. 임대차 계약과 조건에 따라 양측은 15일의 기간을 갖고 그 사이에 계약 갱신 여부에 관한 의사를 전달하기로 되어 있어, 이에 저희는 월세 인상분에 관해 조기 통보를 통해 미리 알려 드리고자 합니다.

저희는 귀하가 저희 세입자로서 계속 남아주셨으면 합니다만, 새로운 임대 기간에는 150달러 인상분이 적용될 것입니다. 현재 월세는 1,500달러이며 새로운 임대차 계약 하에서는 1,650달러 140 까지 인상하게 되었습니다. 임대차 갱신은 귀하의 갱신 여부 15일 서면 통보 141 여부에 따라 성사될 것입니다.

이 기간 동안 저희는 4월 10일 이전까지 임대물의 상태를 142 업데이트하기 위한 검사를 시행합니다. 당사자는 관리나 보수가 필요한 사항에 대해서 확인하게 될 것입니다.
귀하가 모쪼록 가정과 이웃에 정착하셨기를 바랍니다.

tenant 세입자 lease 임대차 계약 party 당사자 intent 의도 extend ~ the courtesy of ~의 호의를 베풀다 inspection 검사 relevant 관련 있는 settle 정착하다 revise 수정하다 effective 효과적인 upon ~하자마자 toward ~즈음에, ~을 향하여 responsive ~에 응답하는, 반응하는 eligible ~할 자격이 되는 contingent ~의 여부에 따라 insolvent 파산한

139 (A) 논의한 바와 같이, 귀하는 이제 집을 판매하실 수 있을 것입니다.
(B) 저희는 귀하에게 수정된 계약서를 보내 드리게 되어 기쁩니다.
(C) 아시다시피 저희와의 임대 계약이 4월 1일에 종료가 됩니다.
(D) 지금부터 즉시, 모든 세입자 분들은 어떤 문제점이든 보고하셔야 합니다.

빈칸 뒤에 나오는 문장의 맥락이 양측이 15일간의 기간을 두고 임대 계약을 갱신(renew the lease)할지 안 할지를 결정할 수 있다는 것이므로 갱신을 하는 것과 가장 문맥상 맞는 것은 임대 계약이 종료된다는 내용의 (C)가 가장 적절하다.
정답_(C)

140 빈칸 뒤에 $1,650이라는 정확한 액수가 나와 있으므로 이를 이끌 수 있는 전치사가 들어가야 할 자리이다. 액수, 수치 등을 이끌 수 있는 대표적 전치사 (A) to가 정답이며, to가 수치를 이끌 때는 '~까지, ~로'라는 의미로 주로 쓰인다. (B) by의 경우 차이를 나타낸 수가 나와야 한다. 나머지 전치사들은 수치를 전혀 이끌지 않으므로 모두 오답이다.
정답_(A)

141 형용사 어휘들은 명사를 수식하기도 하지만 전치사와 함께 구조상 세트를 이루는 경우도 있는데, 동사 respond에서 파생된 형용사 responsive는 to와, eligible은 주로 전치사 for나 to부정사와, contingent는 on과 결합한다는 것을 알면 아주 빠르게 풀 수 있는 문제이다. insolvent의 경우 따로 전치사를 동반하지는 않으므로 오답이다. 의미적으로도 서면 통보의 여부에 따라 계약 성사가 결정된다는 맥락이므로 정답은 (C)이다.
정답_(C)

142 빈칸 뒤로 명사 the statement가 이미 있고, 빈칸 앞으로는 전치사 of가 있기 때문에 자신의 뒤에 오는 명사를 목적어로 취급하며 전치사의 목적어 역할을 하는 동명사가 와야 한다. 따라서 (A) updating이 정답이다. 형용사가 명사를 수식할 경우 그 사이에 관사 a나 the가 들어갈 수 없다는 점에서 (C) updated는 오답이다.
정답_(A)

[143-146]

수신: 카메론 실리 〈cameronseely@efron.com〉
발신: 샘 험프리 〈shumphrey@efron.com〉
날짜: 8월 15일
제목: 이직 관련

카메론에게,

143 당신이 우리 유럽 지점에 합류한다는 소식에 저는 흥분을 감출 수가 없었습니다. 당신이 우리 부서에 소중한 자산이 될 것임을 믿어 의심치 않습니다. 이곳으로 출근하는 첫날 주간 직원 회의가 있을 예정인데 그때 동료들과 회사 임원들을 만날 기회가 있을 겁니다. 회의 후에 바로 회사 시설에 144 접근할 때마다 경비원에게 제시해야 하는 신분증을 받게 되실 것입니다.

여기 오시기 전에 145 어떠한 질문이나 요청 사항이 있으신가요? 146 만일 그렇다면, 전화 031-555-7890으로 저희 담당 직원 중에 한 명에게 연락 주시거나 shumphrey@efron.com으로 저에게 이메일 주시기 바랍니다.

샘 험프리

addition 추가된 사람 executive 임원, 경영진 security personnel 보안 요원 representative 대표자, 대리인 commemorate 기념하다, 축하하다 promising 유망한 in addition 게다가, 덧붙여 for instance 예를 들어 in the end 마침내, 결국 if so 만일 그렇다면

143 (A) 당신의 10년간의 근무를 축하하기 위해 파티를 열 것입니다.
(B) 당신이 우리 아시아 지점에 합류한다는 소식에 저는 흥분을 감출 수가 없었습니다.
(C) 우리 회사는 몇 개의 회의실을 포함한 시설을 확장할 것입니다.
(D) 몇몇 유망한 지원자들이 최종 인터뷰 대상이 될 것입니다.

문맥상 가장 적절한 문장을 고르는 문제이다. 지문의 첫 문장이 빈칸이므로 글 초반부를 읽고 정답을 찾아야 한다. 빈칸 바로 뒤에서 '우리 부서에 소중한 자산이 될 것이다'라는 것으로 보아 이 사람이 합류하여 매우 기쁘다는 내용의 (B)가 가장 적절하다.
정답_(B)

144 빈칸 앞의 every time은 '~할 때마다'라는 의미로 whenever와 유사한 접속사이다. 접속사 뒤에는 〈주어+동사〉의 절이 와야 하므로 (A) you access가 정답이다.
정답_(A)

145 의미상 '어떤 질문이나 요청 사항이 있으십니까?'라는 의미가 되어야 하므로 의문문에서 질문이나 요청이 있는지 모르는 상황에 '무슨, 어떤'이란 의미로 사용되는 (B) any가 정답이다. (A) main(주요한)은 main topic(주요 주제) main problem(주요 문제) 등과 같이 사용되며 (C) this는 뒤에 단수 명사가 와야 하므로 오답이다.
정답_(B)

146 접속부사를 고르는 문제이다. 앞에서는 질문이나 요청 사항이 있는지 물어봤고, 뒤에서는 전화를 주거나 이메일을 보내라고 하는 것으로 보아 '질문이나 요청 사항이 있다면 전화를 주거나 이메일을 보내라'는 의미가 되어야 한다. 따라서 (D) If so(만일 그렇다면)가 정답이다.
정답_(D)

Part 7

[147-148]

빅토리 애틀레틱 사

최근 주문 내역서입니다.
업데이트된 주문 내역은 www.vatheltic.com에서 확인하실 수 있습니다.
저희와 거래해 주셔서 감사합니다.

주문 내역

고객 이름: 글렌 힐 골프 & 컨트리 클럽
고객 번호: LJ2378CM

주문 번호: 105-3675384-3692230
주문 날짜: 12월 12일
작성 날짜: 12월 17일

물건: 회사 로고가 박힌 주문 제작된 모자들
색상: 검은색과 흰색
크기: 조절 가능
수량: 300

summary 요약 view 보다 place 주문을 하다 fill 주문을 이행하다 adjustable 조절 가능한 reporting 보도 agency 대행사 tracking 추적 courier 택배 apparel 의류 outsource 외부에 위탁하다

147 빅토리 애틀레틱 사는 어떤 회사인가?
(A) 뉴스 보도 기관
(B) 택배 추적 조회 서비스 업체
(C) 스포츠 의류 제조업체
(D) 업무 서류 외주 업체

148 주문 날짜는 언제인가?
(A) 12월 12일
(B) 12월 13일
(C) 12월 17일
(D) 12월 30일

[149-150]

타운 어젠더

'타운 어젠더'는 클리블랜드 주 내 다양한 지역 행사와 활동들을 홍보하기 위해서 〈아트 & 라이프〉 잡지의 주말 판에 실릴 겁니다. 이야기나 행사 공고를 내고 싶다면, 짐 캠벨 씨에게 jimc@anl.com으로 이메일이나 440-555-9123으로 팩스를 보내세요. 아래에 적힌 우편 주소도 이용 가능합니다. 잡지에 꼭 실리기 위해선, 매주 수요일 아침까지는 보내셔야 합니다. 그러나 딱히 정해진 마감 일자는 없습니다. '타운 어젠더'가 매주 새롭고 다양한 문화적 행사와 활동들에 관한 소식들을 담을 수 있기를 기대합니다.

아트 & 라이프
12200 페어힐 로드
클리블랜드, 오하이오 44120-1058

publish 출간하다 edition 판, 본 promote 홍보하다 notification 알림 direct 보내다 circulation 발행 부수

149 이 공고의 목적은 무엇인가?
(A) 기자에게 기사 아이디어를 보내기 위해서
(B) 지역 사회의 행사와 활동을 홍보하기 위해서
(C) 잡지로 제출할 것을 요청하기 위해서
(D) 〈아트 & 라이프〉 지의 발행 부수를 증가시키기 위해서

150 타운 어젠더에 관하여 언급된 것은 무엇인가?
(A) 모든 예술 분야의 일자리를 홍보한다.
(B) 각종 행사와 활동에 관한 지역 소식을 매일 전한다.
(C) 정해진 마감일이 없다.
(D) 지역 주민으로부터의 반응을 보장한다.

[151-153]

야생 동물 재활 기구(WRO)
사서함 1004, 그랜햄, 링컨셔 MG11 0AG

12월 5일

알렉시스 램스덜
왓슨 네이처 재단 대표
미쉘린 하우스, 81 펄햄 로드, 런던, SW3 6RD, 영국

램스덜 씨께

야생 동물 재활 기구를 대신해서 17번째 연례 행사를 후원해 주셔서 깊이 감사드립니다.

연례 야생 동물 행사에 참가하는 수가 지난 몇 년간 급격히 늘어났기 때문에 올해는 더 많은 참가자들과 봉사자들을 수용할 수 있도록 이상적인 장소를 찾아야만 했습니다. 그랜드 밸리 호텔은 저희가 작년 행사를 개최했던 WRO 회의장보다 훨씬 더 크고 쾌적한 곳이었습니다. 귀하의 넉넉한 기부 덕분에 행사는 아주 큰 성공이었습니다. 귀하의 도움 없이 그렇게 큰 성공을 거두기는 어려웠을 겁니다.

다시 한 번 도움과 지원에 감사드립니다.

회장이자 최고경영자
롭 헐스 드림

rehabilitation 재활 sincere 진심의 appreciation 감사 sponsorship 재정적 후원 on behalf of ~을 대신하여 search for ~을 찾다 ideal 이상적인 accommodate 수용하다 volunteer 자원봉사자 spacious 널찍한 pleasant 쾌적한 generous 후한, 넉넉한 contribution 기부 support 지지 conservation 보호 gratitude 감사 infrastructure 사회 기반 시설 sponsorship 후원 organize 주최하다 benefit 혜택을 주다 attention 주목

151 헐스 씨는 램스덜 씨에게 왜 편지를 썼나?
(A) 야생 동물 보호 단체를 홍보하기 위해서
(B) 연례행사를 위한 회의장을 예약하기 위해서
(C) 넉넉한 기부에 감사를 표하기 위해서
(D) 후원 기회를 위한 기반 시설을 개선시키기 위해서

152 램스덜 씨에 관해서 무엇을 추론할 수 있는가?
(A) 그는 야생 동물 축제를 매년 주최한다.
(B) 그는 야생 동물 재활에 헌신적이다.
(C) 그는 다양한 자선 단체에 자주 후원한다.
(D) 그는 야생 동물 재활 기구를 설립했다.

153 연례 야생 동물 축제에 관해 언급되지 않은 것은 무엇인가?
(A) 야생 동물 재활 기구에 혜택을 주기 위한 것이다.
(B) 많은 사람들로부터 더 많은 관심을 받고 있다.
(C) 왓슨 네이처 재단으로부터 후원을 받았다.
(D) 매년 같은 장소에서 개최된다.

[154-155]

저스틴 메이더 **오후 5:15**
우리 화요일 열차표를 사놓았나요?

롭 브라운 **오후 5:21**
물론이죠. 금요일에 돌아오는 오스틴 행 11시 30분 고속 왕복표 2장 사놓았어요.

저스틴 메이더 **오후 5:26**
오, 안돼요! 안타깝게 됐네요!

롭 브라운 **오후 5:27**
무슨 일이죠? 제가 표를 잘못 샀어요?

저스틴 메이더 **오후 5:30**
아니요. 그렇지만, 제가 여행자 골드 신용 카드로 표를 샀으면 20% 할인을 받았을 수 있었다는 걸 몇 분 전에야 알았어요.

롭 브라운 **오후 5:35**
아, 그렇군요. 별일 아니에요. 그 표가 값이 꽤 싸요. 제가 온라인으로 각각 30달러에 샀거든요.

저스틴 메이더 **오후 5:38**
생각보다 싸네요.

롭 브라운 **오후 5:44**
오스틴에 도착하는 건 오후 3시쯤이에요. 그러면 우리는 제이콥을 만나 저녁을 먹기 전에 호텔을 찾고 느긋하게 쉴 시간이 충분할 거예요.

round-trip 왕복 여행의 express 급행열차 it's no big deal 별일 아니다 settle in 쉬다, 휴식하다

154 메이더 씨와 브라운 씨에 관해 암시되지 않은 것은 무엇인가?
(A) 열차표 비용은 다해서 60달러 들었다.
(B) 목적지는 오스틴이다.
(C) 오후에 도착할 것이다.
(D) 한 주 동안 머무를 것이다.

155 오후 5시 35분에 브라운 씨가 "별일 아니에요"라고 쓴 의미는 무엇인가?
(A) 표가 너무 비싼 것 같다.
(B) 그 문제는 중요하지 않다.
(C) 신용 카드는 승인되지 않았다.
(D) 여행은 중요하지 않다.

[156-158]

집필 쪽으로 직업을 가질 생각이시라면,
당신을 성공적으로 도와 드리기 위한 적절한 수단이 여기 있습니다.

writersclinic.com은 당신이 작문 능력과 창의력을 증진시키는 데 도움이 될 인터넷 코스를 제공합니다. 당신의 목표는 시, 단편, 장편 소설, 심지어 대본을 완벽하게 쓰는 것일 수 있습니다. 이 모든 것이 당신의 집에서 편안하게 해결될 수 있습니다.

저희는 저명한 작가들이 이끄는 세 달 과정을 제공합니다. 그들은 당신의 요구 사항에 맞게 강의 내용과 자료를 맞출 것입니다. 당신은 작문 능력을 향상시킬 수 있는 개인별 피드백 및 코멘트를 받을 것입니다. 모든 참가자들은 생각과 작문에 대한 의견을 비교하기 위한 토의를 할 수 있을 것입니다.

집필 능력을 키우고 싶으십니까? 더 이상 지체하지 마세요! 저희 사이트를 방문해 12월 31일까지 등록하시고 1월에 개강하는 모든 강의에 한해 20퍼센트를 할인받으세요.

더 많은 정보를 위해 지금 바로 writersclinic.com을 방문하시거나, 555-1352로 전화 주세요.

career 직업 advance 발전시키다 talent 능력 modify 수정하다 tailor 맞추다

156 이 광고는 누구를 위한 것인가?
(A) 여행 가이드를 찾고 있는 사람들
(B) 티칭 클리닉에서 일하는 사람들
(C) 집필 쪽 직업에 관심 있는 사람들
(D) 성공적인 사업을 경영 중인 사람들

157 수업의 장점으로 알맞지 않은 것은?
(A) 개별적인 관리
(B) 무료 온라인 등록
(C) 참가자들과의 의견 교류
(D) 전문 작가들이 진행하는 강의

158 연말까지 등록하는 사람들에게 제공되는 혜택으로 알맞은 것은?
(A) 모든 강의에 대한 할인
(B) 수업 자료 무료 제공
(C) 강사진과의 무료 상담
(D) 각 수업에 대한 자세한 정보

[159-161]

개인 사물함 & 세탁 서비스

개인 사물함의 열쇠를 분실하실 경우, 열쇠 재발급 비용으로 10달러를 지불하셔야 합니다. 자물쇠 교체가 필요한 경우에는 25달러의 자물쇠 교체 비용이 청구됩니다. 분실되거나 제자리에 두지 않아 찾지 못한 세탁물 주머니는 15달러에 다른 것으로 교환해 드립니다. 개인 사물함의 열쇠를 잃어버린 경우 근무 중인 저희 프런트 데스크 직원에게 가능한 한 빨리 말씀해 주시고 열쇠 분실 양식을 작성해 주시기 바랍니다.

운동복은 세탁물 주머니에 넣으시고 잘 닫아 주십시오. 여러분의 운동복이 분실될 위험을 줄일 수 있습니다. 남성분들을 위한 세탁물 바구니는 세탁실 입구에, 여성분들을 위한 세탁물 바구니는 샤워실 입구에 배치되어 있습니다. 세탁된 옷은 24시간 이내에 개인 사물함에 넣어 드립니다.

주의: 고가의 의류나 신발을 세탁물 주머니에 두지 말아 주십시오. 피트니트 센터를 나가실 때 여러분의 개인 소지품은 각자의 사물함에 안전하게 보관하십시오.

제이즈 피트니스 센터는 분실이나 도난에 대한 어떠한 책임도 지지 않습니다.

laundry 세탁물 misplaced 잘못 둔 on duty 근무 중인 workout 운동 entrance 입구 assume 책임을 맡다 liability 법적 책임

159 위와 같은 공지를 찾을 수 있는 곳은?
(A) 의류 상점
(B) 호텔
(C) 세탁소
(D) 체육관

160 개인 사물함 열쇠를 잃어버리거나 제자리에 두지 않아 찾지 못하면 무엇을 가장 먼저 해야 하나?
(A) 분실물 신고 양식 작성하기
(B) 사물함 교환 요청하기
(C) 직원에게 알리기
(D) 열쇠 교환 비용으로 10달러 지불하기

161 세탁된 운동복은 어디로 돌려주는가?
(A) 개인 보관함
(B) 안내 데스크
(C) 세탁물 주머니
(D) 세탁물 바구니

[162-164]

베스트 오퍼 팩토리
모즈 덴먼
3828 리브스 스트리트
애플턴, 위스콘신 주 54913

덴먼 씨에게

귀하의 주문에 관한 저희의 실수에 대해 진심으로 사과드립니다. 주문하신 전기면도기를 파손된 상태로 받으셨다고 들었습니다. 저희 회사는 최고의 고객 서비스로 견고한 명성이 있습니다. 그래서 저희는 파손된 제품을 주문하신 것과 동일한 새 제품으로 기꺼이 바꿔 드리도록 하겠습니다.

저희는 귀하의 편리를 위해 선불 반송 라벨과 함께 새 제품을 이미 발송해 드렸습니다. 평일 기준으로 3일에서 5일 이내로 받으실 수 있을 겁니다. 새로운 전기면도기를 받으실 때, 택배를 수령하기 위해 사인하시기 전에 반드시 그 제품이 깨지지 않고 잘 도착했는지 확인하시기 바랍니다. 파손된 전기면도기를 저희에게 보내 주시면, 저희가 택배 회사에 보상을 청구하도록 하겠습니다.

다시 한 번 불편을 끼쳐 드린 것에 대해 깊이 사과드립니다. 고객님은 언제나 저희의 소중한 고객입니다. 저희와 거래해 주셔서 정말 감사드립니다.

멜리사 폴딩
고객 서비스 담당자
베스트 오퍼 팩토리

reputation 평판 unparalleled 비할 데 없는 along with ~와 함께 label 표, 딱지 make a claim 청구하다 process 처리하다 descriptive 서술하는 file a complaint 불만을 제기하다

162 덴먼 씨에게 어떤 문제가 일어났는가?
(A) 주문이 처리되지 않았다.
(B) 파손된 제품이 배달되었다.
(C) 교환품이 제공되지 않았다.
(D) 주문한 물건의 재고가 없었다.

163 새 전기면도기와 함께 무엇이 배송되었나?
(A) 반송 코드
(B) 새로운 보상 청구 양식
(C) 제품 설명서
(D) 선불 처리된 반송 용품

164 덴먼 씨는 무엇을 할 것으로 예상되는가?
(A) 불만을 제기한다.
(B) 주문을 새로 한다.
(C) 폴딩 씨에게 다시 전화한다.
(D) 파손된 제품을 돌려보낸다.

[165-166]

제레미 루크 [오전 9:41]	안녕하세요. 저를 도와줄 사람이 필요해요. 제 일정이 갑작스럽게 변경되어서, 내일 오전에 앨런 박사님을 공항에 태우러 갈 자원자가 필요해요.
제임스 가너 [오전 9:42]	제가 기꺼이 그분을 데려올게요, 루크 씨.
케서린 키너 [오전 9:42]	제가 할 수 있어요. 저는 내일 아침 일정이 여유로워요. 회사 차를 빌릴 수 있을까요?
제레미 루크 [오전 9:47]	그게 문제예요. 제가 내일 회의에 가는 데 회사 차가 필요하거든요. 여러분 중 한 분이 개인 차량을 갖고 있지 않나요?
케서린 키너 [오전 9:48]	죄송하지만, 저는 없어요.
제임스 가너 [오전 9:49]	저는 SUV를 가지고 있어요. 그렇지만, 만약 케서린이 그분을 태우러 가는 것이 낫다고 생각하시면, 제가 기꺼이 빌려드릴 수 있어요.
제레미 루크 [오전 9:51]	고마워요, 제임스. 그렇지만 당신은 혼자서 그 일을 처리할 수 있을 거예요.
제임스 가너 [오전 9:53]	물론이죠, 문제없어요. 몇 시에 그분이 도착하죠? 그분의 항공편 번호를 아시나요?
제레미 루크 [오전 9:54]	제가 깜빡했네요. 제 비서한테 가서 알아보세요. 비서가 모든 세부 사항에 대해 알려줄 거예요.
제임스 가너 [오전 9:55]	알겠어요. 제가 그녀와 얘기해 볼게요.

unexpected 예상치 못한 volunteer 자원자 pick up ~를 태우다 vehicle 자동차 SUV 스포츠 유틸리티 차량(= sport utility vehicle) on one's own 스스로 slip one's mind 깜빡 잊다 fill A in on B A에게 B에 대해 모든 일을 알려주다

165 가너 씨가 다음에 할 일은 무엇인가?
(A) 항공기 정보 얻기
(B) 공항으로 SUV 운전해 가기
(C) 앨런 박사에게 연락하기
(D) 집으로 귀가하기

166 오전 9시 41분에 루크 씨가 "저를 도와줄 사람이 필요해요"라고 쓴 의미는 무엇인가?
(A) 그는 교통 체증으로 꼼짝 못 하고 있다.
(B) 그는 약간의 자료를 원한다.
(C) 그는 도움이 필요하다.
(D) 그는 프로젝트를 걱정한다.

[167-170]

조셉 키드먼
인수부
레인골드 회계
19188 6번가
디트로이트, 미시간 48207

키드먼 씨에게,

지난 금요일에 디트로이트 사무실에서 귀하와 직원들을 만나서 기뻤습니다. 귀사에 보안 장비와 모니터링 서비스를 제공하는 것에 관해 논의했던 대로, 저희 대표이사의 승인을 받은 정식 가격 견적서를 보내드립니다. -[1]-. 저희가 귀사에 제공해 드리는 서비스가 이 할인의 한계 기준을 충족시키지는 못하지만, 저희 대표이사가 귀사의 성장을 기대하여 할인을 제공하는 데에 동의하셨습니다. -[2]-. 이 계약 조건에 동의하신다면, 계약서에 서명한 시점부터 1년 동안 이 할인이 유지될 것입니다. -[3]-. 이 기간이 만료되면, 저희는 귀사가 요청하신 서비스가 저희의 표준 최소 기준을 충족시키거나 그 이상인 때에만 대량 구매 할인을 계속 제공해 드릴 것입니다. -[4]-. 첨부된 견적서를 검토하시고 저에게 되도록 빨리 연락주세요.

진심으로

패트릭 젠센
하우스맨 보안 서비스

acquisition 인수 as per ~에 따라 security 보안, 안전 equipment 장비 monitoring 감시, 감독 formal 정식의, 형식의 estimate 견적(서) scale 규모 meet the threshold (한계) 수준을 충족하다 extend 주다, 연장하다 in anticipation of ~을 예상하고, 기대하여 forecasted 예상되는 in place 준비된, 이용할 수 있는 expire 만료되다 surpass 능가하다 minimum 최소 attached 첨부된 at one's earliest convenience 되도록 빨리 follow up 후속 조치를 하다 proposal 제안 confirmation 확인 approximation 견적, 추정 revised 개정된, 수정된 reflect 반영하다 bulk discount 대량 구매 시 할인 large customer 대량 매매 고객 reassess 다시 평가하다

167 이 편지의 목적은 무엇인가?
(A) 회의 후속 조치를 하려고
(B) 새로운 서비스를 소개하려고
(C) 제안을 거절하려고
(D) 확인을 요청하려고

168 이 편지와 함께 동봉된 것으로 암시된 것은 무엇인가?
(A) 소개 편지
(B) 비용 견적서
(C) 수정된 계약서
(D) 제품 목록

169 [1], [2], [3], [4]로 표시된 곳 중 다음 문장의 위치로 가장 적절한 곳은 어디인가?

"이 가격은 대량 구매 고객들께 제공해 드리는 15%의 대량 구매 할인이 반영된 것입니다."

(A) [1]
(B) [2]
(C) [3]
(D) [4]

170 만약 합의에 도달한다면 1년 후에 무슨 일이 있을 것인가?
(A) 대량 구매 할인이 증가할 것이다.
(B) 계약이 자동으로 갱신될 것이다.
(C) 대표이사가 또 다른 회의를 요청할 것이다.
(D) 계약 조건이 다시 평가될 것이다.

[171-175]

칼슨 비즈니스 트래블
23 이반 스트리트
렉싱턴, 메사추세츠 02420-1437

9월 10일

데럴 크롬프튼
4534 로마노 스트리트
케임브릿지, 메사추세츠 02141

크롬프튼 씨께

이 편지는 지난번에 전화로 논의한 대로 여행 일정을 바꿔달라는 귀하의 요청에 대한 응답입니다. 10월 2일 보스턴에서 포틀랜드로 가는 당신의 비행은 취소되었고 대신 화요일 10월 12일 오전 10시 20분 비행기로 예약되었습니다. -[1]-. 예정대로 포틀랜드에 저녁 6시 40분에 도착할 예정입니다. 이 비행기는 포틀랜드로 떠나기 전에 텍사스의 휴스턴에 한 시간 머무는 환승 비행기입니다. 앞으로 7일 이내로 예약을 확정하시지 않으면 이 예약은 취소될 겁니다. -[2]-.

시내에 아침 식사를 제공하는 그레이트 웨스턴 호텔에 방을 예약해 두었습니다. 10월 15일 금요일이 체크아웃할 날짜입니다. 호텔 비즈니스 센터에서 팩스, 복사기, 프린터기, 노트북 등 각종 기기를 사용하실 수 있습니다. -[3]-. 또한, 요청하신 대로 10월 13일날 회의실도 잡아두었습니다. 그러나 호텔 관리상 10월 13일에서 14일까지 무선 인터넷 네트워크 점검이 있을 겁니다. 객실, 로비, 회의장, 심지어 비즈니스 센터까지 호텔 내부 어느 곳에서든 인터넷을 24시간 동안 접속하실 수 없습니다. 만약 이것이 심각한 문제라면, 즉시 저에게 알려 주십시오. -[4]-.

항공편과 호텔 예약을 확정지으시기 위해선 최대한 빨리 저에게 연락 주시기 바랍니다. 이해해 주셔서 정말 감사드리고 일정에 지장을 드려서 진심으로 사과드립니다.

산드라 스태포드 올림
고객 지원 매니저

in response to ~에 답하여 itinerary 여행 일정 transfer 환승 confirm 확정하다 downtown 시내의 check out 퇴실 access 이용하다 disturb 방해하다 closure 폐쇄

171 크롬프튼 씨가 스태포드 씨에게 전화로 요청한 것은?
(A) 새로운 리조트 추천하기
(B) 여행 일정 변경 보고하기
(C) 호텔 접근성에 관해 질문하기
(D) 항공편 일정 변경하기

172 포틀랜드행 비행편은 언제 출발하나?
(A) 10월 2일
(B) 10월 12일
(C) 10월 13일
(D) 10월 14일

173 [1], [2], [3], [4]로 표시된 곳 중 다음 문장의 위치로 가장 적절한 곳은 어디인가?

"귀하의 비즈니스에 방해되지 않도록 다른 호텔을 알아보도록 하겠습니다."

(A) [1]
(B) [2]
(C) [3]
(D) [4]

174 크롬프튼 씨는 스태포드 씨에게 왜 가능한 한 빨리 연락해야 하나?
(A) 호텔의 사무 장비를 사용을 신청하기 위해
(B) 예정된 유지 보수를 하기 위해
(C) 숙박 선택 사항들을 제공하기 위해
(D) 여행 일정을 확정하기 위해서

175 이 편지에서 어떤 걱정을 하고 있나?
(A) 일시적 인터넷 장애
(B) 회의실 예약
(C) 호텔 비즈니스 센터 폐쇄
(D) 회의실 이용에 관한 문제

[176-180]

임시직 취업 알선 사무소
3층, 애쉬다운 로드 35, 카터햄
전화: 414-555-4465
팩스: 414-555-6693

이름: 오스틴 스미스 임시직 알선 사무소 직원: 잉게 블랙맨
시작일: 2월 8일 배치: 칼톤 은행 그룹

요일	날짜	시작	종료	시간/ 분
월	2월 8일	오전 7시	오후 4시 30분	8/ 30
화	2월 9일	오전 7시	오후 7시 30분	11/ 30
수	2월 10일	오전 8시 30분	오후 5시 30분	8/ 00
목	2월 11일	오전 7시	오후 4시	8/ 00
금	2월 12일	오전 7시 30분	오후 5시	8/ 30
			총	44/ 30

서명: 오스틴 스미스 날짜: 2월 15일

* 직원들은 매일 2회, 30분의 휴식 시간을 가지며, 이는 무급이다.
* 직원들이 시간외 근무(주당 45시간 이상)를 했을 경우, 지정된 직속 상사에게 서면 허가를 받아야 한다. 관리자들은 임시직 알선 사무소의 직원에게 이메일을 보내야 한다.

수신: 오스틴 스미스
발신: 잉게 블랙맨
참조: 클레오 래톤
제목: 주간 업무 보고서
날짜: 2월 16일

지난주에 제출하신 칼톤 은행 그룹 임시직 주간 업무 보고서에 관해 편지를 씁니다. 추가 근무한 시간을 저희에게 알리는 것을 잊으신 것 같습니다. 클레오 래톤 씨가 2월 9일 저녁에 귀하가 시간외 근무로 회사 행사를 도울 수 있도록 저희에게 허락을 구하기 위해 연락했었습니다. 그러나 이 추가 3시간이 귀하의 업무 기록표에 기록되어 있지 않았습니다. 시간외 근무 시간 3시간을 반영하여 업무 보고서를 수정하시면 승인하도록 하겠습니다. 저희는 귀하가 올바른 보수를 받도록 확실히 하고 싶습니다.

temporary staff 임시 직원 assignment 배치 signature 서명 unpaid 지불이 되지 않는 written approval 서면 허가 appointed 지정된 line manager 직속 상사 placement 배치 permission 허락 function 행사 work log 업무 기록표 amend 수정하다 reflect 반영하다 permanent 영구적인

176 업무 보고서에 있는 정보를 통해 스미스 씨에 대해 알 수 있는 것은?
(A) 매일 저녁 오후 5시에 일을 끝냈다.

(B) 업무 기록을 매일 제출했다.
(C) 업무 일정이 매일 같았다.
(D)매일 2회 30분의 휴식을 갖는다.

177 이메일에 따르면 스미스 씨가 업무 시간을 틀리게 기록한 날은 언제인가?
(A) 월요일
(B)화요일
(C) 수요일
(D) 금요일

178 래톤 씨는 누구일 것 같은가?
(A) 정규 직원
(B)칼톤 은행 그룹의 관리자
(C) 채용 담당자
(D) 임시직 알선 사무소 직원

179 이메일에서 첫째 단락, 여섯째 줄의 단어 reflect와 가장 가까운 의미를 가진 단어는?
(A)보여 주다
(B) 돌려주다
(C) 복사하다
(D) 허용하다

180 블랙맨 씨가 스미스 씨에게 요청하는 것은?
(A) 다른 작업 배치를 수락하기
(B) 임시직 알선 사무소와 계약 갱신하기
(C) 회사 기념식 돕기
(D)자신의 업무 기록 수정하기

[181-185]

www.hamidzafreen.uk

콘서트 관련	공연자 관련	행사 및 출연	하미드 씨의 업적에 대한 찬사

영국 날짜

• 5월 21–22일: 에든버러의 지그문트 센터
콘서트는 매일 저녁 오후 7시에 시작합니다. 더 많은 정보 또는 표 구매는 www.edevents/concert를 방문하세요.

• 5월 24일: 클리어워터의 칼슨 대학
행사는 오후 5시에 시작합니다. 사인회가 오후 7시 30분에 이어집니다.

• 5월 26일: 리버풀의 카론 극장
상세 정보는 매표소 (0161) 555–5734로 전화하세요.

• 5월 28일: 맨체스터의 할톤 컨퍼런스 센터
자프린 씨 행사의 표를 예매하실 분들은 4월 17일까지 예매하시면 HCC에서 15퍼센트 숙박 할인을 받으실 수 있습니다. 마리아 칼렌에게 (0181) 555–3567로 연락하세요.

모든 콘서트 표는 이 웹 사이트가 아닌 개별 장소를 통해 직접 예매하셔야 합니다. 모든 행사에는 콘서트와 질의응답 시간이 있습니다. 세부 정보는 각 행사 설명을 확인하세요. 자프린 씨를 귀하가 사는 지역의 공연에 초청하시려면, 마크 월에게 mwall@hamidzafreen.uk로 연락하세요.

마지막 업데이트: 5월 13일

발신: srider@cccharity.com
수신: mwall@hamidzafreen.uk
날짜: 6월 3일
제목: 다가오는 콘서트

월 씨께,

저는 자프린 씨를 지난달 할톤 컨퍼런스 센터에서 만났습니다. 만나는 동안 제가 위원장으로 있는 자선 행사에서 그가 공연할 가능성에 관해 이야기를 나눴습니다. 자프린 씨는 동의하는 것처럼 보였지만, 가능 여부에 관해 당신과 이야기할 것을 제안했습니다.

연례 플라이포드 자선 행사는 동물 보호 연맹의 후원을 받습니다. 9월 15일에서 18일까지 버밍햄의 국립 실내 경기장에서 개최될 것입니다. 자프린 씨가 9월 16일 저녁에 세계적인 연주자들과 함께 공연하실 수 있는지 알고 싶습니다.

여행 경비와 호텔의 1박 숙박비는 저희 후원 단체에서 지불합니다. 안타깝지만 다른 추가 지불은 제공해 드릴 수 없습니다. 그러나 자프린 씨는 공연하기로 예정된 날에 국립 실내 경기장의 시설을 하루 동안 무제한으로 이용하실 수 있습니다. 남은 행사 기간 동안 머물기 바라신다면 호텔 이용 할인을 마련해 드릴 수 있습니다.

자프린 씨의 가능 여부를 늦어도 7월 21일까지는 확인해 주시고, 그동안 질문이 있으시면 제게 알려 주십시오.

스티브 라이더

appearance 출연 praise 찬사 autograph session 사인회 eligible 적합한 individual 개별의 charity function 자선 행사 chair 의장 agreeable 동의하는 sponsor 후원하다 league 연맹, 동맹 arena 경기장 line-up 참석 예정자들 rate 가격 no later than 늦어도 ~까지 in the meantime 그동안

181 자프린 씨는 누구일 것 같은가?
(A) 작가
(B)공연인
(C) 자선단체 직원
(D) 컨벤션 기획자

182 웹 사이트에 5월 행사에 관해 언급된 것은?
(A) 모든 행사 후에 사인회가 있을 것이다.
(B)표는 자프린 씨의 웹 사이트에서 구매할 수 없다.
(C) 모두 리버풀에서 열린다.
(D) 구매 가능한 표가 충분하다.

183 라이더 씨가 자프린 씨를 만난 곳은?
(A) 리버풀
(B) 에든버러
(C)맨체스터

(D) 클리어워터

184 라이더 씨의 이메일의 목적은?

(A) 음악 그룹 멤버들의 지불을 조정하기 위해

(B) 예술가에게 공연을 하도록 초청하기 위해

(C) 호텔 숙박 시설을 업데이트하기 위해

(D) 콘서트 공연의 표를 주문하기 위해

185 자프린 씨가 국립 실내 경기장의 시설을 무료로 사용할 수 있는 날은?

(A) 9월 18일

(B) 9월 17일

(C) 9월 16일

(D) 9월 15일

[186-190]

주목해 주세요! 도서관 직원 여러분!

제5회의 연례 국제 도서 협회 총회가 8월 7일 호주의 멜버른에서 개최될 것입니다. 우리는 이 행사에 우리 협회를 대표할 네 명의 자원자를 찾고 있습니다. 여러분들은 이틀의 추가 여행을 포함해 호주에서 3일을 지낼 것이며, 총회에서 돌아오자마자 여러분이 얻은 정보에 대해 다양한 발표를 할 것입니다. 대학 측은 왕복 항공 요금과 2박 동안의 메리톤 호텔 개별실을 제공할 것입니다. 그러나 식사 비용은 참석자들이 부담해야 하며, 발생한 그 어떤 추가 비용도 배상되지 않을 것입니다. 만약 여러분이 참석에 관심이 있거나 더 많은 정보를 알고 싶으시다면, kjames@uta.edu로 케빈 제임스에게 이번 금요일까지 연락 주십시오.

수신: 케빈 제임스 〈kjames@uta.edu〉
발신: 멜 브룩스 〈mbrooks@uta.edu〉
날짜: 6월 10일
주제: ILA 총회

안녕하세요 제임스 씨.

저는 대학교 도서관을 대표해 올해 ILA 총회에 참석하는 데 관심이 있다는 걸 말씀드리기 위해 글을 쓰고 있습니다. 귀하가 기억하다시피, 우리는 런던에서 열린 3차 ILA 총회에 함께 참석했었습니다. 일정 중복 때문에 제가 지난해에 덴버 총회를 놓쳤지만 말입니다. 멜버른에 제 가족이 있으므로, 올해의 행사가 제 눈길을 끌었습니다. 그러나 몇 가지 특별한 부탁이 있습니다. 첫째, 저는 리치먼드보다 마이애미에서 출발했으면 합니다. 이렇게 한다고 해서 표 가격이 달라지지 않을 것으로 생각합니다. 또 메리톤 호텔 대신 스페이스 호텔 숙박이 가능할까요? 메리톤 호텔은 제가 찾아뵈려 하는 제 부모님 집과 꽤 멀기 때문입니다. 마지막으로, 제 가족과 함께 더 많은 시간을 보낼 수 있도록 여행의 마지막에 2일의 휴가를 덧붙이고 싶습니다. 다음 월요일에 총회에 관한 발표를 하도록 준비할 것을 약속드립니다. 제 부탁을 고려해 주셔서 감사합니다!

멜 브룩스

호주 도착 카드

이름:	멜 브룩스
시민권:	미국인
동반인:	0명
여권 번호:	00237181
체류 기간:	5일
주요 방문 목적:	총회 참석
호주에서의 주소:	메리톤 호텔, 멜버른
탑승 공항:	마이애미, 미국
비행기 또는 선박 번호:	호주 항공 13번 항공기

annual 연례의 association 협회 conference 총회 represent 대표하다 institution 협회, 단체 a variety of 다양한 round-trip 왕복 여행 air fare 항공 요금 attendee 참석자 compensate for ~을 보상하다 incur (비용이) 발생하다 on behalf of ~ 대신에 conflict 중복; 갈등 catch one's eye 눈길을 끌다 request 요청 citizenship 시민권 accompany 동반[수반]하다 embarkation 탑승 aircraft 항공기 vessel 선박

186 공지에서 첫 번째 단락 일곱 번째 줄의 compensated와 의미상 가장 가까운 것은 무엇인가?

(A) 배상된

(B) ~에 포함된

(C) ~에 관해 상담된

(D) ~에 관해 문의된

187 총회 참석자들의 요구 조건으로 나타난 것은 무엇인가?

(A) 본인의 휴가 기간을 써야만 한다.

(B) 호텔 객실을 같이 써야 한다.

(C) 그들이 알게 된 것을 공유해야만 한다.

(D) 총회에서 발표해야 한다.

188 브룩스 씨에 관해서 암시된 것은 무엇인가?

(A) 매년 ILA 총회에 참석한다.

(B) 이제 대학교 도서관에서 일하지 않는다.

(C) 이전에 제임스 씨를 만난 적이 있다.

(D) 호주의 시민권자이다.

189 네 번째 연례 ILA 총회가 열린 장소는 어디인가?

(A) 멜버른

(B) 런던

(C) 덴버

(D) 마이애미

190 브룩스 씨의 요청 중 제임스 씨가 거절한 것은 무엇인가?

(A) 회의에 참석하기

(B) 다른 호텔로 바꾸기

(C) 추가 휴일 갖기

(D) 다른 공항에서 떠나기

[191-195]

캐피털 은행 고객들을 위한 중요한 업데이트

6번가에 있는 저희 시내 지점은 4월 16일부터 5월 12일까지 보수 공사로 문을 닫을 것입니다. 로비에 있는 두 대의 자동 현금 인출기는 여전히 이용할 수 있지만, 은행 직원과 상담을 원하는 고객님들은 2번가와 버지니아 거리 교차로에 있는 다른 시내 지점을 방문하셔야 합니다. 불편을 끼쳐 죄송하게 생각하지만, 6번가 지점이 소파와 회의 테이블, 그리고 터치스크린 정보 모듈을 갖춘 최신식의, 고객 친화적인 시설로 개선될 것을 발표하게 되어 기쁩니다. 이것은 모든 고객에게 은행 업무를 더 빠르고, 더 편안하고, 더 즐겁게 해 줄 것입니다. 동시에 지점이 있는 1세기가 된 건물의 전통적인 특징은 유지될 것입니다. 여러분은 캐피털 은행 웹 사이트에서 보수 공사 계획에 관한 더 많은 세부 사항들을 찾아볼 수 있습니다.

즉석 고객 평가 – 워싱턴 – 은행 업무와 재무

여러분들이 듣지 못했을까 봐서 그러는데, 6번가의 캐피털 은행이 마침내 문을 다시 열었고, 완전히 탈바꿈했다고 말씀드릴 수 있습니다. 그것은 전통적인 은행이라기보다는 마치 신규 첨단 기술 업체의 휴게실 같은 모습입니다. 새로운 구조가 처음에는 정이 안 갈 수도 있겠지만, 저는 순식간에 그것에 반하게 되었습니다. 구식 번호표 기계는 터치스크린으로 교체되었고, 직원들은 이제 큰 카운터 뒤에 숨어 있지 않습니다—그들은 바로 앞으로 나와 있고 얼굴을 맞대고 여러분들의 일을 처리해 줍니다. 로비에 있는 ATM은 똑같은 옛날 모델들이지만, 지점 안에는 3개의 새로운 것들이 있습니다. 심지어 여러분들이 기다리는 동안에 페이스트리 빵과 무료 커피도 즐길 수 있습니다. 저는 보수 공사가 공지했던 것보다도 몇 주 더 오래 걸려 꽤 실망했었지만, 기다릴 만한 가치가 있었습니다!

윌리엄 메카도 – 2016년부터 캐피털 은행 고객

수신: 리타 모레노 〈moreno@capital-corporate.com〉
발신: 제리 월쉬 〈walsh@capital-la.com〉
날짜: 6월 15일
주제: 회신: 보수 공사

안녕하세요 모레노,

저는 단호한 의견을 가진 사람으로서, 제가 틀렸을 때 이를 인정하기가 쉽지 않다는 것을 알고 있습니다. 그러나 이번에는 그것을 피할 수 없을 것 같습니다. 저는 로스앤젤레스 지점을 새로운 라운지 스타일을 위한 시험대로 삼으려는 당신의 시도에 대해 강력하게 반대했었습니다. 한 번에 모든 걸 시도하는 것은 단지 너무나 많은 변화라고 생각했었던 것이죠. 그러나 제가 워싱턴 지점을 방문하고 막 돌아왔는데, 저는 그 결과에 너무나 반해버렸습니다. 새로운 구조가 진정으로 효율성을 개선했으며, 지점장인 멜라니 브라운이 저에게 보여준 고객 만족 설문은 깊은 인상을 남겼습니다. 저희가 여기서 비슷한 보수 공사 실행을 논의할 회의 일정을 잡을 수 있을까요? 편하실 때 되도록 빨리 저에게 알려 주세요.

제리 월쉬
지점장
캐피털 은행, 로스앤젤레스

accessible 사용할 수 있는 representative 직원, 대표 inconvenience 불편(함) state-of-the-art 최신식의 module 모듈(= 정해진 일을 수행하는 프로그램) result in ~ 결과를 내다 retain ~인 채로 유지하다 feature 특징점 instant 즉석[즉시]의 finance 재무 undergo 겪다 transformation 변화, 변형 breakroom 휴게실 tech 첨단 기술(의) start-up 신규 업체 layout (건축물의) 구조, 시설 off-putting 정이 안 가는, 좋아하기 힘든 number-ticket dispenser 번호표 자동 발매기 face to face 얼굴을 맞대고 indulge in ~을 탐닉하다 frustrated 실망한, 좌절한 unavoidable 피할 수 없는 resist 저항하다 serve as ~의 역할을 하다 prototype 프로토타입(= 시행되기 앞서서 미리 제작해 보는 형태) blow A away A에 너무나 반하다 efficiency 효율성 impressive (깊은) 감동을 주는 implementation 실행, 시행 annoyance 짜증

191 6번가의 캐피털 은행에 대해 언급되지 않은 것은 무엇인가?
(A) 5월에 재개장하기로 일정이 잡혀 있었다.
(B) 로비에 ATM 2대를 보유하고 있다.
(C) 2번가로 이전할 것이다.
(D) 오래된 건물에 있다.

192 메카도 씨가 짜증 난 이유는 무엇인가?
(A) 예상치 못한 장기간의 폐점
(B) 놀랍도록 무례한 은행 직원
(C) 신기술 부족
(D) 불편한 위치

193 보수 공사 이후에 6번가 캐피털 은행이 보유한 ATM은 몇 개인가?
(A) 없음
(B) 2개
(C) 3개
(D) 5개

194 새로운 은행으로 바꾸는 것에 대한 월쉬 씨의 원래 의견은 무엇인가?
(A) 그것에 대해 기대했었다.
(B) 너무나 과도하다고 느꼈다.
(C) 비용이 너무나 많이 든다고 생각했다.
(D) 안전에 대해 염려했다.

195 월쉬 씨가 모레노 씨에게 원하는 것은 무엇인가?
(A) 그녀의 무례한 행동에 대해 사과하기
(B) 워싱턴 지점 둘러보기
(C) 고객 만족 설문 조사하기
(D) 지점을 보수하는 것에 대해 그와 이야기 나누기

[196-200]

수신: 노엘 클라크 〈clarke@junoelectrical.com〉
발신: 빅토리아 해밀턴 〈hamilton@hotmail.com〉
날짜: 4월 5일
제목: findjobs.com의 구인광고에 응답

클라크 씨에게,

주노 전기회사를 대표해서 귀하께서 findjobs.com의 취업 검색 엔진에 올린 광고를 보고 이 글을 씁니다. 우선, 전기공학 분야에서의 저의 경력을 설명해 보겠습니다. 저는 노스캐롤라이나 기술대학에서 전기공학 석사 학위를 취득했습니다. 대학원생 시절에는 캐서린 포브스 박사님 아래서 연구실 조교로 일했습니다.

저는 2019년에 듀크 대학에서 박사 학위를 취득했습니다. 그 당시에 노스캐롤라이나 전력 회사의 연구 개발 부서에서 인턴사원으로 근무했습니다. 박사 학위 취득 이후에도 그곳에서 근무했고 확실한 기여를 해왔지만, 저는 새로운 기회에 대해 열린 자세를 가지고 있습니다. 그래서 저는 주노 전기회사에서 일하는 것에 관심이 있습니다. 저는 주로 대형 전력 발전기를 위한 전기 회로 기판을 제작하는 데 주력하고 있습니다. 첨부된 이력서와 추천서 3통이 증명하듯, 저는 믿음직하고 활동적인 직원입니다.

제 구직 신청서를 진지하게 고려해 주시기 바랍니다. 곧 소식 듣길 바랍니다.

진심으로
빅토리아 해밀턴

수신: 빅토리아 해밀턴 <hamilton@hotmail.com>
발신: 노엘 클라크 <clarke@junoelectrical.com>
날짜: 4월 15일
제목: 회신: findjobs.com의 구인광고에 응답

해밀턴 박사에게,

주노 전기회사에 관심을 가져 주셔서 감사합니다. 3통의 추천서와 함께 당신의 이력서를 검토해 보았습니다. 당신이 강력한 교육적 배경을 가지고 있다는 것에는 의심의 여지가 없습니다. 당신은 전기기사로 우리가 찾고 있는 모든 자격을 명백히 갖추고 있습니다.

그러나 당신의 이력서 중 제가 확실히 했으면 하는 부분이 하나 있습니다. 당신은 대형 전력 발전기의 전기 회로 기판을 제작한 경험이 있다고 하셨는데요, 하지만 말씀하신 것이 어떤 종류의 발전기인가요? 증기 터빈 발전기, 방사성 동위 원소 발전기, 핵발전기, 기타 종류도 있습니다.

당신의 경력 중에 설계된 다양한 발전기에 관한 더욱 구체적인 정보를 이메일로 보내 주시기 바랍니다. 일단 우리가 이와 관련된 사실을 확보하고 있다면, 당신을 면접에 부를 것인지 결정할 수 있을 것입니다. 시간 내 주셔서 감사합니다.

진심으로
노엘 클라크

발신: 주노 전기회사
043-555-1029

----------------------- 2019년 4월 15일 월요일 -----------------------

안녕하세요, 해밀턴 박사님. 저는 주노 전기회사의 노엘 클라크입니다.

우리는 귀하가 보낸 서류를 신중하게 검토하였습니다. 무엇보다도, 귀하가 만든 방사성 동위 원소 발전기가 특히 인상적이었습니다. 그러므로 저는 귀하를 만나서 더 많은 대화를 나누고 싶습니다. 비서인 자넷 포트만 씨가 오늘 오후쯤에 전화할 것입니다. 그러면, 이번 주 안에 가능한 시간을 선택하시고, 저의 사무실을 방문해 주세요. 또 다른 질문이 있으시면 그녀에게 질문해 주세요. 곧 봅시다.

오후 5:38 메시지

on behalf of ~을 대신해서 electrical engineering 전기공학 master 석사 doctoral degree 박사 학위 research and development 연구 개발 solid 견고한, 충실한 contribution 공헌 specialize in ~을 전문적으로 다루다 circuit board 회로 기판 generator 발전기 attest 증명하다 energetic 활동적인 pedigree 계통 quality 자격 steam turbine 증기 터빈 radioisotope 방사성 동위 원소 thermoelectric 열전기의 nuclear 핵의 pertinent 관련된, 적절한 core business 주력 사업 dissertation 논문

196 노엘 클라크는 누구인가?
(A) 노스캐롤라이나 기술대학 학생
(B) 노스캐롤라이나 전력 회사의 직원
(C) findjobs.com의 직원
(D) 주노 전기회사의 직원

197 해밀턴 박사가 전문적으로 다루는 것은 무엇인가?
(A) 홍보
(B) 포브스 박사를 돕는 것
(C) 대학원생을 가르치는 것
(D) 전기 회로 기판을 제작하는 것

198 클라크 씨가 구체적으로 요청하는 정보는 무엇인가?
(A) 해밀턴 박사가 언제 인터뷰에 올 수 있을 건지
(B) 해밀턴 박사의 박사 학위 논문의 주제
(C) 해밀턴 박사의 학력
(D) 전력 발전기에 대한 정보

199 문자 메시지에서 알 수 있는 것은 무엇인가?
(A) 클라크 씨는 해밀턴 박사와 여러 번 일했다.
(B) 주노 전기회사는 4월에 신제품을 출시할 것이다.
(C) 해밀턴 박사는 4월 15일에 클라크 씨에게 이메일을 보냈다.
(D) 클라크 씨는 최근에 매니저로 고용되었다.

200 해밀턴 박사에 관해 추측할 수 있는 것은 무엇인가?
(A) 그녀는 노스캐롤라이나 전력 회사에서 정규직으로 근무한다.
(B) 그녀는 findjobs.com에 이력서와 지원서를 제출하였다.
(C) 그녀는 항목별 광고에서 매우 큰 도움을 받았다.
(D) 그녀는 전화상으로 포트만 씨와 대화할 것이다.

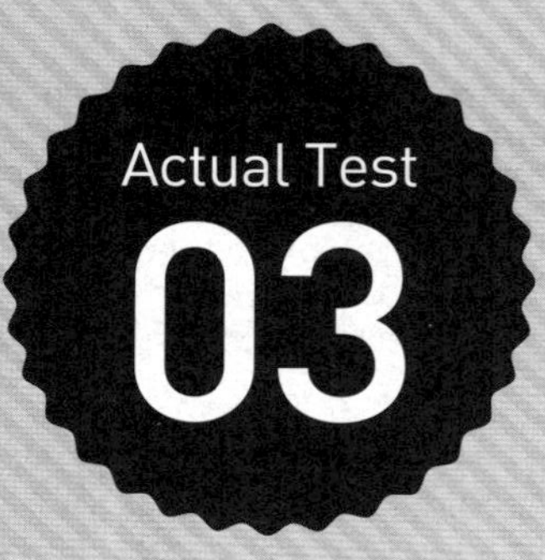

Listening Comprehension

PART 1

1 (C)	2 (B)	3 (A)	4 (D)	5 (A)	6 (C)				

PART 2

7 (A)	8 (A)	9 (B)	10 (C)	11 (B)	12 (B)	13 (C)	14 (A)	15 (C)	16 (A)
17 (C)	18 (C)	19 (B)	20 (A)	21 (B)	22 (B)	23 (A)	24 (C)	25 (A)	26 (C)
27 (C)	28 (B)	29 (A)	30 (B)	31 (A)					

PART 3

32 (D)	33 (B)	34 (A)	35 (A)	36 (D)	37 (C)	38 (D)	39 (B)	40 (C)	41 (C)
42 (D)	43 (B)	44 (D)	45 (B)	46 (C)	47 (D)	48 (B)	49 (D)	50 (C)	51 (A)
52 (C)	53 (B)	54 (A)	55 (C)	56 (A)	57 (B)	58 (D)	59 (B)	60 (D)	61 (A)
62 (D)	63 (A)	64 (B)	65 (C)	66 (C)	67 (C)	68 (D)	69 (A)	70 (C)	

PART 4

71 (D)	72 (A)	73 (A)	74 (A)	75 (B)	76 (A)	77 (A)	78 (B)	79 (A)	80 (C)
81 (D)	82 (B)	83 (D)	84 (A)	85 (A)	86 (B)	87 (B)	88 (A)	89 (A)	90 (C)
91 (D)	92 (B)	93 (C)	94 (B)	95 (A)	96 (C)	97 (D)	98 (A)	99 (D)	100 (B)

Reading Comprehension

PART 5

101 (D)	102 (C)	103 (A)	104 (C)	105 (B)	106 (A)	107 (C)	108 (B)	109 (D)	110 (A)
111 (D)	112 (C)	113 (D)	114 (B)	115 (A)	116 (C)	117 (B)	118 (C)	119 (A)	120 (B)
121 (A)	122 (A)	123 (D)	124 (B)	125 (D)	126 (A)	127 (A)	128 (D)	129 (A)	130 (B)

PART 6

131 (B)	132 (A)	133 (B)	134 (A)	135 (C)	136 (A)	137 (A)	138 (C)	139 (C)	140 (A)
141 (B)	142 (A)	143 (C)	144 (D)	145 (A)	146 (B)				

PART 7

147 (D)	148 (B)	149 (A)	150 (C)	151 (D)	152 (B)	153 (B)	154 (D)	155 (C)	156 (D)
157 (D)	158 (D)	159 (C)	160 (C)	161 (B)	162 (A)	163 (D)	164 (B)	165 (C)	166 (B)
167 (D)	168 (A)	169 (B)	170 (D)	171 (C)	172 (A)	173 (B)	174 (B)	175 (D)	176 (C)
177 (D)	178 (A)	179 (D)	180 (B)	181 (D)	182 (B)	183 (D)	184 (C)	185 (A)	186 (A)
187 (B)	188 (D)	189 (D)	190 (B)	191 (D)	192 (B)	193 (A)	194 (C)	195 (C)	196 (B)
197 (C)	198 (A)	199 (A)	200 (D)						

Part 1

1 호M
(A) A woman is washing a car.
(B) A woman is repairing a road.
(C) A woman is riding a bicycle.
(D) A woman is changing a tire.

(A) 한 여자가 자동차를 청소하고 있다.
(B) 한 여자가 도로를 수리하고 있다.
(C) 한 여자가 자전거를 타고 있다.
(D) 한 여자가 타이어를 교환하고 있다.

safety goggles 안전 보호 안경 workbench 작업대 cloth 천

2 미W
(A) The man is hanging some tools on the wall.
(B) The man is drilling a hole in some wood.
(C) Safety goggles are being removed from a cabinet.
(D) A workbench has been covered with a cloth.

(A) 남자가 벽에 연장을 걸고 있다.
(B) 남자가 목재에 드릴로 구멍을 뚫고 있다.
(C) 보호용 안경이 캐비닛에서 옮겨지고 있다.
(D) 작업대가 천으로 덮여 있다.

safety goggles 안전 보호 안경 workbench 작업대 cloth 천

3 미M
(A) A woman has a bag over her shoulder.
(B) They are putting together some bookshelves.
(C) A librarian is organizing materials on a shelf.
(D) There are shelves on both sides of the people.

(A) 여자가 그녀의 어깨에 가방을 메고 있다.
(B) 사람들이 책꽂이들을 조립하고 있다.
(C) 사서가 선반 위에 물건들을 정리하고 있다.
(D) 사람들의 양쪽에 선반이 있다.

put together (부품을) 조립하다 bookshelf 책꽂이 organize 정리하다 material (물건의) 재료

4 호M
(A) A woman is placing food in a basket.
(B) A woman is paying for her purchase.
(C) A woman is planting some vegetables.
(D) A woman is pushing a shopping cart.

(A) 한 여자가 바구니에 음식을 담고 있다.
(B) 한 여자가 물건값을 지불하고 있다.
(C) 한 여자가 채소를 심고 있다.
(D) 한 여자가 쇼핑 카트를 밀고 있다.

pay for 지불하다 push 밀다

5 미W
(A) Some people are relaxing around the fountain.
(B) Some people are lying on the grass to read.
(C) Some people are resting at the bottom of the steps.
(D) Some workers are watering trees in a park.

(A) 몇몇 사람들이 분수대 주변에서 휴식을 취하고 있다.
(B) 몇몇 사람들이 잔디 위에 누워 독서를 하고 있다.
(C) 몇몇 사람들이 층계의 아래에서 쉬고 있다.
(D) 몇몇 인부들이 공원 안의 나무에 물을 주고 있다.

relax 휴식을 취하다 fountain 분수대 lie 눕다 rest 쉬다 step 계단 water 물을 주다

6 미M
(A) Some instruments are being carried outside.
(B) Some pianos are being repaired.
(C) Some guitars are hanging on a wall.
(D) Some musicians are playing instruments.

(A) 몇몇 악기가 밖으로 옮겨지고 있다.
(B) 몇몇 피아노가 수리되고 있다.
(C) 몇몇 기타가 벽에 걸려 있다.
(D) 몇몇 음악가가 악기를 연주하고 있다.

instrument 악기 carry 옮기다 hang 걸다, 매달다

Part 2

7 미W 미M
Who's the head of the sales department?
(A) Ms. Gupta.
(B) For the sales presentation.
(C) You go ahead.

영업부 부서장은 누구죠?
(A) 굽타 씨요.
(B) 판매 발표를 위해서요.
(C) 먼저 가세요.

어휘 head 대표, 우두머리 sales department 영업부

8 미W 미M
Where will the national book fair be next year?
(A) In Beijing.
(B) Next November.
(C) The National Museum.

내년 전국 도서전은 어디에서 하나요?
(A) 북경이요.
(B) 내년 11월이요.
(C) 국립 박물관요.

어휘 national 전국적인, 국가의 book fair 도서전

9 미M 미W
Where can I obtain a parking permit?
(A) Yes, you can park here.
(B) It's free for visitors for 2 hours.
(C) Maybe it's not permitted here.

주차 허가증은 어디에서 받나요?
(A) 네, 여기에 주차하시면 됩니다.
(B) 방문객들은 2시간 무료입니다.
(C) 아마 그것은 여기서 허락되지 않을 겁니다.

어휘 obtain 얻다 parking permit 주차 허가증 permit 허가하다

10 호M 미M
Mr. Goldman hasn't signed the contract, has he?
(A) Yes, I have already signed it.
(B) From seven to four.
(C) No, not yet.

골드먼 씨가 아직 계약서에 서명 안 했죠, 그렇죠?
(A) 네, 벌써 제가 서명했어요.
(B) 7시에서 4시까지요.
(C) 아니요, 아직요.

어휘 sign the contract 계약서에 서명하다

11 미M 호M
Are you ready for the press conference?
(A) No, I think I'm ready to do it.
(B) Not if the script is not completed.
(C) It wasn't an important meeting.

기자 회견 준비가 되셨나요?
(A) 아니요, 전 준비가 된 것 같아요.
(B) 원고부터 끝내야 해요.
(C) 그건 중요한 회의는 아니었어요.

어휘 press conference 기자 회견 script 원고 complete 끝내다

12 미W 미M
This printer is out of order.
(A) No, I ordered three.
(B) Why don't you try the one on the third floor?
(C) Ms. Rose has printed them.

프린터기가 고장 났어요.
(A) 아니요, 제가 3개 주문했는데.
(B) 3층에 있는 프린터를 사용해 보는 건 어때요?
(C) 로즈 씨가 그걸 인쇄했어요.

어휘 out of order 고장 난 order 주문하다 print 인쇄하다

13 Why is Mr. Singh running so late in approving the
미M expense report?
미W (A) There seems to be pretty simple.
(B) Because he runs at the gym after work.
(C) Some of the receipts were missing.

싱 씨가 비용 보고서를 승인하는 데 왜 이리 늦나요?
(A) 아주 간단한 것 같은데요.
(B) 퇴근 후 체육관에서 달리기 때문이에요.
(C) 영수증 일부가 분실되었거든요.

어휘 run late 늦다 approve 승인하다 expense 비용 pretty 매우 receipt 영수증 miss 빠뜨리다

14 May I see your boarding pass, please?
미W (A) Sure, here you are.
미M (B) You can board soon.
(C) It's just passed.

탑승권 좀 보여 주시겠어요?
(A) 네, 여기 있습니다.
(B) 곧 타실 수 있어요.
(C) 막 통과했어요.

어휘 boarding pass 탑승권 board 타다 pass 통과하다

15 Who's on the new construction project?
미M (A) We project an annual growth rate of 10%.
미W (B) It's going ahead of schedule.
(C) I'm afraid it was cancelled at the last minute.

누가 새로운 공사 프로젝트를 맡고 있나요?
(A) 우리는 10퍼센트의 연 성장률을 예상하고 있어요.
(B) 일정보다 앞서 진행 중입니다.
(C) 마지막 순간에 취소된 것 같아요.

어휘 project 프로젝트, 예상[추정]하다 annual 연간의 growth rate 성장률 ahead of schedule 일정보다 앞서 at the last minute 막판에

16 Where did you see the commercial?
미M (A) On the company Web site.
호M (B) It is too commercial.
(C) I saw it yesterday.

어디서 그 광고 봤어요?
(A) 회사 홈페이지요.
(B) 그건 너무 상업적이죠.
(C) 어제 그걸 봤어요.

어휘 commercial 광고, 상업적인

17 Would you like to give me a ride to the airport this
미W afternoon?
미M (A) Yes, I'll ride a bus there.
(B) He's going to fly out to Japan next week.
(C) If you don't mind a long drive.

오늘 오후에 제가 당신을 공항까지 태워 드릴까요?
(A) 네, 저는 거기에 버스를 타고 갈 겁니다.
(B) 그는 다음 주에 비행기 타고 일본에 갈 겁니다.
(C) 오래 차를 타고 가도 괜찮으시다면요.

어휘 give a ride 차로 태워 주다 fly out 비행기로 출발하다 mind 꺼리다

18 How will you get to the subway station?
미M (A) Probably by e-mail.
미W (B) It's an expressway.
(C) One of my friends is driving me.

지하철역에 어떻게 가실 거예요?
(A) 아마 이메일로요.
(B) 그건 고속 도로예요.
(C) 제 친구가 차로 태워 줄 겁니다.

어휘 get to 도착하다 subway station 지하철역 expressway 고속 도로 drive 태워다 주다

19 Who do you think will be the new secretary?
호M (A) The documentary film was pretty informative.
미M (B) We may go without one for the time being.
(C) Renew the contract, please.

누가 새로운 비서가 될 거라고 생각하세요?
(A) 그 다큐멘터리 영화는 꽤 유익했어요.
(B) 당분간 비서 없이 지내야 할 거예요.
(C) 계약을 갱신해 주세요.

어휘 informative 유익한 for the time being 당분간 renew 갱신하다

20 Haven't you ever seen Ms. Chu before?
미M (A) I don't think so.
미W (B) No, it's after the ceremony.
(C) Yes, I've seen him once.

전에 추 씨를 본 적 있지 않나요?
(A) 아닌 것 같은데요.
(B) 아니요, 식 끝나고요.
(C) 네, 그를 한 번 봤어요.

어휘 ceremony 기념식 once 한 번

21 Please turn off your electronic gadgets before
호M departure.
미M (A) I need your signature here.
(B) I will. Thanks for reminding me.
(C) The technician will take a look at them.

출발 전에 전자 기기는 꺼 주세요.
(A) 여기에 당신의 서명이 필요합니다.
(B) 그럴게요. 상기시켜줘서 고마워요.
(C) 기술자는 그들을 살펴볼 겁니다.

어휘 turn off 끄다 gadget 장비 departure 출발 signature 서명 remind 상기시키다 technician 기술자

22 Is the president arriving this week or next week?
미M (A) Oh, the accounting department.
미W (B) He'll be here on the 15th.
(C) Yes, four of these presents.

사장님이 이번 주에 도착하시나요, 아니면 다음 주인가요?
(A) 아, 회계팀이요.
(B) 여기 15일에 오세요.
(C) 네, 이 선물들 중 4개요.

어휘 president 사장, 회장 present 선물

23 Isn't Mr. Eastman back from his business trip yet?
미W (A) Yes, he had to cut it short.
미M (B) I had a great time there.
(C) It's hard to start a new business.

이스트먼 씨는 출장에서 아직 안 돌아왔나요?
(A) 네, 중간에 취소하고 돌아왔습니다.
(B) 거기서 즐거운 시간을 보냈어요.
(C) 새로운 사업을 시작하기는 어렵네요.

어휘 business trip 출장 cut ... short ~을 갑자기 끝내다

24 Who needs a copy of the final report?
미M (A) Yes, the limousine goes to the airport.
미W (B) Recent sales figures.
(C) I think Harrison does.

최종 보고서 한 부 필요한 사람이 누구죠?
(A) 네, 리무진이 공항까지 가요.
(B) 최근 판매액이요.
(C) 해리슨일 것 같네요.

어휘 copy 복사본, 한 부 final report 최종 보고서 recent 최근의 sales figure 판매 수치

25 Why is the Thomson & Gray office closing this month?
미M (A) Because of their remodeling.
미W (B) The office is open from 10 to 5.
(C) The entire staff makes me feel comfortable.

톰슨 앤 존슨 사무실이 이번 달에 왜 문을 닫죠?
(A) 리모델링 때문에요.
(B) 그 사무실은 오전 10시에서 오후 5시까지 열어요.
(C) 전 직원들이 절 편안하게 느껴요.
어휘 close 닫다 remodel 개조하다 entire 전체의

26 What is it like working for a publishing company?
미M (A) That publisher wants the lowest costs.
호M (B) A 6-hour office job sounds good to me.
(C) Meeting the deadline is always stressful.

출판사에서 일하는 건 어떤가요?
(A) 그 출판업자는 가장 낮은 비용을 원해요.
(B) 6시간 근무하는 사무직이라니 저한테는 괜찮네요.
(C) 시한을 맞추는 일이 항상 스트레스네요.
어휘 What is it like ~는 어떤가? publisher 출판업자 meet the deadline 시한을 맞추다 stressful 스트레스를 주는

27 Why are you putting these brochures in the boxes?
미M (A) Because it's far from the store.
미W (B) There are too many boxes.
(C) We're putting them in storage.

왜 상자에 이 안내 책자를 넣고 있죠?
(A) 가게에서 멀어서요.
(B) 상자가 너무 많은데요.
(C) 창고에 넣으려고요.
어휘 brochure 안내 책자 far 먼 storage 창고, 보관소

28 Isn't there a fire inspection scheduled for today?
미M (A) No, we need to order more fire safety devices.
호M (B) Yes, and they'll be coming to your office.
(C) The fire alarm will ring at regular intervals.

화재 점검이 오늘 아닌가요?
(A) 아니요, 우리는 더 많은 화재 안전 장비들을 주문해야 합니다.
(B) 네, 저희가 당신의 사무실에 들어갈 거예요.
(C) 화재 경보는 주기적으로 울릴 겁니다.
어휘 fire inspection 화재 점검 safety device 안전장치 fire alarm 화재 경보 ring 울리다 interval 간격

29 Do I need my fur coat today, or is a jacket okay?
호M (A) It's pretty warm.
미M (B) No, thank you.
(C) You can find it in the closet.

오늘 털 코트 필요할까요, 아님 재킷으로 괜찮을까요?
(A) 오늘 날씨 아주 따뜻해요.
(B) 아니요, 괜찮아요.
(C) 벽장에서 찾으시면 돼요.
어휘 fur 털 pretty warm 아주 따뜻한 closet 벽장

30 Could you help me make an inventory?
미W (A) Sure, I'd like to see the invention.
미M (B) I know it is not a small job to do.
(C) He always puts everything in order.

재고 정리 하는 거 도와줄래요?
(A) 물론이죠, 그 발명품을 보고 싶어요.
(B) 그게 하는 게 쉽지 않다는 걸 알죠.
(C) 그는 항상 모든 것을 정돈해 둡니다.
어휘 inventory 재고 목록 invention 발명품 small 사소한, 대수롭지 않은 put ... in order 정돈하다

31 We should register for the online workshop by
미M Wednesday.
미W (A) Thanks for reminding me.
(B) It was a short walk.
(C) The store is downtown.

수요일까지 온라인 워크숍 등록해야 됩니다.
(A) 상기시켜 줘서 고마워요.
(B) 얼마 걷지 않았어요.
(C) 상점은 시내에 있어요.
어휘 register 등록하다 remind 상기시키다 short walk 단거리의 보행 downtown 시내에

Part 3

Questions 32-34 refer to the following conversation. 미M 미W

M Kelly, I'm wondering if you can help me out. I have had a toothache since last week and since I'm new here, I can't find a dentist in the neighborhood.
W Oh, that's too bad. You have to get it taken care of before it gets worse.
M I know. Do you know someone I can just walk in to right away? I know that I have to make an appointment, but I just can't wait any more.
W Actually, I know a dentist who lives next door to my place so let me call her after lunch and see if you can see her today or tomorrow.

남 켈리, 혹시 저 좀 도와줄 수 있는지 궁금하네요. 지난주부터 이가 아팠는데, 제가 여기 온 지 얼마 안 되어서 근처에 치과를 찾을 수가 없네요.
여 저런, 안됐네요. 더 악화되기 전에 치료하셔야만 해요.
남 그렇죠. 제가 예약 없이 바로 가서 볼 수 있는 의사가 있을까요? 예약을 해야 하는 건 알지만 더 이상 기다릴 수가 없네요.
여 사실 제 옆집에 사시는 의사 한 분을 알아요. 점심 이후에 전화를 해서 오늘이나 내일 당신이 그녀를 볼 수 있는지 알아볼게요.

toothache 치통 neighborhood 주변 get worse 악화되다 walk in to 예약 없이 바로 ~로 들어가다 make an appointment 예약하다 next door 옆집에

32 What does the man want to do?
(A) Take the woman out for lunch
(B) Postpone his appointment with a dentist
(C) Move out of the town tomorrow
(D) Go to a dental clinic on short notice

남자는 무엇을 하고 싶어 하는가?
(A) 여자에게 나가서 점심을 사 준다.
(B) 치과 예약을 연기한다.
(C) 내일 다른 곳으로 이사 나간다.
(D) 급히 연락하고 치과에 간다.

33 What does the man ask the woman for?
(A) A dental record
(B) A recommendation
(C) A ride to the dentist
(D) A phone number

남자는 여자에게 무엇을 요청하는가?
(A) 치과 기록
(B) 추천
(C) 치과까지 태워 주기
(D) 전화번호

34 What does the woman offer to do?
(A) Contact a neighbor
(B) Go to a dental clinic
(C) Print a city map
(D) Book a different seat
여자는 무엇을 해 주려고 하는가?
(A) 이웃에게 연락하기
(B) 치과 가기
(C) 도시 지도 인쇄
(D) 다른 자리 예약

Questions 35-37 refer to the following conversation. 미M 미W

M Good morning! Where to?
W Could you drive me to the Westwood Station? And I'm very short on time, so please get there as soon as possible. I have a train to catch.
M What time does your train leave? It's rush hour, so it will take at least half an hour to get there. Do you know the exact departure time?
W I'm supposed to be on the train at 8:55 A.M., so I have 45 minutes left. I think I can make it.
남 좋은 아침입니다! 어디로 가세요?
여 웨스트우드 역까지 가 주세요. 시간이 너무 없으니까 가능한 한 빨리 가 주세요. 기차를 타야 하거든요.
남 기차가 언제 출발하나요? 차가 막히는 시간이라 가는 데 최소 30분은 걸릴 거예요. 정확한 출발 시간을 아세요?
여 아침 8시 55분 기차를 타야 하니까 45분 남았네요. 갈 수 있을 것 같아요.

where to 택시에서 기사가 행선지를 묻는 표현 be supposed to ~해야 한다 make it 시간에 맞게 도착하다 car race 자동차 경주 under construction 공사 중인 broken 고장 난 ride 차를 타고 가는 여정 work shift 근무 교대 be over 끝나다

35 Who most likely is the man?
(A) A taxi driver
(B) A ticket agent
(C) A market clerk
(D) A delivery man
남자는 누구일 것 같은가?
(A) 택시 기사
(B) 티켓 판매원
(C) 시장 점원
(D) 배달 직원

36 Where does the woman want to go?
(A) To an airport
(B) To a bus station
(C) To a car race
(D) To a railroad station
여자가 가고자 하는 곳은?
(A) 공항
(B) 버스 정류장
(C) 자동차 경주
(D) 기차역

37 What does the man tell the woman?
(A) The station is under construction.
(B) Her watch is broken.
(C) The ride will take some time.
(D) His work shift is over.
남자가 여자에게 말하는 것은?
(A) 역이 공사 중이다.
(B) 여자의 시계가 고장 났다.
(C) 가는 데 시간이 걸릴 것이다.
(D) 그의 근무 교대가 끝난다.

Questions 38-40 refer to the following conversation. 미M 영W

M Hello, Jenna. Did you check the e-mail from the manager? It says that he is going to give a presentation at two o'clock today and this time, it is mandatory to attend.
W Yes, I know about it. It's in the conference room as usual, right?
M Oh, no. They changed the venue because there is a scheduling conflict. The accounting department is going to hold a budget meeting there, so the presentation will be in the smaller meeting room. Why don't you post a notice on the change for the rest of the people?
W I will do that. I don't want anybody to go to a wrong place and waste time.
남 안녕, 제나. 부장한테서 온 이메일 받았어요? 오늘 오후 2시에 그가 발표를 한다고 합니다. 그리고 이번에는 의무적으로 참석해야 한다고 하더군요.
여 네, 알고 있어요. 예전처럼 회의실에서 하는 거죠, 그렇죠?
남 아닙니다. 시간이 겹쳐서 장소를 변경했어요. 회계부서에서 예산 관련 회의를 한다고 하더군요. 그래서 발표는 더 작은 회의실에서 합니다. 변경된 사항에 대해 공지를 올리는 게 어때요?
여 그럴게요. 직원들이 잘못된 장소로 가서 시간 낭비하게 하고 싶지 않네요.

mandatory 의무적인, 필수적인 as usual 예전처럼 venue 장소 scheduling conflict 시간이 겹치는 것 budget 예산 post 공지하다 notice 공지사항 waste 낭비하다

38 What are the speakers talking about?
(A) A speech
(B) A farewell party
(C) An accounting policy
(D) A compulsory meeting
화자들은 무엇에 관해 이야기하고 있는가?
(A) 연설
(B) 송별회
(C) 회계 정책
(D) 의무적인 모임

39 What does the man say about the event?
(A) The registration is mandatory.
(B) There was a problem with the first location.

(C) Tickets must be purchased ahead of time.
(D) The speaker is going to be changed.

남자가 행사에 관해 말하는 것은?
(A) 등록이 의무적이다.
(B) 첫 번째 장소에 문제가 있다.
(C) 표는 미리 구입해야 한다.
(D) 발표자가 변경될 것이다.

40 What will the woman probably do next?
(A) Set up a new appointment
(B) Email the presenter about the change
(C) Inform her coworkers of the change
(D) Delay the presentation to next week

여자는 다음에 무엇을 할 것인가?
(A) 새로운 약속을 잡는다.
(B) 연사에게 변경 사항을 이메일로 보낸다.
(C) 동료들에게 변경 사항을 알린다.
(D) 발표를 다음 주로 미룬다.

Questions 41-43 refer to the following conversation. 미M 미W

M Antonio's Italian Cuisine. This is Max Irons. How may I help you?
W Mr. Irons, I found a wallet in the subway and there was your business card in it. Is it yours?
M Yes! What a relief! I thought I left it at the dentist's office where I had a check-up this morning. I never thought about the subway.
W Well, that's where it was. I see from your card that your restaurant is on Young Street. I actually work at a camera shop right on Kyle Street, which is just a block away from your restaurant. So you can come over to my store any time to pick up your wallet.

남 안토니오 이탈리아 퀴진입니다. 저는 맥스 아이언스입니다. 어떻게 도와 드릴까요?
여 아이언스 씨, 제가 지하철 역에서 지갑을 발견했는데 안에 당신의 명함이 있었어요. 이 지갑이 당신 것인가요?
남 네! 다행이네요! 아침에 제가 검진 받았던 치과에 두고 온 줄 알았어요. 지하철 역일 줄은 몰랐네요.
여 지하철 역에 있었답니다. 명함에 보니까 당신의 레스토랑이 영 가에 있네요. 저는 바로 카일 가에 있는 카메라 상점에서 일하는데 그 레스토랑에서 한 블록 떨어진 곳이에요. 언제든 여기로 오셔서 지갑을 가져가도록 하세요.

relief 안도, 안심 check-up 검진

41 What does the man mention about the dentist's office?
(A) He works there.
(B) He found his wallet there.
(C) He had a check-up there today.
(D) It is located on Andrew Street.

남자는 치과에 대해서 무엇을 언급하는가?
(A) 그곳에서 일한다.
(B) 지갑을 그곳에서 찾았다.
(C) 오늘 그곳에서 검진을 받았다.
(D) 그것은 앤드류 가에 있다.

42 What does the man imply when he says, "Yes! What a relief"?
(A) He can make a reservation for dinner.
(B) A new subway line will start operating.
(C) He can make it to the dental clinic on time.
(D) He is glad to hear that his wallet has been found.

남자가 "네! 다행이네요"라고 말한 의미는 무엇인가?
(A) 그는 저녁 예약을 할 수 있다.
(B) 새 전철 노선이 운행을 시작할 것이다.
(C) 그는 치과에 늦지 않게 갈 수 있다.
(D) 그의 지갑이 발견되었다는 것을 듣고 기쁘다.

43 What does the woman suggest the man do?
(A) Contact a restaurant
(B) Visit the woman's workplace
(C) Purchase a new wallet
(D) Order more business cards

여자는 남자에게 무엇을 할 것을 제안하는가?
(A) 레스토랑에 연락하기
(B) 여자의 근무지에 방문하기
(C) 새 지갑 구입하기
(D) 명함 더 주문하기

Questions 44-46 refer to the following conversation. 미M 영W

M This house is the largest of the three I've shown you so far. It has a separate dining area and the bathroom is spacious as well.
W Wow, and the view is great. But the best thing about it is that my office building is very close to here. I can even walk to work. How much is the rent?
M It is 1,500 dollars per month.
W Hmm... That's more than I was hoping to spend. Could you give me some time to think it over? I'll call you early next week.

남 이 집은 지금까지 보여 드린 3개 중에서 가장 큽니다. 식사 공간이 분리되어 있고 화장실 역시 매우 넓습니다.
여 와, 게다가 경치도 좋네요. 그렇지만 가장 좋은 점은 제 사무실이 매우 가깝다는 거예요. 걸어갈 수도 있거든요. 임대료는 얼마죠?
남 한 달에 1,500달러입니다.
여 흠… 제가 쓰려고 한 것보다 많네요. 생각할 시간을 좀 주시겠어요? 다음 주 초에 전화를 드릴게요.

so far 현재까지 separate 분리된 spacious 넓은

44 Who most likely is the man?
(A) A tenant
(B) A home builder

(C) A designer
(D) A real estate agent

남자는 누구일 것 같은가?
(A) 세입자
(B) 주택 건축업자
(C) 디자이너
(D) 부동산 중개인

45 What does the woman say about the apartment?
(A) It is fully furnished.
(B) It is conveniently located.
(C) The rent is reasonable.
(D) The living room needs repairs.

여자는 아파트에 대해 뭐라고 말하는가?
(A) 가구가 완비되어 있다.
(B) 편리한 위치에 있다.
(C) 임대료가 적절하다.
(D) 거실이 수리가 필요하다.

46 What does the woman mean when she says, "That's more than I was hoping to spend"?
(A) The apartment is unnecessarily large.
(B) She has spent a lot of money on furniture.
(C) The rent is more expensive than she expected.
(D) She does not have time to think.

여자가, "제가 쓰려고 한 것보다 많네요"라고 말한 의미는 무엇인가?
(A) 아파트가 불필요하게 넓다.
(B) 여자는 가구에 돈을 많이 썼다.
(C) 임대료는 여자의 예상보다 비싸다.
(D) 여자는 생각할 시간이 없다.

Questions 47-49 refer to the following conversation with three speakers. 영W 미M 호M

W Simon and Zachary! I appreciate the both of you taking time out of your busy schedules today to discuss this consumer survey.
M1 It's no trouble at all.
M2 We know how important the research will be in developing a successful promotional strategy.
W What do you think of the initial draft of our questionnaire?
M1 Well, the questions are all very good, but some seem a bit repetitive. I'd recommend dropping a few.
M2 That makes two of us. Plus, you'll probably get a lot more responses if the form doesn't take long to complete.
W Those are convincing points. I'll be sure to pass them along to the project manager at our next meeting.

여 사이먼하고 재커리! 이 소비자 설문 조사 논의를 위해 바쁜 일정에도 시간을 내주신 두 분께 감사드려요.
남1 전혀 어려운 일이 아닙니다.
남2 저희는 성공적인 프로모션 전략을 개발하는 데 있어서 이 조사가 얼마나 중요한지 알고 있어요.
여 우리 설문지의 초안에 대해 어떻게 생각하시나요?
남1 음, 질문들이 아주 좋긴 하지만 몇 가지가 약간 반복되는 부분이 있는 것 같아요. 조금 삭제할 것을 추천해 드립니다.
남2 저도 같은 생각입니다. 게다가, 아마도 이 양식을 작성하는 데 시간이 오래 걸리지 않는다면, 더 많은 응답을 받게 될 겁니다.
여 설득력 있는 지적이네요. 다음 회의에서 프로젝트 매니저에게 꼭 전달하겠습니다.

consumer survey 소비자 설문 조사 promotional strategy 광고 전략 initial 처음의, 초기의 draft 원고, 초안 questionnaire 설문지 repetitive 반복적인, 반복되는 drop ~을 빼다 That makes two of us 나도 마찬가지이다, 같은 생각이다 convincing 설득력 있는 pass along 전달하다, 알리다

47 What are the speakers mainly discussing?
(A) A research budget
(B) A consumer campaign
(C) A managerial promotion
(D) A marketing survey

화자들이 주로 논의하는 것은 무엇인가?
(A) 연구 예산
(B) 소비자 캠페인
(C) 경영 촉진
(D) 마케팅 설문 조사

48 What do the men suggest?
(A) Extending a deadline
(B) Shortening a form
(C) Conducting longer interviews
(D) Emphasizing particular points

남자들이 제안하는 것은 무엇인가?
(A) 마감일을 연장하는 것
(B) 양식을 단축시키는 것
(C) 더 긴 인터뷰를 실시하는 것
(D) 특정 포인트 강조하는 것

49 What does the woman decide to do?
(A) Alter the schedule for a meeting
(B) Find a way to satisfy customers
(C) Make a few revisions to a document
(D) Relay some feedback

여자는 무엇을 하기로 결심하는가?
(A) 회의 일정을 변경하는 것
(B) 고객들을 만족시킬 방법을 찾는 것
(C) 문서를 몇 군데 수정하는 것
(D) 피드백을 전달하는 것

Questions 50-52 refer to the following conversation. 미M 영W

M Hi, Jena. Didn't you just begin your own business manufacturing swimwear for children? How is it going?

W Well, it has been difficult because it's a new venture. We will rely initially on word of mouth from relatives and colleagues and families. But this week, we sent out some brochures to leisure centers, so I expect that will bring us quite a bit more trade.

M Oh, I'm sure it will. In fact, maybe I can be of assistance. My wife is planning a swimming party for my daughter. I'd be delighted to take along some samples and display them to other parents.

남 안녕하세요, 제나. 당신은 어린이용 수영복을 만드는 본인의 사업을 막 시작하지 않았나요? 어떻게 돼 가나요?

여 음, 새로운 벤처 사업이라서 힘들었어요. 처음에는 친지, 동료와 가족들의 입소문에 의존하겠죠. 하지만 이번 주에, 레저 센터에 안내책자를 좀 보낼 거라서 꽤 많은 거래가 더 있을 것 같아요.

남 오, 저도 그럴 것이라고 확신해요. 실은, 제가 도움이 될 수도 있을 것 같아서요. 아내가 딸을 위해 수영 파티를 계획 중인데 제가 기꺼이 샘플을 몇 개 가지고 가서 다른 부모들에게 보여 주겠습니다.

manufacture 만들다, 제작하다 venture 벤처 (사업), (사업상의) 모험 rely on ~에 의지하다 initially 처음에 word of mouth 구전, 구두 relative 친척 colleague 동료 send out (많은 사람들 · 장소로) ~을 보내다[발송하다] brochure (안내 · 광고용) 책자 quite a bit 많은 trade 거래 be of assistance 도움이 되다 take along 가지고 가다

50 What kind of business does the woman run?

(A) A catering firm
(B) A swimming school
(C) A clothing firm
(D) An advertising company

여자가 운영하는 사업은 어떤 종류인가?

(A) 요리 조달업체
(B) 수영 학원
(C) 의류 회사
(D) 광고 회사

51 What does the woman hope will happen?

(A) That advertising will bring more trade
(B) That she will relocate her office
(C) That she joins a leisure center
(D) That additional employees will be hired

여자가 발생하길 바라는 것은?

(A) 광고가 더 많은 거래를 불러오는 것
(B) 그녀의 사무실을 이전하는 것
(C) 레저 센터에 가입하는 것
(D) 추가 직원들이 채용되는 것

52 What does the man offer to do?

(A) Contact his friends
(B) Distribute some brochures
(C) Recommend the woman's business
(D) Learn how to swim

남자는 무엇을 하기로 제안하는가?

(A) 그의 친구들에게 연락하기
(B) 안내책자 나눠주기
(C) 여자의 사업 추천하기
(D) 수영하는 법 배우기

Questions 53-55 refer to the following conversation. 미W 미M

W Hi! Julian, listen! I found a possible transport solution. A local company can provide a car and driver to us at short notice so I'm going to visit their garage this morning and won't be able to come into the office.

M A local chauffeur firm will be perfect. You really don't have to come in this afternoon. Everything appears to be under control for tomorrow's press reception. The meeting room's fully equipped and the client is ready for the presentation.

W That's excellent. It seems as if you have thought of everything. I'll arrive first thing in the morning to organize any last minute items. Is there anything else to do for the new product launch?

M I don't think so. In fact, some of our staff are on the phone calling potential interested customers to tell them of the innovative new product that will be launched in the morning.

여 안녕하세요! 줄리안, 있잖아요! 제가 가능성 있는 교통편 해결 방안을 찾았어요. 지역 회사가 우리에게 바로 차와 운전수를 제공할 수 있어서, 제가 오늘 아침에 그 정비소를 방문하느라 사무실에 가지 못할 거예요.

남 지역 기사 서비스 회사는 완벽할 겁니다. 당신이 오늘 오후에 반드시 들어올 필요는 없어요. 내일 언론 연회를 위한 준비는 모두 제대로 된 것처럼 보이네요. 회의실의 장비는 모두 갖춰져 있고, 의뢰인은 발표할 준비가 되어 있습니다.

여 훌륭해요. 당신이 모든 것을 다 생각해 두었던 것 같아요. 제가 막바지 사항을 준비하러 아침 일찍 갈게요. 새 제품 출시를 위해 더 해야 할 게 있나요?

남 없을 거예요. 사실, 저희 직원 중 몇 명은 관심 있는 잠재 고객에게 아침에 출시될 혁신적인 새 제품에 관해 전화를 걸고 있습니다.

transport 운송수단, 교통수단 at short notice 촉박하게, 갑자기, 바로 chauffeur 기사 (서비스) be under control 잘 관리되다 press 언론의, 보도의 reception 연회 fully 완전히 equipped 장비가 갖추어진 client 고객 presentation 발표 last minute 막판의 product launch 제품 출시 drive through 드라이브 스루(차에 탄 채로 이용할 수 있는 식당) leaflet 전단 potential 잠재적인

53 Who does the woman say she has to meet with?

(A) A new employer
(B) A transport supplier
(C) A catering firm
(D) A convention venue

여자가 만나야 한다고 말하는 사람은 누구인가?

(A) 새 고용주
(B) 차량 제공자
(C) 요리 조달업체
(D) 컨벤션 장소

54 What event are the speakers preparing for?

(A) A press reception
(B) An anniversary celebration
(C) A drive through facility
(D) A community event

화자들은 어떤 행사를 준비 중인가?

(A) 언론 연회
(B) 기념일 축하

(C) 드라이브 스루 시설
(D) 지역 사회 행사

55 How is the event being publicized?
(A) By promoting it online
(B) By handing out leaflets
(C) By calling potential customers
(D) By promoting it on television

행사는 어떻게 홍보되고 있는가?
(A) 온라인으로 홍보함으로써
(B) 안내 책자를 나눠줌으로써
(C) 잠재 고객들에게 전화함으로써
(D) 텔레비전에 홍보함으로써

Questions 56-58 refer to the following conversation. 미W 미M

W Hi, Chris. Do you have time to go over this press release I just drafted?
M Certainly. What's it about?
W It describes some updates that we plan for our Web site.
M Oh, yeah? I read about that in the company newsletter. I bet a lot of our customers will be making use of the new financial services we'll be offering. So many people are doing their banking online these days.
W Well, who can blame them? It's so much more convenient than going into a branch.

여 안녕하세요, 크리스, 제가 방금 작성한 보도 자료 초안을 검토해 주실 시간이 있으신가요?
남 물론입니다, 무엇에 관한 거죠?
여 우리가 계획한 웹 사이트 업데이트에 관한 내용입니다.
남 아, 그런가요? 사보에서 그에 대해 읽었어요. 많은 고객들이 우리가 제공할 새로운 금융 서비스들을 사용할 거라고 저는 장담해요. 요즘 많은 사람들이 온라인 뱅킹을 하고 있잖아요.
여 맞아요, 누가 그들을 탓할 수 있겠어요? 그것이 지점에 가는 것보다 훨씬 더 편리하니까요.

press release 보도 자료 newsletter 소식지 blame ~을 탓하다, ~책임으로 보다

56 What does the woman ask the man to do?
(A) Review her work
(B) Draft a report
(C) Release some records
(D) Update a Web site

여자는 남자에게 무엇을 하라고 요청하는가?
(A) 여자의 작업을 검토하는 것
(B) 보고서 초안을 작성하는 것
(C) 음반을 발매하는 것
(D) 웹 사이트를 업데이트하는 것

57 What kind of organization do the speakers work for?
(A) A newspaper
(B) A banking firm
(C) A marketing company
(D) A software company

화자들이 근무하는 곳은 어떤 종류의 회사인가?
(A) 신문사
(B) 금융 회사
(C) 마케팅 회사
(D) 소프트웨어 회사

58 What does the woman mean when she says, "who can blame them"?
(A) Customers did not cause the problem.
(B) Customers' confusion was expected.
(C) Customers are likely to make some complaints.
(D) Customers' behavior is understandable.

여자가 "누가 그들을 탓할 수 있겠어요?"라고 말하는 의미는 무엇인가?
(A) 고객들이 문제를 일으키지 않았다.
(B) 고객들의 혼란이 예상되었다.
(C) 고객들이 불만을 제기할 가능성이 있다.
(D) 고객들의 행동은 당연한 것이다.

Questions 59-61 refer to the following conversation. 미M 영W

M Susan, I've been checking the outcome of the research group we arranged to get reaction to our new toddler seat and we might have a problem. Most of the feedback reported that the seat is too large and complicated to fit.
W Oh! I see. Well perhaps we should focus more on the ergonomics to ensure the seat is less complicated.
M Um maybe, but we've already allocated the majority of our design funding. We will really require more money if we are proposing to redesign the seat to alter the complexity. At tomorrow's meeting, I can inquire about increasing the funds.

남 수잔, 우리가 새로운 유아용 의자에 대한 반응을 얻기 위해 마련했던 연구 그룹의 결과를 확인해 왔는데, 어쩌면 문제가 있을 수도 있어요. 대부분의 피드백은 의자가 너무 크고, 맞추려면 너무 복잡하다고 보고했습니다.
여 오! 그렇군요. 어쩌면 우리는 의자가 덜 복잡하도록 하기 위해, 인체공학에 더 집중해야 할지도 모르겠네요.
남 음, 어쩌면요. 하지만 이미 우리는 디자인 자금의 대부분을 할당했어요. 만약 복잡함을 고치기 위해 의자를 재디자인하는 것을 제안한다면, 정말 더 많은 돈이 필요할 거예요. 내일 회의에서 자금을 늘리는 것에 대해 물어보면 되겠네요.

outcome 결과 research group 연구 그룹 get reaction 반응을 얻다 toddler 걸음마를 배우는 아이 complicated 복잡한 focus on ~에 집중하다 ergonomics 인체공학 allocate 할당하다 majority of 다수의 funding 자금 redesign 다시 디자인하다 alter 변경하다 complexity 복잡함 inquire 문의하다

59 What item are the speakers discussing?
(A) A mobile phone
(B) A child seat
(C) A television
(D) A watch

화자들이 이야기하고 있는 제품은?
(A) 휴대폰
(B) 유아용 의자
(C) 텔레비전
(D) 손목시계

60 What does the woman suggest?
(A) Reviewing an advertising strategy
(B) Canceling production
(C) Delaying a consumer survey
(D) Altering a product design

여자는 무엇을 제안하는가?
(A) 광고 전략 검토
(B) 생산 취소
(C) 고객 설문조사 지연
(D) 제품 디자인 변경

61 What topic does the man say he will bring up at the meeting?
(A) A request for funding
(B) More time for research
(C) A changed schedule
(D) An alternative product

남자는 회의에서 어떤 화제를 말할 것이라고 하는가?
(A) 자금 요청
(B) 연구를 위한 더 많은 시간
(C) 바뀐 일정
(D) 대체 상품

Questions 62-64 refer to the following conversation. 미M 미W

M So Mwambi, you've been here a month now. What do you think of our three story office format?
W Well, I used to work in the Nairobi branch at an open-plan office across one floor. So, sitting in a separate room enclosed by four walls is a new experience. There's not much interaction and sometimes the office can get quite lonely.
M It took us all a while to get familiar with it. But perhaps using the shared common room will make you get to know people better.
W I'm sure I will get used to it. Some people suggest turning on the radio to help them cope. I think I will try that.

남 참, 므왐비 씨, 당신은 이제 여기에 온 지 한 달이 되었네요. 저희 3층 사무실 공간에 대해 어떻게 생각하세요?
여 글쎄요, 저는 나이로비 지사의 1층 탁 트인 사무실에서 일했었죠. 그래서 4면의 벽으로 둘러싸인 분리된 공간에 앉아 있는 것이 새로운 경험이네요. 상호 작용이 많지 않고 때로는 사무실이 다소 적막해질 때가 있어요.
남 저희도 익숙해지는 데 시간이 좀 걸렸어요. 하지만 공용 휴게실을 사용하는 것이 당신이 사람들을 더 잘 알아가는 데 아마 도움이 될 거예요.
여 저도 분명 익숙해질 거라 믿어요. 어떤 사람들은 라디오를 트는 것이 대처하는 데 도움이 된다고 권하네요. 저도 그렇게 해 볼까 해요.

story 층 format 형식 open-plan office 오픈 플랜식 사무실(탁 트인 사무실) separate room 각방, 분리실 enclosed 둘러싸인 interaction 상호 작용 shared 공용, 다 같이 사용하는 common room 휴게실 cope 대처하다, 대응하다 agenda 의제, 안건 layout 배치 isolate 격리하다, 고립시키다

62 What are the speakers mainly discussing?
(A) A job opportunity
(B) A program reformat
(C) A work agenda
(D) An office layout

화자들은 무엇을 주로 논의하고 있는가?
(A) 고용 기회
(B) 프로그램 재포맷
(C) 업무 안건
(D) 사무실 배치

63 What problem does the woman mention?
(A) The work area is isolated.
(B) She is moving to Nairobi.
(C) Renovations are too expensive.
(D) The radio is noisy.

여자는 무엇을 언급하는가?
(A) 근무 공간이 고립되어 있다.
(B) 그녀는 나이로비로 이사 갈 것이다.
(C) 개조가 너무 비싸다.
(D) 라디오가 시끄럽다.

64 What will the woman probably do next?
(A) Transfer her office
(B) Listen to the radio
(C) Use specialist equipment
(D) Speak to management

여자는 다음에 무엇을 하겠는가?
(A) 그녀의 사무실 이전하기
(B) 라디오 듣기
(C) 전문 장비 사용하기
(D) 경영진에게 말하기

Questions 65-67 refer to the following conversation and list. 미M 영W

Southtown Fitness Club	
Class	Trainer
Power Yoga	Jessica
Spinning	Tim
Cardio Dance	James
Boxing	Jonathan

M Welcome to Southtown Fitness Club. How can I help you?
W Hi. I'd like to get some information about the exercise classes you offer.
M Absolutely. We offer private lessons and group exercise classes. Which would you prefer?
W My work schedule is pretty erratic and I lack the motivation to work out on my own. So I think private sessions would work better for me.
M Do you happen to have a particular instructor in mind?
W Actually yes. A close friend of mine strongly recommended a trainer who works here. But the problem is that I can't remember his name.
M But do you remember what class he teaches? We have three male instructors.
W I think he teaches some kind of dance class.

사우스타운 피트니스 클럽	
수업	강사
파워 요가	제시카
스피닝	팀
카디오 댄스	제임스
복싱	조너선

남 사우스타운 피트니스 클럽에 오신 걸 환영합니다. 어떻게 도와 드릴까요?
여 안녕하세요. 여기서 제공하는 운동 수업에 대해 정보를 얻고 싶습니다.
남 물론이죠. 저희는 개인 레슨과 그룹 운동 수업을 제공합니다. 어떤 것을 선호하시죠?
여 제 업무 스케줄이 불규칙한 편이고 저 혼자는 운동에 동기 부여가 약한 편이에요. 그래서 제 생각에는 개인 레슨이 더 잘 맞을 것 같아요.
남 혹시 생각하고 계신 특정 트레이너가 있으세요?
여 실은 그렇습니다. 저와 친한 친구 한 명이 여기서 일하는 트레이너 한 분을 강력 추천했어요. 그런데 문제는 그의 이름이 기억이 안 나네요.
남 그렇지만 그가 가르치는 수업을 기억하시나요? 남자 강사는 세 명이 있어요.
여 무슨 댄스 수업을 가르친다고 했던 것 같아요.

erratic 불규칙한, 일정치 않은 motivation 동기 on one's own 스스로 have ~ in mind ~를 염두에 두다

65 Why is the woman at the fitness club?
(A) To cancel a membership
(B) To provide some feedback
(C) To learn about exercise classes
(D) To participate in a competition

여자는 왜 피트니스 클럽에 있는가?
(A) 멤버십을 취소하려고
(B) 피드백을 제공하려고
(C) 운동 수업에 대해 알려고
(D) 경기에 참여하려고

66 Why does the woman prefer private lessons?
(A) She has worked at the gym before.
(B) There is no wait for exercise machines.
(C) Her work schedule is quite irregular.
(D) She is highly motivated to work out regularly.

여자는 왜 개인 레슨을 선호하는가?
(A) 여자는 전에 체육관에서 일해본 적이 있다.
(B) 운동 기기를 기다리지 않아도 된다.
(C) 그녀의 업무 스케줄이 일정하지 않다.
(D) 규칙적으로 운동하려는 동기 부여가 잘 되어 있다.

67 Look at the graphic. Which trainer does the woman want to learn from?
(A) Jessica
(B) Tim
(C) James
(D) Jonathan

시각 정보를 보시오. 여자는 어떤 트레이너로부터 배우길 원하는가?
(A) 제시카
(B) 팀
(C) 제임스
(D) 조나단

Questions 68-70 refer to the following conversation and advertisement. 미W 미M

The Great Kings Sale SAVE 50% OFF EVERYTHING IN THE SHOWROOM!		
	Regular Price	Sale Price
Diamond Necklace	$500	$250
Ruby Necklace	$300	$150

W Hi, this necklace is absolutely gorgeous. I saw an advertisement in today's newspaper that said every item in your showroom is fifty percent off.
M Oh, I'm afraid that sale begins on Saturday. You may want to come back in two days to get a necklace at a discounted price.
W That won't work for me. I've been in Brussels for a medical conference for the last few days and I fly back to the United States tomorrow afternoon. But I still want to get a nice necklace to wear for a banquet tonight. Could you show me this one here?
M Oh, that's a great choice! The ruby mounted in it is genuine so it will last a life time.
W It is just beautiful. I'll take it.

그레이트 킹스 세일 진열장의 전 품목 50퍼센트 할인!		
	정가	할인가
다이아몬드 목걸이	500달러	250달러
루비 목걸이	300달러	150달러

여 안녕하세요. 이 목걸이는 정말 아름답네요. 오늘 신문에서 이 진열장에 있는 전 품목이 50퍼센트 할인된다는 광고를 봤어요.
남 아, 안타깝게도 그 세일은 토요일에 시작됩니다. 목걸이를 할인가에 구매하시려면 이틀 후에 다시 오시는 게 좋겠네요.
여 그럴 수가 없어요. 저는 지난 며칠 동안 의학 컨퍼런스 때문에 브뤼셀에 와 있었는데 내일 오후에 다시 미국으로 돌아갑니다. 그렇지만 여전히 오늘 저녁 연회 때 할 예쁜 목걸이를 사고 싶네요. 여기 이 제품을 보여 주시겠어요?
남 아, 훌륭한 선택이세요. 거기 박혀 있는 루비는 진품이라 평생 갈 겁니다.
여 정말 아름답네요. 이걸로 주세요.

absolutely 완전히 gorgeous 예쁜, 아름다운 showroom 전시장, 진열

공간 banquet 연회 mount (보석 등을) 박다 genuine 진품, 진짜

68 What was advertised in the newspaper?
(A) A fashion show
(B) A job opening
(C) A musical performance
(D) A half-off sale

신문에 무엇이 광고 되었는가?
(A) 패션쇼
(B) 일자리 공석
(C) 음악 공연
(D) 반값 세일

69 What is the purpose of the woman's visit to Brussels?
(A) To attend a conference
(B) To purchase some jewelry
(C) To open a business
(D) To write an article

여자가 브뤼셀에 방문한 목적은 무엇인가?
(A) 컨퍼런스에 참석하려고
(B) 보석을 구입하려고
(C) 개업하려고
(D) 기사를 쓰려고

70 Look at the graphic. How much will the woman pay for a necklace?
(A) $150
(B) $250
(C) $300
(D) $500

시각 정보를 보시오. 여자는 목걸이에 얼마를 낼 것인가?
(A) 150달러
(B) 250달러
(C) 300달러
(D) 500달러

Part 4

Questions 71-73 refer to the following telephone message. 미M

Hi, this message is for Al Masino in the rental office. My wife and I are very interested in the apartment in your brochure that you sent us last week. But we have one final question. The last owner said he was not renewing the fee for using the communal leisure facilities on the same site. Well, my wife and I are both fitness enthusiasts. So, would we need to rent two leisure passes? I wonder if you could call me back and tell me how much the monthly cost would be. We just want to have the costs before we make a final choice about renting the apartment. Thanks so much for your help. Talk to you later.

안녕하세요, 이 메시지는 임대 사무소의 앨 마시노에게 남깁니다. 아내와 저는 지난주 당신이 보내 준 책자에 나온 아파트에 매우 관심이 많습니다. 하지만 마지막 질문이 하나 있습니다. 지난번 주인이 같은 장소에 있는 공동 레저 시설 이용료를 갱신하지 않았다고 말했습니다. 음, 제 아내와 저는 건강 관리에 열의가 많은 사람들입니다. 우리가 레저 시설 출입증 두 개를 빌려야 할까요? 당신이 제게 전화해서 월간 이용료가 어떻게 되는지 알려 주실 수 있나 궁금합니다. 우리는 아파트 임대에 관한 최종 선택을 내리기 전에 그 비용을 알고 싶습니다. 도움에 매우 감사드립니다. 나중에 이야기합시다.

rental office 임대 사무소 communal 공용의, 공동의 leisure facility 레저 시설 site 장소 fitness 건강 관리 enthusiast 열렬한 지지자 make a final choice 최종 선택을 하다 application 지원서

71 Who most likely is the listener?
(A) A fitness trainer
(B) A leisure center owner
(C) A bank loan officer
(D) A leasing agent

청자는 누구일 것 같은가?
(A) 건강 관리 트레이너
(B) 레저 센터 주인
(C) 은행 대출 담당 직원
(D) 임대 대리인

72 What is the speaker inquiring about?
(A) Joining a leisure center
(B) Renting parking spaces
(C) Renewing a contract
(D) Reducing a payment

화자는 무엇에 관해 묻고 있는가?
(A) 레저 센터 가입
(B) 주차 공간 임대
(C) 계약 갱신
(D) 지불액 인하

73 What does the speaker ask the listener to do?
(A) Provide price information
(B) Check the security
(C) Review an application
(D) Employ a personal trainer

화자는 청자에게 무엇을 요청하는가?
(A) 가격 정보 제공하기
(B) 보안 확인하기
(C) 지원서 검토하기
(D) 개인 트레이너 고용하기

Questions 74-76 refer to the following excerpt from a meeting. 미W

As most of you know already, we are in the middle of making the entry process to the theme park faster by installing a fast track scanner on all rides. Beginning on Saturday, visitors can scan their tickets every time they want to enjoy a ride. So as to make this change effective, please ensure that everyone going through the entrance gates keeps their ticket on their person. This way, we'll be able to test the process to reduce waiting times before the holiday season begins on Monday.

이미 여러분들 대부분이 아시다시피, 우리는 모든 놀이기구에 초고속 판독 장치를 설치하여 테마파크로 입장할 때 더 신속하게 하는 중입니다. 토요일에 시작하여, 방문객들은 놀이기구를 타고 싶을 때마다 그들의 표를 스캔할 수 있습니다. 이 변화가 시행될 수 있도록, 입구를 지나가는 모든 분들이 각자 자신의 표를 소지하고 있는지 확인해 주세요. 이렇게 하면, 우리는 월요일에 시작하는 연휴 전에 대기 시간을 줄이기 위한 과정을 시험해 볼 수 있을 것입니다.

in the middle of ~의 도중에 entry process 입장 과정 theme park 테마파크, 놀이공원 fast track 빠른 코스 scanner 판독[기록] 장치 ride 탈 것 effective 시행되는; 효과적인 entrance gate 입구 waiting time 대기 시간 instruction manual 취급 설명서

74 What is the talk mainly about?
(A) Entrance improvements
(B) Security upgrades
(C) Work availability
(D) A training timetable

담화는 주로 무엇에 관한 것인가?
(A) 입장 문제 개선
(B) 안전 업그레이드
(C) 근무 가능성
(D) 교육 시간표

75 According to the speaker, what will take place on Monday?
(A) A stock take will begin.
(B) The holiday season will start.
(C) The theme park will be closed.
(D) New rides will be announced.

화자에 따르면, 월요일에 일어날 일은?
(A) 재고 조사가 시작될 것이다.
(B) 휴가철이 시작될 것이다.
(C) 테마파크가 문을 닫을 것이다.
(D) 새로운 놀이기구가 발표될 것이다.

76 What must employees do on Saturday?
(A) Ensure visitors have their tickets
(B) Update their emergency training
(C) Have their photos taken
(D) Review an instruction manual

직원들은 토요일에 무엇을 해야 하는가?
(A) 방문객들이 표를 소지하고 있는지 확인하기
(B) 그들의 비상 훈련 업데이트하기
(C) 그들의 사진 촬영하기
(D) 취급 설명서 검토하기

Questions 77-79 refer to the following telephone massage. 영W

Hi, Ms. Warr. This is Juno Temple from Catering Supplies Express. I'm calling about the food order for your daughter's wedding. Your main course has been approved but we are still waiting for your selection of starters and desserts. So I would like to know if you prefer us to go ahead and advise the chef to get all the ingredients for the main course or if you'd prefer to wait and tell him about the other courses at the same time? Please email me back and let me know how you would like to proceed. Thanks and enjoy your day.

안녕하세요, 워 씨. 저는 케이터링 서프라이즈 익스프레스의 주노 템플입니다. 따님의 결혼식을 위한 음식 주문에 관해 전화했습니다. 당신의 메인 요리는 승인되었지만, 전채 요리와 후식으로 엄선할 요리들은 아직 대기 중입니다. 그래서 당신은 우리가 그대로 진행하여 주방장이 메인 요리의 재료를 준비하길 바라시는지, 아니면 기다리면서 동시에 주방장과 다른 코스들에 관해 이야기하길 원하시는지 알고 싶습니다. 이메일을 다시 보내 주시고 어떻게 진행하길 바라는지 알려 주세요. 감사드리며 즐거운 하루 보내세요.

catering 요리 조달 supply 공급; 보급품, 물자 express 속달 main course 주요리 selection 선발, 선정, 선택; 엄선된 것 starter 전채 요리 go ahead 시작하다, 밀고 나가다 ingredient 재료 at the same time 동시에 proceed 진행하다 via 경유하여, 거쳐

77 Where does the speaker most likely work?
(A) At a catering company
(B) At a printing studio
(C) At a cake shop
(D) At a hotel

화자는 어디에서 일할 것 같은가?
(A) 요리 조달업체
(B) 인쇄 스튜디오
(C) 케이크 가게
(D) 호텔

78 What does the speaker say about the order?
(A) It has already been cancelled.
(B) It is partially approved.
(C) An ingredient is out of stock.
(D) A price has changed.

화자는 주문에 관해 말한 것은?
(A) 이미 취소되었다.
(B) 일부만 승인되었다.
(C) 재료의 재고가 없다.
(D) 가격이 바뀌었다.

79 What does the speaker ask the listener to do?
(A) Contact via email
(B) Taste a range of food
(C) Make a credit card payment
(D) Arrange another caterer

화자는 청자에게 무엇을 해 달라고 요청하는가?
(A) 이메일로 연락하기
(B) 다양한 시식하기
(C) 신용 카드로 지불하기
(D) 다른 요리 조달업체 준비하기

Questions 80-82 refer to the following talk. 미W

I called this meeting to assign everyone with a new task. But first I'd like to share some good news. It is with great pleasure that I can announce that this has been the most profitable year in the history of SC Electronics. It is all because of everyone here. The company's profits have increased by 30% since last year thanks to your hard work. And we're planning to release our new smart phone, the Universe 7, on December 1st, which we have high hopes for. Now Anthony Jacobs will tell you more about the marketing strategies you will use to attract customers to purchase the Universe 7. Please come up to the stage, Anthony.

제가 이 회의를 소집한 이유는 여러분에게 새로운 업무를 배정해 주기 위함입니다. 그러나 먼저 좋은 소식을 알려 드리겠습니다. 올해가 SC 일렉트로닉스 역사상 가장 높은 수익을 올린 해였다는 것을 발표하게 되어 기쁩니다. 이것은 모두 여러분 덕분입니다. 여러분들이 열심히 일하신 덕분에 작년부터 한 해 동안 회사의 수익은 30퍼센트 증가하였습니다. 그리고 많은 기대를 하고 있는 우리의 새로운 스마트폰 더 유니버스 7의 출시를 12월 1일로 계획하고 있습니다. 이제 앤서니 제이콥스 씨가 여러분이 더 유니버스 7을 구입하도록 고객들을 끌어 올 마케팅 전략에 대해서 더 얘기를 할 것입니다. 앤서니, 무대 앞으로 나와 주세요.

profitable 수익성이 좋은 thanks to ~ 덕분에

80 Who most likely are the listeners?
(A) Sales representatives
(B) Store customers
(C) Marketing staff
(D) Magazine reporters

청자들은 누구일 것 같은가?
(A) 판매 사원
(B) 매장 고객
(C) 마케팅 직원
(D) 잡지 기자

81 What does the speaker mean when she says, "It is all because of everyone here"?
(A) Employees have developed a new product.
(B) Employees have organized tonight's event.
(C) Employees are able to multi-task.
(D) Employees have helped the company succeed.

화자가 "이것은 모두 여러분 덕분입니다"라고 말한 의미는 무엇인가?
(A) 직원들은 신제품을 개발했다.
(B) 직원들은 오늘 밤의 행사를 주관했다.
(C) 직원들은 여러 가지 일을 동시에 할 수 있다.
(D) 직원들은 회사가 성공하도록 도왔다.

82 What will the company do on December 1?
(A) Celebrate an anniversary
(B) Launch a new product
(C) Conduct a marketing survey
(D) Open a branch overseas

회사는 12월 1일에 무엇을 할 것인가?
(A) 기념일을 축하한다.
(B) 신제품을 출시한다.
(C) 마케팅 설문조사를 한다.
(D) 해외 지점을 연다.

Questions 83-85 refer to the following recorded message. 미M

Thank you for calling Henwick Travel Agency. Your call is very important to our company. However, due to unprecedented seasonal demand, all of our travel representatives are engaged. Please note you are held in a line and will be answered as soon as possible. If you are calling about today's flight delays, we ask you to check airlines direct as they regularly update information. We anticipate that the backlog will be cleared by 9 o'clock tonight. If you are calling concerning any other travel issue, please hold on, and we will pass you to the next available operative.

헨윅 여행사로 전화해 주셔서 감사합니다. 귀하의 전화는 저희 회사에 매우 중요합니다. 그러나 전례에 없던 계절적인 수요로 인해, 저희의 모든 여행 담당자들이 업무를 보고 있습니다. 귀하가 통화 대기 중이며 가능한 한 빨리 통화가 될 것입니다. 만약 귀하께서 오늘의 비행 연착을 알아보기 위해 전화하셨다면, 항공사가 정보를 정기적으로 업데이트하기 때문에 그곳을 통해 직접 알아보도록 요청드립니다. 밀린 통화량이 오늘 밤 9시까지는 처리될 것으로 예상합니다. 만약 귀하께서 다른 여행 사항에 관련하여 전화하셨다면, 잠시 대기해 주시면 통화 가능한 다음 직원에게 연결해 드리겠습니다.

unprecedented 전례 없는 seasonal 계절적인 representative 대표, 대리인 be engaged 볼일이 있다 note ~에 주목하다, ~에 유의하다 be held in a line 통화 대기 중이다 flight delay 비행 연착 airline 항공사 regularly 정기적으로 anticipate 예상하다 backlog 밀린 일 clear (움직임·흐름 등이) 다시 원활해지다 concerning ~와 관계된 hold on 기다리다

83 Who is the message intended for?
(A) Online shoppers
(B) Internet users
(C) Call center representatives
(D) Travel agency customers

메시지는 누구를 대상으로 하는가?
(A) 온라인 쇼핑객
(B) 인터넷 사용자
(C) 콜센터 담당자
(D) 여행사 손님

84 According to the speaker, why is there a wait?
(A) There is a backlog of calls.
(B) A telephone system has failed.
(C) A flight has been delayed.
(D) The payment system is faulty.

화자에 따르면, 대기가 발생한 이유는?
(A) 통화가 밀려 있다.
(B) 전화 시스템이 실패했다.
(C) 비행 편이 지연되었다.
(D) 지불 시스템이 고장 났다.

85 What will likely happen by nine o'clock tonight?
(A) Telephone help will be available.
(B) Normal flight schedules will resume.
(C) A computer system will be restored.
(D) A call center will close.

오늘 밤 9시에 무슨 일이 일어날 것 같은가?
(A) 전화 안내가 이용 가능할 것이다.
(B) 정상적인 비행 일정이 시작될 것이다.
(C) 컴퓨터 시스템이 복구될 것이다.
(D) 콜센터가 문을 닫을 것이다.

Questions 86-88 refer to the following news report. 미W

In the newspapers today, the Alhambra Mining Company announced that they will be relocating its main production plant to Hurghada once construction is finished on the site. A company spokesperson said that Alhambra Mining chose Hurghada for the location of its new factory because of the increased mining potential and excellent weather conditions. Hurghada's mayor, Klaus Herman, welcomed the move but accepted that some local residents have shown concern about heightened pollution levels in the local environment. However, Mayor Herman commented that he believes that when the local population sees the final blueprints for the development, their apprehension will be allayed. The plans will be posted on the company's Web site early in the new year.

오늘 신문에서, 알함브라 광산업체는 현장에서 공사가 완료되자마자 그들의 주요 생산 공장을 후르가다로 이전할 것이라고 발표했습니다. 회사의 대변인은 알함브라 광산업체가 증대된 광산 잠재력과 탁월한 기상 조건 때문에 후르가다를 새 공장의 부지로 선택했다고 했습니다. 후르가다의 시장인 클라우스 허먼은 이전을 반갑게 맞이했지만 일부 지역민들이 지역 환경의 높아진 오염 수준에 대한 우려를 표했다고 시인했습니다. 그러나 허먼 시장은 지역 주민들이 개발을 위한 최종 청사진을 보게 되면 그들의 걱정이 가라앉을 것으로 믿는다고 말했습니다. 그 계획은 내년 초 회사의 웹 사이트에 게시될 것입니다.

mining company 광산업체 relocate 이전하다 production plant 생산 공장 site 장소; 현장 spokesperson 대변인 mayor 시장 local resident 지역민 heightened 높아진 comment 평하다, 견해를 밝히다 blueprint 청사진 apprehension 걱정 allay 가라앉히다, 달래다 post 게시하다, 게재하다 occupancy 사용 go under 가라앉다 commence 시작되다[하다]

86 What is the news report mainly about?
(A) A desert construction project
(B) The relocation of the production facility
(C) Occupancy of a production factory
(D) Economic projections for a country

뉴스 보도는 주로 무엇에 관한 것인가?
(A) 사막 건설 프로젝트
(B) 생산 시설의 이전
(C) 제조 공장의 사용
(D) 한 국가의 경제 전망

87 Why are residents concerned?
(A) Some businesses may go under.
(B) Urban pollution may increase.
(C) Streets may become overcrowded.
(D) Property values may decline.

주민들이 걱정하는 이유는?
(A) 일부 사업들이 도산할 수 있다.
(B) 도시의 공해가 증가할 수 있다.
(C) 거리가 너무 붐빌 수 있다.
(D) 부동산 가치가 떨어질 수 있다.

88 What does the mayor say residents should wait for?
(A) Architectural drawings to be posted
(B) A regional decision to be made
(C) Updated employment figures to be released
(D) Road improvements to commence

시장은 주민들이 무엇을 기다려야 한다고 말하는가?
(A) 게시될 건축 도면
(B) 내려질 지역 결정
(C) 공개될 갱신된 고용 수치
(D) 개시할 도로 개선 공사

Questions 89-91 refer to the following talk. 미M

Welcome to Multnomah Falls. My name is Liam and I'll be your tour guide today. I am very excited to show you the majestic Multnomah Falls, which I'm sure you will not forget. Our tour will last about 4 hours and we will walk about 3 kilometers along the scenic Multnomah Pathway. You are welcome to take pictures during the tour, but you must stay with the group at all times. You're not allowed to wander around on your own. Due to the natural moisture from the falls, the surrounding area is very wet and slippery. So, please watch your step. One final note, please leave any food or beverages on the tour bus because we're going to have a lunch buffet at a nearby restaurant at noon. Okay everyone, let's begin our tour!

멀트노머 폭포에 오신 것을 환영합니다. 저는 리엄이고, 오늘 여러분의 투어 가이드입니다. 여러분께 앞으로 절대 잊지 못하실 이 엄청난 멀트노머 폭포를 보여 드릴 생각에 매우 신이 납니다. 투어는 4시간 정도 소요되고 3킬로미터 정도 경치 좋은 멀트노머 산책로를 따라서 걷게 될 것입니다. 투어 중에 얼마든지 사진을 찍어도 좋지만 항상 그룹과 함께 다니셔야만 합니다. 혼자서 다니시는 것은 허용되지 않습니다. 폭포로부터 나오는 자연적인 습기 때문에 주변이 매우 축축하고 미끄럽습니다. 그러니, 발을 조심하십시오. 마지막 공지는, 정오에 근처 레스토랑에서 점심 뷔페를 먹을 예정이므로 음식과 음료는 투어 버스에 놓고 내려 주세요. 자 여러분, 이제 투어를 시작합시다!

falls 폭포 majestic 위대한, 엄청난 pathway 산책로 surrounding area 주변 지역 slippery 미끄러운

89 What is the main purpose of the talk?
(A) To describe a nature tour
(B) To give directions to a tower
(C) To recommend a travel agency
(D) To introduce a speaker

공지의 주 목적은 무엇인가?
(A) 자연 투어에 대해 설명하려고
(B) 타워까지 가는 길 안내를 하려고
(C) 여행사를 추천하려고
(D) 화자를 소개하려고

90 What are listeners not allowed to do?
(A) Take photographs
(B) Swim in some areas
(C) Explore the site alone
(D) Use cell phones

청자들은 무엇을 하는 것이 허용되지 않는가?
(A) 사진 찍기
(B) 일부 장소에서 수영하기
(C) 혼자 그 장소 다니기
(D) 휴대 전화 사용하기

91 Why does the speaker say, "So, please watch your step"?
(A) To encourage them to enjoy the beautiful view
(B) To ask them to wear a life vest
(C) To tell them to look around the falls
(D) To warn them not to slip

화자는 왜 "그러니, 발을 조심하십시오"라고 말하는가?

(A) 아름다운 경치를 보라고 권하려고
(B) 구명 조끼를 입으라고 요청하려고
(C) 폭포 주변을 살펴보라고 말하려고
(D) 미끄러지지 말라고 경고하려고

Questions 92-94 refer to the following news report. 미M

And for today's local news, Akron City Council announced yesterday that it has approved the construction of the proposed Greenburgh multiplex cinema and shopping mall complex located in the southwest of Summit County. The project will cost an estimated three million dollars and is expected to take four years to complete. Controversy has swirled around the project, as many citizens wanted the land to remain protected open space. However, the Mayor of Akron argued that once completed, the complex will bring in millions of dollars in revenue for the city every year. "This project will be a boon to our city," he said. The groundbreaking ceremony for the complex will take place next Monday at 10 A.M.

이어서 오늘의 지역 뉴스입니다. 애크런 시 의회는 어제 서밋 카운티의 남서쪽에 위치한 멀티플렉스 영화관과 복합 쇼핑몰인 그린버그의 건설 제안을 승인했다고 밝혔습니다. 이 프로젝트는 3백만 달러의 비용이 들 것이며, 완공되는 데 4년이 걸릴 것으로 예상됩니다. 많은 시민들은 그 땅이 공공용지로 남아 있기를 원했기 때문에 이 프로젝트를 둘러싸고 논란이 일고 있습니다. 그렇지만 애크런 시장은 복합몰의 공사가 완성되면 매년 도시에 수백만 달러의 수익을 가져올 것이라고 주장하며 "이 프로젝트는 우리 도시에 큰 혜택이 될 것이다"라고 말했습니다. 기공식은 다음 주 월요일 오전 10시에 진행될 예정입니다.

announce 발표하다 approve 승인하다 controversy 논란 swirl 소용돌이치다, 빙빙 돌다 open space 공공용지 revenue 수익 boon 혜택, 은혜 groundbreaking ceremony 기공식, 착공식 tear down ~을 허물다

92 What was announced yesterday?
(A) A protest is going to be held.
(B) A proposal has been approved.
(C) A new business has opened.
(D) A construction project has been completed.
어제 발표된 것은 무엇인가?
(A) 시위가 열릴 것이다.
(B) 제안이 승인되었다.
(C) 새로운 사업이 시작된다.
(D) 공사 프로젝트가 완료되었다.

93 What can be understood from the report?
(A) Construction has already started.
(B) The tax will be increased next month.
(C) Many residents are against the project.
(D) The shopping mall will be torn down.
이 보도를 통해 알 수 있는 것은 무엇인가?
(A) 공사가 이미 시작되었다.
(B) 다음 달에 세금이 인상될 것이다.
(C) 많은 주민들이 프로젝트에 반대한다.
(D) 쇼핑몰을 허물 것이다.

94 What did the Mayor of Akron mean when he said, "This project will be a boon to our city"?
(A) The tax increase will be worth it.
(B) The development will generate more income.
(C) The construction will cost a lot of money.
(D) The land should remain as open space.
애크런의 시장이 말한 "이 프로젝트는 우리 도시에 큰 혜택이 될 것이다"가 의미하는 것은 무엇인가?
(A) 세금 인상은 가치가 있을 것이다.
(B) 개발로 인해 더 많은 수입을 발생시킬 것이다.
(C) 공사에 많은 비용이 들 것이다.
(D) 그 땅은 공공용지로 남아 있을 것이다.

Questions 95-97 refer to the following message and program. 영W

Workshop Program	
Presenter	Time
Jack Huston	10:00 ~ 10:50
Emily Tennant	11:00 ~ 11:50
Lunch	12:00 ~ 13:50
Ryan Lee	14:00 ~ 14:50
Melissa Leo	15:00 ~ 15:50

Good morning and welcome to the 15th Annual Professional photographers Conference. Today, we have a lot of interesting workshops prepared for you. And you can find a copy of the program at the registration desk. Before we start, I have an announcement for those of you planning to attend Huston's 10 o'clock workshop. Due to a mechanical problem, Mr. Huston's flight was delayed in Denver. He's on his way now but he won't be arriving until noon today. So there will be a change in the schedule. Please note that the last speaker will present first and the first speaker will be the last. We apologize for any inconvenience this may cause you. If you must leave before 3 P.M., you may request a full refund at the registration desk. Thank you for your understanding.

워크숍 프로그램	
발표자	시간
잭 휴스턴	10시 ~ 10시 50분
에밀리 테넌트	11시 ~ 11시 50분
점심	12시 ~ 13시 50분
라이언 리	14시 ~ 14시 50분
멜리사 레오	15시 ~ 15시 50분

안녕하세요. 15번째 연례 전문 사진 작가 컨퍼런스에 오신 것을 환영합니다. 오늘 우리는 여러 가지 흥미로운 워크숍을 준비하였습니다. 등록 데스크 가시면 프로그램지를 보실 수 있습니다. 시작하기에 앞서, 휴스턴 씨의 10시 워크숍에 참석하려고 하시는 분들께 공지 사항이 있습니다. 휴스턴 씨가 탄 비행기가 기계 결함으로 덴버에서 지연되었습니다. 그는 지금 오는 중이지만 오늘 정오가 되어야 도착할 것입니다. 그래서 스케줄에 변경이 있을 예정입니다. 마지막 연사가 처음 발표를 하고 첫 번째 연사가 마

지막이 될 것임을 알아두세요. 불편을 끼쳐 사과드립니다. 만약 오후 3시 전에 가셔야만 한다면 등록 데스크에서 전액 환불을 요청하시면 되겠습니다. 이해해 주셔서 감사합니다.

registration desk 등록 데스크 mechanical problem 기계 결함, 기술적인 문제

95 What kind of event is taking place?
(A) An annual conference
(B) A television show
(C) A cooking competition
(D) An awards ceremony

어떤 종류의 행사가 열리는가?
(A) 연례 컨퍼런스
(B) 텔레비전 쇼
(C) 요리 경연대회
(D) 시상식

96 What is the problem?
(A) A flight is fully booked.
(B) A venue has been changed.
(C) A presenter will arrive late.
(D) A food festival has been canceled.

무엇이 문제인가?
(A) 항공편 예약이 꽉 찼다.
(B) 장소가 변경되었다.
(C) 발표자가 늦게 도착할 것이다.
(D) 푸드 페스티벌이 취소되었다.

97 Look at the graphic. According to the revised schedule, who will be the day's first speaker?
(A) Mr. Huston
(B) Ms. Tennant
(C) Mr. Lee
(D) Ms. Leo

시각 정보를 보시오. 바뀐 스케줄에 따르면, 누가 오늘의 첫 번째 연사가 될 것인가?
(A) 휴스턴 씨
(B) 테넌트 씨
(C) 리 씨
(D) 레오 씨

Questions 98-100 refer to the following announcement and chart. 미W

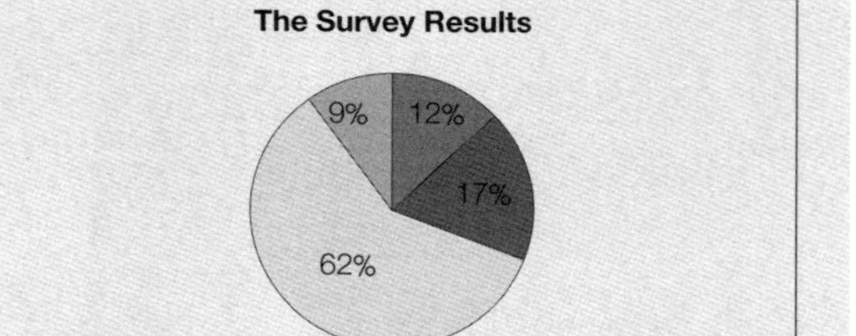

Before I end today's sales seminar, I'd like to give you one last tip. Many new sales representatives just assume that our customers are more interested in low prices than quality. But that is not true. The market research group conducted a survey of a thousand customers who have purchased our home appliances and this is what they found. Take a look at the chart and see what the most important factor in their buying decision was. When people make major purchases that will last for many years, they want to get the best product for their money. So from now on, you should tell customers how long our refrigerators last and how durable our microwaves are.

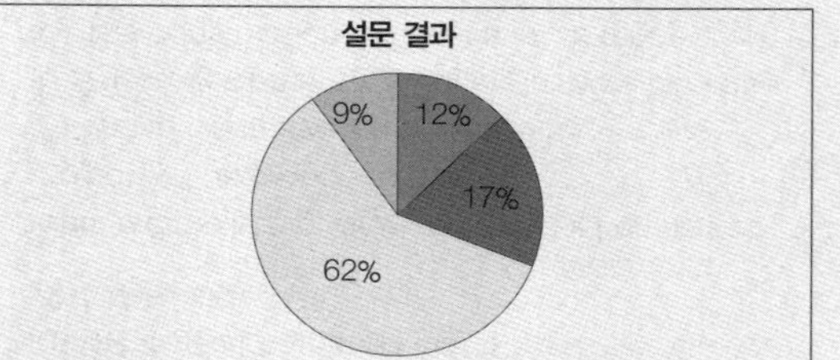

오늘의 영업 세미나를 끝내기 전에, 여러분에게 마지막 조언을 해주고 싶습니다. 많은 신입 영업 사원들은 고객이 질보다 낮은 가격에 더 관심이 있을 거라고 추측합니다. 그러나 그것은 사실이 아니죠. 시장 조사팀이 우리 가전제품을 구매한 경험이 있는 천 명의 고객들에게 설문 조사를 하였고 다음 사실을 알게 되었습니다. 차트에서 그들의 구매 결정에서 가장 중요한 요인이 무엇이었는지 보세요. 사람들은 오래 쓰는 물건을 구매할 때에는 돈의 가치를 하는 상품을 사고 싶어 하죠. 그러니 이제부터는 고객들에게 우리 냉장고가 얼마나 오래가는지 우리 전자레인지가 얼마나 내구성이 좋은지 알리도록 하십시오.

assume 추정하다, 예측하다 market research 시장 조사 conduct a survey 설문 조사하다 home appliances 가전제품 factor 요인 buying decision 구매 결정 durable 내구성이 좋은

98 What merchandise does the speaker's company sell?
(A) Home appliances
(B) Motor vehicles
(C) Office equipment
(D) Cleaning products

화자의 회사는 어떤 상품을 파는가?
(A) 가전제품
(B) 자동차
(C) 사무기기
(D) 청소용품

99 What does the speaker say about the market research group?
(A) They designed new products.
(B) They put together a product manual.
(C) They researched a competing brand.
(D) They conducted a customer survey.

화자는 시장 조사팀에 대해서 뭐라고 하는가?
(A) 신상품을 개발했다.
(B) 상품 매뉴얼을 만들었다.
(C) 경쟁 상품을 조사했다.
(D) 고객 설문 조사를 진행했다.

100 Look at the graphic. Which survey item accounts for 62 percent?
(A) Customer reviews
(B) Product quality
(C) Free shipping
(D) Competitive prices

시각 정보를 보시오. 어떤 조사 항목이 62퍼센트를 차지하는가?
(A) 고객 후기
(B) 상품 품질
(C) 무료 배송
(D) 경쟁력 있는 가격

Part 5

101 **해설** 뒤에 longer와 함께 쓰이는 표현은 (D)이며, 관용 어구로 쓰인다. 참고로 no longer, not ~ any longer, not ~ any more도 알아 두자.

에덴 철물점은 더 이상 상품에 대한 지불로 신용 카드를 받지 않는다.

hardware shop 철물점 payment 지불, 지급 goods 상품, 물건

102 **해설** appear가 2형식으로 쓰이면 보어로 to부정사를 쓸 수 있다. 따라서 (C)가 정답이며 appear, remain, seem 등의 2형식 동사는 to부정사를 보어로 취하기도 한다는 것을 알아 둔다.

둘리 씨의 보고서는 건설 산업 부활의 초기 단계를 보여주는 것 같다.

early phase 초반, 초기 단계 resurrection 부활

103 **해설** 명사 어휘 문제로 such as 이하에서 클럽의 일원이 되었을 때의 혜택에 관해 말하고 있으므로 가장 적절한 선택지는 (A)이다.

샤프슈팅 클럽의 일원이 되면 안내 책자에 실리는 등 많은 이점이 있다.

become part of ~의 일부가 되다 directory (이름·주소 등의 관련 정보를 보통 알파벳순으로 나열한) 안내 책자 principle 원칙 renewal 재개, 부활

104 **해설** 명사 어휘 문제로 빈칸 뒤의 building과 어울려 쓰일 수 있는 명사는 (C)이다.

리더스 앤 손즈 주식회사는 루비 로드의 새 카센터 건물의 건설을 시작하도록 고용되었다.

application 지원, 적용 distribution 유통 distraction 방해

105 **해설** 관사(the)와 전치사(from) 사이는 명사 자리로 contractors와 contracts가 정답 후보이다. 문맥상 '계약서를 받았는지 확인해 주세요'가 적절하므로 (B)가 정답이다. contracting은 분사 혹은 동명사이고, contracted는 분사 혹은 동사로 빈칸에 들어갈 수 없다.

오늘 오후에 회의에 참석이 예상되는 모든 사람들이 하웰 씨로부터 계약서를 제공받았는지 확인해 주세요.

verify 사실임을 확인하다 copy (책·신문 등의) 한 부 contractor 계약업자, 도급업자

106 **해설** 부사 문제로 beyond와 between은 전치사로 뒤에 반드시 명사와 함께 해야 하므로 정답에서 제외되고, 문맥상 '5미터 이상 떨어져 있어야 한다'가 적절하므로 (A)가 정답이다.

트렌튼의 상법 규정에 따르면, 록커 애비뉴에 건설될 건물은 5미터 이상 떨어져 있어야 한다.

commercial code 상법 규정 unit 단위, 공동 주택의 한 가구 apart 떨어져, 따로

107 **해설** 명사 responsibility 앞의 빈칸은 형용사 자리이다. One another, The others는 대명사이므로 정답에서 제외되고, 형용사 역할도 하는 Other와 Another가 정답의 후보이다. Other는 뒤에 가산 복수와 불가산 명사가 오고 Another 뒤에는 단수 가산 명사가 와야 하는데 responsibility는 단수 가산 명사이므로 (C)가 정답이다.

싱어 씨가 보안부의 책임자로서 가진 또 다른 책임은 네트워크 기밀을 유지하는 것이다.

responsibility 책임감 head (단체·조직의) 책임자 preserve 유지하다 confidentiality 기밀성, 기밀

108 **해설** 빈칸 뒤에 형용사가 있으므로 이를 수식하는 부사 (B)가 정답이다. slightest는 형용사 최상급, slighter는 형용사 비교급, slight는 형용사로 빈칸에 올 수 없다.

소비자 의견에 응하여, 다우니 데코레이터 주식회사는 그들의 오션 블루 인테리어용 광택 페인트를 조금 더 밝은 빛으로 바꿨다.

in response to ~에 답하여 decorator 장식가, 도배업자 interior 내부, 인테리어 gloss paint 광택 페인트 light 밝은; 가벼운 shade 빛; 그늘

109 **해설** 숫자와 복수 명사 앞에 오면서 '6개월마다 바꾸도록 요구한다'라는 의미로 쓸 수 있는 것은 (D)이다. every 다음에 단수 가산 명사가 오면 '모든'이란 의미라는 것을 알아 둔다. along은 전치사로 뒤에 기간 표현과 함께 쓸 수 없고, even과 only는 부사로 명사구를 강조할 수 있으나 문맥상 적절하지 않다.

IT 부서는 직원들이 비밀번호를 6개월마다 한 번씩 바꾸도록 요구한다.

department 부서, 팀

110 **해설** 명사 어휘 문제로 문맥상 '그 구역들의 연례 점검을 수행하기 위해'가 자연스러우므로 정답은 (A)이다.

안전 관리자는 그 구역들의 연례 점검을 수행하기 위해, 오전 8시에 도착할 것이다.

safety officer 안전 관리자 carry out 수행하다 annual 연례의 premise 구역, 부지

111 **해설** 부사 문제로 문맥상 앞에 이미 언급된 것을 다시 가리키는 역할을 하면서 '이달 말까지 그렇게 해 주세요'로 쓸 수 있는 것은 (D)이다. them, those, one은 모두 대명사 역할을 하므로 do 뒤에 와서 목적어가 될 수 있지만 문맥상 적절하지 않다.

만약 당신이 아직 당신의 관리자에게 당신의 신상 정보를 제출하지 않았다면, 이달 말까지 그렇게 해 주세요.

personal detail 개인 정보, 신상 정보 supervisor 감독관, 관리자

112 **해설** 동사 어휘 문제로 문맥상 영수증과 함께 결함 상품을 반품하거나 교환 받기 위해 해야 하는 행동을 서술하는 가장 자연스러운 동사는 (C)이다.

소비자가 반품이나 교환을 받으려면 결함이 있는 제품은 첫 판매 영수증과 함께 되돌려 줘야 한다.

faulty 결함이 있는 initial 처음의, 초기의 substitute 대체하다

113 **해설** Judy's ~ fried goods는 문장의 필수 성분을 모두 갖춘 완전한 문장이므로 빈칸부터 costs까지는 수식 역할이다. 빈칸 뒤에 명사(rise)가 있으므로 빈칸은 전치사 자리로 (D)가 정답이다. as soon as, in order that, even if는 부사절 접속사로 뒤에는 완전한 절이 와야 한다.

도맷값의 인상 때문에 주디스 패스트푸드는 튀김류의 가격을 올릴 계획이다.

rise 상승 wholesale 도매의 fried 튀긴 goods 상품

114 **해설** 동사 문제로 '~에 적절하다, 적합하다'라는 의미로 쓰이는 be suited for가 적절하므로 정답은 (B)이다.

세법 학위가 있는 제임스 싱어는 법인세 컨설턴트의 직책에 이상적으로 알맞다.

hold a degree 학위를 갖고 있다 tax law 세법 ideally 이상적으로 company tax 법인세 suit 맞다, 적합하다; 정장 suitor 구혼자(남자); 타 기업 인수를 원하는 기업

115 **해설** 관계절 동사(housed) 앞의 빈칸은 부사 자리이다. 문맥상 '과거에 루빅스 컴퓨터에 거처를 제공했던 부지'가 적절하므로 (A)가 정답이다. once가 부사일 때 '과거의 한때, '한 번'의 의미로 쓰이는 것을 알아 둔다. 또한, ever는 at any time의 부정문이나 의문문에 쓰인다. since가 부사일 때는 '그 이후로'란 의미이다.

켐프트 텍스타일즈는 루빅스 컴퓨터스에 거처를 제공했던 부지를 사려고 계획 중이다.

premises 부지, 구역 house 거처를 제공하다, 살 곳을 주다

116 **해설** 명사(fans) 앞은 명사를 수식하는 형용사 자리로 (C)가 정답이다. devoted는 명사 앞에서 과거분사로 쓰이는 분사이다.

미시 마가렛의 범죄 소설의 헌신적인 팬들은 6월 8일에 그 시리즈의 다섯 번째 책이 출간된다는 것을 염두에 두어야 한다.

note 기억하다 devote 헌신하다 devotion 헌신

117 **해설** 전치사로 쓰이는 because of 뒤에는 명사(구)가 오므로 명사 (B)가 정답이다. affordable은 형용사, afford는 동사, afforded는 동사 혹은 분사로 명사 자리에 쓸 수 없다.

새 노반타스 지게차는 주로 그것의 적정한 가격 때문에 시장에서 인기를 얻고 있다.

forklift truck 지게차 popularity 인기 mainly 주로 affordable 입수 가능한, (가격이) 알맞은 affordability 적당한 가격으로 구입할 수 있는 것; 감당할 수 있는 비용 afford (~을 사거나 할 금전적·시간적) 여유가 되다

118 **해설** 명사 어휘 문제로 문맥상 '예정된 출발 3일 전에'가 가장 자연스러우므로 (C)가 정답이다.

당신의 여행 보험 서류들을 출발하기로 한 날로부터 최소한 3일 전에 커버 씨에게 건네주세요.

hand 건네주다 travel insurance 여행 보험 intended 의도된 efficiency 효율성 progression 진행, 진전

119 **해설** 동사 어휘 문제로 주어 piece와 가장 자연스럽게 연결되는 동사는 assemble이므로 정답은 (A)이다.

모든 맥슨 가구는 배달되기 전에 완전히 조립된다.

assemble 조립하다; 집합시키다 establish 설립하다

120 **해설** 문장에 동사 is subject to가 있으므로 빈칸은 주어 자리이다. 주어 역할을 하는 것은 명사이므로 (B)가 정답이다. To price도 명사 역할을 하나, 뒤에 price의 목적어가 없고 의미상 적절하지 않으므로 오답이다.

오븐 수리 서비스의 가격 책정은 필요한 수리에 따라 변동될 수 있다.

be subject to ~의 대상이다, ~할 수 있다 pricing 가격 책정

121 **해설** 조동사(will) 뒤는 동사원형 자리이므로 (A)가 정답이다. surprisingly는 부사, surpassing은 동명사 혹은 현재분사, surpassed는 과거분사로 동사원형 자리에 쓸 수 없다.

오늘 태양이 빛나는 것으로 보아, 로드 크리켓 경기 주최자들은 오늘의 참석률이 어제보다 높을 것으로 예상한다.

given ~을 고려해 볼 때 match 경기, 시합 organizer 조직자; 주최자 attendance 참석, 참석률 surpass 능가하다, 뛰어넘다 surpassing 빼어난

122 **해설** 빈칸은 monthly passes와 weekly passes를 연결해 주는 접속사 자리이다. owing to는 전치사이고, by the time과 so that은 부사절 접속사로 뒤에 문장이 와야 하므로 (A)가 정답이다. A as well as B는 not only B but also A로 바꿔 쓸 수 있다는 것을 알아 두자.

7월 21일부터 셀리톤 수영장의 주간 정기 출입증뿐만 아니라 월간 정기 출입증의 입장료도 웹 사이트에서 구매할 수 있다.

pass 출입증 admission 입장료 owing to ~덕분에

123 **해설** 주어가 many employees이고, 동사는 have been reporting이다. 주어와 동사 사이는 수식어구가 와야 하므로 현재분사인 (D)가 정답이다. are working과 have worked는 동사, work는 동사 혹은 명사이므로 수식 역할을 할 수 없다.

도장 공장에서 일하는 많은 직원들이 지난 4개월 동안 안전하지 않은 관행을 보고해 오고 있다.

painting shop 도장 공장 practice 관행, 관례; 관습

124 **해설** 부사 어휘 문제로 빈칸 뒤의 large와 어울려 크기를 표현하는 부사로 (B)가 가장 자연스럽다.

마기니 박사는 병원의 상급 암 병동에서 수술이 필요한 비정상적으로 큰 종양을 발견했다.

identify 발견하다; 구분하다 tumor 종양 surgery 수술 advanced 상급의; 발달한 unit (병원의) 부서 outwardly 겉으로는, 표면상으로 unusually 비정상적으로 insecurely 불안하여

125 **해설** 형용사 문제로 문맥상 '고객의 조언이 중심이 되도록 노력한다'가 가장 자연스러우므로 (D)가 정답이다.

아주어 피싱은 고객의 의견을 중심으로 제품을 개발하려 노력한다.

strive 분투하다 input 조언 product development 제품 개발 moderate 보통의, 중간의

126 **해설** 전치사(prior to) 뒤에 올 수 있는 것은 명사 installation과 동명사 installing인데 빈칸 뒤의 명사(the water purifier)를 목적어로 가질 수 있는 것은 (A)이다. installed는 과거분사로 명사를 수식할 수는 있지만 관사(the)와 명사(water purifier) 사이에 와야 하므로 오답이다.

정수기 설치 전에 안내 설명서를 봐 주세요.

guideline 지침 manual 설명서 prior to ~ 이전에 water purifier 정수기

127 **해설** 알맞은 전치사를 고르는 문제로 문맥상 '고객들을 위해 다양한 디자인의 케이크를 만든다'가 가장 자연스러우므로 (A)가 정답이다.

알렉산드라 베이커리는 고객들을 위해 여러 가지 다양한 디자인의 케이크를 만든다.

a variety of 다양한, 여러, 많은

128 **해설** 명사 문제로 빈칸은 see 뒤에서 목적어 역할을 하면서 형용사(steady)의 수식을 받는 명사 자리이므로 (D)가 정답이다. grow는 동사, grown은 분사로 목적어 역할을 할 수 없다.

전자기기 매장의 국내 영업 수익은 계속해서 꾸준한 성장을 보이고 있다.

domestic 국내의; 집안의 steady 안정적인, 꾸준한

129 **해설** 상관 접속사 문제로 and와 함께 쓰이는 것은 both A and B이다. 상관 접속사 표현으로 either A or B, neither A nor B, not only A but also B, B as well as A, not A but B 등을 알아 둔다.

밍갈리스 씨는 교육생들이 목요일의 교육 과정과 금요일의 워크숍에 둘 다 참석했으면 하는 그녀의 바람을 표현했다.

trainee 교육생

130 **해설** 형용사 문제로 빈칸 뒤에 명사 treatments가 있으므로 빈칸은 명사를 수식하는 형용사 자리로 (B)가 정답이다. difference는 명사, differently는 부사, differ는 동사로 명사를 수식할 수 없다.

알버트슨 인터내셔널은 당신의 의학적인 질환을 해소하기 위해 다양한 치료약을 생산한다.

treatment 치료, 처치 medical complaint 의학적 질환

Part 6

[131-134]

수신: 잭 브라프 〈zachbraff@uptonhotel.com〉
발신: 크리스틴 벨 〈kristenbell@kos.com〉
제목: 연회장

안녕하세요, 브라프 씨. 저는 크리스틴 벨이며, 연회장에 관해서 이메일을 씁니다. 귀하의 호텔 연회장이 12월 9일에 이용 가능 131 한지 아닌지 궁금합니다.
저희 회사 회장님을 위한 은퇴 파티를 열기 위해 저녁 7시쯤부터 10시까지 최대 200명을 수용할 수 있는 방을 132 찾고 있는데요. 적어도 50개의 테이블과 200개의 의자가 필요합니다. 133 또한, 빔 프로젝터를 포함한 장비를 빌리고 싶습니다. 저희가 빌리는 장비는 문제없이 선명한 그래픽을 보여줄 만큼 다목적 장비여야 합니다.
행사 5일 전 12월 4일까지 저에게 연락 주실 수 있을까요? 제 사무실 번호는 555-7890입니다. 곧 연락 주시기를 134 기다리겠습니다.

banquet 연회, 축하연 available 이용할 수 있는 accommodate 수용하다 device 장치, 기구 versatile 다용도의, 다목적의 equipment 장비 alternatively 양자택일로, 그 대신에

131 빈칸 앞의 wondering과 어울리며 문맥상 '연회장이 이용 가능한지 아닌지 궁금하다'라는 의미가 되어야 하므로 '~인지 어떤지'를 뜻하는 (B) if가 가장 적절하다.
정답_(B)

132 빈칸 뒤의 전치사 for와 어울리는 동사를 골라야 한다. '~를 찾다'는 뜻의 look for가 적절하므로 (A)가 정답이다. (B) seeking은 '찾다'라는 의미이지만 전치사 없이 쓰는 타동사이며, (C), (D) 역시 전치사 for와 어울리지 않기 때문에 오답이다.
정답_(A)

133 (A) 저를 위해 이 문제를 처리해 주셔서 감사합니다.
(B) 또한, 빔 프로젝터를 포함한 장비를 빌리고 싶습니다.
(C) 그것들은 그 사람들을 수용할 만큼 크지 않습니다.
(D) 대신에, 더 큰 테이블을 예약하실 수 있습니다.
문맥상 가장 적절한 문장을 고르는 문제이다. 빈칸 바로 뒤에 The devices(장비)라는 단어가 나오므로 '장비'와 관련된 내용이 와야 한다. 따라서 빔프로젝터를 포함한 장비를 빌리고 싶다는 (B)가 정답이다.
정답_(B)

134 적절한 시제를 고르는 문제이다. 연락을 받을 것을 지금 기대하고 있다는 의미로 현재시제 look이 적절하므로 (A)가 정답이다. (B) will have looked는 미래완료로 현재 진행되고 있는 동작이나 상태가 미래 어떤 시점에 완료된다는 의미이므로 오답이다.
정답_(A)

[135-138]

근무하거나 공부하시는 동안 심각한 언어 장벽으로 고생하고 계신가요? 그렇다면, ANC 인터내셔널 어학원으로 오세요. 여기 저희가 135 제공해 드릴 수 있는 특별한 혜택들이 있습니다.
첫째, 모든 인터넷 사용자 분들은 직장에서든 집에서든, 어떤 컴퓨터로도 언제든 저희 프로그램에 접속하실 수 있습니다. 둘째, 귀하에게 보내지는 저희 교육 자료는 최상의 수준입니다.
136 게다가, 저희 전문 강사들은 모두 자격증을 수료했으며 최소 10년간의 강의 경력이 있습니다. 마지막으로, 저희는 이 지역에서 처음으로 다음 달에 입문용 중국어 수업을 개설할 예정입니다.
이 수업은 6달 동안 일주일에 2회씩 137 진행됩니다. 138 이번 주말까지 수업을 등록하시면 20% 할인을 해드립니다. 추가 정보를 위해서는 저희 고객 서비스 데스크 555-9086로 전화 주세요.

suffer from ~로 고통받다 barrier 장벽 exclusive 독점적인 access (컴퓨터에) 접속하다 licensed 면허를 받은 introductory 소개의 schedule 예정하다 commence 시작하다 intensive 집중적인 eligible 자격이 있는 conflict 갈등, 충돌

135 선택지의 빈칸이 동사인 것으로 보아 we 이하는 선행사 some exclusive benefits를 수식하는 절로 볼 수 있다. 목적격 관계대명사 which나 that이 생략된 관계대명사절이므로 빈칸은 선행사 some exclusive benefits를 목적어로 받을 수 있는 타동사가 되어야 한다. 따라서 수동태 동사 (D)는 오답이고, (A)와 (B)는 '제공해 드렸던'의 과거를 뜻하므로 문맥상 어색하고, '제공해 드릴 수 있는'을 뜻하는 (C)가 되면 제공되는 혜택들이 뒤에 언급되므로 빈칸의 조건에 가장 적합하다.
정답_(C)

136 적절한 접속부사를 고르는 문제이다. 지문 초반에 제공할 수 있는 혜택이 있다고 했으므로 이런 혜택들을 나열하고 있다. 빈칸 앞까지 두 가지가 언급되었고, 빈칸 뒤에서도 혜택에 대한 내용이 이어지므로 부가적인 내용을 덧붙이고 있음을 알 수 있다. 따라서 (A) Besides(게다가, 더욱이)가 정답이다.
정답_(A)

137 동사 어휘 문제이다. 수업이 6달 동안 일주일에 2회씩 진행된다는 의미이므로 '(모임 등이) 열리다'를 뜻하며 수업, 회의, 모임 등의 빈도와 함께 쓰이는 동사 meet이 가장 적절하다. 따라서 (A)가 정답이다.
정답_(A)

138 (A) 집중 코스는 동시에 다양한 언어 능력을 배우는 데 더 나을 것입니다.
(B) 고급반 학생들은 무료 토론 클럽에 가입하실 수 있는 자격이 있습니다.
(C) 이번 주말까지 수업을 등록하시면 20% 할인을 해드립니다.
(D) 일정이 겹치는 관계로 강사를 교체하는 것은 어려울 것입니다.
어학원 광고로 마지막에는 어학원 등록을 유도하기 위한 혜택을 제시하는 것이 적절하다. 따라서 선택지 중에서 이번 주말까지 등록하면 할인이 적용된다는 (C)가 가장 적절하다.
정답_(C)

[139-142]

수신: 데이브 프랭코 〈davefranco@msm.com〉
발신: 레베카 스펜스 〈rebeccaspence@seattleweekly.com〉
날짜: 7월 15일
제목: 구독 현황

안녕하세요, 프랭코 씨. 저는 〈시애틀 위클리 지〉의 레베카 스펜스입니다. 저는 귀하의 신문 구독이 7월 31에 종료될 것임을 알려드리고자 이 이메일을 씁니다. 이번 달 139 내에 구독을 갱신하시면, 저희가 30% 할인을 해 드릴 것입니다. 이 특별가는 지난 10년간에 걸친 귀하의 성실한 140 애용에 감사 드리고자 이루어진 것입니다.
또한, 저희는 귀하께서 수표로 지불해 오셨음을 알게 되었습니다. 141 모든 온라인상의 결제는 추가로 5%를 더 할인해 드림을 알려 드리고 싶습니다. 이 방식이 더욱 편리하시다면, 신용 카드를 이용한 온라인 결제를 위하여 이 방식을 이용해 주세요.
추가 정보를 얻기 위해서는, 주저 마시고 저희 웹 사이트 www.seattleweekly.com을 방문해 주시거나 추가 질문 사항이 있으신 경우 555-7780으로 저희에게 전화 주세요. 이 훌륭한 142 특별가의 기회를 이용하시기 바라며, 앞으로도 저희와 계속 거래해 주시기를 희망합니다.

subscription 구독, 신청 loyal 성실한, 충실한 convenient 편리한 take advantage of ~을 이용하다 patronage 단골거래, 애용 patron 단골, 후원자 deal 거래, 계약 position 직책, 위치 market 시장 selection 선택

139 빈칸 뒤 this month와 어울리는 전치사를 고르는 문제이다. 특정 기간 앞에 올 수 있는 전치사 (C) within이 정답이다. (A), (B)는 기간을 연결할 수 없는 전치사이고, (D) after를 쓰면 이번 달 이후에 갱신하는 것이므로 이런 경우 특별가를 제공한다는 것은 의미상 어색하므로 오답이다.
정답_(C)

140 소유격 your 뒤에 오는 명사를 골라야 한다. 동명사 또는 분사형인 (D)를 먼저 제외하고 (A), (B), (C) 모두 명사이므로 해석을 통해 정답을 골라야 한다. your 자체가 사람을 뜻하는 소유격이기 때문에 그 뒤로도 사람 명사인 patron(고객)이 오는 것이 아니라, 고객으로서의 '애용'이라는 의미가 적절하다. 따라서 정답은 (A) patronage이다.
정답_(A)

141 (A) 이 기간 동안에는 추가 20% 할인을 더 받으시게 됩니다.
(B) 모든 온라인상의 결제는 추가로 5%를 더 할인해 드림을 알려 드리고 싶습니다.
(C) 이 서비스가 중단되었음에 매우 유감입니다.
(D) 일단 제품이 배송이 되면 배송지를 변경하는 것은 불가능합니다.

빈칸 앞에서 지금까지 수표로 지불을 해왔다고 했고 빈칸 뒤로는 신용 카드를 통한 온라인 결제를 원하면 그렇게 하라고 했으므로 결제 방식에 대한 안내가 나와야 한다. 따라서 정답은 (B)이다. 빈칸 앞에 특정 할인 기간이 언급된 바가 없으므로 기간을 받아 연결한 문장인 (A)는 오답이다.
정답_(B)

142 명사 어휘 문제이다. 빈칸 앞에 지시형용사 these가 있으므로 빈칸에 들어갈 명사는 앞에서 언급된 내용이어야 한다. 앞에서 금액 할인에 대한 내용이 나왔으므로 '거래'뿐 아니라 특별하게 제공하는 '거래 가격'의 의미로도 쓰이는 (A) deals가 정답이다.
정답_(A)

[143-146]

드류 포웰
112 인사동
종로구, 서울 12005

포웰 선생님께,

저희 영업 부서 매니저 직에 관한 귀하의 지원서를 (143) 수령했음을 알려드리며, 저희 회사에 대한 귀하의 관심에 대해 진심으로 감사드립니다. (144) 저희의 구인 공고에 엄청난 지원이 있었습니다.

따라서 각 지원서를 검토하고 저희의 요구 사항에 맞는 자격을 갖고 (145) 계신 지원자를 선정하는 데 더 오랜 시간이 걸릴 수 있습니다.

저희는 6월 30일까지는 이 자리를 충원하고자 합니다. 이 날짜까지 저희로부터 연락을 받지 못하신다면, 자리가 충원되었다고 (146) 생각하시면 됩니다.

가르시아 인터내셔널에 대한 관심 감사드립니다.

제인 아담스
인사부장

acknowledge (받았음을) 알리다 **candidate** 후보자, 지원자 **note** 언급하다 유념하다 **assume** 가정하다, 생각하다 **ensure** 보장하다 **request** 요청하다

143 동사 acknowledge 뒤로 목적어인 명사의 자리이므로 (C) receipt(수령, 수취)가 정답이다. acknowledge receipt of는 '~를 수령했음을 알리다'라는 표현이다.
정답_(C)

144 (A) 10명의 최종 선발 명단의 지원자로서, 귀하께서는 최종 면접을 보실 자격이 있습니다.
(B) 귀하의 업무와 관련된 몇 가지 샘플을 저희 매니저에게 보내주십시오.
(C) 귀하의 확고한 직업 윤리와 뛰어난 전략 때문에 귀하를 선정했습니다.
(D) 저희의 구인 공고에 엄청난 지원이 있었습니다.

문맥상 가장 적절한 문장을 고르는 문제이다. 빈칸 다음 문장이 Therefore(따라서)로 시작하므로 이에 근거가 되는 내용이 와야 한다. 지원서를 검토하고 지원자를 선정하는 데 더 오랜 시간이 걸릴 수 있다는 것은 일자리 공고에 많은 사람이 지원했다는 것을 알 수 있다. 따라서 (D)가 정답이다.
정답_(D)

145 빈칸 바로 뒤에 명사(qualifications)로 이어지는 절이 앞의 선행사 candidates를 수식하려면 관계대명사가 필요한데 빈칸에 소유격 관계대명사 (A) whose가 들어가면 선행사의 의미를 받으면서 qualifications를 수식하므로 가장 적절하다.
정답_(A)

146 문맥상 '연락을 받지 못할 경우 자리가 충원되었다고 생각하면 된다'라는 의미가 적절하므로 '생각하다, 가정하다'라는 뜻의 (B) assume이 정답이다.
정답_(B)

[147-148]

SAC 대학교
대학 평의회 학부 연구 위원회
제2회 연례
연구 리셉션

학부 연구에서의 우수함을 기리기 위해
더글러스 M 버만 교수님을 특별 초청 연사로 모십니다.

2019년 11월 29일 목요일

오전 10시 칵테일 리셉션, 오전 11시 시상식
랜덜 홀

준 정장

11월 19일 화요일까지 research_committee@mail.com으로 회신 바랍니다.

senate 상원, 대학 평의회 **undergraduate** 학부 **award ceremony** 시상식 **cocktail attire** 비즈니스 복장, 준정장 **RSVP** 회답 주시기 바랍니다

147 행사는 얼마나 자주 열리는가?
(A) 하루에 한 번
(B) 일주일에 한 번
(C) 한 달에 한 번
(D) 일 년에 한 번

148 연구 리셉션에 관해 언급되어 있는 것은?
(A) 교내에서 처음 열렸다.
(B) 입을 수 있는 복장 규정이 있다.
(C) 시상식이 끝난 후 칵테일 리셉션을 제공한다.
(D) 박사 학위 프로그램과 연구를 포함한다.

[149-150]

맥켄지 브리지스 오전 11:44
안녕, 앨버트. 우리의 새 동쪽 건물의 도면을 검토했니?

앨버트 브룩스 오전 11:45
응, 했어. 그런데 그렇게 큰 공간이 주차장으로 필요할 것인지는 의문이야.

맥켄지 브리지스 오전 11:47
맞아. 하지만 우리가 성장함에 따라 더 많은 환자가 우리를 찾아올 거야.

앨버트 브룩스 오전 11:48
내 생각엔 가까운 시일 내에 그렇게 될 것 같진 않아.

맥켄지 브리지스 오전 11:50
장기적인 요구를 진지하게 고민하는 것이 중요해. 이 건물은 의료 서비스 확장을 위한 대체 공간을 제공한다고.

앨버트 브룩스 오전 11:52
네 말이 맞아. 우리의 요구는 특히 최신 의료시설을 사용하기 시작할 때 바뀔 수도 있으니까.

floor plan 도면 wing 부속 건물 property 소유물, 건물 alternative 대체의, 대안의 expansion 확장 especially 특히 up-to-date 최신의

149 브리지스 씨가 종사할 것 같은 사업은 어떤 분야인가?
(A) 병원
(B) 건축회사
(C) 부동산
(D) 지역 제조업체

150 오전 11시 52분에 브룩스 씨가 "네 말이 맞아"라고 썼을 때 무엇을 의미하는 것 같은가?
(A) 의료 장비가 대여되어야 한다.
(B) 새로운 서비스가 너무 비쌀 것이다.
(C) 그 건물은 앞으로의 요구에 적합할지도 모른다.
(D) 그 건물은 구조적인 개조가 필요하다.

[151-152]

특별 연말 할인 행사

- 월요일부터 목요일! 어서 오세요, 스키터즈로!

외투, 후드 티, 스웨터와 같이 겨울을 대비하는 따뜻한 옷들을 최대 50퍼센트까지 절약하세요.
다 나가기 전에 빨리 오셔서 최고의 겨울옷들을 가져가세요!

편하신 때에 저희 상점을 방문해서 돈을 절약하세요.
로즈 테라스, 펄 하버, 브로큰 애로우

구매자분들은 기억해 주십시오.

- 신발과 장신구들은 할인 행사에 포함되지 않습니다.
- 저희 상점은 연례 할인 기간이 끝날 때까지는 오전 9시부터 오후 10시까지 영업합니다.

평소 영업시간은 오전 10시에서 오후 6시까지입니다.

스키터즈

outwear 외투 hoody 후드 티 selection 선별된 것들 supply 공급품 savings 절약, 저축 footwear 신발류 accessories 장신구 take place 발생하다 comprise 구성하다, 차지하다 extend 연장하다

151 연말 할인 행사에 관해 무엇이 제시되어 있는가?
(A) 매년 열리는 행사이다.
(B) 다음 공지가 있을 때까지 계속될 것이다.
(C) 사계절 제품 모두를 할인한다.
(D) 할인 행사 기간 동안 영업시간을 연장한다.

152 할인 품목에 포함되지 않는 것은 무엇인가?
(A) 외투
(B) 장갑
(C) 후드 티
(D) 스웨터

[153-154]

직원 구내식당 직원들께

피나클 주식회사의 모든 구내식당 직원들은 주목해 주십시오. 안전이 최우선입니다. 항상 좋은 업무 습관을 연습하기 위한 기본 법칙을 따르십시오. 하나의 작은 실수가 심각한 부상을 일으킬 수 있기 때문에 당신이 부엌에서 무엇을 하고 있는지에 주의를 기울이십시오.

- 날카로운 기구는 나무 블록이나 서랍에 저장합니다.
- 단정한 옷을 착용하고 긴 머리는 뒤로 묶으십시오. 옷이 물건에 걸리고 문제가 발생할 수 있으므로 옷을 헐렁하게 입어서는 안 됩니다.
- 온도에 민감한 음식은 내놓지 마십시오. 매우 빠르게 상할 것입니다.
- 음식을 취급하기 전이나 고기 및 가금류를 취급한 후에는 비누로 손을 씻으십시오. 손에는 세균이 가득합니다.
- 비상 사태의 경우 사용할 수 있도록 소화기의 위치와 사용법을 알고 계십시오. 당신은 불 속에서 설명서를 읽는 시간을 낭비할 수 없습니다.

안전 점검은 매주 예고 없이 그렉 나퀸이나 패티 루빈에 의해 실시됩니다. 항상 집중해 주십시오!

이러한 안전 수칙에 관한 질문이나 우려 사항은 다음으로 연락 주십시오.

안전부, 새이나 게바라
피나클 주식회사, 12542 로즐레어 드라이브,
휴스턴, 텍사스 77066

priority 우선사항 at all times 항상 pay attention to ~에 집중하다 utensil 기구 tidy 단정한 sensitive 민감한 sit out 내놓다 spoil 상하다 poultry 가금류 fire extinguisher 소화기 emergency 비상사태 be on your guard 경계심을 늦추지 않다 janitorial 잡역부의 instruct 가르치다 regulate 조성하다

153 이 지시 사항은 누구를 대상으로 하는가?
(A) 구내식당 이용자
(B) 주방 직원
(C) 잡역부
(D) 안전 부서

154 공지의 목적은 무엇인가?
(A) 새 복장 규정을 발표하기 위해
(B) 소화기 사용법을 가르치기 위해
(C) 새로운 안전 요건의 개요를 서술하기 위해
(D) 더욱 안전한 환경을 조성하기 위해

[155-157]

수신: sharon@interprete.com
발신: jwilson@wilsontrading.com
날짜: 6월 3일
제목: 프로젝트 마무리

셰런 씨께

당신의 엄청난 솜씨와 프로 의식에 감사드립니다. 저는 앞으로도 당신과 함께 일하고 싶습니다. 저는 국제 금속 박람회에서 귀하의 동시 통역에 매우 감동받았습니다. -[1]-. 저는 금속 무역 업계의 고객들로부터 오직 긍정적인 의견만을 받았습니다. 당신의 의무를 이행하는 동안, 저는 제 임무를 완료하지 못했습니다. 우리의 계약을 완료하려면, 당신의 협조가 필요합니다. -[2]-.

요구하신 대로 계좌로 통역비를 이체해 드리지 못해 대단히 죄송합니다. -[3]-. 제 이메일 계정에서 받은 메일을 정리할 때, 실수로 귀하의 은행 계좌번호가 포함된 메일을 삭제했습니다. 최대한 빨리 이메일로 그 정보를 제게 알려 주시기 바랍니다. -[4]-. 양해해 주셔서 감사합니다.
곧 다시 함께 일할 수 있기를 바랍니다.

조니 윌슨 드림

wrap up 끝내다 tremendous 굉장한 work 솜씨 professionalism 전문 직업의식 simultaneous 동시의 interpretation 통역 fulfill 완수하다 cooperation 협조 transfer 이체하다 remit 송금하다 agency 대행사 provider 공급업체 remittance 송금

155 조니 윌슨은 어떤 종류의 회사를 다니는가?
(A) 금융 기관
(B) 통역 회사
(C) 금속 무역 회사
(D) 이메일 서비스 공급업체

156 셰런 씨는 이메일을 받은 후 무엇을 하도록 부탁받았는가?
(A) 은행 계좌 개설한다.
(B) 송금 이체를 요청한다.
(C) 미스터 윌슨에게 받은 모든 이메일 삭제한다.
(D) 그녀의 계좌 정보를 온라인으로 제공한다.

157 [1], [2], [3], [4]로 표시된 곳 중 다음 문장의 위치로 가장 적절한 곳은 어디인가?
"받는 즉시 계좌로 금액을 송금해 드리겠습니다."
(A) [1]
(B) [2]
(C) [3]
(D) [4]

[158-160]

몬트리올에서의 구인 공고

캐나다 몬트리올에 있는 저희 중간 규모의 사립 학교에서 7월에 근무를 시작할 영어 교사를 모집하고 있습니다. 저희의 검증된 커리큘럼을 이용해 초등과 중등 학생들을 가르치게 될 것입니다. 급여는 한 달에 1,800달러로, 동일한 위치에 평균을 훨씬 웃도는 수준입니다. 매주 월요일부터 금요일, 오후 2시부터 8시까지 30시간을 가르치게 될 것입니다. 저희 학교에서 단 10분 거리에 가구가 비치된 아파트도 제공받게 될 것입니다. 저희는 몬트리올이 불어를 주로 사용하는 도시라는 점을 감안해, 영어 원어민을 찾고 있습니다.

이곳에 채용되려면, 적어도 공인된 대학에 학사 학위(분야 무관)를 소지하고 있어야 합니다. 교사 경력이 있다면 이점이 있지만 반드시 필요한 것은 아닙니다. 그러나 전과 기록이 없다는 것은 입증할 수 있어야 합니다.

저희 학교 선생님들은 모두 우호적이고, '요령을 터득하도록' 기꺼이 도와줄 것입니다. 때로 선생님들이 한 교실에 함께 들어가, 학생들의 영어 학습을 용이하게 하기도 합니다. 저희는 학생들을 주의 깊게 가려내고 있어, 시끄럽게 떠들거나 공격적인 아이들이 교육적 노력을 방해하는 일은 없을 것입니다.

82-2-555-3371번으로 장 프랑소와에게 연락하세요.

job opening 구인 moderately 중간 정도의 elementary 초등의 tried-and-true 검증된, 신뢰할 수 있는 above the average 평균을 웃도는 a bachelor's degree 학사 학위 accredited 공인된 absolutely 절대적으로, 반드시 criminal background 전과 기록 learn the ropes 요령을 배우다 screen 가려내다 belligerent 공격적인 publicize 홍보하다, 알리다 throughout 도처에, 전역의 recruit 모집하다 obedient 말을 잘 듣는, 순종적인 respectful 공손한 immigrant 이민자

158 공고의 목적은 무엇인가?
(A) 캐나다 전역의 학생들에게 학교를 홍보하기 위해
(B) 학교에 해외 학생들을 모집하기 위해
(C) 영어의 중요성을 확인하기 위해
(D) 영어 수업을 가르칠 외국인을 고용하기 위해

159 선생님들의 근무 시작 시간은 몇 시인가?
(A) 오전 10시
(B) 정오
(C) 오후 2시
(D) 오후 8시

160 학생들에 관해 제시된 내용은 무엇인가?
(A) 선생님들을 기꺼이 도와줄 것이다.
(B) 영어 학습에 무엇이든 관심이 없다.
(C) 선생님들 말을 잘 듣고 존중한다.
(D) 캐나다에 온 프랑스 이민자들 출신이다.

[161-164]

헬렌 포이 [오후 2:15]	토론에 참여해 주셔서 감사합니다. 행사 준비가 어떻게 되어가고 있는지를 공유하고 싶습니다. 톰, 새로운 소식 좀 있나요?
톰 스터리지 [오후 2:16]	네, 굉장한 소식이 있습니다. 현지의 상공회의소에서 마침내 우리 회사가 직업 박람회를 여는 것을 승인했습니다.
지나 로드리게즈 [오후 2:17]	놀랍네요!
세스 그린 [오후 2:18]	굉장한 소식이네요! 저는 그것 때문에 걱정했었습니다.
톰 스터리지 [오후 2:19]	제가 그들에게 우리가 현지 회사에 행사 참가 우선권을 줄 계획이라고 알려줬어요. 그것이 그들을 납득시킨거죠.
헬렌 포이 [오후 2:20]	오, 굉장해요! 다른 소식은요?
지나 로드리게즈 [오후 2:21]	데일리굿 사는 이미 그 박람회에서 부스 5개를 설치하는 데 동의를 했습니다. 또 저는 나머지 현지 업체들에 여러 차례 연락을 취하고 있습니다. 목요일까지 다른 참가자들로부터 응답을 받도록 노력할 것입니다.
세스 그린 [오후 2:22]	저는 아직 이 행사를 위해 우리가 계획 중인 강습회를 위한 더욱 적합한 강연자를 확보하는 중입니다. 다니엘 웨버 씨는 "더 나은 대화를 하는 5가지 방법"이라는 강연을 진행하는 것에 잠정적으로 동의하였습니다.
헬렌 포이 [오후 2:23]	그거 괜찮을 것 같습니다. 저도 그가 이 분야에서 유명한 전문가라고 알고 있습니다.

preparation 준비 chamber of commerce 상공회의소 hold 개최하다 job fair 직업 박람회 priority 우선권 convince 납득시키다 suitable 적합한 tentatively 잠정적으로 lead 이끌다

161 글쓴이들이 논의하는 것은 무엇인가?
(A) 지역 회사
(B) 박람회
(C) 강연
(D) 공공기관

162 오후 2시 18분에 그린 씨가 "저는 그것 때문에 걱정했었습니다."라고 쓴 의미는 무엇인가?
(A) 그 제안이 승인될 것으로 생각하지 않았다.
(B) 그 기관이 행사에 참여할 것으로 생각하지 않았다.
(C) 그 회의가 취소될 것으로 생각했다.

(D) 현지 사업체가 제외될 수도 있다고 생각했다.

163 로드리게즈 씨가 기다리는 것은 무엇인가?
(A) 승인에 관한 공지
(B) 강연자로부터의 응답
(C) 계획의 변경
(D) 여러 업체로부터의 응답

164 웨버 씨는 누구인가?
(A) 새로운 공무원
(B) 강연자
(C) 행사 조직자
(D) 심사위원단

[165-167]

리더스 트레저 아일랜드
3116 버치 스트리트
인디애나폴리스, 인디애나 46268

독서를 좋아하십니까? 무엇을 기다리세요?
리더스 트레저 아일랜드에 회원으로 등록하시고
놀라운 가격으로 수상 작품을 즐기세요!

우리는 언제나 인기 있는 어린이용 시리즈 <진짜 꿈! 진짜 모험!>부터 시작해서 추리 소설 작가 말빈 벤슨, 그랜트 매톡스, 켈리 켈러 등이 쓴 뛰어난 작품들까지 여러분이 푹 빠질 추리 소설, 공상 과학 소설, 공상 소설들을 전문으로 하고 있습니다.

리더스 트레저 아일랜드 회원들을 위한 특권:
- 정상가에서 최대 60퍼센트까지 할인되는 가격으로 책 구입하기
- 우리 서점과 웹 사이트에서 수천 권의 책들을 즐기기
- 회원 전용 웹 사이트를 언제든 이용하기

그밖에, 우리 회원들은 무료 주간 소식지를 받게 되실 겁니다. 각 소식지에는 신간 소식, 금주의 할인 품목, 우리 편집자들이 쓴 서평이 실릴 겁니다. 회원권을 유지하시기 위해선 매달 최소 한 권의 책을 구입하셔야만 합니다.

등록하셔서 www.treasurebook.com에서 리더스 트레저 아일랜드를 즐기세요.

feature 특징으로 삼다 addicted to ~에 푹 빠진, 중독된 superior 우수한 achievement 업적 privilege 특권 gain 얻다 access 이용 exclusively 독점적으로 newsletter 소식지, 회보, 사보 book review 서평, 서평 at least 최소한 overnight 익일의

165 리더스 트레저 아일랜드에 언급된 제품이 아닌 것은 무엇인가?
(A) 공상 소설
(B) 추리 소설
(C) 참고 서적
(D) 공상 과학 소설

166 리더스 트레저 아일랜드의 회원은 어떤 혜택을 받는가?
(A) 무료 익일 배송
(B) 특별 할인 가격
(C) 어린이용 도서 대여 서비스
(D) 도서관 데이터베이스 이용권

167 회원 자격을 유지하기 위해서, 회원들은 어떻게 해야 하는가?
(A) 편집자로 구성된 팀과 일한다.
(B) 새로 발행된 책의 서평을 쓴다.
(C) 매주 소식지를 정기 구독한다.
(D) 매달 최소 책 한 권을 구입한다.

[168-171]

더 데일리 이코노미스트

SLU 스틸즈 분기별 재정 보고서

런던(4월 19일) - SLU 스틸즈의 최고 재무 책임자인 루크 피셔 씨는 오늘 올해 첫 분기의 회사 수익이 지난해 수익률보다 7% 앞섰다고 보고하였다. 이것은 시장의 현재 상황을 고려할 때 충격적인 성과이다. -[1]-. 또, 피셔 씨는 붉은 화살표가 느리지만 꾸준히 올라가는 그래프를 보여주는 회사의 대차대조표를 덧붙였다. 이 결과는 지난 12월 미국 기업인 락포트 스틸즈와 SLU 스틸즈의 제휴로부터 예측된 것이다. -[2]-. 더욱 긴밀한 제휴를 통해서, 이 두 회사는 자동차 제조업체와 조선업체에 우수한 제품을 공급하는 그들의 사업을 강화하는 것을 목표로 한다.

피셔 씨는 기자회견에서 SLU 스틸즈의 붉은 화살표가 하락하는 것을 막을 수 있도록 다른 방안을 마련할 것이라고 밝혔다. SLU 스틸즈는 기간산업의 중요한 공급업체로서 1970년대 이래로 영국의 경제 성장에 원동력이 되어 왔다. -[3]-. 기반을 강화하는 것을 넘어서 현재는 급속하게 변하는 세계 철강 업계를 선도하기 위해 새로운 기술 발전으로 초점을 옮겨 한 발짝 더 나아가고 있다.

피셔 씨는 향후 몇 년간 이 회사가 기술과 제품의 다양화에 집중할 것임을 밝혔다. SLU 스틸즈를 포함하여 세계에는 철강회사들이 몇 개 안 되지만 그렇다고 다른 시장에 비해 경쟁이 더 약한 것은 아니다. -[4]-. 피셔 씨는 SLU 스틸즈가 여전히 철강업계에서 우위를 차지하려고 노력하고, 국가의 경제를 끌어 올릴 것이라고 언급했다.

CFO (= chief financial officer) 최고 재무 책임자 earnings 수익 precede 앞서다 apply 적용하다 balance sheet 대차대조표 alliance 제휴, 동맹 strengthen 강화하다 automaker 자동차 제조업체 driving force 추진력 shift 옮기다 diversification 다양화 steelmaker 철강업체 pull up 끌어올리다 accuse 고소하다 share 주식 counterbalance ~을 균형 잡히게 하다 stem from ~에서 기인하다 consolidation 통합 steel industry 철강업계 boost 촉진시키다 union 결합

168 이 기사의 목적은 무엇인가?
(A) 회사의 재정 성과를 공표하기 위해서
(B) 합병을 발표하기 위해서
(C) 회사의 신제품을 소개하기 위해서
(D) 범법으로 한 회사를 고소하기 위해서

169 [1], [2], [3], [4]로 표시된 곳 중 다음 문장의 위치로 가장 적절한 곳은 어디인가?
"이 두 회사 모두는 철강업계에서의 통합에서 기인하는 난제들을 상쇄시키기 위하여 서로의 부가적인 주식을 매입하는 거래를 해 왔다."
(A) [1]
(B) [2]
(C) [3]
(D) [4]

170 SLU 스틸즈의 성장을 촉진한 것은 무엇인가?
(A) 새로운 재료의 개발
(B) 시장 점유율 증가
(C) 주식에 올바른 투자
(D) 또 다른 회사와의 결합

171 SLU 스틸즈에 관해 암시되지 않은 것은 무엇인가?
(A) 회사의 수익률이 올라가고 있다.
(B) 산업 변화에 대응할 계획이다.
(C) 현재 세계에서 가장 강력한 철강회사이다.
(D) 1970년대 이래로 경제 성장을 선도하는 역할을 해 왔다.

[172-175]

하이 엔드 로지스틱스

HEL 해외 배송 I 특송 화물 I 자원 센터 I 고객 서비스 자주하는 질문들

• 특송 화물 고객 서비스 자주하는 질문들

HEL은 언제나 고객들에게 최상의 서비스와 신뢰를 제공하고 있습니다.

1. 지점은 어디에 있나요?

지점 위치를 찾으시려면 여기 www.highendlogistics.com/storelocator를 클릭하시거나 1-800-555-2050으로 전화해 주십시오. 저희는 북미, 유럽, 아시아에 걸쳐 가장 저렴한 가격에 신뢰할 수 있는 맞춤화된 서비스를 제공하는 1,000개 이상의 지점이 있습니다. 또한, 저희 지점에는 모든 표준 규격 포장용품과 규격 외 특별 포장용품과 그와 관련된 비품들을 갖추고 있고 300가지 크기의 배송용 포장 상자, 포장지, 기포가 들어 있는 비닐 포장재, 완충재로 보강된 튼튼한 봉투, 그리고 우송용 원통까지 고객의 상품을 배송하는 데 필요한 모든 것을 갖추고 있습니다.

2. 배송해야 할 물건을 집이나 사무실에서 보낼 수 있나요?

네, 저희는 픽업 서비스를 근무 시간과 근무 외 시간에도 제공합니다. 계신 곳에서 배송품을 픽업해 주길 원하신다면 픽업 서비스를 예약하세요. 여기 www.highendlogistics.com/pickups에 들어가셔서 계신 곳에서 픽업 서비스가 가능한지 확인하시고 그 후에 예약해 주십시오. 당일 픽업 서비스도 요청하실 수 있습니다. 픽업을 위한 픽업 서비스 가능 지역이나 예약에 관해 질문은 1-800-555-2032로 연락 주십시오.

3. 배송 조회는 어떻게 하나요?

배송 추적 번호로, 저희 웹 사이트에서 배송 상황을 간단히 확인하실 수 있습니다. 여기 www.highendlogistics.com/track을 클릭하시고 '추적과 확인' 항목에 배송 추적 번호를 입력하신 후 엔터를 누르십시오. 그러면 보내신 배송품에 관한 배송 상태 정보를 보실 수 있습니다. 배송 추적 번호는 주문하실 때 받은 주문 확인 이메일에서 찾으실 수 있습니다.

4. 분실 또는 파손된 제품에 관한 보상 청구는 어떻게 하나요?

어떤 이유에서든 배송이 제대로 되지 않을 경우, 배송을 의뢰한 물품과 포장 상태에 대한 상세한 정보를 가지고 저희 고객 서비스 센터에 가능한 한 빨리 연락 주십시오. 저희는 분실된 제품을 찾을 수 있도록 모든 노력을 다할 겁니다.

reliability 신뢰도 unbeatable 타의 추종을 불허하는 trustworthy 신뢰할 수 있는 bubble wrap 기포가 들어 있는 비닐 포장재 padded envelope 완충재로 보강된 튼튼한 봉투 mailing tube 우송용 원통 accurate 정확한 description 설명 vendor 판매 회사, 노점상 coated 방수 처리한

172 누가 이 정보에 가장 관심 있을까?
(A) 고객들
(B) 우표 수집가들
(C) 배송업체들
(D) 우편배달부들

173 픽업 서비스를 이용하기 위해서 가장 먼저 해야 할 일은 무엇인가?
(A) 고객 서비스 센터로 전화한다.
(B) 온라인으로 픽업을 요청한다.
(C) 배송 날짜를 바꾼다.
(D) HEL 택배원을 기다린다.

174 HEL 지점에서 이용할 수 없는 물품은?
(A) 기포 비닐 포장재
(B) 밀봉 테이프
(C) 다양한 우편물용 원통
(D) 포장지

175 잃어버리거나 파손된 제품을 보고할 때 고객들은 무엇을 제공하라고 요청받고 있나?
(A) 택배 물건의 가격
(B) 고객의 개인 정보
(C) 택배 물건을 위한 추적 정보
(D) 택배 물건에 대한 상세한 정보

[176-180]

4월 2일
인디아 칼로스
리버뱅크 하우스
스완 레인 2
런던 EC4R 3BF

칼로스 씨께,

저는 〈더 스테이지〉의 6월 20일 자에 광고된 〈맨 오브 스틸〉의 주연 오디션을 보기 위해 연락을 드립니다. 저는 리즈의 엠파이어 극장에서 3년간 공연되고 있는 연극 〈자이언트 커즈웨이〉에서 현재 주연을 맡고 있습니다. 런던 연기 학교에서 졸업하자마자 그 역할을 제안받았습니다.

런던 연기 학교와 엠파이어 극장 두 곳에서 저는 가수 겸 무용수로서의 재능을 보일 기회를 얻었고, 제 포트폴리오가 그 다재다능함을 보여 줍니다. 저는 또한 감독 기술을 공부해 왔습니다. 두 달 전에 저는 가장 영향력 있는 공연 예술 잡지 중 하나인 〈워킹 더 보즈〉에 특집으로 실렸습니다. 이력서와 귀하가 볼 수 있도록 제 공연이 담긴 DVD를 동봉합니다. 더 많은 정보나 공연 작품을 필요로 하신다면 제공해 드릴 수 있습니다. 연락을 기다리겠습니다.

아마나 알바레즈

4월 8일
아마나 알바레즈
큐 브리지 로드 62
런던 W4 3AF

알바레즈 씨께,

오디션에 관한 당신의 편지를 받아 읽어 보았고, 이력서(특히 당신의 뮤지컬 경력)를 보니 당신을 정말 만나 보고 싶습니다. 이곳 리버뱅크 하우스의 주연을 위한 오디션을 당신에게 제안하고 싶습니다. 5월 30일 화요일에 약속을 잡을 수 있는지 연락해 주세요. 또, 5월 21일까지 당신 공연의 DVD를 보내 주시면 매우 감사하겠습니다. 동봉했다고 하셨지만, 보내신 소포에는 포함되어 있지 않았습니다.

인디아 칼로스
인사부장

audition 오디션을 보다 lead role 주연 edition (잡지 등의) 호, 판 exhibit 전시하다, 보이다 portfolio (특히 구직 때 제출하는 사진·그림 등의) 작품집, 포트폴리오 versatility 다재다능 direct 감독하다 feature 특집으로 다루다 influential 영향력 있는 performing arts 공연 예술 enclose 동봉하다 appointment 약속 senior position 상급직

176 리버뱅크 하우스에서 전문으로 하는 것은?
(A) 춤
(B) 감독
(C) 연기
(D) 출판

177 알바레즈 씨는 그녀의 교육을 언제 마쳤는가?
(A) 지난주
(B) 지난달
(C) 1년 전
(D) 3년 전

178 알바레즈 씨가 최근 그녀의 일에 대해 인정받은 일은?
(A) 잡지 기사의 대상이었다.
(B) 런던 연기 학교에서 주연을 땄다.
(C) 회사에서 상급직으로 승진했다.
(D) 업계에서 중요한 회의의 연설을 요청받았다.

179 칼로스 씨는 언제 알바레즈 씨와 면접을 하길 원하는가?
(A) 5월 14일
(B) 5월 17일
(C) 5월 21일
(D) 5월 30일

180 칼로스 씨가 알바레즈 씨에게 받은 것은?
(A) DVD

(B)이력서
(C) 포트폴리오
(D) 기사 한 부

[181-185]

수신: 모든 부서의 부장
발신: 일롱 바티스티
날짜: 4월 8일
제목: 설명회

인사부는 이곳 소아메스 백화점에서 3개월 미만 근무한 직원들에게 다른 부서에 관해 교육하기 위한 강좌를 고안했습니다. 12월 31일, 또는 그 후에 고용된 귀하의 부서의 모든 직원은 지금쯤 강좌 일정표를 받았을 것입니다. 책임자로서 귀하는 반드시 직원들이 다른 부서의 책임자들에 의해 운영될 강좌를 참석하도록 해야 합니다. 또한 강좌의 피드백이 필요하므로 귀하의 직원들에게 그들이 참석하는 마지막 강좌 후에 양식을 작성해야 한다는 것을 알려 주십시오. 양식은 매 강좌 후 발부될 것이며, 일주일 이내로 자그 빌딩 22호실의 잉게 조하니스에게 제출해야 합니다.

아래의 전체 일정표를 확인해 주세요. 모든 강좌는 드웨인 로지의 2층 회의실에서 열립니다. 점심은 매 강좌마다 제공될 것입니다.

부서	발표자	날짜와 시간
영업	하미르 칸	7월 10일 오전 11시 15분-오후 12시
요리 조달	카일 잭스	7월 17일 오전 10시 45분-오전 11시 30분
제품 개발	마리세 로드	8월 20일 오전 11시 15분-오후 12시
마케팅	칼 에버톤	8월 29일 오전 10시 45분-오전 11시 30분

감사합니다.

일롱 바티스테
인사부 부장

설명회 피드백 양식

직원 이름: 안드레 부숑

어느 강좌에 참석했나요?
✔ 영업 ✔ 요리조달 ✔ 제품 개발 ___ 마케팅

어느 강좌가 가장 효과적이었고, 그 이유는 무엇인가요?
저는 제품 개발 강좌의 발표자가 집에 갖고 갈 수 있는 신제품에 우리의 새로운 아이디어를 시험하도록 한 것이 마음에 들었습니다. 그 부서에는 어떤 일이 있는지 배울 수 있는 좋은 방법이었습니다.

강좌가 어떻게 향상되면 좋을까요?
저와 제 동료 3명은 7월 17일 강좌에서 일찍 나와야 했습니다. 제 담당 매니저는 매주 수요일 11시 15분에 재고 조사를 합니다. 인사부에서 추후 강좌의 일정을 잡을 때 타 부서장들과 확인하면 도움이 될 것 같습니다.

information session 설명회 devise 고안하다 educate 교육하다 practice 관행, 관습 trainee 훈련 받는 사람 employ 고용하다 itinerary 일정표 ensure 확실히 하다 hand out 발부하다 board room 회의실 presenter 발표자 stock take 재고 조사 schedule 일정을 잡다 prospective 유망한 reminder 상기시키는 것 nominate 지명하다 questionnaire 설문지

181 메모가 쓰인 이유는?
(A) 세미나가 왜 이전되었는지 설명하기 위해
(B) 부장들에게 발표를 요청하기 위해
(C) 물망에 오른 후보자들의 면접을 위한 새 정책을 소개하기 위해
(D)부장들이 직원들에게 상기시키도록 요청하기 위해

182 모든 강좌에 대해 사실인 것은?
(A) 부장들은 후보자들을 지명해야 한다.
(B)강좌에 참석하는 직원들은 식사를 제공받는다.
(C) 오후 12시 15분에 시작한다.
(D) 훈련을 받는 사람들은 참석하기 전에 설문 조사를 작성해야 한다.

183 안드레 부숑에 관해 알 수 있는 것은?
(A) 그의 사무실은 자그 빌딩에 있다.
(B) 그의 책임자는 하미르 칸이다.
(C) 그는 소아메즈 백화점의 요리 조달 부서에 근무하고 있다.
(D)그는 소아메스에 고용된 지 3개월이 안되었다.

184 강좌 중에 시험을 허용한 사람은?
(A) 하미르 칸
(B) 카일 잭스
(C)마리세 로드
(D) 칼 에버톤

185 안드레 부숑이 일찍 나가야 했던 강좌는?
(A)요리 조달
(B) 영업
(C) 제품 개발
(D) 마케팅

[186-190]

수신: 매들린 해리스 〈mharris@apex.com〉
발신: 사무엘 조슬린 〈sjoslin@apex.com〉
날짜: 3월 25일
제목: 이메일 사용

매들린에게,

저는 지금이 직원들에게 우리 회사의 이메일 사용 규정을 상기시킬 때라고 생각합니다. 저는 직원들이 대부분 시간에 이메일을 올바르게 사용하고 있다고 믿지만, 이메일이 업무 목적으로만 쓰이고 있지 않은 것 같습니다. 그래서 기존의 직원들에게 기억을 되살리고 신입 직원들에게 분명히 알리기 위해서 이메일 규정에 관한 발표가 필요합니다. 에이펙스는 이메일 사용이 업무를 위한 필수 수단이라는 것을 인정합니다. 그러나 이 도구를 남용하는 것은 우리 업체의 명성에 안 좋은 영향을 줄 수 있습니다.

저는 우리 직원들이 어떤 종류의 이메일이 적합한가 아닌가를 명확하게 이해하도록 확실한 조치를 취하고 싶지만, 그들이 엄격하게 통제된다고 느끼길 원하는 것은 아닙니다. 그래서 당신이 저 대신 직원들이 읽어 볼 메모를 작성해 주신다면 감사하겠습니다. 되도록 빨리 작성하셔서 이번 달 말까지 정책이 발표되길 바랍니다.

미리 감사드립니다.

잭 그랜트
에이펙스

메모

직원들에게,

이 글은 현행 이메일 사용 정책에 관한 것입니다. 우리 회사와 여러분의 안전을 위해 이메일 사용 규정을 읽고 숙지하는 시간을 가지십시오.

이 메모를 경고로 오해하지 마십시오. 이메일의 사용은 이러한 이메일의 이용이 사업의 이익을 위한 목적이라면 적극적으로 허용되며 지원받게 됩니다. 그러나 우리는 직원들이 알았으면 하는 하나의 정책이 있습니다. 그러므로, 우리 웹 사이트에 있는 정책에 대한 안내 지침을 다운을 받으시고, 여러분의 책상에 붙여 놓고 계속 확인해 주세요.

매들린 해리스

이메일 사용 정책

이메일 사용 시 다음 사항에 유념해 주세요:

- 현재의 규정을 지키세요
- 용인되는 방식으로 사용하세요
- 이메일을 남용하지 마세요

용납될 수 없는 사용

1. 불법성이 있는 사진, 글 혹은 자료를 유포하거나 저장하는 것
2. 개인적인 용무를 위해 이메일과 인터넷을 사용하는 것
3. 허가되지 않는 비밀번호와 우편함을 사용하는 것
4. 저작권을 위반하는 것
5. 직원들의 업무나 통신 자원을 낭비할 수 있는 고의적인 행동을 하는 것
6. 불필요한 상업·광고성 자료를 보내는 것
7. 불쾌하거나, 차별적이거나 혹은 학대하는 글을 보냄으로써, 인신공격하거나 협박을 하는 것

감시

회사 이메일 자원은 단지 업무 목적을 위해서만 제공된다는 것을 알아두십시오. 그러므로 회사는 시스템에 기록된 어떠한 정보도 조사하고 검사할 수 있는 권한을 가집니다. 이 정책을 수행하기 위해서 에이펙스는 이메일 내용과 쓰임을 검토하기 위한 감시 소프트웨어를 사용할 권한을 가집니다. 이러한 감시 활동은 단지 정당한 목적을 위한 것이고 직원들이 동의한 절차를 준수하며 실행될 것입니다.

usage 사용(법) remind 상기시키다 protocol 규약 enlighten 알리다, 계몽하다 acknowledge 인정하다 misuse 남용 impact (up)on ~에 영향력 reputation 평판 regulate 규정하다, 통제하다 on one's behalf ~을 대신해서 in advance 사전에 familiarize A with B A를 B에 익숙하게 하다 warning 경고 affirmatively 적극적으로 legislation 법률, 규정 tolerable 참을 수 있는 unacceptable 용납될 수 없는 in possession 소유하고 있는 spread 퍼뜨리다 illegal 불법의 personal business 개인적인 용무 copyright 저작권 undertake 착수하다 deliberate 고의적인 squander 낭비하다 unsolicited 필요치 않은 commercial 상업적인 attack 공격 threat 협박 offensive 불쾌한 discriminatory 차별적인 abusive 학대하는 inspect 조사하다 carry out 수행하다 legitimate 정당한 implement 실행하다 in accordance with ~에 따라서 compliance with ~을 준수해서

186 이메일에 따르면, 조슬린 씨가 해리스 씨에게 하길 바라는 것은 무엇인가?
(A) 안내 지침을 보내는 것
(B) 이메일을 감시하는 소프트웨어를 찾는 것
(C) 정책을 위한 제안을 하는 것
(D) 정책을 준수하는지 감시하는 것

187 가이드라인에서 세 번째 단락 네 번째 줄에 단어 "legitimate"과 의미상 가장 가까운 것은 무엇인가?
(A) 특별한
(B) 타당한
(C) 공통의
(D) 주요한

188 이메일 사용 정책에 관해 암시된 것은 무엇인가?
(A) 해리스 씨가 보낸 메모에 첨부되어 있다.
(B) 갱신될 필요가 있다.
(C) 첨부는 특정 분량으로 제한될 것이다.
(D) 3월 말쯤에 발표되었을 것이다.

189 이메일 사용 위반으로 판단되는 것이 아닌 것은 무엇인가?
(A) 개인적 목적으로 이메일을 사용하는 것
(B) 인종차별주의 글을 보내는 것
(C) 불법 사진을 유포하는 것
(D) 직장 동료들 사이에 파일을 교환하는 것

190 이메일 감시에 관해 언급된 것은 무엇인가?
(A) 회사는 월별 검사를 갖는다.
(B) 회사는 이메일 감시 권한을 가진다.
(C) 검사 절차는 외부 업체에 의해 이루어질 것이다.
(D) 부적절한 정보를 가진 직원은 해고될 것이다.

[191-195]

수신: 피에스타 온천
발신: 제시카 그린, 파라다이스 타운사
날짜: 12월 7일

파라다이스 타운사는 피에스타 온천을 인수했다는 것을 발표하게 되어 기쁩니다. 우리는 이미 경영을 인수받았고 지금은 피에스타 온천과 관련된 모든 일을 책임지고 있습니다. 우리는 우리 직원 모두와 생산적인 사업 관계가 유지 될 것을 높이 기대하고 있습니다. 만약 도움이 필요하시면, 동봉된 서류의 목록에 있는 직원들에게 연락할 수 있습니다.

다음은 우리 회사의 중요 직책의 사람들의 연락처 목록입니다.

인사 부서
인사 담당자, 스텔라 스톤 〈stellastone@paradisetown.com〉

서비스 유지 관리 부서
유지 관리부 감독자, 놀런 딘 〈n_dean@paradisetown.com〉

시설 관리보수 부서
시설 서비스 담당자, 루카스 반즈 〈lucasrepairs@paradisetown.com〉

기술 유지관리 부서
기술 서비스 담당자, 딜런 웨스트 〈techdylan@paradisetown.com〉

업무 관리 부서
행정 업무 담당자, 제시카 그린 〈green@paradisetown.com〉

파라다이스 타운사
555-6756

수신: 루카스 반즈 〈lucasrepairs@paradisetown.com〉
발신: 에밀리 햄프셔 〈hampshire@paradisetown.com〉
날짜: 12월 11일
제목: 사우나 문제

안녕하세요. 제 이름은 에밀리 햄프셔입니다. 그리고 저는 피에스타 온천의 일본식 노천탕의 접수대에서 일하고 있습니다. 최근에 온천 사우나 중 하나에 관한 불만 사항을 접수하였습니다. 그 고객은 온도가 충분히 높지 않은데 습도의 밀도가 너무 높다고 말했습니다. 저는 그 사우나를 확인했는데 온도가 섭씨 77도라고 표시되어 있었지만, 실제 온도는 섭씨 60도를 넘지 못했습니다. 또한, 환풍기의 팬 중 하나가 멈췄습니다. 제 생각에 이것이 높은 습도를 일으킨 원인으로 보입니다. 그 사우나는 현재 폐쇄되었지만 온천의 필수 시설이므로 빨리 수리되어야 합니다. 언제 수리될 수 있는지 알려 주십시오.

에밀리 햄프셔

spa 온천 acquisition 인수 finalize 결말짓다 take over 인수하다, 인계하다 look forward to -ing ~할 것을 학수고대하다 business relationship 사업 관계 representative 직원 personnel department 인사부

human resource 인적자원, 인사부 **maintenance** 유지 관리 **supervisor** 감독관, 관리자 **facility** 시설 **coordinator** 조정자 **office operations** 행정 업무 **lately** 최근에 **complaint** 불만 사항 **temperature** 온도 **humidity** 습도 **dense** 밀도가 높은 **Celsius** 섭씨 **ventilating** 환기의 **density** 밀도 **put up for auction** 경매에 부치다

191 파라다이스 타운사는 어떤 사업체에 속하는가?
(A) 전문적인 마사지 치료사를 훈련한다.
(B) 기업체에 전문적인 조언을 해준다.
(C) 공석에 적절한 사람을 소개한다.
(D) 온천 시설을 관리한다.

192 메모에서 언급된 것은 무엇인가?
(A) 피에스타 온천은 회비를 올릴 것이다.
(B) 도움을 위해 전문가들과 연락할 수도 있다.
(C) 피에스타 온천은 경매에 부쳐질 것이다.
(D) 인력 감축은 곧 시행될 것이다.

193 햄프셔 씨는 어느 부서에 연락하고 있는가?
(A) 시설 관리보수 부서
(B) 인사 부서
(C) 업무 관리 부서
(D) 기술 유지관리 부서

194 햄프셔 씨가 이메일을 쓴 목적은 무엇인가?
(A) 직책에 지원하기 위해서
(B) 온천 이용 비용에 관해 문의하기 위해서
(C) 문제를 보고하기 위해서
(D) 검사를 실행하기 위해서

195 이메일에서 첫 단락 네 번째 줄의 "dense"와 의미상 가장 가까운 것은 무엇인가?
(A) 가벼운
(B) 거친
(C) 진한, 밀집한
(D) 헐거운

[196-200]

항공사 정책 업데이트

팬 퍼시픽 항공의 국제 항공기 위탁 수화물 정책 변경이 즉시 발효됩니다. 특히 국제 여행객 1인당 위탁 수화물 허용량을 한 개에서 두 개로 늘렸습니다. 게다가 각 가방에 대한 무게 제한도 20kg에서 25kg으로 상향 조정했고, 중량 초과 가방에 대한 벌금을 100달러에서 50달러로 낮췄습니다. 그러나 두 개의 허용량 이상의 추가 위탁 가방에 대한 청구 요금은 4개의 추가 가방까지 가방당 25달러로 유지하기로 했습니다. 이러한 변경 사항은 국내 항공기 정책에는 전혀 영향을 미치지 않을 것입니다 — 한 개의 무료 가방, 20kg 제한, 그리고 중량 초과 가방에 대한 100달러 벌금의 정책은 현재도 계속 똑같이 남아 있습니다. 만약 여러분이 질문이 있으시다면, 저희 탑승 수속 창구 직원에게 말해주세요.

감사합니다.

Flyin.com 항공사 여행객 온라인 후기

저는 최근에 홍콩에서 제 고향 시카고로 가는 팬 퍼시픽 항공의 새 직항편 중 하나를 이용했습니다. 전반적으로 비행은 만족스러웠습니다. 팬 퍼시픽 항공은 저가 항공사와 표준 국제 항공사의 중간쯤 되는 수준이었습니다. 즉 가격은 저렴하고, 가격만큼 누릴 수 있었습니다. 그런데 저는 두 번째 위탁 수화물에 대해서 요금을 받지 않는다는 것을 알고 매우 기뻤습니다. 이것은 새로 도입된 변화인 것 같았고, 매우 환영할 만했습니다.

그러나 최근 LA에서 뉴욕으로 팬 퍼시픽 항공을 타고 간 친구가 저에게 국내 여행에 대해서는 기존의 한 가방 정책이 유지된다는 말을 들었는데, 이는 매우 실망스럽습니다. 저는 항공사가 새 수화물 정책이 모든 항공편으로 확대하는 것을 고려해 주시기 바랍니다.

수신: 빌 팩스톤 〈paxton@jazzco.com〉
발신: 스티븐 루크 〈luke@ppa.com〉
날짜: 12월 10일
주제: 귀하의 후기

고객님께서 Flyin.com 웹 사이트에서 팬 퍼시픽 항공을 최근 이용해 주신 경험에 대해 시간을 내어 평가해 주셔서 감사합니다. 저희는 여행객에게 더 가까이 다가설 수 있도록 마련된 새 수화물 정책에 대해 우리만큼 고객님께서 반가워하시는 것을 들으니 기쁩니다. 소비자 반응이 압도적으로 긍정적이었고, 그것은 매우 기쁜 일이었습니다. 국내 항공편까지 정책을 확장하는 것에 대한 고객님의 제안은 미국 연방 항공국이 요구하는 제한 때문에 불가능하다는 점을 말씀드리게 되어 유감입니다. 그렇지만, 저희는 2020년을 시작으로 국내 승객들에게 중량 초과 수화물 벌금을 25%까지 줄일 것입니다. 저희는 또한 저희의 국제 여행객들이 기대하는 수준까지 국내 서비스의 질을 올릴 방법을 계속 찾을 것입니다.

진심으로

스티븐 루크
팬 퍼시픽 항공

initiate 시작하다, 개시하다 **checked-baggage** 위탁 수화물 **effective** (법, 규정 등이) 발효되는, 유효한 **specifically** 특히 **allowance** 허용량 **additionally** 추가로, 게다가 **weight** 무게 **penalty** 벌금 **overweight** 중량 초과의 **lower** 낮추다 **charge** 요금, 수수료 **domestic** 국내의 **in effect** 시행[발효] 중인 **address** 말하다 **check-in counter** (공항의) 탑승 수속 창구 **take advantage of** ~을 이용하다 **direct flight** 직항편 **overall** 전반적으로 **satisfactory** 만족스러운 **budget airline** 저가 항공사 **standard** 표준의 **carrier** 항공사 **charge for** ~에 대해 청구하다 **apparently** 명백히 **disappointing** 실망스러운 **expand** 확장하다 **cover** 포함하다 **consumer** 소비자 **response** 반응 **overwhelmingly** 압도적으로 **positive** 긍정적인 **extremely** 매우 **gratifying** 기쁜 **as for** ~에 관한 **suggestion** 제안 **regarding** ~에 관한 **be unable to do** ~할 수 없다 **restriction** 제한 **impose** 부과하다 **Federal Aviation Administration** 미국 연방 항공국

196 국제 항공기에서 승객 1인당 무료로 맡길 수 있는 현재의 가방의 수는 몇 개인가?
(A) 한 개
(B) 두 개
(C) 세 개
(D) 네 개

197 항공사에 대한 팩스톤 씨의 전반적인 의견은 무엇인가?
(A) 저렴하지만 승객들을 형편없이 대접한다.
(B) 대부분의 국제 항공사들보다 더 좋다.
(C) 낮은 가격을 고려하면 품질이 좋다.
(D) 빠르고 편리하나 값이 너무 비싸다.

198 이메일에서 첫 번째 단락 네 번째 줄의 gratifying과 의미상 가장 가까운 것은 무엇인가?
(A) 기쁘게 만드는

(B) 무서운
(C) 당황스러운
(D) 깜짝 놀라게 하는

199 새로운 정책 덕분에 팩스톤 씨가 절약했던 금액은 얼마인가?
(A) 25달러
(B) 50달러
(C) 75달러
(D) 100달러

200 2020년도에 국내 승객에 대한 중량 초과 가방 벌금은 얼마인가?
(A) 없음
(B) 10달러
(C) 50달러
(D) 75달러

나혼자 끝내는 新 토익

FINAL 실전 모의고사 3회분

- ★ 실제 시험지 형태 그대로, 신토익 실전 모의고사 3회분 수록
- ★ 문제의 키워드를 단숨에 파악하는 알짜 해석·해설
- ★ 실전용 · 복습용 버전의 2종 MP3 무료 다운로드 >> QR코드 & 홈페이지 다운로드
- ★ 문제풀이 후 바로 채점할 수 있는 자동 채점 방식 제공 >> QR코드
- ★ 신토익 빈출 어휘 리스트 제공 >> www.nexusbook.com